MODERN AMERICAN HISTORY ★ A

Garland
Series

Edited by
FRANK FREIDEL
Harvard University

THE MODERNIZATION
OF AMERICAN REFORM ★ Structures
and Perceptions

Steven Kesselman

Garland Publishing, Inc.
New York & London ★ 1979

Library of Congress Cataloging in Publication Data

Kesselman, Steven.
  The modernization of American reform.

  (Modern American history)
  Bibliography: p.
  Includes index.
  1. United States—Social policy—Addresses, essays,
lectures.   2. Social reformers—United States—History—Addresses, essays, lectures.   3. United States—
Social conditions—1865–1918—Addresses, essays, lectures.   4. United States—Social conditions—1918–
1932—Addresses, essays, lectures.   5. Industrialization—History—Addresses, essays, lectures.   I. Title.   II. Series.
HN64.K36   309.1'73'08   78-62386
ISBN 0-8240-3635-2

All volumes in this series are printed on acid-free,
250-year-life paper.
Printed in the United States of America

THE MODERNIZATION OF AMERICAN REFORM

by

Steven A. Kesselman

To my mother
and to the memory of my father

CONTENTS

INTRODUCTION

"Evolution works for sheep or roses or even for steam engines," A. J. P. Taylor once observed; "it does not work for men's ideas. These do not improve; they change."[1] The prevailing styles of thinking of one's own age, however, often seem the final phase of a progressive process. For more than half a century, the mode of thought and action usually called "pragmatism," "pluralism," or "relativism" characterized mainstream American reform. Within the past few years, the possibility has been raised that this style was itself only an interlude. Since nothing has clearly emerged as its successor, the current intellectual fluidity makes it timely to examine the route by which it achieved its preeminence. The description of the origin, development, communication, transmutation, and disappearance of ideas is the complex material of intellectual history. The timing of these events and the process by which styles of thinking rise and fall in public acceptance are the problems of the relationship between intellectual and social change, the problem of why particular

- 1 -

ideas have social resonance at particular times.

The startling intellectual transformation of American
social reform between 1870 and 1940 from "rationalistic,"
"idealistic," "absolutistic," and "romantic" modes of thought--
modes that William James grouped together as "monism"--to the
modern "pluralistic" modes occupied the same era as a startling
social transformation--the emergence of modern industrial
society. The relationship between the two events has been
difficult to pin down in a satisfactory way. The character-
istically modern modes of thought were available at least as
early as the 1880's, but are generally regarded as not dominating reform thinking until after the Progressive Era; and the
dominant modes of the 1870's and 1880's were still available
in the mid-twentieth century, but were usually dismissed as
archaic. The questions to be answered, therefore, are why a
set of ideas, available at one time, does not become a coercive
truth for society at large until another; and why, of all the
intellectual alternatives available at any time, one configu-
ration of ideas meets a popular response.

The reformers of the interwar period and their successors
had their own answer to those questions. Pragmatism or experimentalism, they argued, was the only style of reform

appropriate to an industrial society, and the delay in its
acceptance from its first discovery was only a matter of
cultural lag. The modernization of patterns of thinking happened to be slower than the modernization of social and economic life; but the appropriateness of the new style would
finally impel society to catch up to its economic or its
technological base.

There are, however, questions about the relationship
between intellectual and social change that "cultural lag"
does not answer, because William Ogburn invented the concept
in 1922 partly so that his contemporaries would not have to
answer them. Lag implicitly assumes increasing sophistication as the dynamic force in modern intellectual history.
It thus generally fails to credit "pre-modern" and interim
modes of thinking with serving legitimate social purposes.
It treats the old modes as archaic and the interim modes as
incomplete, and it fails to consider the social purposes
they served in their own times, the factors that made them
convincing when they were dominant. Lag similarly does not
explain why historical figures and their contemporaries do
not see the gaps and inconsistencies in their own social
thinking that are apparent to their successors. Nor does it

explain the timing of the rise and decline of intellectual styles, nor the order in which their constituent parts are adopted or abandoned, nor why some parts are accepted while others are ignored.

Similarly, there are limits to the usefulness, particularly in social thought, of explaining intellectual change by the internal logic or "working out" of certain ideas. It is not always profitable to see social ideas as "playing themselves out," as evolving on their own to a point of excessive complication or rigidity and then breaking down, or as being governed by cycles or the swings of a pendulum. There is no "logical" reason, for example, why the evolutionary relativism of the Progressives had to give way to the purer relativism of the New Dealers. Nor is there a logical reason why the oft-noted contradictions of Progressive social thought could not have been maintained--unless the conditions comprehended by those contradictions had altered. Similarly, cyclical explanations rarely take account of the historical dimension: the fact that the lengths of cycles vary enormously. It seems more likely that a style of thinking would become compelling--and remain so--only under certain social conditions, irrespective of the "real" merit of the style itself.

This book proposes an alternative method of understanding the relationship between intellectual and social change in the period of modernization: the relationship between changes in intellectual structures and changes in perceptions of society. The first step toward understanding the correlation between "pragmatism" and "industrialism" is to date the stages of the intellectual transformation with some precision, and then to correlate those stages with a social dimension. For that purpose, focused intellectual biographies offered an underlying continuity of perspective that could allow the changes to be seen with greatest clarity and to be pinpointed accurately in time. In addition, biography offered an element of concreteness for an account that required a degree of abstraction in order to cross the line from the individual to the general, from the idiosyncratic to the social experience. Particularly in this period, when social reform was preeminent at three discrete times, the change in intellectual style could be most graphically seen in the differences among the people to whom their contemporaries responded as the articulators of the experience of their age. Studies of contrasting figures whose lives paralleled the trajectories of each of the

reform episodes--figures who were preeminent when reform itself was preeminent and who lived to see that preeminence
decline--could allow at least some part of the collective experience to be abstracted from the minds of individuals.

For the 1880's, the wide circulation of Progress and
Poverty and Looking Backward made Henry George and Edward
Bellamy clearer choices than the New Economists or Dynamic
Sociologists whose impact would be felt two decades later.
Their writings not only educated millions of their contemporaries, but George's New York mayoral campaign of 1886 was
the high point of omnibus labor politics in American history,
and Bellamy's influence on the Populist movement was strongest
when it seemed closest to victory. For the Progressive Era,
Jane Addams of Hull House, the "most famous woman in America"
in 1912, and Herbert Croly, ideologue of the New Nationalism
and founding editor of the New Republic, were appropriate
subjects. And for New Deal liberalism, the strongest candidates were Rexford Tugwell, the Brain Trust's spokesman for
national planning, and Thurman Arnold, trustbuster and
theorist of random experimentalism. They were all sensitive
to social changes, and their careers were in large part responses to them. They were not thinkers to whom we return

again and again for guidance, but they solved significant
personal and historical problems simultaneously and thereby
became salient figures in the liberalism of their own age.
As reformers, they all took as their primary concern "the
social problem" (generally defined as the inequitable distribution of wealth and power), the broadest problem reform
can address and the one concern that might conceivably define
a reform tradition. Their influence was both activist and
intellectual, and their greatest impact was immediate, and
so they could be taken as representative, as people who
spoke to and for their contemporaries. They had both popular appeal and intellectual depth, giving them resonance on
many levels of society; and succeeding generations of reformers regarded them as forebears, even though they had been
superseded. Finally, within each wave of reform, each of the
figures represented different brands of liberalism, and thus
any discoveries that their thinking changed in similar ways,
at about the same times, and in response to the same things,
would indicate a degree of generalizability beyond the figures
themselves and their narrowest constituencies.

Social reform is essentially a moral enterprise. If the
experiences of these six people are in fact generalizable,

then reform emerges as the ultimate solution to the problem
of morality--that of integrating one's beliefs and one's actions in the specific context of one's age. The question of
what makes one answer to the moral problem relevant and popular at a particular time is also the question of what out-
dates it. The careers of the three generations overlapped--
the first and second during the 1890's, the second and third
during the 1920's, each of them periods of reordering for
American liberalism, when the resonance of one generation
was waning and another was rising. And so their integra-
tions of thought and action--their intellectual structures--
rather than their more concrete reform proposals, had to be
the focus of analysis.

An intellectual structure is the attribution to society
of an ideal of natural order borrowed from a particular type
of philosophy or conception of science, and the modes of
thought and action conceived to be appropriate to it. With
appropriate qualifications, it will include elements of what
has been meant at different periods by habits of mind,
climate of opinion, universe of discourse, definitive terms
of knowledge, cognitive style, and paradigm. It is reflected
in mode of reasoning, use of language, underlying structure

of articles and books, and both the style and the substance of recommended reforms. William James identified two alternative intellectual structures: the monistic (encompassing all forms of rationalism and idealism) and the pluralistic (the expression of pragmatism). Simon Patten, the early twentieth-century economist who influenced the theorists of the New Deal, made the same distinction, identifying the pluralistic as the only structure appropriate to modern conditions. Its declining resonance now permits us to treat it with as much distance as the other, to ask what made it convincing, and to identify an intermediate but independent structure--the dualistic, which unconsciously combined conflicting elements of monism and pluralism in changing proportions--that occupied the middle years of the period. It also permits us to ask what relationship the complex process of change from one intellectual structure to another--and from one pair of representative reformers to another--had to the contemporary social changes.

The critical mechanism connecting the social transformation to the intellectual appears to have been changes in perceptions of society. Social perceptions are contemporaries' descriptions of the factual state of their own societies at

particular times. Two books with identical titles and published forty years apart illustrate the change in perception
from shortly after the beginning of the period of modernization to just before its end. In August 1889, David A. Wells
introduced his Recent Economic Changes by observing, "The
economic changes that have occurred during the last quarter
of a century--or during the present generation of living men--
have unquestionably been more important and varied than during
any former corresponding period of the world's history." And
he concluded with the note that "the epoch of time under con-
sideration [the quarter century before 1889] will hereafter
rank in history as one that has no parallel . . ."[2]

Four decades later, the President's Committee on Recent
Economic Changes contrasted its own era with Wells's:
"Acceleration rather than structural change is the key to an
understanding of our recent economic developments. Gradually
the fact emerged during the course of this survey that the
distinctive character of the years from 1922 to 1929 owes
less to fundamental change than to intensified activity."
After contrasting that statement with Wells's, the Committee
observed: "Each generation believes itself to be on the
verge of a new economic era, an era of fundamental change,

but the longer the committee deliberated, the more evident it became that the novelty of the period covered by the present survey rested chiefly on the fact that developments such as formerly affected our old industries have been recurring in our new industries. The changes have not been in structure but in speed and spread."[3]

The description of society given by the President's Committee is encapsulated as a perception of stasis: an assumption, based on certain concrete phenomena, that the underlying structure of society had matured, that future developments would be only the completion of identifiable existing trends, that a final stage of social history had been reached. A perception of chaos encapsulates the description of society during the two decades of upheaval whose conclusion Wells recorded: a loss of moorings resulting from a series of social shocks that made the world seem to be in a period of rapid, unpredictable, and uncontrollable change. The experience of our own era makes it easier to appreciate the depth and power of such a perception now than it was forty years ago, when the millennial and cataclysmic literature of response to chaos was taken as an example of lack of sophistication. Recent experience helps affirm that the most devastating

social crisis can be the loss of the common vocabulary of social change, the destruction of the set of reference points
with which people understand, or can take for granted, the
nature of their society. And thus the story of the shift in
social perception between 1870 and 1940 is the story of the
destruction of one set of reference points and the discovery
of another, the story of the change from uncertainty to certainty. And just as there was an interim intellectual structure between the monistic and the pluralistic, so there seems
to have been a distinctive perception during the Progressive
Era, a perception of transition, bridging both detachment
from and attachment to the past, certainty and uncertainty
about the future, a growing sense of order and a sense of
ever-increasing complexity.

The social context of social thought, then, appears also
to have been a phenomenon of the mind. "Modern industrial
society," for example, is as much an idea as a fact; it has
a history and an impact as an idea; and it was the perceived
contours of the phenomena for which industrial society became
the label that affected this level of intellectual life.
Changing perceptions appear to have been the filter through
which substantive social changes caused particular intellectual

structures to have resonance at particular times. For each
of the three generations of reformers, one intellectual
structure was characteristic, presumably learned, though possibly innate. Their resonance peaked when their characteristic structure bore a particular congruence to their perceptions of society. As the pressure of events created
changes in perception, it in turn created pressures toward
modifications in intellectual structure that the salient generation resisted or adopted only with great difficulty. At
that point, their resonance began to decline; and a group of
thinkers for whom the intellectual structure appropriate to
the new perception was both natural and congenial rose to
prominence.

The process of intellectual change was not orderly or
logical or inevitable. It depended, at least in part, upon
events, upon channels of communication, and upon the inventive
genius and moral stamina of the people involved. There does
emerge one significant pattern, and that is a persistent
polarity between intellectual structure and social perception
throughout the period of the transformation. At each stage,
the reformers attributed to society an ideal of natural order
that was the polar opposite of the factual order that they

described in society, and their reforms were geared to the attributed universe rather than to the perceived one. Those attempting to reform a chaotic society operated intellectually in a monistic universe; those reforming a static society, in a pluralistic universe. The reformers of the interim period with their complex dualistic intellectual structure used remnants of monism where flux and uncertainty persisted and pluralism where development appeared to have ended.

If the polarity is in fact there--and it is a polarity, not a contradiction that should be taken as vitiating the moral enterprise--it reinforces the impression that the intellectual history of reform in this period cannot be treated as autonomous. At higher levels of intellectual life, where the ideas of the future are sometimes prepared, intellectual change might be treated as if it were strictly internal. The desire, for example, because of personal or professional ambitions, to break an intellectual oligopoly, might lead younger thinkers to attribute to society a character that would make their own intellectual structure more attractive than that of an entrenched establishment. But at least in the instance of social reform, the case for looking outside intellectual life for a social correlate is strong. The reformers were not adopting an intellectual style and then perceiving in society an order that neatly suited it. They were in fact at each point perceiving in society an order that was the polar opposite of their intellectual structure.

Whether this kind of analysis is fruitful beyond this very special and compact period is open to investigation. But it does seem to have the virtues of keeping historical figures firmly in their age, of illuminating far corners as well as the centers of their thinking, and of avoiding the distortions that result when people are implicitly judged for lacking hindsight about what was really happening during their era. And it may be useful in understanding the roots of the current intellectual fluidity and in exploring what may become the preferred resources for its resolution.

PART I

A WORLD WITHOUT SUBJUNCTIVES

CHAPTER I

INTRODUCTION: THE HISTORY OF

"MODERN INDUSTRIAL SOCIETY"

In September 1934, Ida M. Tarbell, one of the formidable journalists of the Muckraking Era, published an article entitled, "New Dealers of the 'Seventies: Henry George and Edward Bellamy." While she did not try to prove George's and Bellamy's direct relevance to the 1930's, she did see them as the forerunners of modern liberalism. There was in fact a revival of interest in Looking Backward (1888) at the time Ida Tarbell was writing. Accompanying the rise of social planning among liberal reformers in the New Deal, Bellamy Clubs were organized in various parts of the country; and, promoted by the novelist's widow, "Nationalism" enjoyed a brief flurry of renewed popularity. The doctrines that supported the Single Tax were simultaneously being spread by Henry George Schools in some of the nation's largest cities. The two movements had little patience with each other. In fact, one ardent Single Taxer protested Tarbell's association

of the two. "George was an uncompromising individualist,"
he wrote the editor of _Forum_, "while Bellamy was an extreme
collectivist. They cannot both be right." The Single Tax on
rent and the utopia of the year 2000 had radically different
pictures both of human nature and of the reformed society,
he argued. "George and Bellamy were as far apart as the two
poles."[1]

The two men would have agreed with that assessment, and
during their own lifetimes they occasionally criticized each
other on similar grounds. And yet their major works were
published less than a decade apart; the height of their popularity overlapped; and they influenced many of the same
people. Historians as well have usually felt justified in
lumping them together as an intermediate stage between ante-
bellum romantic reform and Progressivism, as reformers whose
concern was "the social problem" rather than the less comprehensive problems of currency, tariff, and civil service that
preoccupied many of their liberal contemporaries. Conservatives in their own time often opposed them both for the same
reasons. Later critics felt similarly justified in treating
a utopia and a panacea as belonging in a single category,
usually because they seemed expressions of the same

phenomenon--lack of sophistication. But sophistication about social problems is a very relative quality. Neither George nor Bellamy was less intelligent, less perceptive, less intellectually able than their later critics. George probably and Bellamy possibly may be classed with the commanding intellects of American history. Among their followers as well were men and women whom any contemporary would have included among the best informed and most sensitive people of the day. And yet they were "unrealistic."

Vernon L. Parrington, in the unfinished third volume of his popular and influential Main Currents in American Thought (1930), devoted a sympathetic chapter to each of these "early progressives." Of the Bellamy Nationalist movement, he concluded that it "was naive, no doubt it sprang from a social inexperience that underestimated the complexity of the problem." Of the author of Progress and Poverty (1879), he made a similar judgment. "No doubt," Parrington wrote, "like his progenitors [the classical economists], he oversimplified the problem. Society is more complex than he esteemed it; individual motives are more complex." Rexford Tugwell, the planners' spokesman in the first New Deal administration, found the early appeal and final irrelevance of

George's program in its "perfect simplicity." From the
perspective of 1930, then, the difference between sophistication and naivete about social problems was the difference
between a complex and a simple picture of society. Since
neither simplicity nor complexity is "objectively true,"
that one should seem coercively true at one time and the
other at another may be attributable not to increasing
sophistication, but to a change in perspective.[2]

From the perspective of the reformers of 1930--indeed,
from the perspective of those of 1914--George's and
Bellamy's unrealism seemed to derive from inadequate foresight, from insufficient realization of the transformation
their society was then undergoing: the birth of modern
industrial society. Charles Beard made such an attack on the
politicians of the seventies and eighties as early as 1905,
he included it in a college textbook in 1914. Walter Lippmann
made similar charges a year earlier. And one recent historian
of the liberals of the Gilded Age concluded that they "never
grasped the realities of the Industrial Revolution" and that
they failed to see the necessity for "adaptation to new conditions and absorption of new ideas."[3]

Such judgments rest on at least three implicit

assumptions. The first is that societies are to be described according to what is distinctive about them, rather than what is universal, and that therefore "new ideas" are necessary for "new conditions." The second is that "industrialism" is the distinctive organizing fact of modern society. And the third is that people in the 1870's and 1880's should have realized that they were "modernizing."

The first assumption involves changing conceptions of the nature of social science, and part of the task of the following chapters is to examine how and for what purposes, on the popular level, those changing conceptions took hold. What seems obvious at one time may seem absurd at another. Edwin L. Godkin, editor of the "old liberal" Nation and Evening Post, recalled near the end of the nineteenth century that in the 1840's, when he went to school, "political economy was taught as a real science, which consisted simply in the knowledge of what man, as an exchanging, producing animal, would do, if left alone. On that you can base a science, for the mark of science is that it enables you to predict. Since then, what is called political economy has become something entirely different. It has assumed the role of an adviser, who teaches man to make himself more comfortable through the help of his government, and has no more claim to be a science than philanthropy or what is called 'sociology.'"[4]

The second assumption is no less controversial. Apart from the fact that social critics have classified societies not only by their economic, but also by their political, moral, intellectual, esthetic, and even psychological features, the question of whether "industrial society" is in fact a distinct "type" of society has been a central question to critics who have analyzed the problem of "convergence" of capitalist and socialist systems.[5] In addition, the phrase "industrial society" has not always been used to designate an "industrialized society," a distinctively modern society whose central economic fact is the dominance of complex, highly organized manufacturing enterprises employing machines and factories. "Industrial society" had, in fact, a long history before it emerged in the first decade of the twentieth century as the name for a new era in social development.

The name had first been used early in the nineteenth century, most notably in the works of Henri de Saint-Simon. But while Saint-Simon associated the name with "modern" society, with the rise of the bourgeoisie, and with a "scientific" or "positive" ideology, he did not associate it with machine technology. He distinguished between military and industrial societies, but he traced the birth of the latter to the eleventh and twelfth centuries, not to what was later called the "Industrial Revolution."[6] Auguste Comte followed Saint-Simon's classification of societies and also did not identify "industry" with factories. "Industry" meant free labor, which was incompatible with war and therefore with a military state. Comte also regarded, not 1760, but "the opening of the fourteenth century" as the period "we must fix upon as the time when the organic industry of modern society began to assume a characteristic quality. All the chief tokens of civilization indeed concur in marking that era as the true origin of modern history."[7]

Though neither Saint-Simon nor Comte was widely read in America, both Jane Addams and Herbert Croly were influenced by Positivism, and Herbert Spencer, who was influenced by Comte, helped popularize the Frenchmen's schema in the English-speaking world. Spencer, however, eliminated the historical dimension that had been prominent in their account. His attempt to find natural laws of organization and ideal or natural types at first precluded his use of the name "industrial society" for something distinctively modern. In 1876,

in the first volume of The Principles of Sociology, he proposed two "natural" ways of classifying societies. The
primary way, consistent with the law of development, was to
group them according to degree of composition or complexity:
simple, compound, doubly compound, and trebly compound. All
the "great civilized nations"--both ancient and modern--were
trebly compound, and no society could reach that stage without passing through all the others. The secondary way was
to classify societies according to whether they were
"predominantly militant" or "predominantly industrial."
Here again there was no distinction between ancient and
modern, since examples of each type could be found in all
periods and in each degree of composition. The types represented not stages of history, but ideals useful for scientific analysis.[8]

Both types of society could be treated as organisms,
and Spencer applied his general laws of evolution to both of
them. Both exhibited "high" and "low," complex and simple,
degrees. In both, progressive differentiation of structure
followed increase of size and was accompanied by progressive
differentiation of function. In both, all systems became increasingly interdependent as the complexity of society

increased. Spencer found, however, that as social development went on, there was a differentiation between two systems:
the "outer" and the "inner." He also called these the regulating and the sustaining and, more significantly, the
political-military and the industrial.[9] He defined the two
types of society--militant and industrial--according to
whether they emphasized one system at the expense of the
other, and he could thus argue that societies tended toward
the pure types. The militant society (also called the
predatory) was characterized by an identity of the political
with the military organization, centralized control, strict
hierarchies, a closely regulated industrial organization
serving as a "permanent commissariat" for the military structure, rigid control of civilian life, a militant religion
stressing revenge and obedience, and total subordination of
the individual to the state. An industrial society (of
which Spencer could not find a pure example) was characterized by democratic or representative political institutions
with leadership by the best, decentralized control, a
proliferation of voluntary associations run on democratic
principles, an unregulated industrial structure that existed
to satisfy private wants, religious freedom, and subordination

of the state to the will of the individual.

The distinction between the two types, then, centered not on whether society contained great industries, but on the type of regulation that the "sustaining" or "industrial" system was subject to. In a militant society, cooperation was compulsory, conscious, and closely regulated. In an industrial society, cooperation was voluntary, spontaneous, and free. That Spencer did not regard "industrial society" as distinctively modern is evidenced by the fact that he listed the Hanse Towns among the "most advanced" industrial societies, that he included socialism and communism in the militant rather than the industrial category, and that he found a reversion to the militant type among highly industrialized modern societies such as Germany and, to a lesser but still alarming extent, England. Since structure followed function, modern states, no matter how dedicated to manufacturing, would become less and less "industrial" as they prepared for war or adopted socialistic measures.[10]

Spencer declared that the industrial type was "higher" than the militant type. Societies "become high," he wrote in a postscript, "in proportion to the evolution of their industrial systems, and not in proportion to the evolution

of those centralized regulating systems fitting them to carry
on wars."[11] Spencer's measure of "height" was the extent to
which a society served individual welfare; and that by definition was the central fact of industrial society. By the
mid-nineties, however, when Spencer issued volume III, which
dealt specifically with industrial institutions, he was associating "higher" with "later" and industrialism with the
late nineteenth century. A change in perception had apparently taken place, causing Spencer to inject a historical
dimension into his analysis to account for the rise of a
substantively complex society that was also distinctively
modern. Industrial progress, he noted, exhibited "compound
acceleration." The chief fact of technological advance was
"the cooperation of appliances," something distinctively
modern; and the unique achievement of the nineteenth century
was a rate of progress so much greater in degree than that
achieved by earlier types of society (nomadic, pastoral,
agricultural--itself a new way of classifying societies,
according to a historical progression of productive systems)
as to be almost different in kind. "Only in modern times,"
Spencer noted, had industrial progress become rapid.[12] He
also analyzed phenomena that were modern because consonant

with the highest "degree of composition" or complexity:
compound labor (factories) and compound capital (corporations).
And when in 1896 he published the revised edition of volume I,
first issued twenty years before, he made industrialism the
culmination of evolution, a position earlier assignable to
either of the pure types. "Social organization is to be considered high in proportion as it subserves individual welfare,"
he wrote, "because in a society the units are sentient and the
aggregate insentient; and the industrial type is higher because, in that state of permanent peace to which civilization
is tending, it subserves individual welfare better than the
militant type."[13]

In the years between the two editions of volume I, the
name "industrial society" was acquiring the connotation
Spencer was trying to accommodate in his last work. When
William Graham Sumner, following Spencer, referred to the
"modern industrial system" in 1879, it did not mean to him,
as it would mean to Jane Addams and her contemporaries after
1900, that society itself had changed or that existing institutions, arrangements, social knowledge, and scientific
"laws" were thereby outdated.[14] Even the "New Economists,"
for whom the distinctive modernity of factory production was

an article of faith, did not use "industrial society" in the 1880's to describe only their own age. When Henry Carter Adams began teaching at Johns Hopkins in 1881, for example, he noted that while classical economists referred to political economy as the science of wealth, he preferred to call it the science of industrial society because "this definition is more comprehensive." It forced the economist to deal with all the institutions and attitudes that affected the economic life of any society. "Industrial society" thus meant "society seen from the perspective of political economy." There were, according to Adams, three stages in the history of "industrial society," which corresponded to the primacy in production of land, labor, or capital: the nomadic and pastoral, the agricultural, and the manufacturing or commercial. This last was "the stage of development at which the Western world has now arrived." But that stage had begun four or five centuries before, not at the time of the Industrial Revolution.[15] When, five years later, Adams sought the causes of modern social agitation, he did not contrast the 1880's with, for example, the 1830's; he contrasted the nineteenth century with the fourteenth century.[16]

By the mid-eighties, however, the name can be read in

three ways: in the universal or generic sense of the early
Spencer or the early New Economists, in the "modern" (post-
medieval) sense of Comte and Saint-Simon, and in a sense that
involved a very recent beginning and implied "industrialization." Carroll D. Wright, for instance, combined the last
two in his historical review of wages and prices of 1885.
Wright put the beginning of the "modern industrial system"
in 1830, listed its distinctive features as the "development
of invention" and changes in the juridical status of labor,
and referred to the period before 1815, the period prior to
the factory system and the use of machines as the "early
[but not the pre-] industrial period."[17]

Henry Carter Adams was running the School of Applied
Ethics at which Jane Addams delivered two important speeches
in the summer of 1892. The lectures were delivered in the
School's Economics Department, which Henry C. Adams called
"a recognition of the fact, that, inasmuch as the most significant changes of the nineteenth century are industrial in
character, the most pressing of the practical questions of
right and wrong find their root in industrial relationships."
Lectures on economic theory, delivered during the same summer
session, had been intended "to leave the impression that the

economist is gradually changing his point of view, and that
political economy, while ceasing to be an industrial philosophy of a class, is coming to be a comprehensive philosophy of
industrial society."[18]

Finally, Richard T. Ely, Henry C. Adams's former colleague and a leader of the new school of historical economists,
began his Studies in the Evolution of Industrial Society (1903)
with the generic definition. "The term 'industrial society' is
merely a short way of saying, 'society viewed from the industrial standpoint.'" But he also noted that the pace of social
change had vastly accelerated in the nineteenth century. "It
is, in fact, only within the last one hundred years that the
industrial ties binding men together have become so extensive
and intensive that the term 'industrial society' has become
familiar." Furthermore, where earlier the New Economists had
distinguished historical stages of "industrial society"
(nomadic, agricultural, etc.), Ely distinguished "economic
stages" and gave the name "industrial stage" only to the last
one, the specifically modern stage of mechanized production.[19]

In the first dozen years of the twentieth century,
"industrial society" became increasingly commonplace as the
label for a new era in social history that, from the

perspective of 1912, seemed to have begun in 1870 or 1880. Its easy use by critics, historians, and reformers from the Progressive Era to the mid-1960's implied a sense of assurance about the nature of modern society, a complete, though not always articulated, set of reference points, which the reformers of the 1870's and 1880's necessarily lacked. In any case, if the careers of the later Progressives are evidence, "industrial society's" role in the modernization of intellectual life came less through the concrete phenomena implied by "industrialization" than through configurations or patterns perceived in those phenomena: the perceptions that industrial society was distinctively modern and that it was substantively, irreducibly complex.

The one tool that might have helped the Gilded Age reformers understand the events of their own age as symptoms of a transition would not have helped them perceive it in this "modern" way. That tool was the example of Britain, where the industrial revolution seemed to be almost a completed process. A comparison with England might have indicated the significance of such symptoms as factories, increasing population, and urbanization, even before they had gone very far in America. But Arnold Toynbee's famous lectures, the first to

treat "Industrial Revolution" as a comprehensive concept
denoting a change in the nature of society, were not published until 1884.[20] And the historical school of economists,
to which Toynbee belonged, had little immediate influence in
Britain and the United States. The historical school, in
fact, was not British, but German, in origins. Since classical (British) economics had triumphed simultaneously with the
British industrial revolution, there was little incentive for
an economist like Henry George to abandon the classical model
on the grounds that a "new society" had arisen to belie the
universals of the old theory when the industrial revolution
came to America.

Whatever the date chosen for the beginning of industrialization, historians of the Progressive Era and later noted
that its transforming effects on social life, politics, and
modes of thought did not begin to crystallize until the late
1870's and 1880's and first burst into public consciousness
in the explosive railroad strikes of 1877, the first of the
great "industrial wars" of the postbellum period. Since a
social transition is unlikely to be experienced in the same
way at its inchoate beginnings as at its well-defined end,
it may be less reasonable to judge the reformers of the

Gilded Age as shortsighted than to look at them in the context
of their own age with a view to discovering the problem that
they solved successfully enough to attract such a wide and
enthusiastic audience.

Since the transition to "modern industrial society" was
first experienced as a series of "earthquakes,"[21] it is not
surprising that George and Bellamy would respond to a perception of "anarchy" and "chaos" rather than to "modernization" and "development." The unexpectedly large and violent
labor agitation focused attention on other symptoms of social
breakdown as well as on widespread failures of policy.
Among the symptoms that George and Bellamy and such varied
contemporaries as Washington Gladden, David Wells, Andrew
Carnegie, Henry D. Lloyd, William Dean Howells, and even
Herbert Croly's parents pointed to, were an increasingly
visible population of vagrants, growing vigilantism, urban
disorders, agricultural dislocations, massive immigration,
breakdowns of municipal services, and extensive political
corruption that destroyed faith in all levels of government
and seemed to bespeak a breakdown of "self" government as
well. And if the concrete symptoms of industrialization
appeared in America as a series of disorders, intellectual

and moral life displayed an anarchy of their own; and the breakdown of authority could only make the material breakdown all the more threatening. Issues in literature, art, architecture, politics, religion, philosophy, economics, and science face in one direction in the early 1870's and in another by the late 1890's. In the interim, the bonds of common understanding were broken.

It was in this context that George and Bellamy unexpectedly found their intellectual opportunity. It was their struggle to be moral in a setting of social upheaval that ultimately led them to reform. For George, morality was the small enterpriser's ethic of justice, the right to a full and fair return for one's labor. For Bellamy, it was the demand of the Calvinist conscience that self-fulfillment be sought through self-sacrifice. These traditional values were challenged not only by the crass materialism of the Gilded Age--and by the materialism of the new biological and physical sciences--but also by social chaos itself. Chaos broke the predictable relationship between accepted beliefs and their fulfillment in acceptable forms of action, between one's motives or intentions and the consequences of one's behavior. It meant that previously reasonable expectations had suddenly been destroyed, that, for example, careers that would have satisfied the conscience's demands in an earlier era were no longer satisfactory. It was indeed possible, as the work of the pragmatists, New Economists and Dynamic Sociologists showed, to regard chaos as "complexity," to accept the world as pluralistic, as random, unpredictable, and filled with novelties, and still be a reformer. It was possible to treat industrialism as something distinctively modern and irreducibly complex and to carry on a search for new and "relevant" values without being paralyzed by ignorance and uncertainty. George himself in the years after Progress and Poverty, and Bellamy as well, displayed elements of that pattern. But it would be at least a decade before those ideas had any measure of popular resonance, after the perception of chaos had passed into a less frightening perception of transition. Indeed, the extremity of the response to Darwinism in the seventies and eighties may have been less a result of its challenge to the Bible than to the fact that the religious issue made it the most prominent of a number of theories in the natural and social sciences that made chaos the salient feature of the universe, implying that the social anarchy of the period might be a permanent condition.

If the moral effect of upheaval was the disruption of the connection between intentions and consequences, the universe of Darwin implied that the connection never existed. By rejecting the argument from design, the new pluralistic sciences would have broken the hard-won alliance between religion and science that had made it possible to conceive of a monistic science of society, one that was both "natural" and "moral." They would thus only have ratified the connection between material chaos and moral anarchy.

It was to those uncertainties that George and Bellamy provided answers. They rescued traditional and authentic values by embedding them in the kind of monistic intellectual structures that seemed most under attack. If they had created a science without morality, their arguments would have included neither the values they were trying to rescue nor the incentive for reform. The monistic structure thus served as an antidote to the social perception, and it made social reform a live option for an age that could have been inhibited by the attack on moral absolutes and paralyzed by the uncertainties of unpredictable change.

CHAPTER II

THE LAW OF PARSIMONY

Henry George

During the years 1877-79, while Henry George was revis-
ing classical economics in California, Richard T. Ely, a
founder of the pragmatistic New Economics, was learning to
reject the classical block universe under the tutelage of
Karl Knies at Heidelberg. When he disembarked in New York in
1880, the year Progress and Poverty was first widely distributed, Ely "became aware that our country was experiencing
a crisis in which the potentialities for good or for evil
were great beyond precedent. This was a time when either
optimism or pessimism was easy, but both were dangerous.
There was enough that was alarming to excite one to vigorous
action; there was enough that was promising to encourage the
brightest hopes." The sense of "genuine crisis" was evident
in the widespread conclusion that "the very foundations of
the social order" had somehow to be reconstructed.[1]

Lester F. Ward, in the nation's capital in 1881, sensed

the same stirrings. There was, he noticed, a growing demand for positive social action, and yet the little that was done was wrong-headed and ignorant because laissez-faire economists had convinced people that governmental interference would incite reprisals from nature. New forms of social control were inevitable, Ward observed; they were impelled by "blind sentiment," and social changes had opened an irrevocable and ever-widening gap between "prevailing theories" and "prevailing practices." The practices were new and the theories old, and the disjunction between the two indicated an "approaching crisis in social opinion," a "critical period . . . full of dangers to society."[2] Ward had finished Dynamic Sociology by the summer of 1880, the year of Progress and Poverty and Ely's return; and he expected the compelling force of his argument to derive from a similar perception of crisis and uncertainty. It was a time for Answers. If Ward's answer, artificial selection, were not begun soon, he warned, there would eventually be a cataclysm, a period of "reaction and degeneracy" with no possibility of ever progressing again.[3]

For Dynamic Sociology, as for the New Economics, the social chaos--the disjunction between prevailing theories and prevailing practices--implied that new modes of thought and

action were necessary for social survival and progress. Action
had to be geared not to the theoretical block universe of the
monists, but to a universe that accurately matched society as
it was perceived--and indeterminate, pluralistic universe in
which the consequences of actions would be random and unpredictable unless consciously controlled. The goal was to fit
the intellectual structure to the perception--to match chaos
with chaos, as Rexford Tugwell later described it[4]--and thereby
create what they conceived to be the only valid and possible
theory of reform. Given the support that conservatives derived from entrenched intellectual structures, it was not surprising that Ely and Ward would think that a whole new universe
of discourse was needed for a modernized liberalism. Their
concern was evidence that the new universe was an intellectual
option in the early 1880's; but the fact that they did not
have a significant public impact for almost a generation indicated that their proposed match between perception and structure was not a live option to the public at large. Instead,
center stage was taken by such thinkers as William Graham
Sumner and especially Henry George, who, while having little
but contempt for each other, were distinguishable from the
new social scientists in similar ways. Neither George nor

Sumner would accept as real or ultimate the chaotic and disorderly state of society. Both assumed that behind apparent chaos there was a permanent and unitary body of laws to explain and resolve it and that social thought had to assume a harmony between natural law and the social good. Sumner and George shared as well a belief that the universe contained permanent values, that new values geared to distinctively modern times were not required; and that a proper conception of science could overcome the "feebleness and vacillation in regard to economic doctrine" that arose during the "distress, uncertainty, and disorder" of the contemporary crisis.[5]

The values that both Sumner and George regarded as permanently valid were those of the small enterpriser. Sumner called him the "forgotten man." "He will be found to be worthy, industrious, independent, self-supporting. He is not, technically, 'poor' or 'weak'; he minds his own business, and makes no complaint. . . . He passes by and is never noticed, because he has behaved himself, fulfilled his contracts, and asked for nothing. . . . he is just what each one of us ought to be."[6] Both George and Sumner came from such backgrounds, and both rejected demands for absolute equality in favor of equal opportunity. Not happiness, but only its

pursuit, had to be guaranteed. Both assumed that there was
an economy in the universe, a principle of reciprocity that
guaranteed that when an unproductive man gained something he
had not produced, a productive man lost the value of his labor.
Yet for Sumner, the salvation of the productive man came
through inaction, and the block universe served as a bridge
between the liberating creativity of classical liberalism and
the self-protective defenses of modern conservatism. It required, in his mind, a rigid separation of morality, which he
derided as "sentiment," from science and therefore a refusal
to correct social evils on a social scale. Sympathetic action
had to be limited to the personal relationships between two
people. Anything larger flew in the face of nature, which
took prompt revenge. For the New Economists and Dynamic
Sociologists, morality was social, not merely personal; the
truths of social ethics and social science had to be identical; and thus "sciences" like Sumner's were persuasive evidence that the block universe, while perhaps appealing in a
chaotic era, could never promote reform.

Henry George's considerable intellectual feat was to
prove that judgment wrong, to make social reform seem possible
and necessary with a monistic intellectual structure.

Progress and Poverty showed that there was an alternative to
Sumner's belligerency in the conflict between science and
morality, between the individual and the social, and between
"natural" social equilibrium and conscious progress; and the
volume won an immediate and enthusiastic public reception.
It provided a reform alternative to the chaos and uncertainty
of the late 1870's and 1880's, a perception the newer social
scientists wanted to treat as a permanent reality; it
rescued a set of traditional American values; and it inspired
an international generation of future reformers, many of whom
would later regard it as too simple for modern times. For
when a new perception of society, as distinctively modern
and substantively complex, began to take hold, George's universe of discourse began to seem old-fashioned and unsophis-
ticated, the values he sought to rescue seemed irrelevant,
his own intellectual structure began to crack, and his Single
Tax was subjected to the ultimate degradation of a panacea--
to be considered simply one reform proposal among many.

I

The small enterpriser's conception of justice is probably as close as America has ever come to a generally accepted

economic ideal. Associated with the "workingman-producer"
in the literature of Jacksonianism, its relevance to wage
labor in the rising industrial collectivism of the late nineteenth century seemed increasingly tenuous and, in retrospect,
increasingly mythical. Yet it had strong personal and social resonance in the America in which Henry George and many
of his contemporaries had been raised. The Philadelphia in
which he was born in 1839 was, though the country's second
largest city, still a manageable and relatively homogeneous
trading community, and the values of market, church, and home
meshed comfortably in the George household.[7] Both of Henry
George's parents had been children of tradesman and artisans,
and both were resourceful, if never entirely successful,
enterprisers themselves. His mother, Catherine George, was
running a small school at the time of her marriage. His
father began as a sailor, had a dry goods business, became a
clerk in the Customs House, was a small publisher of religious books, and finally returned to his clerkship. St. Paul's
Episcopal Church, to which the family belonged, had a reputation for a simplicity of ritual that avoided, as distracting
and wasteful, the extravagance of the high-church service.
It stood for standards of Christian behavior that enabled the

small enterpriser to make ends meet and possibly to rise,
demanding not asceticism, but thrift, not renunciation, but
delayed gratification, not submissiveness, but self-reliance,
not the ambiguities of choosing between good and evil, but
steady habits and industry. A family recollection of an
early Sunday-School lesson revealed a Golden Rule that was
phrased negatively and had two parts: Do not do unto others
what you would not have them do unto you; and, just as important, do not allow yourself to be done unto.[8]

While the George family was rarely in need, finances
were apparently a strong undercurrent in its routines. Henry
George, as the second of ten children and the eldest of four
sons, seems to have realized very early that he could demand
only what he deserved. In such a large household with limited
resources, it was easy for the children to see the effects of
selfishness. There was an "economy" or "efficiency" in the
family unit that illustrated a principle of reciprocity: if
one member received more than his fair share, someone else was
being deprived. At the age of ten or eleven, Henry George refused to remain at a private Episcopal academy when he found
that he was no longer entitled to reduced tuition. At thirteen, he insisted on leaving school entirely and began to earn

his own way. Neither family recollections nor early letters reveal a concern with self-sacrifice for its own sake, even in a religious connection. The opposite of selfishness was not self-sacrifice, but justice.

Henry George began his serious pursuit of a livelihood in the wake of the panic of 1857, when opportunities for the tradesman seemed to have suddenly closed. After trying a variety of occupations, he settled on printing, worked his way to California, and, still in his early twenties, found himself with a family and no income. In his diary, he blamed himself for not following the patterns of behavior that were supposed to produce a just return. "To sum up for the present," he concluded in 1865, ". . . it is evident to me that I have not employed the time and means at my command as faithfully and advantageously as I might have done, and consequently, that I have myself to blame for at least part of my non-success. And this being true of the past, in the future like results will flow from like causes."[9] But the experience of California--the rapid closing of an open society, the rise of a few inordinately wealthy and powerful families, the straitened circumstances of talented people like himself, who wanted only the chance to work--quickly forced him to look elsewhere for the factor that made the relationship between "like causes" and "like results" unpredictable.

The occasion was an article that he published in 1868, weighing the advantages and problems of the growth that would accompany the transcontinental railway. The railway, he noted, would only increase the tendency of wealth to concentrate, for production would expand at the expense of wages and interest rates. High wages and interest, however, were "evidences of social health," "indications that the natural wealth of the country was not yet monopolized, that great opportunities were open to all." As opportunities declined, he argued, the benefits of growth would accrue more and more to those who were already well off. "Those who have lands, mines, established businesses, special abilities of certain kinds, will become richer for it and find increased opportunities; those who have only their own labour will become poorer, and find it harder to get ahead."[10]

George did not yet know a solution; nor did he preclude natural forces arising in the future to counterbalance the dangerous tendencies. But his argument had two features that were indications of his cognitive style. First, he refused to regard progress of any sort as more desirable than the

individual's opportunity to work, a test of social health that
was independent of growth. Second, he found a principle of
reciprocity acting in the economy; he treated the increasing
wealth of some as dependent upon the increasing poverty of
others, implying a unitary and static view of reality. He
saw these phenomena as accompanying growth, but not as
causally related to it. The dynamic factor in his analysis
was not growth at all, but the tendency of wealth to concentrate.

In his own enterprises, he could see that the principle
of justice in which he had been raised could produce its predicted results only where artificial restraints on opportunity
did not exist. In the course of the 1860's, he was connected
with journals that failed because the supply of news from the
East was monopolized by the Associated Press. He therefore
urged the construction of competing telegraph lines and then
government ownership. He attacked the importation of Chinese
labor as a tool of the railroad magnates to keep wages low.
He converted from protection to free trade and left the
Republican Party in 1868. He attempted unsuccessfully to get
a Democratic nomination for Assemblyman on an antimonopoly
platform. As editor of Governor Henry Haight's Sacramento

Reporter, he attacked the subsidies granted the Central
Pacific Railroad as a hindrance to industry, a source of corruption and inefficiency, and a violation of individual freedom. In 1871, he ran, again unsuccessfully, for the State
Assembly. Also in 1871, he wrote his first book.

II

By Victorian standards, Our Land and Land Policy was a
pamphlet--48 tightly packed pages in the original, 130 as
printed in the collected works--and it had the logic and
structure of a pamphlet. Its major focus was a policy proposal, and so the enemies were personalized and the language
dramatic. The book resulted, George later reported, from two
visions he had had. In 1869, in New York City, he had been
struck by the paradoxes of modern society, and he had vowed
to resolve them. In 1870, in Oakland, California, the answer
had been revealed.[11] George's recollections came after years
of proselytizing, during which he had been trying to make the
Single Tax a religious duty, and so the revelatory nature of
the insights could sanctify his ideas against those who might
believe that truth was provisional.

The paradoxes that struck George were the coexistence of

extreme wealth and extreme poverty, and the apparent fact that industrial advance, while increasing national wealth, had also aggravated the problems of the working poor. "A very Sodom's apple seems this 'progress' of ours to the classes that have the most need to progress."[12] The cause, which he had not pinpointed in the Overland article, was the progressive monopolization of the nation's land. George showed the extravagant squandering of the usable national domain and its capture by the wealthy and the powerful, especially, in California, by the railroads. He predicted that the remaining portion would be wiped out by 1890--the year in which the census-taker did in fact record the end of the continuous frontier. He foreshadowed Turner's thesis as well in relating the national domain to American character. That character could be preserved only if two remedial steps were taken: a more effective homestead system and a tax on the unearned value of land, the value resulting from the growth of the community rather than from improvements made by the landowner.

George kept abstract economic theory to a minimum in Our Land and Land Policy, since he was as yet largely unfamiliar with it. But he did adopt some economic concepts, and the scientific models that gave force to his argument also resulted in dualisms that would have permitted him to take either of two strikingly different intellectual paths after 1871.

"Wealth," George wrote, "is the product--or to speak more precisely, the equivalent of labor." A labor theory of value was very congenial to the "producer" ideology that persisted among labor and agrarian reformers to the end of the century. There were, however, two kinds of labor theory then current, and the dash in George's definition of wealth connected both of them. One, a theory of absolute value, defined all "real" or "natural" value as a product of labor. The other, a theory of exchange value, was more concrete and quantifiable, measuring the value of a thing by the amount of labor it could be exchanged for in the marketplace. The two definitions lent themselves to different types of arguments. Absolute value was suited to an abstract, deductive argument and was virtually useless for an argument dependent upon particulars, such as George's analysis of the situation in California. For that, exchange value was tailored. The ambiguity in his theory of value extended to his definitions of land and labor themselves. On the one hand, he treated them as abstract and aggregate factors of production, and, on the other, as discrete physical and moral things--places

to live and work and the actual people who did the living and
working. George explained the causes of the land problem in
California on the basis of exchange value; he justified his
proposed remedies on the basis of absolute value. The unin-
tentional ambiguity of his definitions made the arguments
seem one.[13]

Up to a point, the two forms of argument were mutually
reinforcing. George embedded his conception of justice in
the two themes that he expected to have the most bite: the
wastefulness of the current policy and the personal dependence
resulting from it--the two things most likely to disturb a
parishioner of St. Paul's. Thus, efficiency and personal
freedom (the opportunity to be one's own boss) derived their
force from both exchange and absolute value. The argument
from exchange value reduced to a statement about objective
economic power. Since the laborer had to live somewhere, the
landlord could extort his labor in the form of rent, while
the scarcity of land denied him the one retreat that could
free him from economic dependence. As the concentration of
ownership proceeded, the landlord's appropriation would expand until the worker was left with bare subsistence, making
him in effect a slave. The problems were thus the power of

the monopolist to fix rents and the laborer's lack of alternatives. The situation caused inefficiency as well as personal dependence since large grants and speculation kept
enormous amounts of land unproductive. Land-value taxation,
George argued, would force landowners to make land available
for productive use and for places to live, thus yielding both
efficient use of the nation's resources and opportunities for
independence. Similarly, by giving land without charge only
to actual settlers and only in the limited amounts that a
person could actually use without hired help, a revised homestead system would also guarantee personal freedom and national efficiency.[14]

Deduction from the theory of absolute value gave moral
and scientific backing to these particulars. By declaring
all wealth the product of labor, rather than simply measured
in terms of labor, George could declare land, the other
"term" of production, to be inherently valueless. Given by
God, land became wealth only when transformed by work. The
wealth of landowners, therefore, was "fictitious" and made
the country seem wealthier than it really was, while restricted access to land prevented an increase of real wealth.
The theory of absolute value thus justified the expropriation

of the expropriators. Not owning "real" wealth, landowners had no "right" to extort any labor and thereby deprive a man of his natural freedom, his ownership of his own labor.[15]

Neither of George's arguments gave capital more than a secondary role. The argument from exchange value depended upon his treatment of the landlord and the monopoly capitalist as a single interest (a contention fairly well supported by his data for California); otherwise, there would have been no connection between landlordism and low wages. The argument from absolute value depended upon there being only two factors of production; otherwise, there would have been no reason to confiscate rent alone. In ignoring the possible primacy of capital--an indifference that would persist in various forms throughout his career--George was ignoring the one factor of production that had undergone substantive changes in the course of history. Thus, the possibility that there was arising a distinctively modern type of economy, one that in-volved a permanent wage-earning class and large aggregations of industrial capital, was outside his analysis. Economic systems were not typed. The same natural laws governed all of them. The situation that caused the downfall of Rome would cause the downfall of the United States. Although

George did mention that the new modes of production had made
it harder for a man to go into business for himself, he did
not include that observation in his theoretical analysis,
where capital was fixed, or in his particular argument, where
independence was permanently assured by the crucial "fact"
that there was no foreseeable limit to the number of people
who could be supported on American land.[16]

Thus, the "dynamic" factor in Our Land and Land Policy
was not technological progress (changing forms of capital),
but the increasing concentration of wealth, which in turn
was the result of specific policies. George's reforms were
ultimately political and particular rather than scientific
and universal. Even his theoretical speculations did not explain the conjunction of progress and poverty, the paradox
whose resolution he had sought. Progress played a role only
in the guise of increasing population, which created the
unearned increment in the price of land. What George had
explained, therefore, in both forms of his argument, was the
conjunction of the increasing wealth of some people with the
increasing poverty of others, not the conjunction of increasing poverty with increasing aggregate wealth. Since there
were only two "terms" of production, land and labor, and

only two interests, monopoly and workers, George had only
demonstrated the static principle of reciprocity. He had
the powerless producers competing with the powerful non-
producers for the available wealth. Whatever the state of
the productive arts, the greater the share that went to one,
the less that was left for the other. Thus, land policy was
only the "main cause" of the problem in California' it explained not everything everywhere, but "most of the perplex-
ing phenomena."[17]

While the principle of reciprocity indicated George's
ultimate preference for a static analysis, the particularism
of his reforms did result in an uncomfortable contradiction
that could have led him along another path. Freedom and
efficiency were intimately connected in the small enterpriser's
version of justice. They could not exist apart, since they
made each other possible; but the inherent conflict between
George's two modes of argument emerged to set them against
each other. Under the theory of absolute value, for example,
land, with only a fictitious worth, should not have been
morally exchangeable for labor, since that would subtract
from the worker's natural freedom, his right to a full return.
On the other hand, exchange value gave land a value in terms

of labor and implicitly guaranteed private property in land, because a free man had a right to himself, to his labor, and to whatever he exchanged his labor for. In that case, efficiency had to restrict freedom on pragmatic grounds. Because the quantity of land was fixed (though sufficient), rightful title had to be limited to the amount needed to "satisfy a reasonable need," to sustain life when efficiently used.[18] That was the sort of measure that did not lend itself to universals, that would require continuous administrative oversight, and that depended upon a balance of political power among competing groups to keep in check the tendency of wealth to concentrate. The contradictions between a person's natural freedom and his limited right to the land, between the theory of absolute value and the right of title to something labor did not create, arose because George was less concerned in 1871 with land and labor as abstract factors of production than with a particular problem in California. Thus private ownership of land in limited quantities was an institutional guarantee of personal independence that George was yet unwilling to abandon.

There were two ways he could have resolved the intellectual problem after 1871: either by holding strictly to

exchange value and making a pragmatic, political argument for
his reforms, the only sort of argument that could both support
a right of title and limit it at the same time, or by ending
private landownership entirely and developing a consistent
deductive argument from absolute value and natural right.
The choices were not merely technical, since they pointed to
radically different modes of discourse. The tension between
the scientific and the personal, between the power analysis
based on exchange value and the moral surety based on absolute value, reflected the emerging conflict between two
styles of economic and social thought. The argument on the
personal and particular level of specific classes, institutions, and economic mechanisms might have led George to a
historical, comparative, or institutional New Economics,
rather than to the classical conception of political economy,
which the scientific analysis of the pamphlet tried to imitate. In the eight years between Our Land and Land Policy
and Progress and Poverty, George developed in the latter
direction, and the enormous popularity of his second book may
indicate that he chose wisely.

The options were live ones; and had George not rejected
the former path and adopted the latter, he might have been

more "modern"--though less popular--than he was. In 1877, the year he began <u>Progress and Poverty</u>, George, in a vain attempt to get a professorship, delivered a lecture at the University of California on the science of political economy. In the century since Adam Smith's <u>Wealth of Nations</u>, George complained, and especially in the sixty years since Ricardo's theory of rent, no substantial improvement had been made in political economy, and its very status as a science was in question. George blamed the lack of progress on vested interests, who found it useful to believe that economic truths were not only final, but nearly all known, especially since those truths affirmed the futility of trying to help the poor or strengthen the wage-earner. Instead, George argued, political economy ought to be directed to lighten "the dark side of our boasted progress," to find the "causes of social weakness and disease," and to demonstrate remedies, to solve, in sum, the "labor problem."[19]

George's radical views kept him from the professorship, but his complaints against economic orthodoxy were paralleled point by point in the tracts that were to be written during the eighties by the rising school of reformist New Economists, who had been training in the late seventies in Germany.

Richard T. Ely, for example, introduced one collective
manifesto by arguing that vested interests had given traditional economists academic positions in order to refute dangerous doctrines. The pretensions to finality and completeness served as a scientific ratification of the existing
system. Like George, the founders of the American Economic
Association rejected the idea that political economy and
public policy were separate. Like George, they argued that
social science could not ignore moral values; and they emphasized the agency of motives other than selfishness in economic life. Their goal, which was also George's, was to solve
the "paramount question of political economy to-day"--the
"question of distribution," the "question of the laborer,"
the "social problem."[20]

From this common vantage point, however, George and the
New Economists chose opposite conceptions of social science.
Both saw social history at a crisis point, but they interpreted "crisis" differently, lent credence to different modes
of understanding and dealing with it--and their public recep-
tions were vastly different. George's impact was direct and
immediate; the New Economists did not begin to reach a com-
parable audience until the mid-nineties or later; and thus

their triumph in the Progressive Era should not obscure the
fact that George should be taken as the salient figure in the
American liberalism of the early 1880's. Their different interpretations of the prevailing crisis centered on two crucial issues: modernity and complexity. For the new school,
political economy had to acknowledge both; for George, neither.
The New Economists held that economic theories were relative
to the time and place in which they arose and to the conditions they sought to explain and reform. Classical economics,
they argued, had arisen when close mercantilistic regulation
had become obstructive of economic growth, and thus the idea
of a natural order in society that was itself inherently constructive had helped break mercantilism down. It had been
useful, the New School admitted, but it had never been true,
and its usefulness as fiction was outdated. Times had changed.
The sense of crisis indicated not mere disorder, but a new
beginning for society, a transition to a distinctively
modern era. The classical system, Ely noted, could have
"nothing to say" when "new economic formations" created new
problems; and so a science that dealt with universals was,
as Mayo-Smith argued, "on the face of it absurd." And
Henry C. Adams capped the relativity of the discipline by

asserting that for all practical purposes a "lego-historical fact" had the same impact as a "fact of nature," and so all the distinctive traits of a given age had to be part of the body of the science.[21]

Similarly, the New Economists deplored as self-contradictory the classical economists' argument that social life was too complicated to be understood by the inductive method, that only deduction from "a few simple truths" could comprehend the source of disorder. "For the confusing, the bewildering complexity of the economic phenomena surrounding us," Ely complained of the classicists, "they substituted an enticing unity and an alluring simplicity." They allowed the ordinary man to think he could be an expert, and thus they maintained the legitimacy of amateurism against the rising claims of professional scholars. The only method of wending a way through the real universe, the pluralistic universe, the New Economists argued, was not with laws, but with the tentative empirical hypotheses of an inductive science. "Experience," they said, "is the basis"--"step by step" reforms would be made and their consequences studied before the process continued. Predictability was out of the question, since economic arrangements "are founded partly on the

nature of things, but are also due in part to the present
state of civilization and, to a certain extent, to accident
and chance." The sole realistic aim could be to "solve concrete problems as they arise." After 1883, Lester Ward provided the New Economists with an appropriate model of the
progress of a complex organization. Society was a "continuous conscious organism capable of placing before itself an
ideal structure to be attained."[22]

The New Economists' model of social progress foreshadowed
the one used by Jane Addams and Herbert Croly in the Progressive Era, when the perception of transition to a distinctively
modern and substantively complex society seemed compelling.
Henry George himself would display some elements of that model
in the mid-eighties, when he, too, began to react to a similar
perception. But his intellectual needs in 1877-80 were very
different. Richard Ely interpreted the disorder that he
found on his return from Germany in 1880 as a symptom of a
transition to modernity and complexity, requiring new values
and methods. George described it as chaos in Progress and
Poverty and felt he had to explain it away. There had been
a continuous rise in social tensions since the Panic of 1873,
and George began to write Progress and Poverty during the

climactic railroad strike of 1877, the first of the great
"industrial wars" of the postbellum period. The episode had
created a wave of near hysteria, with the popular press al-
ternating between demands for "law and order" and calls for
"reform."[23] In retrospect, the salient feature of both
approaches has seemed to be their irrelevance to the actual
transformation to modern industrial capitalism that was then
occurring. Transitions, however, are not often seen as having a direction until they are almost over. The first industrial war is not likely to be taken as symptomatic of the
same condition as the fourth or fifth. In its midst, transition is experienced as disorder, upheaval, chaos, and uncertainty about the future. An historical economics might have
pointed out where a later generation of Americans saw society
as headed--an industrial order with a permanent working class.
But while that might not have required much more evidence
than was available in 1870, it would have required a frame
of mind receptive to such an analysis Outside of anthropol-
ogy, however, evolutionary thought was only beginning to be
used in America to explain substantive changes in economic
systems; and the epochal event separating medieval from modern
times was not "industrialization" but the substitution of

contract for status several centuries before. The New Economics itself did not appear in an American university curriculum until 1881, when Ely and Adams brought it to Johns
Hopkins; none of the New Economists found it easy to get a
sympathetic public hearing (or a job) in the eighties; and
their most influential public works did not appear until
almost a decade later. As late as 1898, Veblen was complaining about the dominance of the old conception of science in
economics.[24] And "Industrial Revolution" as a coherent concept had not yet been formulated in 1880. As long as the
great age of invention could be dated to the 1760's (before
Adam Smith wrote his epochal treatise) there was no need to
think that the methods of classical political economy had
been recently outdated--though some of its laws might have
been wrong.

Thus for George, claims of complexity allowed charlatans
to "palm off" either quack remedies for social problems or
excuses for letting people starve. Although like the new
school he criticized classical economists for their misguided
doctrines and poor reasoning, he found no grounds to reject
their mode of explanation. "Although political economy
deals with various and complicated phenomena," he told the

students of California in 1877, "yet they are phenomena which may be resolved into simple elements, and which are but the manifestations of familiar principles." He praised the "simplicity and certainty of a science too generally regarded as complex and indeterminate." Such a science would find "in the constantly changing phenomena the evidence of unchanging law." It was possible to reduce the context of an economic problem to what Ely dismissed as "isolated barbarous conditions" and still reach conclusions valid for modern society.[25]

Such a thoroughly deductive science would permanently lock out such inductive perceptions as "distinctive modernity" and "substantive complexity"--the peculiar, the special, the local, the historically changing or evolving--and thus chaos and upheaval would not be seen as symptoms of a new birth of society. Nor would they demand, as the pluralistic model implied, the invention of new and tentative values for a new and complicated age, values whose authenticity would therefore be in doubt. Not only did George not see a distinctively new age emerging, but he saw his task as reasserting in the midst of uncertainty the permanent and authentic values of the historic system. By immersing himself in the classical universe, by universalizing his argument, by, for example, writing about factors of production (land, labor, capital) rather than classes of people (landowners, workers, capitalists), George could rescue the values of the "workingman-producer," show the natural link between labor and capital, obviate class conflict, and undermine the landlord-business alliance that he had found in California. His belief that America would always have enough land minimized substantive social change itself and permanently underwrote free enterprise. By raising his values and beliefs--the enterpriser's values of freedom and efficiency that had pervaded Our Land and Land Policy--to the level of scientific axioms and moral absolutes, as he set out to do in Progress and Poverty, he could fix them forever in God's universe.

III

The impetus to universalization is thus traceable to George's perception of chaos in all of American society in the late 1870's and from his impulse to tackle that problem rather than just the victimization of California workers by special interests. George wrote Progress and Poverty in the last years of the longest depression in American history, but as the experience of the 1930's would show, it was possible

to interpret the significance of depression in different
ways. To liberal economists of the New Deal years, their
depression was a symptom of social stasis, a sign of the
final emergence of a mature industrial society, in effect
the last stage of social history. Henry George saw his
contemporaries regarding theirs as evidence of just the op-
posite--social chaos with possibilities of cataclysm. The
liberals of the 1930's took the nature of society and its
future for granted and went about their reforms with an
alacrity and self-assurance that were stunning. For George
and his public, the pervasive uncertainty about the future
inhibited any such approach. "There is a vague but general
feeling of disappointment," George observed; "an increased
bitterness among the working classes; a widespread feeling
of unrest and brooding revolution. If this were accompanied
by a definite idea of how relief is to be attained, it would
be a hopeful sign; but it is not." The institutional bul-
warks of traditional values were losing their influence.
The decline of religion and the resulting spiritual malaise
indicated that "the mightiest actions and reactions" were
preparing. Such symptoms "have heretofore always marked
periods of transition." They accompanied the French

Revolution and the decline of ancient civilization. "What change may come, no mortal man can tell, but that some great change must come, thoughtful men begin to feel. The civilized world is trembling on the verge of a great movement." A year and a half later, he reiterated his prognosis "that even now, in modern civilization, the causes which have destroyed all previous civilizations are beginning to manifest themselves, and that mere political democracy is running its course toward anarchy and despotism."[26]

George codified the chaos as the frightening paradox that social problems were greatest where material progress (increases in population, production, and the social attributes affecting production) was most advanced, that poverty actually increased as newer communities progressed toward the material conditions of older ones. That the United States would become like Europe had long been an American nightmare, and George did not feel compelled to adduce evidence to convince his readers that it was beginning to come true. Modern studies have supported the contention of economists of the 1870's and 1880's that real wages had increased since the late eighteenth century. But the same authorities were also certain that despite the increase, labor's share of wealth

had declined, while productivity and profits had risen.
Labor was absolutely better off but relatively worse off than
it had been.[27] That, despite the other resonances of the
word, was George's definition of "poverty."[28] His concern
was for laborers, not for indigents. Poverty was the lack of
a fair wage, a violation of the workingman-producer's value
of justice, of his right to a full return for his labor. It
was a name for the disjunction between accepted values and
actual practices. An apparently increasing tramp population
in the late seventies and eighties served as a vision of the
ultimate end of the process in which both the land and the
laborer's productivity were engrossed by the monopolist. The
early predictions of an industrial golden age had proven
false, and the future itself was a threat. Material progress,
George wrote, "does not merely fail to relieve poverty--it
actually produces it."[29]

George's task was to make this increasingly dangerous
form of social change no longer incomprehensible and threatening, and to make it possible to interfere with it so that its
results would be just. Evolutionary thought could do the
first without the second--understanding without reform--as
conservative Darwinism showed. It could also do both, but in

a way that George found uncongenial. The New Economists, for
example, with their perception of "modern" society, their
piecemeal description of its emerging characteristics, and
their consequent argument for experimental action, offered
the sort of thinking that would capture the future. George
offered another way and captured his contemporaries.

George's alternative to both passivity and experimentalism was a panacea that came to be known as the Single Tax.
He occasionally denied that it was a panacea. Indeed, it
was no more of a cure-all--and no less--than other measures,
such as free trade and currency reform, that gained popular
attention in the 1870's and 1880's by promising to be a sufficient solution to social problems. Their attraction was
their panacean flavor. It was necessary to find, as George
put it, "a solution which accounts for all the facts and
points to [a] clear and simple remedy." George's clear and
simple remedy was to assert the principle of common ownership
of land by taxing land-values to their full extent and abolish-
ing all other taxes. That it was clear and simple--that it
denied the very existence of complexity--is apparent. That
it was attractive because it seemed to be a panacea is also
convincing: "What I, therefore, propose as the simple yet

sovereign remedy, which will raise wages, increase the earnings of capital, extirpate pauperism, abolish poverty, give
remunerative employment to whoever wishes it, afford free
scope to human powers, lessen crime, elevate morals, and
taste, and intelligence, purify government, and carry civilization to yet nobler heights, is--to appropriate rent by
taxation."[30]

Less important than George's specific proposal (to which
he devoted only a minute portion of his volume) was the mode
of reasoning by which he connected the broad world of social
chaos to a pinpoint reform. George's real service was to
create a monistic intellectual structure out of three sets
of polar ideas that seemed to his contemporaries to be locked
in mortal combat, a combat that reinforced the perception of
social chaos with an appearance of intellectual and moral
anarchy: the static vs. the dynamic; the scientific vs. the
moral; and the individual vs. the social.

George's "statics"--his economic analysis--was a radical
revision of classical political economy. Though as a form of
explanation it followed the classical model rather closely,
it replaced what Veblen, who was influenced by George, called
a system of "constraining normality" with one of liberating

regularity.

George based his science on two implicit assumptions: a
condition of freedom and an axiom of efficiency. The state
of perfect freedom from which his laws were derived was the
equivalent of the frictionless universe in Newtonian physics.
To George and the classical economists, it was the one thing
that made political economy "as exact a science as geometry."
As statements of the relationship between cause and effect,
economic laws could not be limited by context, for "the
fundamental truth, that in all economic reasoning must be
firmly grasped, and never let go, is that society in its most
highly developed form is but an elaboration of society in its
rudest beginnings, and that principles obvious in the simplest
relations of men are merely disguised and not abrogated or
reversed by the more intricate relations that result from the
division of labor and the use of complex tools and methods."
George's science was thus one of stripping away complexities,
reducing situations to their simplest and freest forms, deriving the laws, and then applying them to modern society
because there was nothing scientifically accountable or distinctive about modern life. To reach the simplest, most
natural, and therefore truest case, all the excrescences that

might obscure the operations of the laws had to be removed. These excrescences, called "history," formed the materials of the New Economics. For George to have taken them into account would have destroyed the absolute and universal character of his science.[31]

Thus, even were the emergence of an industrialized society objectively obvious, it would not have been intellectually relevant to him. The differences between two forms of economic organization, the historical factors, were not as real as the scientific factors, their similarities. The consequential transition for George was not from one mode of production to another, but from an open society to a closed one, from a society that resembled the freest, simplest, and most natural operation of the laws, to one in which freedom was hobbled and which therefore faced destruction. Since George set up his laws to operate "under conditions of freedom," they naturally prescribed freedom as necessary for the survival of society and as a standard by which progress had to be judged.

George's second assumption, which may be called the axiom of efficiency or economy, was more explicit. "The fundamental principle of human action--the law that is to

political economy what the law of gravitation is to physics--
is that men seek to gratify their desires with the least exertion."[32] The axiom made possible a social science of individual actions, but it was not a statement of hedonism. For
George, it expressed the scientific discountability of wasted
effort, an individual equivalent of the harmonious economy of
the universe, logically necessary for a deductive science of
"economy," meaning the direct connection between means and
ends. Put more concretely, it was the labor theory of absolute value. The natural value of a good was the amount of
labor devoted to its production or procurement. There was a
second half to this axiom: the sufficiency of the material
universe. In contrast to the classical economists and Darwinians, George assumed that the earth was equipped with
enough resources to sustain all life as long as they were
efficiently employed. This had to be the obverse of absolute
value, for if land were insufficient, then demand-value (rent)
might be legitimate as a form of rationing. The crucial
American "fact" of Our Land and Land Policy had to be a
permanent attribute of the universe.

The assumptions of freedom and efficiency allowed George
to knock down the props of classical economics and create a

reform alternative. Two classical arguments had explained the persistence of poverty in a context of progress: the theory that wages were drawn from a fixed fund of capital, and the Malthusian law that population tended to outstrip productivity. Both contradicted George's axioms. By defining land (the entire material universe except man) as given, and labor as human exertion, George could show that wealth (the union of land and labor) and capital (the portion of wealth used to produce more wealth) had to be derivative and sufficient. A man's wages, instead of being drawn from a fixed amount of capital, were a draft upon the general stock of wealth, which had been increased by the amount of his labor. To try to reduce poverty, therefore, either by increasing capital (technological progress) or by decreasing the number of workers would be illogical. Mathusianism violated the same logic. As long as land was available for work, the more mouths there were to feed, the more hands there were to produce. There was no inevitability in the struggle for survival.[33]

The same two elements underlay George's most radical reversal of orthodoxy: his unification of the three laws of distribution with each other and with the laws of production. Since the factors of production were sufficient to preclude

poverty, the cause had to be in the mechanics of distribution.
Classical economics had divorced the two, treated the three
elements of the latter (wages, interest, and rent) as distinct, and thus separated the problem of poverty from that
of productive progress. George, in contrast, concluded that
all three elements of distribution came directly out of the
returns of production. Since labor and capital by definition
produced their own full return, rent, resulting only from demand, had to come out of their shares. Thus wages and interest, labor and capital, were not in conflict with each other,
as the wage-fund theory indicated, but both were in conflict
with rent. Rents rose when progress increased the demands on
the material universe, lowering the margin of cultivation.
Depression resulted when the prospect of progress caused land
speculation to so raise rents that the returns to capital and
labor were not sufficient to continue production. By restrict-
ing access to natural resources, the landowner got something
for nothing, violating both economy and freedom. It was thus
an unnatural social mechanism--private ownership of the given--
that brought poverty with progress. Common ownership, effected
through land-value taxation, would "make wages what justice
demands they should be--the full earnings of the laborer."[34]

In forming production and distribution into a single process and linking all economic laws to each other through the
axiom of efficiency[35]--itself a statement of production for
distribution--George had created a system more complete, more
unitary, more universal, and therefore in his eyes more scientific than that of the classical economists.

Similar pressures to create a monistic social science in
the seventies and eighties were evident in the work of George's
archrival, William Graham Sumner of Yale, who attacked Progress
and Poverty in 1881 for misunderstanding economic laws and sociological principles.[36]   Like George, Sumner used science to
secure old values. But he also succeeded in defining the barrier between classical and modern liberalism, both George's
version and that of the New Economists. In 1878, Sumner
called the latters' attempt to trace in detail the complicated
problems of modern economic life a "mistaken" conception of
scientific method. The "constraining normality" of classical
economics, pre-Darwin, was a permanent propensity toward
equilibrium. Since Sumner accepted that idea, he could "not
believe that the advance of economic science depends upon
fuller and more minute description of complicated social
phenomena as they present themselves in experience, but on a

stricter analysis of them in order to get a closer and clearer knowledge of the laws by which the forces producing them operate." He distinguished between universal forces of nature, whose operation in society was described by laws of political economy, and arbitrary patterns and complexities, which had no place in the discipline. One was science, and the other was history; and nothing could be gained by mixing them up.[37]

Unlike George, Sumner seemed to acknowledge certain new conditions of modern industrial life, its complexity, its interdependence, its extreme sensitivity; but that only strengthened his insistence that economic science had to be both natural and deductive. His great fear, in fact, was the very thing George exploited: that people would mistake "the phenomena of a new era for the approach of calamity," that they would "lose their heads and begin to doubt the economic doctrines which have been most thoroughly established."[38] What defined Sumner's classical liberalism as a new con- servatism, therefore, was his denial of the scientific rele- vance of his own perception of society.

Sumner's assumption that complete knowledge of economic laws, when attained, would preclude control, was an odd posi- tion for a scientist to take, but it did give an indication of

how his conception of natural law differed from George's.
The laws of evolution, which Sumner accepted from Herbert
Spencer, were processes with effects of their own. The laws
of economics described the permanent relationships among
natural forces. Both were self-consciously, if inaccurately,
patterned after the laws of Newtonian physics. George
thought he was following the same pattern, but he denied the
existence of natural forces in society and of "ideal points"
toward which actions tended. His laws were simply statements
of cause and effect, in a sense "media" through which all
actions passed in order to have consequences. Laws had no
results of their own, but they could foretell the effects
of any arrangement. In that way, George could give complete
predictive certainty (which the New Economists were willing
to live without, as the price of reform) and still be a reformer.

Similarly, Sumner could absorb the idea of substantive,
irreducible complexity as just another argument against reform and still retain the idea of a natural equilibrium.
George could not absorb it without disrupting his intellectual
structure or giving up the possibility of reform. If his laws
had been the "working hypotheses" of the New Economists or the

Pragmatists, scientific reform, as he understood it, would not have been possible. Like Sumner, he saw science and history as inherently separate disciplines. The consequences of actions were determined by natural law, not by their historical context. But because he was a reformer, George did not face the dilemma of conservative monists like Spencer and Sumner: the acceptance of complexity as substantive for one purpose (to discourage reform) and as only apparent for another (the definition of science). The New Economists did not face the dilemma either, since for them complexity was substantive for both purposes and caused a redefinition of social science to deal with a pluralistic universe. In the 1870's and 1880's, however, the preeminent conception of social science was the one shared by George and Sumner, that the real universe was unitary and therefore so must be the intellectual structure that comprehended it. But only George used it comfortably for reform.

Thus, the dynamic thing, progress--either material or spiritual--was not at the center of George's science. He had reconciled the static and the dynamic by using the former to relieve the latter of its threatening side-effects. Material progress worked <u>through</u> the laws, making its effects predictable; with a small social adjustment, they could also be just. Material progress itself, if it was "caused" at all, was the result of things outside George's science, such as an innate desire for more and better things or a tendency for technical knowledge to expand. All forms of progress other than the material resulted from volition and the accumulation of intelligence. While that took them out of the unknown and brought them within human control, it did not bring them within the purview of natural law. George could not legitimately say that continuous improvement would result from his reform. Not adopting it would produce an increasingly inequitable distribution of wealth until civilization toppled. Adopting it would revise the distribution until it was equitable. Since "equitable" meant a full return to the laborer of the amount of wealth his labor created, there was nothing "progressive" in it. George's Law of Human Progress--association in equality--simply summed up his statics to show that equity was necessary for the survival of society. Making society better was a separate problem and might require whole new sciences of the sort George would not accept as scientific. The antidote to perceive chaos had to be theoretical stasis.

The second polarity George faced was as difficult as
that between the static and the dynamic. Understanding that
while scientific materialism might command the intellect, moral
idealism commanded the will, he felt he had to supplement scientific certainty with a moral incentive for reform. If these
two arguments had been based on conflicting assumptions,[39] the
book might not have had the same reception, especially the
welcome from Social Gospelists and the criticism from academic
economists. Nor could John Dewey have praised it as an example of a fusion of scientific and ethical arguments.[40] Nor,
indeed, could it have served George's apparent purpose of
uniting all truths, scientific and moral, into a single intellectual structure. A "pure" science could obstruct reform.
Classical economists, for example, rigidly separated the
"pure" and the "applied," "science" and "art," natural law
and morality. In order to get people to act, rather than re-
frain from acting, George had to make morality identical with
his science. Since the conflict between "idealism" and
"materialism" loomed large in intellectual arguments of the
1870's and 1880's, his identification of the two was an
attractive intellectual feat.

On one plane, he simply adapted the natural theology
that had reconciled Newtonian physics and Christian ethics.
The universality of scientific laws made them morally absolute, the laws of a just and beneficent God, harmonious and
economical. Thus, the fact that Malthus had pitted two
natural laws against each other--reproduction and the world's
ability to sustain life--was an "impiety far worse than
atheism."[41] God's laws could not cause poverty--indeed,
laws did not cause anything--only human action could. Thus,
George's statement that the wisest policy was also the most
just was an expression, not of utilitarianism, but of faith
in the universality of natural law. It was possible to
translate scientific questions into questions of morality
without losing anything in the translation.

On a deeper level, the two implicit assumptions of
George's science had exact counterparts giving force to his
moral argument. The assumption of freedom had a twin in the
natural right of title. The simplest and freest case in
George's science was that of a man working on the land to
produce something and then exchanging it for the value of
his labor. He was entitled to that value because he was
naturally free: he had a right to himself, and his labor

was part of him. By extension, no man could claim as his that
which he had acquired without labor; so no man had rightful
title to God's gift of land. Thus, George's scientific
"ceteris paribus" and his social ideal were the same: freedom
to work on the material universe. His famous "paean to
liberty" expressed his belief that when civilizations declined
it was that freedom that was lost.

Similarly, perhaps no ethical value could have had a
clearer material origin than George's justice: the small
enterpriser's demand for full and fair returns. The axiom of
efficiency--that men seek to gratify their desires with the
least exertion--did not imply a selfishness that conflicted
with morality. As an expression of the labor theory of absolute value, it stated that the work required to satisfy a
desire was the natural worth of the thing desired, the amount
of labor that could legitimately be expected in return for it.
Exertion produced a full return. The ideal of justice was
its moral equivalent, adding only the demand that the return
go to the laborer who created it. The axiom of efficiency
and its counterpart were thus sufficient to impel the single
tax and to moralize the society that adopted it. Anything
else--such as George's ingenious proof of immortality, which

he added to the book just before publication[42]--was superfluous. His reconciliation of materialism (science) and idealism
(morality) was made according to the demands of the former.

The third polarity that George faced pitted the individual against the social. The "social problem"--the inequitable distribution of wealth--was, as he saw it, a disjunction
between individual intentions and social results. All the
things people naturally did to earn a living were only increasing their own misery or that of others. Poverty as a
social evil was expressed in the question of priorities:
what makes a nation great. But for the purposes of science,
George defined it individualistically, in terms of a fair
wage. Similarly George's political economy was a social
science of individual actions. The existence of natural
law could be validated only in society, but the science itself was derived from an axiom of individual behavior. In
the 1930's, liberal economists used statistical probability
and group psychology to treat the collective person as real
and still guarantee individual freedom. George and the
classical economists could deal scientifically with "men in
the aggregate" only by assuming some uniformity in the

economic behavior of individuals. Classical economics had
assumed hedonism or self-interest; George, the axiom of efficiency, a statement for the labor theory of value, of logically calculable behavior. But "logically calculable" was
the same as "natural" in his conception of science, and so
the natural actions of individuals could not be held responsible for the misery they seemed to cause. Poverty had to be
the result of a social mechanism: individual property in
land. The remedy was social in content--common ownership--
and in execution, and therefore George would have to organize
a movement. But its ultimate effect would be to give individuals equal access to the material world, restoring competitive individualism.

In this intertwining of the social and the individual,
George was in fact treating only one (the individual) as fundamental. Since that was also the case with the other polarities,
a bond existed across all three of them. George was not only
reconciling three polar pairs: individual-social, material-
ideal (or scientific-moral), and static-dynamic (or static-
progressive). He was also unifying two triads: individual-
scientific-static and social-ideal-progressive. And he was
unifying them by establishing the fundamentality of the former.

His only science was his statics, derived from an axiom about individual behavior in the freest and most natural, the least social, state. Society was indeed the repository of progress, but it therefore embodied history and change, things George's conception of science could not handle. Society and progress were not logically calculable. Private property in land was a relic not of an outmoded individualism, but of an artificial social interference in the perfect individual freedom of the natural state. The remedy was less "common ownership" of land than non-ownership and equal access to it. A social movement was necessary, but once the single act of reform--legislating the tax--was achieved, collective action would cease, and the resulting society would be the height of purified individualism. People would be rewarded only for the amount of work they did. Justice was simply a statement of individual rights, and the apparently collective ideal of "fraternity," under which George said the reformed society would operate, was individualistic as well, an idealistic label for the totality expressed by the principle of reciprocity: in the closed society, the increasing wealth of some depended upon the increasing poverty of others. In the reformed society, the economic behavior of individuals would remain unchanged--it

was axiomatic; it would not become "social" or "collective."
Fraternity was merely the absence of jealousy and need. It
was not the "cooperative commonwealth" that would become popular in the late 1880's.[43]

George thus unified two competing triads, representing
competing modes of thought and action, by putting one of
them at the center of the universe. After 1880, when he was
starting to organize a reform movement, the beginnings of a
perception of society as distinctively modern and substantively complex would force the progressive triad on his attention as an independent mode of discourse. It would then
compete within his own writings with the static mode, in much
the way that the pluralistic New Economics and Dynamic Sociology competed with monistic classical economics and social
physics for the adherence of society at large. The resulting
dualisms would foreshadow the intellectual structure of leading Progressives, for whom the coexistence of competing modes
of discourse was not only congenial, but useful and soothing.
George, however, would be uncomfortable with it, and his
unconscious attempts to eliminate the irritants would ultimately mark him as old-fashioned to his successors. In 1880,
however, he presented to a responsive public a nearly perfect

example of a perception of social chaos creating pressures to form a monistic intellectual structure out of the anarchy of contemporary intellectual life.

The elegant unity of Progress and Poverty made it a complete reform document in the context of that perception. Its structural unity refuted the perceived state of society and focused attention on a pinpoint reform. It made an appeal that many Americans, reformers and conservatives alike, have often taken as universal: the appeal to the tradition of the small enterpriser. This may have been the last decade in which such an appeal could be legitimate, though not, certainly, the last in which it was made. That America was entering a new era in its social history, that memories of Jacksonian America were no longer useful, was not yet a widespread perception. Even in national politics, the Jacksonian issue of tariff, currency, and civil service, still virtually monopolized attention.

The small enterpriser's standards of behavior had been calculated to produce success in an open society. In Progress and Poverty, those standards appeared as the axiom of efficiency; the open society appeared as the condition of freedom. George took them as self-evident assumptions, derived laws

from them, recommended a reform that embodied them, and tested
the reform by using them as standards. Social sciences can
often work in this circular way. Values result in laws or
models that not only verify, but assume, the values, yielding
proposals already contained in the assumptions. Explicitly
deductive reasoning, like George's, is especially susceptible
to it. But the shortcomings of deductive reasoning are less
important than the question of why people find it convincing
at one time and not another. For George, its usefulness was
that it provided an Answer, a way of coming to terms with
random, inexplicable, threatening social change, not by
abandoning monism and traditional values, conforming his
theoretical structure to his perception of chaos, taking random change as characteristic of the universe and calling it
pluralism, but by using what he took to be the model of
liberal science: by depriving change of its randomness, its
inexplicability, and its resistance to control. Society
might seem to be in a period of chaos; but the "real" society--
the society embodied in scientific theory--was in fact static
and comprehensible. As long as chaos remained the prevailing
perception, the prevailing malaise would be traceable to
uncertainty about the future. And as long as there was a

willingness to lock out the perceptions of distinctive
modernity and substantive complexity, then the monistic intellectual structure of Progress and Poverty would be congenial.

IV

When the circulation of Progress and Poverty reached
the hundreds of thousands, through additional printings, cheap
editions, and newspaper serializations, George could reasonably feel that his work had answered a real need. To restore
the world to some degree of human control, however, he had
left substantive social change outside the realm of science.
He had, in depicting man as a social animal, made society a
natural thing. But its laws were static and unitary, not
developmental. The single tax would not create progress; it
would only prevent decline.

E. L. Youmans caught the unprogressive nature of George's
laws and the "unnatural" character of his conception of
progress; and he attacked George for being unscientific.
Youmans' passive Darwinism offered no solution to social problems, as George well knew; and George did not "think his
criticisms very serious." Nevertheless, in The Land Question
(1881), his first strategic guide for a reform movement,

George did stress the scientific naturalness of social development according to a law of integration that tied specialization to interdependence. But he distinguished between a natural integration (interdependence in equality) and an unnatural one (dependent inequality), introducing a wedge of normality and an element of will and choice that a truly "scientific" evolutionism of the type Youmans demanded would not have allowed. The distinction made natural and necessary a society with all the characteristics that the single tax would confer.[44]

Thus, George made it clear that he was not about to give up statics in political economy. His reform was more than a radicalization of capitalism on terms favorable to workers. The reform was no more historically determined in The Land Question than it had been in Progress and Poverty. His science still described society in general. He traced the inequities of modern life not to industrialization but to the era when the feudal class of landholders threw off its responsibilities and burdens and yet managed to retain its privileges and political power. The natural laws were not affected by the change, and science did not have to take it into account.

As George became increasingly involved in social

agitation, however, and looked more and more closely at modern life, the tension between the static laws of political economy and the dynamic law of development became more apparent. By 1883, it had forced the reemergence of the progressive triad in its own right. Our Land and Land Policy, George's 1871 book, had pointed in two possible directions: a particularistic science or a universal one, intellectual pluralism or intellectual monism. In Progress and Poverty, George had chosen the latter as a response to social chaos, and that had contributed to the volume's success. But George's reform was not so popular as his book, and three years of unsuccessful reform agitation raised the options again. For George found that he had to argue for what he had naturally assumed in 1879: not only that one should support his reform, but that one should become a reformer at all, that things should be changed, and that it had to be done now. The "now" sowed the seeds of discord.

In response to the new demand to justify reform in general--and in direct response to Sumner's attack on reformers-- George wrote Social Problems (1883), a book twentieth-century readers have often found more congenial than Progress and Poverty. It contained his most extensive discussion of the

peculiar problems of modern society, using the dynamic law of
integration to particularize those problems and thereby create
an objective necessity for immediate reform. Modern society,
he argued, was sensitive, interdependent, complex, and yet
diffuse and incohesive; and it was tending to become more so.
It differed from primitive society in the complexity that
forced an individual to be dependent upon others. People
could no longer directly apply their own labor to the satisfaction of their desires, and they no longer had "direct recourse to nature" in a social breakdown. The direct economy,
the direct connection between means and ends, upon which, as
a description of the "natural" society, George's science was
based, no longer existed; and the reason was apparently in
the nature of modern society rather than just in the form of
land ownership.[45]

Such a startling perception--the acknowledgment of real
social transition, the discovery in social life of distinctive
modernity and substantive complexity--could not but jar the
structure of George's thought. The new emphasis did not,
significantly, cause him to abandon either his political
economy or his social value of justice. He simply, but warily,
raised new conceptions beside them, and the progressive triad

took on independent strength, an adumbration of the intellectual style of the progressives, for whom such dualisms were
much more natural. George's "First Principles" remained the
same as before; the labor theory was still absolute; and he
retained the small enterpriser's standards of personal freedom and a full return.[46] But none of the problems of
modern life, which George was at such pains to depict, could
b e solved by land-value taxation alone; and he observed
that technological change had outmoded the personal freedom
of the small enterpriser. Constantly increasing complexity
required the constant application of social will and intelligence, not the once-for-all-time institution of the single
tax. In an argument similar to Lester Ward's in Dynamic
Sociology, published during the same year, George used the
law of integration to mean that at every stage of evolution,
individual and social, the decisive factor in survival had
been, not an accidental advantage, but the deliberate adjustment of intelligence to current conditions.[47]

George's two triads, so skillfully allied in 1880, became separated to handle these ideas, because each of the
triads could perform a separate role. The individual-science-
statics triad, into which the arguments of Progress and

Poverty had been ultimately resolved, was universal, not peculiarly modern. Derived from a state of nature in which the individual labored freely and alone, it denied the validity of a social science catering specifically to complexity, and it proposed true laissez-faire as the ideal social state. An independent social-ideal-progressive triad, on the other hand, could cater to any set of conditions. It could make possible, indeed demand, the exercise of social will, independently of any formal science, to adjust to current conditions and to effect reform. It offered not perfect freedom, but deliberate and conscious adjustment.

Thus, while George wrote Social Problems to advocate reform and specifically to press for the single tax, the advocacy of the single tax and the advocacy of general social progress were inherently separate roles, involving different modes of action, different conceptions of the natural order, and different perceptions of where society stood in relation to the past and the future. As indicated by the progressive law of integration, the new social complexity was substantive and irreducible. It could not be resolved, even for the purpose of science, into something simpler. As indicated by the science of political economy, complexity was only apparent and could be explained

through the operations of a few simple laws. Thus, the social intelligence required by progress was distinct from the
natural laws of political economy, for the latter were independent of evolution, could not explain it, and required no
distinctively modern intelligence to apply. The stress on
modernity and complexity thus forced George to raise, alongside his long-standing identification of the reformed society
with individual freedom, an identification of reform with
social control.

Matching these divergences in his science, George also
split his moral values along static-dynamic, scientific-
religious, and individual-social lines. "Justice," the labor
theory of absolute value, belonged to his statics and could
serve as the incentive only for the single tax. Something
else was needed to impel the kind of progress made by deliberate acts of will, the progress that modern problems made
necessary and modern conditions possible. Thus, beside the
scientific, universal, and natural ethic of justice, George
raised the religious, progressive, and collective ethic of
love and duty. Although he occasionally treated the latter
as simply "a keener sense of justice," more frequently and in
his most extensive discussion, the two ethics represented

different conceptions of society. Justice was for the freely
competitive, spontaneously cooperative society that functioned
with only land-value taxation. Love and duty were for the
broad and deep and conscious cooperation of the cooperative
commonwealth.[48]

The separation of the two triads was an antinomy that,
like all antinomies, was uncongenial to George's cognitive
style. He assumed, even in Social Problems, that reform had
to follow from a complete and unified set of ideas, something
that could replace the certainties of religion and science
and thereby provide a center for society to gather around,
an alternative to the panic that occurred when people felt
threatened by social chaos. Ideas were the surrogate for
the actual social stability that no longer seemed to exist.
George had provided such a center in Progress and Poverty,
but capitulating to the alien ideas of modernity and complexity challenged the unity of his intellectual structure
by contradicting the ideas of universality and economy that
had dominated it. Through most of the 1880's, he resolved
the antinomy by arranging its elements in temporal sequence,
having them represent different stages of world history.
The single tax had to precede all other reforms, he said

again and again, expanding an idea that had appeared in
Progress and Poverty. Justice would yield the single tax;
love and duty would create the cooperative commonwealth.
Justice had to precede love as Moses preceded Christ.[49]

Even this much-compromised antinomy, however, could
not be maintained. George's intellectual structure was
ruled by a unitary conception of truth, and his primary commitment was to the single tax. He had no other significant
program that was not resolvable into land-value taxation,
and his elaborate political economy, the only science he
had, inexorably pointed to land reform alone. As his agitation met with resistance, land-value taxation became more
and more central, and the temporal or sequential resolution
of the antinomy was gradually discarded in a three-pronged
process. First, the collective and religious ethic of duty
and love doubled back and became the incentive for the
single tax itself.[50] Second, he abandoned the cooperative
commonwealth as artificial. While acknowledging that material progress had increased the area requiring social control,
he rejected socialism, which he had identified with the cooperative commonwealth (an identification sealed by Laurence
Gronlund), as "super-adequate" precisely because it presumed

to exercise that control.[51] He then narrowed the area for
control until it virtually disappeared and the single tax
was sufficient.[52] And the kind of "cooperation" he finally
chose was precisely the kind that only the single tax and
not progressive reform could give: spontaneous or unconscious cooperation, the free competition of undirected individuals receiving a full return for their labor--men freed
by justice, not bound by love.[53]

The sequential arrangement disappeared in a third way.
George failed to retool his description of the universe. He
opted for statics and failed to create a progressive political economy. He refused even to glorify the political
economy of Ely and Adams with the name science. The one
scientific treatise he wrote during the 1880's, Protection
or Free Trade? (1886), ignored the distinctiveness of modern
industrialism and used a method of analysis identical with
that of Progress and Poverty. Rejecting all concern for
particularities, George asserted that tariffs had a "nature,"
that they operated according to "laws," and that these could
be found by looking at the simplest or the most complex, the
most natural or the most social state, according to intellectual convenience. Trade had to be free both across and within

boundaries (hence, the single tax was "true free trade"), because trade was "natural," and natural law and justice indicated freedom. Protection could not be valid because it was
particularistic. Its theory was "hard to reconcile with the
idea of the unity of the Creative Mind and the universality
of law."[54] George chose wisely. Of all his books except
Progress and Poverty, on which it was modeled, this dose of
deductive statics was by far his largest seller.

By 1890, when the single tax emerged as the focus of a
movement of its own, the temporal sequence had been wholly
weeded out as a method of resolving the antinomy.[55] In opting
for social statics and in rejecting conscious cooperation,
George discarded substantive progress and replaced it with
"free organic growth."[56] That was a form of social change
that did not affect the substance of society--described by
natural laws--and that was not subject to control. The single
tax could become a panacea again: a single static mechanism
effecting a dynamic thing called progress. At best, however,
it was what Ward had called passive or negative progress,
the kind George had ridiculed in Youmans. And whatever
its usefulness to his own movement, it was the first clear
sign that George was condemning himself to obsolescence.

Despite these "subterranean" readjustments, the pressures
of the perceptions of modernity and complexity kept the antinomy still prominent in George's polemical writings after 1890,
although in a new form. From a decade and more of unsuccessful advocacy, he had concluded that conservatism resulted when
moralists and scientists stepped out of their proper roles and
prescribed for each other. He therefore demanded their separation, allocating to each sphere its own competency and to
each its own truths. He intended the Single Tax Movement to
be their only intersection. Religion could provide the incentive for reform, the social will to act, and the moral
purposes to be served. Indeed, reform movements themselves,
he noted, would replace the churches as foci of Christian
ethics and religious enthusiasm.[57] Science would make the
consequences of social action predictable, thereby providing
certain knowledge about what had to be done.[58] George thus
settled on an instrumental resolution of the antinomy to
replace the sequential resolution, and this made him attractive to later instrumentalists.[59] That attraction, however,
was illusory. George repeatedly rejected antinomies whenever he found them in others,[60] and this instrumental relationship was no more congenial to his intellectual structure

than was the earlier sequential one. This was most clearly illustrated in the very book written to initiate its systematic exposition.

The Science of Political Economy, begun in 1891 and nearly completed by the time of his death in 1897, was George's attempt to write a scientific treatise in a morally neutral way. He would then have completed the process by arguing for reform on a moral basis alone. The attempt failed. The most "progressive" and instrumentalistic aspect of the treatise was its distinction between science and art. George divided every process of action into two parts. On the one hand were the beginning and the end, the motivation and the consequence, the initial desire and its ultimate satisfaction, the first and the final cause. On the other hand were the uniform causal sequences, the natural laws, that connected them. It was only with the latter part, George said, that science was concerned, because only causal sequences were permanent and universal, "in all times and places . . . true and invariable." The other part of the process, the beginning and the end, was the realm of will, of morality, and of reform, the realm of uncaused things. It was the realm of "art." Art was the way people behaved with respect to science; it contained the desires they chose to satisfy. Thus, while there could be only one science, there could be many arts, moral and immoral. As a science, therefore, political economy was morally neutral. It did not deal with the desire or the satisfaction, the first or the final cause, but only with what transpired inbetween: the production and distribution of wealth. "[Its] proper business is neither to explain the difference between right and wrong nor to persuade to one in preference to the other."[61]

George was able to maintain the neutrality of science as long as he was dealing with production. He could logically argue, for instance, that the axiom of efficiency--men seek to satisfy desires with the least exertion--of which the laws of production were simply an extension, had nothing to do with moral judgments. It was an axiom, he noted, about the method of satisfying a desire and had nothing to do with the character of the desire itself. In his discussion of the laws of distribution, however, the neutrality of science was violated. George had naturally assumed that consumption (satisfaction) was the end, the final cause, of the economic process. He assumed that it was beyond science and within art because it was voluntary and variable. But that was

precisely the nature of distribution as well. It was obvious
to him that distribution could be--in fact, always had been--
tampered with. That was what made reform possible. It was
in distribution, after all, that poverty, an unnatural and
therefore unjust apportionment of the returns from production,
arose. George had reached the end of the process before he
had expected to. Distribution, not consumption, was the final
cause of production. And since through final cause the end
was variable (poverty or equity), George's science was no
longer free of the moral concern with the original act of
will. He was forced to distinguish in kind between the laws
of production and those of distribution. Both were natural
laws, but the former, he had to say, were only physical and
descriptive, while the latter were moral and normative as
well. They involved "the perception of right or justice, the
recognition of ought or duty." The end of George's treatise
contradicted its beginning. He could not make his science
morally neutral and purely instrumental.[62]

Art was thus superfluous. George's science contained
as much morality as his system needed. And where art was
intended to offer voluntarism and control, George's science
offered all that he thought to exist. An individual's

behavior with respect to science--the axiom of efficiency--
was inevitable, not voluntary. In social action as well,
natural law had to be obeyed. That was the only way the
consequence of an action could be brought into line with
its intention. It is clear from George's analysis, from
his dismissal of other economic sciences, and from his rejection of socialism and other reforms as false arts, that
it would have been ultimately impossible in George's thought
for a unitary and total science to justify more than a
single art.[63] The relationship between them could not be
truly instrumental if it was functional only with the single
tax.

The characteristic that helped explain the popularity
of Progress and Poverty helps explain these difficulties as
well. The basic structure of George's thought simply was not
congenial to antinomies, and so the dualisms created by the
pressures of the perceptions of modernity and complexity created impossible problems for him. Lester F. Ward, who published The Psychic Factors of Civilization (1893) while George
was working on his final treatise, could make effective use
of the science-art dichotomy, because the structure of his
thought was antinomic. Ward set the natural and human

processes in opposition. Nature was purposeless or "genetic";
social action was purposive or "teleological." Society was
the opposite of nature and therefore controllable. Just as
important, both the genetic and the teleological processes,
the natural and the social, were dynamic--"aggregative,"
cumulative, progressive. Ward's conception was a logical antidote to Darwin's discovery of an uneconomical process in
nature, and so economical or efficient action could be set
in opposition to it. All these conceptions were alien to
George. God's universe was inherently economical, and therefore intelligence followed, not opposed, nature. Society was
controllable because it was natural, and therefore Ward's
conception of reform would be as needlessly artificial as
Sumner's laissez-faire was ungodly. More important, George's
description of the universe was a statics. He objected to
the cosmic processes depicted by evolutionary materialists
and dynamists because they were natural processes without
ends and, in Spencer's case, without beginnings as well.
George, on the contrary, could conceive of eliminating neither
the first nor the final cause, and his science of political
economy was explicitly founded upon their existence. Complex
phenomena could not be understood without them.[64]

The relevant distinction for understanding George's science, therefore, is not that between a teleological process and a genetic one, for both can be cumulative or progressive. Rather, it is the distinction between a progressive process and a completable process; and the former has no place. When George discussed the proper materials for science, he always distinguished between permanent relationships, characteristic of natural law, and transient relationships, established by human legislation. Neither was progressive. For George, the end of a process was always part of its beginning. Whether he would deal with the beginning and the end (now called morality) or only with what transpired inbetween (called science), he was always dealing with the completable processes characteristic of statics and never with cumulative or progressive ones.

When George discovered real transition--the distinctive modernity and substantive complexity stressed in the early 1880's--an alien concept was introduced into his thought, forcing apart the triads that had been so neatly merged in Progress and Poverty. Rather than keeping them in opposition, however, or capitulating to pluralism, George gradually and perhaps unconsciously brought them back together in the kind

of unitary scheme that had explained away the chaos of 1880.
By the early nineties, virtually all the discordant elements
that had attended his new perception of society, elements
for which art and control were perfectly tailored, had been
eliminated or redefined so that the static triad could once
again be all-embracing. Progress and statics, justice and
duty, science and religion, social reform and the single
tax, all were once again under the single umbrella of "nature."
For George, the unity, harmony, and economy of thought had to
reflect the unity, harmony, and economy of God's universe,
and so the alien concepts were either deported or they were,
quite literally, naturalized.

Antinomies, dialectics, dual processes, as offered by
Ward and other not yet popular thinkers, proved to be the kind
of intellectual structures best suited to a perception of
transition to a distinctively modern and substantively complex society, a perception that, if Jane Addams and Herbert
Croly are representative, began to prevail in the middle 1890's.
Thus the monistic intellectual structure that had made George
a popular reform ideologue in the context of perceived chaos
meant that other reformers, with different intellectual predis-
positions, would be required for the decades that followed.

CHAPTER III

THE RECENT FUTURE

Edward Bellamy

In 1897, in Equality, Edward Bellamy's sequel to his
Looking Backward of 1888, the protagonist Julian West recalls
the 1880's. "It was all quite as you describe it," Julian
tells Doctor Leete, his twenty-first-century host, "the industrial and political warfare and turmoil, the general sense
that the country was going wrong, and the universal cry for
some sort of reform. But, as I said before, the agitation,
while alarming enough, was too confused and purposeless to
seem revolutionary. All agreed that something ailed the
country, but no two agreed what it was or how to cure it."[1]

But looking backward makes a difference. Julian West,
having fallen asleep in 1887 and not awakened until the year
2000, could not know what came out of the chaos. To him,
the experience of transition had been the experience of
uncertainty, of "confusion and incoherence and short-
sightedness." His host, with the benefit of a historian's

hindsight, fills him in. The "revolutionary epoch" from the early 1870's to the beginning of the twentieth century, he relates, was divided into two periods. The first or "incoherent" phase was "a time of terror and tumult, of confused and purposeless agitation, and a Babel of contradictory creeds." A year or two after Julian fell asleep, the second or "rational" phase began. Though the two periods overlapped, Doctor Leete says, "from about the beginning of the nineties we date the first appearance of an intelligent purpose in the revolutionary movement and the beginning of its development from a mere formless revolt against intolerable conditions into a logical and self-conscious evolution toward the order of to-day." Bellamy's implication was clear. In bringing order out of chaos, Looking Backward made the difference.[2]

Bellamy was not alone in perceiving that the sense of chaos and uncertainty, to which George had responded with Progress and Poverty, had peaked in the middle eighties before subsiding during the next decade. "Anarchy" was commonly used in the mid-eighties as the label not just for the aims of a small band of agitators, but for the problems of the social system as a whole; and when reformers published

their cures, the most popular were those presented as both
simple and final, the polar opposites of the disease.

Laurence Gronlund, for example, whose Cooperative
Commonwealth of 1884 was an attempt to import "modern" or
"German" socialism into America, identified a fearful consensus that "we are at the brink of an extraordinary change;
that a crisis of some sort is impending, no matter if it is
likely to burst out now or in ten or fifty years from now."
He tried to exploit the perception by declaring the capitalist order itself anarchic and by offering the cooperative
commonwealth as a "clear-cut and definite" solution. With
the social order "tottering" in all advanced countries, he
wrote, Americans had to choose between a descent into barbarism, which would only start the cycles of history going again,
and Cooperation, the only final solution. "When the Cooperative Commonwealth is achieved," Gronlund concluded, "there
will be no room for any more revolutions." Gronlund later
claimed to have cleared the way for the popularity of Looking
Backward, and disputes about plagiarism and influence figured
in both the contemporary and later scholarly literature.[3]

Gronlund's idea that the cycles of history could be
brought to a halt by a simple remedy dominated as well Josiah

Strong's popular tract, <u>Our Country</u>, published by the
American Home Missionary Society in 1885. In introducing the
book, the Congregational minister Austin Phelps singled out
"crisis" as its leading idea. It was, he said, "the critical
moment in the critical battle of the critical campaign for a
nation's endangered life." While a sense of impending crisis
was a historic characteristic of home missionary tracts, the
wider popularity and influence of Strong's volume indicated
a sensitivity to more widespread and contemporary social perceptions. Strong traced the sense of detachment from traditional values and the consequent fear of the future to the
enormously accelerated pace of social change in late
nineteenth-century America, a condensation of the "time
factor" so exaggerated that the last twenty years of the century would be the equivalent of a millennium. He took the
wide circulation of <u>Progress and Poverty</u> as a symptom of
prevailing discontent and disharmony. "Modern civilization,"
Strong admonished, "is called on to contend for its life with
forces which it has evolved." "There is nothing beyond re-
publicanism," he warned, "but anarchism." Evangelization of
the West and Christianization of society were sufficient
remedies for Strong, but his great fear was that "some great

industrial or other crisis" would lead to an open conflict between "conservative" and "destructive" elements. In a society with extremes of wealth and poverty, with congested cities and fenced-in land, with corrupt governments and insensitive capitalists, with armed bands of socialists and anarchists--in that setting, any conflict would become widespread and be the "real test" of Anglo-Saxon character and institutions.[4]

Strong's appeal for evangelization was less concrete than the Social Gospel of Washington Gladden, whom Strong cited as an authority on the social question. Gladden preached the Social Gospel in Springfield, Massachusetts, from 1875 to 1882, overlapping the years when Bellamy was working as a journalist in the same city. Gladden later credited the "terrible" railroad strike of 1877 (which had also given Henry George his sense of urgency) and a coal miners' strike of 1884 with bringing "very strongly before my own mind the critical character of the relations between the men who are doing the work of the world and the men who are organizing and directing it." As early as 1876, in a series of sermons delivered in Springfield, he had accepted the growth of the factory system as part of a divine plan to substitute intelligence for manual labor, but he treated the chaos that attended this process as the problem in greatest need of solution. "All the kingdoms of the world's industry are now in a state of war," Gladden observed; and the all-embracing remedy he proposed, cooperation under the Christian law of love, was the culmination of the same historical succession of systems as Gronlund's cooperative commonwealth. Gladden expanded the theme in his influential volume, Applied Christianity (1886), which identified Christianity with social science on the grounds that both recognized "the fact that men are in a condition of disorder and distress." His perception of social chaos in the Springfield of the 1870's had become even more pressing by 1886. "Such, then, is the state of industrial society at the present time," he wrote. "The hundreds of thousands of unemployed laborers, vainly asking for work; the rapid increase of pauperism, . . . the strikes and lock-outs reported every day in the newspapers; the sudden and alarming growth of the more violent types of socialism, are ominous signs of the times. Any one who keeps his ear close to the ground will hear mutterings of discontent and anger in unexpected quarters."[5]

A sensitive ear was less necessary after 1886. To

opinion leaders across the spectrum, the crisis that Strong
had feared had materialized. The strikes against the Gould
railroad interests by the Knights of Labor in the spring, the
Haymarket Bombing and trial in the summer, and Henry George's
campaign for mayor of New York under a labor banner in the
fall confirmed the perception of chaos, the threat of anarchy,
and the fear of the future that so much of the contemporary
social literature displayed.[6] Andrew Carnegie observed the
panic and attributed to it the popular scrambling for radical
literature advocating cooperative solutions. William Dean
Howells, whose own involvement in the "realist war" did much
to add an impression of intellectual anarchy to the perception of social chaos, found himself thoroughly demoralized
by the events of that year, especially the condemnation of
the anarchists in Chicago. For men of liberal sympathies
like Howells, 1887 was even more distressing, for the anarchists' appeals were not exhausted until a year after their
trial, and they were not executed until November 1887. The
trial and executions--Howells called them civic murders--
pricked liberal consciences and crystallized political and
social opinion to much the same degree as the trial and execution of two anarchists forty year later. In 1888, the year

Looking Backward was published, Howells wrote that his horizons had been "indefinitely widened" by his efforts on behalf
of the Chicago anarchists. He told Hamlin Garland that he
was thinking deeply about social problems for the first time
and that the Single Tax, which Garland espoused, seemed insufficient. Several months later, he observed that civilization
seemed "a state of warfare and a game of chance," that America
seemed to be "the most grotesquely illogical thing under the
sun," that after fifty years of complacency he felt civilization to be "coming out all wrong in the end, unless it bases
itself anew on a real equality." Howells became an early admirer of Bellamy's novel.[7]

Looking Backward not only offered Howells equality and
logic; it also rescued the Puritan values of self-sacrifice
and social devotion to which Strong and Gladden had both appealed, values that seemed suddenly on the defensive in the
materialism of the Gilded Age. Indeed, Bellamy's intellectual
career is the story of successive attempts to end the conflict
between those values and a hostile environment, at first by
fruitlessly attempting to escape both, and finally, in
Looking Backward, by proposing a radically new environment in
which the values were covertly but inextricably tied to the

social system. His utopia also offered the "sufficiency"
that the Single Tax lacked for Howells. Modern readers of
Bellamy's novel would find there what George had provided
only in 1883, three years after Progress and Poverty had appeared: a recognition, as Henry Carter Adams put it, that a
revolution in the management of industry was the "last step
of the development of the idea of modern history" and that
such a revolution was a peculiarly modern possibility because
until the late nineteenth century "there did not exist the
industrial power of the sort which now forms the basis of
modern civilization." Adams's analysis of the "prevalent
discontent" and the "disintegrating tendencies of the present"
had influenced both Gladden and Strong; but his method was too
pragmatistic and inductive, his approach too tentative, partial, and complex--too "advanced"--to have popular impact.
Bellamy seemed to take account of complexity and modernity,
but he subordinated that perception to the perception of chaos
and uncertainty, and the "sufficiency" of his enterprise required a rejection of the pragmatistic notions that chance
and uncertainty characterized the universe and that "history"
was one thing that could never end. He thus responded to his
perception of chaos with the kind of monistic intellectual

structure that George had found so popular in 1880 and 1886--
deductive, final, total, and simple. "[L]ike Mr. George's
great work," Francis A. Walker, bell-wether of respectable
liberal opinion, complained in 1890, "Looking Backward shows,
through its whole structure, the perverting effect of a
single false notion, having the power to twist out of shape
and out of due relation every fact which comes, in any way,
at any point, within the field of its influence."[8]

Looking Backward's circulation marked the end of the
attractiveness of such an approach. The volume itself enjoyed a phenomenal popularity for several years; but the movement, known as Nationalism, that embodied its attempt to resolve "the complex conditions of modern life"[9] on the basis
of the clear and simple, universal principle of equality,
quickly disappeared. It influenced the programs of reformist groups, most notably the Populists, and large numbers of
individual reformers as well; but its distinctive feature--
the possibility of a total and final solution to the "social
problem"--was ultimately ignored; and Bellamy's utopia, like
George's panacea, was regarded as irrelevant to society as
social reformers were increasingly coming to perceive it in
the 1890's.

I

If the Puritan conscience has been as strong a factor in American values as cultural rebels have often contended, then Edward Bellamy was well placed to exemplify the confrontation between that major American tradition and the chaotic birth of modern industrial society. The conflict between his family experience and the larger social environment in which he grew to adulthood graphically displayed the new tensions, allowing him to observe and experience a discrepancy between traditional modes of behavior and the results they were bringing in the modern world. When Bellamy was born in Chicopee Falls, Massachusetts, on March 26, 1850,[10] the area had recently crossed the line separating rural village from factory town. The belief that a community was something based on shared values and patterns of behavior was shattered by the disruptive forces characteristic of early American industrialization: an influx of immigrant laborers, the appearance of a class of conspicuous and apparently permanent poor, and the rise of families whose wealth and power were not associated with any of the traditional New England signs of superiority and who were not responsive to traditional preachings.

In the face of these challenges, Edward Bellamy's

parents maintained a united front in favor of the values associated with Calvinism as a way of life. Both his father and his maternal grandfather were Baptist preachers, evangelicals whose appeal was largely to what had formerly been the lowest independent classes in society, but who were making few converts among the new working masses. There is some vagueness about the character of the father, Rufus Bellamy, descended from a prominent disciple of Jonathan Edwards. A legend of theological liberalism grew up in the family after Edward Bellamy became famous; but Edward himself and his brother Frederick recalled an old-fashioned and strict Calvinist (though perhaps an amiable man) who continually preached to his children about the sin of the "natural man" until they underwent a conversion experience. The mother, Maria Putnam Bellamy, could have felt at home in the Boston of 1635. Within the Bellamy household, she was the dominant figure and the enforcer of asceticism. "She never had any patience with self-indulgence," Frederick Bellamy recalled. "Merely that it was a pleasure to do a thing constituted no recommendation or excuse for it, but rather an objection. She regarded the main purpose of life to be discipline of the heart, soul, and mind, and deprivation of sense

gratifications she regarded not as a misfortune but as a
blessing and benefit." A stern disciplinarian who expected
good behavior as part of the natural course of things, she
sought to instill in her children a commitment to duty and
self-sacrifice without an expectation of reward.[11]

While the strict Calvinism of a family of preachers dis-
couraged the quest for material success, the world's challenge to its values took on particular power as the strength
of the church declined with the transformation of the town.
Edward Bellamy, at least, was more than ordinarily ambitious;
his ambitions did not run to following his father's path into
the church; and yet his fear and dislike of the new world
were palpable. The self-fulfillment offered by the world
and the self-sacrifice demanded by his creed vibrated in his
life with an irregular rhythm, complicated both by external
frustrations and by his own unwillingness to choose between
the two. There was no predisposition toward reform in either
his background or his character, and he resisted the activist
solution with all of his intellectual energy. It was only
his failure, after repeated attempts, to reconcile his values
and the modern world that ultimately led him to write the
most popular literary utopia in American history.

Bellamy's own account of his childhood, written at the age of twenty-five, showed his awareness both of the conflicting impulses and of the attractiveness of passivity in face of them. In his preadolescent years, he reported, he spent a good deal of time reading military history and dreaming of personal glory, dreams that were encouraged by accounts of the Civil War and at the same time countered by feelings of guilt. He questioned whether his ambitions were motivated by an unworthy desire for self-glorification or by the more respectable desire to sacrifice the self as "the servant of God, of humanity." Despite his good behavior, Bellamy recalled, it was taken for granted that he was tainted by original sin; and consequently in his early teens, he "submitted to the emotional experience of a religious conversion," which he also attributed to the "Calvinism in his blood." The event only confirmed passivity. Having submitted to the power of "a very real and sublime being," he temporarily thrust his ambitions aside, a decision he recalled with some discomfort. "The relation established by Christianity between the believer and Christ," he observed in retrospect, "makes a woman of the former, tending as it does peculiarly to cultivate the feminine graces of trustfulness and confidence in protection to be repaid by love. It is better adapted to women than men, on whose minds it has an effect to degenerate the masculine virtues of self-reliance and valor." So dependent did he become on God that he wondered how he had ever got along without Him.[12]

The next several years witnessed a rejection of theological Calvinism, an intellectual reaction against the extreme dependence, and the reassertion and frustration of his ambitions by their apparent incongruence with the era. Bellamy was convinced that his calling in life was greater than that of the ordinary mortals around him. Although these fantasies persisted well beyond his adolescent years, he was never able to define his ambitions, a problem Jane Addams recalled as widespread among sensitive young people of the seventies and eighties, who were unable to reconcile their own goals and values with modern opportunities. "Were the ambition which spurs my labors any of the ordinary ones as for pelf or fame," Bellamy confided to his journal, "I fancy I should be well content to let it go and earn my daily bread in some plodding business such as men ply all about me. But I cannot turn my heart from the great work which awaits me. It is a labor none other can perform." At one point he conceded that he might be

a man of mediocre talents, a discovery that led him to
thoughts of death--a discovery, as well, that he quickly
disowned. His chronic failure to find an appropriate role encouraged retreat from the world entirely. Society seemed to
be changing too rapidly for him to move into traditional channels. Though he did not try the ministry, he did limit himself to the liberal callings consistent with tested values.
He thought of a military career, but was unable to enter West
Point; he sampled philosophy at college for a year, but never
returned; he studied law, but gave up after his first case;
he tried journalism without sticking to any journalistic
enterprise for very long; when he tried literature, he published his first work anonymously. At twenty-four, in the
midst of these changes, he was still attempting to rationalize his "vague yet poignant ambitions to be accomplishing
something though just what the fastidious mind cannot choose."
He saw himself as pursued by a "ministry of disappointment,"
buffeted by the "continual harassment of existence," and
occasionally, more concretely, as unappreciated and thwarted
by fools. He felt, he said, well before beginning his career
in fiction, as if he were suffering the discomforts of a
literary life without the romantic disposition that made such

an existence charming.[13]

For the very reasons that the modern world was discouraging his ambitions, his ancestral Calvinism offered no comfort. Its insistence that he have a calling, that he continually test himself--reinforced by his mother's reminders that he must dedicate his life to self-sacrifice in the service of God--only pushed him back towards the world when he might have sought retreat. Evangelical religion compelled choices; but in an era of unpredictable change, the number of options with uncertain consequences, as Bellamy was acutely aware, was vastly increased. The Calvinist's guilt, as created by the parents, emphasized the forbidden rather than the open. It could function effectively where the channels of action were stable and dependable, where the acceptable callings, which offered self-fulfillment through self-sacrifice, were live options. Bellamy's early experience seemed to show that the connections no longer existed. A man's actions no longer seemed to give reliable evidence of his inner directives. Social turmoil, he decided, in reference to the new businessmen, was allowing the rhetoric of self-sacrifice to cloak lack of self-knowledge and even outright hypocrisy.[14]

Still, religion offered advantages that Bellamy was

unwilling to give up. On the personal level, only a higher
loyalty could rationalize the passivity that had attracted
him at his conversion, and only the existence of a super-
natural reality could overcome his continual obsession with
death. More important, to justify his retreat from the confrontation with the world that his conscience demanded, he
needed a philosophy that could blur the line between self-
assertion and self-abnegation without forcing him to engage
in the unattractive forms of aggression and opportunism required for modern success. Provisional truths would offer
him no security against the harassments of existence, and
utilitarian or pragmatic standards would only aggravate his
uncertainty. The unity of religious belief in his childhood
made him very sensitive to the intellectual and moral anarchy
of his day, and to regard it as a problem to be solved, not
as a promise of intellectual possibility. "I have not the
least inclination to doubt," he asserted, "the existence of
abstract truths because the world has just now discovered the
falsity of those it had always held as such and has not yet
found any better ones." He analyzed his own cognitive style
in some detail. His mind always tended, he observed, to
"comingle levels." He could not deal with a concrete fact

without raising it through successive stages to ultimate abstraction; and, in a sentence prophetic of his later intellectual career, he noted, "I am intensely practical in the
sense that no abstract idea is any satisfaction to me till I
have realized it concretely." Only a unified, metaphysical
approach to the universe could harmonize, by inclusion, conflicting strata. The pluralistic universe that the pragmatists found in Darwin had no appeal to him. He did think
that inconsistency was "the law of the mind" and that writing should reflect it. But in the end, monism--"the law of
the book"--won out. There had to be, he thought, a deeper
unity and harmony behind "the apparent utter chaos" of the
world, and minds that indulged in "contradictories" would
never find them. "Illogical people" might get along better
in the world. But it was the intellectual and moral absolu-
tists, the "logical people," those "to whose minds apparent
incongruities are hateful and who are forever seeking pro-
founder generalizations, analogies more universal, these are
they to whom the world will ever owe all its gains in mental,
moral and material grasp, in short its progress."[15]

Standing hesitantly on the "threshold of life," Bellamy
decided that the Puritan conscience was inconsistent with a

disordered world. He wanted to be free of the claims of a
personal God who could simultaneously demand a life of sacrifice, not guarantee that such a life could be led when traditional paths were not dependable, and still exact punishment
for every false step. When a youth abandons the truths and
duty in which he has been raised, Bellamy noted, "he carries
his loyalty in his hand anxious only to find some fitting
shrine where he may lay it down and be at rest." By the time
he had found his shrine, Bellamy was no longer a youth. The
disorder around him was frustrating his ambitions and making
the Puritan conscience burdensome and unattractive. He
wanted to retreat. His new loyalty would have to offer a
justification for it. But terrible is the power and fearful
the revenge, he observed prophetically, of the moral standards
in which a man is bred.[16]

II

Bellamy found one alternative to the conflict between
Calvinism and modern success that he thought attractive enough
to offer to his contemporaries in fictional form in his first
novel. In Six to One, published anonymously in 1878, Frank
Edgerton, an overworked bachelor journalist of thirty

undergoing a rest-cure on Nantucket, finds himself faced with a choice between the sensitive, retiring Addie Follett, a "nun of the sea" who is perfectly content to commune with the infinite, and Kate Mayhew, a dynamic, passionate, ambitious girl who wants to participate in the world of things and activities. Edgerton chooses Addie and promises himself that he will never work hard again.[17]

Addie personified the shrine that Bellamy had found four years earlier in a "Religion of Solidarity" of his own invention. He remarked of it in 1887, when writing Looking Backward, "I should like this paper to be read to me when I am about to die. . . . [It] represents the germ of what has been ever since my philosophy of life." It did in fact become, once Bellamy had found it unsatisfactory in other fictional settings, part of the intellectual framework of his utopian scheme. But Bellamy in the 1870's still saw himself as too sensitive for the world of things and activities. His proper role was the search for self-knowledge through introspection. When he explored the depths, however, he returned not with self-knowledge, but with the Transcendental oversoul.[18]

Bellamy opened The Religion of Solidarity with a description of the romantic's conflict between the desire to achieve communion with the transcendental reality felt when viewing great natural beauty and the inability to escape the material world. The conflict led him to adopt a version of the Transcendentalists' model of the dual ego. On the one hand was the personality--the isolated, "phenomenal," concrete man, including both body and mind, defined by time and space, mutable, material, atomistic, subjective. On the other, was the impersonal--the "noumenal," universal soul of solidarity, infinite and eternal, permanent and unchanging, and therefore objective and harmonizing. The ultimate aim of all life, Bellamy decided, was escape from the duality by rejecting the dead weight of the "phenomenal" via introspection, communion with the infinite, and approximation of the impersonal mood.

The Religion of Solidarity performed several important functions for its author. By combining the particular with the general, the individual with the universal, it could effectively serve as a substitute for the traditional religion that Bellamy had found too demanding. At the same time, it allowed the privacy of a church with only one member. In addition, by asserting the primacy of the universal, the eternal, and the infinite, it allowed Bellamy to deny the reality of those things that most challenged him. It provided an escape from death, since real life would not end, but only begin, when mind and body died. Most important, it rationalized retreat from the struggles of the material world, that domain in which the personality had been unable to provide even for its physical wants. For one who felt very keenly the rootlessness of an era of change, the Religion of Solidarity satisfied the need for an escape from the uncertainties of making choices in the midst of chaos, when confronted by an irrelevant past and an unknowable future. By annihilating the distinctions among past, present, and future, and ending the necessity for playing out one's life in the realm of time, it removed the need to know the consequences of one's actions, the predictability that conscience required but that the world had destroyed. This, plus the correlative fact that solidarity was achieved in solitude, in a renunciation of action, affirmed--demanded--the passivity that Bellamy was drawn to.[19]

Solidarity did not point toward social reform. Apart from some minor resemblances, it was not a religion of humanity like Auguste Comte's, which attracted a number of Americans--including Herbert Croly's parents--interested in reform in the three decades after 1860. It was instead a

philosophy of privacy. Although it recognized equality in
that each person partook of the soul of solidarity, the concern for mankind ended there. The "Greater Self," as Bellamy
came to call it, was not the abstract concept Humanity; nor
was communion achieved by contemplating the sublimity of the
human ego. All of Bellamy's sympathies were with nature,
not people. The closest approximation of the transcendental
mood was not love, but esthetics--the appreciation of natural
beauty and inanimate objects. Indeed, love, like guilt, was
a tie that bound. The one who loved and was loved, like the
one who was dominated by his conscience, was "morally in
bondage." He was also subject to anxieties arising out of
fear of future loss, just as the conscience-bound communicant
feared the vengeance of the past. The remedy for those
uncertainties lay "in a vast increase of intellectual and
artistic sympathy, and in cultivation of the sense of the
universal life in God." "Sympathy" represented an extension
of being; and for Bellamy this extension could not be in the
direction of other persons if it was to be liberating.[20]

Thus, when Bellamy tried to present the Religion of
Solidarity in a palatable fiction, the most appropriate setting he could find was the timeless wilderness hermitage of

a man who had exiled himself from modern life. The manuscript apparently preoccupied Bellamy during much of the 1870's and 1880's, though none of the various drafts were ever published. Each of them was the narrative of a soul claiming to be alienated from both traditional religious values and the modern world and seeking both self-dependence and social passivity. The earliest version depicts Eliot Carson as a sensitive, rebellious young man, "a poor mechanic," whose desire to "get air for his soul and mind" is hampered by his inability to afford leisure. The next version makes Eliot the promising young manager of a woollen mill, who realizes that in his quest to satisfy material ambitions he has neglected his boyhood desire to solve the problem of life. He quits the mill, breaks his engagement, and resolves to live like a hermit with minimum provision for his material wants. He will devote his life to "the cultivation and the following forth of the majestic intuitions which visit in sympathy with infinite things, intuition in whose elation we tread on stars." He is convinced that what he is doing is what "the world will some day, when it gets done with words, call religion."[21]

The last and longest version begins when Eliot has been

a solitary for a year. The pivotal character is now Edna
Damon, a city girl visiting Eliot's nearest neighbors.
Eliot is Bellamy as an adult; Edna is the adolescent Bellamy;
and their dialogue is Bellamy's autobiography. Having experienced her conversion at fifteen, Edna at the time of
the story is in the period between the falling away from
the church and the discovery of the Religion of Solidarity,
and deeply troubled by her own and the general loss of
faith. She feels an emotional need for prayer, but her
mind objects that no self-respecting God would demand such
total dependence as the Calvinist God whom she had encoun-
tered at her conversion and that no honest paternal God would
neglect, as this one did, the welfare of his children in a
brutal, immoral world. The inconsistency between the chaotic
state of the material world and personalism in religion has
cast her adrift. She carries her loyalty in her hands
anxious only to find some fitting shrine where she may lay
it down and be at rest. Eliot provides that shrine in his
Religion of Solidarity, which he presents as a liberating
"fact of consciousness" attained by a process of education,
rather than a dominating faith achieved by a conversion
experience.[22]

Since both Edna and Eliot--and Bellamy--were originally
troubled by their inability to reconcile their perception of
the world with the idea of a responsive God, it is indicative
of Bellamy's concern at this stage of his life that their
spiritual journeys did not end in a reformist religion like
the Social Gospel. After Edna had left the church and found
herself adrift, she had turned to social action in charity
work. "She felt that Christians could afford to do mean and
hardening things, for they had a forgiver and refresher for
their souls when they had stained them, but she could not afford to risk anything. Believers could find inspiration in
divine communion. She could only seek it in generous actions." Retreat from these activities, however, the security
of inaction, was precisely what Eliot's religion then provided. As social action had been a surrogate for religion,
so the new religion was a surrogate for social action. It
cultivated passivity. The end result of its practice was
peace of mind, not social guilt. Eliot, living alone, need
never feel responsible for any social consequences flowing
from his actions, and the wilderness (and later Edna's wealth)
would provide for his known wants with ready predictability.[23]

By treating the individual as unreal, save as a temporary

physical presence, Solidarity did seem to end the distinction
between selfish and unselfish motives, thus apparently resolving the conflict between self-fulfillment and self-sacrifice
that had set the world at large against the Puritan's conscience. Since the channels that could have satisfied both
the demand for sacrifice and the desire for success no longer
seemed to exist, Bellamy's conscience had not been able to
relieve itself comfortably in action. Solidarity was attractive because it seemed to offer both sacrifice and romantic
inertia. "[On] the theory of the dual life," Bellamy had
written in 1874, "of which the life of solidarity is abiding
and that of the individual transitory, unselfishness is but
a sacrifice of the lesser self to the greater self, an emi-
nently rational and philosophical proceeding per se, and entirely regardless of ulterior considerations."[24] Similarly,
Bellamy made Eliot extol the virtues of generosity and self-
sacrifice. All other virtues, Bellamy had Eliot assert, were
artificial. As responses to the ills of the world, there was
nothing absolute or inherently good in them. Change the character of the world, Eliot said, and since there was no original
sin, they would no longer be needed. But generosity and self-
sacrifice were "natural virtues." There was something

"intrinsically great" about them, because they sprang not from sympathy with others, but from identity with the infinite, from the recognition that individuality was "a very cheap affair to be thrown overboard on small provocation."[25]

Both "per se" and "intrinsically great" were, however, implicit admissions that generosity and self-sacrifice had no logical place in Eliot's garden. There was nothing to sacrifice for and no one to be generous to. Self-fulfillment became passive, and self-sacrifice irrelevant. The conscience's demand for altruism became trivial, and a belief in freedom was substituted for the action of a free agent. Even in a social setting, "natural virtues," conceived in that way, could be a rationale for avoiding reform. Indeed, their ordinary expression, as in Edna's case, took the form of charity, which had always been a bulwark against reform and which was the most passive social way of relieving guilt. And even from that, Edna had sought an escape. And Bellamy regarded "loyalty or patriotism, philanthropy or sympathy" not as examples of Solidarity, nor even as means of attaining it, but only as its analogues.[26] There was thus nothing in the Religion of Solidarity itself that inexorably pointed to reform. Indeed, its intended thrust was in the opposite

direction, toward retreat from the world rather than engagement with it. What did ultimately help push toward reform
was its failure to provide a setting where the Puritan value
of self-sacrifice could be acted on in a more than trivial
way and still have predictable consequences. Whatever
Bellamy's alienation from Calvinist religion, he continued
to let it set the standards for moral action.

A similar phenomenon of rejection and absorption attended his alienation from his own perception of social chaos.
While retreat from the world might have been an attractive
solution, it was not a generalizable one, and thus it could
not solve Bellamy's original problem of acting morally when
social chaos intervened between intentions and consequences.
In looking for an approach to unpredictability that could
work in a more heavily populated romance, not to say world,
Bellamy turned next not to reform, but to a theory of personal identity that incorporated chaos symbolically and tried
to turn its frightening aspects--detachment from the past,
ignorance of the future--into a liberation from Calvinism.
This new theory held not only that the mind and body were
impermanent and finite compared to the soul of solidarity,
but that even in one lifetime they contained no unity. Each

being, Bellamy argued, was a succession of non-identical personalities linked only by memory, with consciousness of only
the present one as essential to personal identity. The discovery of the mutable ego was intended to be Bellamy's ultimate rationale for the rejection of Puritan conscience in a
setting of social chaos. No one needed to feel guilt for the
actions of his previous selves, he claimed, and therefore no
one needed to be paralyzed by fear of the unforeseeable results of his current behavior. "It is in reality," he wrote,
"just as unjust (as we call it) that the sins of youth
should be visited upon age as that those of fathers should be
visited upon their children."[27]

Bellamy's theory of personal identity thus tried to cele-
brate, rather than deny, the irrelevance of the past, and it
sought to transmute the unpredictability of a chaotic society
into the possibility of personal redemption. It became the
theme of his Dr. Heidenhoff's Process (1880), a well-received
novel that inspired William Dean Howells to call Bellamy the
successor to Hawthorne. Bellamy used the novel to bitterly
excoriate the idea that the past could be a legitimate burden
on the present. In a prologue to the romance, a repentant
embezzler named George Bayley informs a church meeting that

he is leaving town. Although the local people have forgiven
him, neither he nor they can forget his crime. The experience
of conversion has not erased the memory of sin, which contin-
ues to exert its tyranny over the conscience-bound communicant.
After the meeting, Bayley commits suicide. In the main plot,
a young woman named Madeline rejects her longtime sweetheart
Henry Burr in favor of a new man in town. She loses her
virtue, is jilted, and runs away to Boston to hide her shame.
Although Henry finds her and courts her again, her sense of
guilt and remorse--evidence of her repentance--keep her from
agreeing to marry him: "her heart was pure; only her memory
was foul." The past was exercising illegitimate power over
the conscience. Hearing of Dr. Heidenhoff's thought-extirpation
process, the couple agree to try to purge Madeline of her op-
pressive memories. The doctor explains that since "repentance
balances the moral accounts" and since only the truly repentant
would want to forget their sins, his process is the only truly
moral solution. Moreover, "there is no such thing as moral
responsibility for past acts, no such thing as real justice
in punishing them," because people are constantly changing,
and the person who receives the punishment is not the one who
committed the crime. Alas, Dr. Heidenhoff is but a dream,

and Henry awakens to find a suicide note from Madeline.[28]

Dr. Heidenhoff's process, Bellamy's metaphorical engine
for turning the sense of detachment from the past and the consequent destruction of accepted values into an instrument of
liberation rather than a cause of fear, turned out to be
neither a real escape from Puritan conscience nor a social
morality. Thought-extirpation, whether by machine or act of
will, could relieve guilt only after it had taken its requisite toll and stimulated repentance. It relieved patients
of only the consequences of their immoral actions and of only
those consequences that affected them personally. It still
relied on the reality of conscience and the threat of guilt--
the persistence of the past and the retribution of the future
--as incentives. Bellamy tried to provide an antidote to
these vestiges of Calvinism in his next novel, the one he
came to regard as the best of his earlier works.[29]

The very existence of the central characters of Miss
Luddington's Sister (1884) is made tolerable only by their
acceptance of Bellamy's theory of personal identity, his belief in successive personalities that die but continue to
exist in the infinite to be reunited after death. Ida
Luddington believes it because she was once beautiful, but

is now disfigured; and her young relative Paul, because he is
in love with his fantasy of the young Miss Luddington. A
young woman who swindles them by materializing as the young
Ida during a seance, is ultimately relieved of blame for her
crime because the repentant swindler is regarded as a different person from the intended swindler. Paul asserts that the
belief in successive identities will add a "new department"
to ethics. While a man will have to honor reasonable obligations undertaken by his past selves, he will also have a duty
"to lead a wise life, to be prudent, to make the best of his
powers, to maintain a good name"; and this "is not a duty to
himself, merely an enlightened selfishness, as it is now
called, but a genuine form of altruism, a duty to others, as
truly as if those others bore different names instead of succeeding to his name."[30]

Having the future thus usurp the past as the incentive
to moral action would be a key element in Bellamy's path toward reform, but it had several shortcomings as an escape
from Calvinist values. It was a version of self-sacrifice--
denying the present self for future selves--that was still
most fitting for a world of solitaries, for in a social
setting, it could justify any sort of behavior, even the

selfishness and materialism that Bellamy found so unconsionable in the world about him. Moreover, it could be seen as not an escape from, but an atavistic affirmation of Puritanism. Jonathan Edwards, for example, of whom Bellamy's great grandfather had been a disciple, had used a similar theory of personal identity to justify not only personal guilt, but original sin, both of which Bellamy was trying to deny.

The persistent presence of self-sacrifice and generosity, Bellamy's inability to dismiss them along with the "artificial virtues" in Eliot's forest, his use of them in the self-centered altruism of his theory of personal identity, were signs that he considered them the only reliable moral standards, however much he struggled to escape the religion whose social centerpiece they were. The two novels together had metaphorically incorporated chaos--reality as Bellamy perceived it--and attempted, vainly, to turn them to moral account--to construct a theory consonant with his perception of society. Heidenhoff argued for the unreliability of the past and Luddington for the unpredictability of the future as morally useful. But this was not Calvinism; and it was the residual strength of Calvinist values, appearing in his work where least necessary, that drove him to seek new

solutions, at first in utopianism and finally in reform.
Bellamy's underlying obsession, whether he labeled it Calvinism or not, was to make its values active, to give them predictable results, a task that seemed impossible in a chaotic
world. In the gratuitous presence of self-sacrifice, his
inherited values were exacting their "fearful revenge" by
repeatedly upsetting the logic of his theories. Yet advance,
he had said, came from logical people. If real self-sacrifice
and real self-fulfillment could not be reconciled in the world
as Bellamy perceived it, retreat to a hermitage or to excul-
patory theories were not the answers. His theories could not
be consonant with his perception.

III

Looking Backward (1888) was presented in a double "time
warp." Julian West, the hero and narrator who sleeps from
1887 until the year 2000, is not the creation of Edward
Bellamy nineteenth-century romancer, but of Bellamy's half-
hidden persona, an unnamed twentieth-century historian writing a popular history in the form of a romance. This double-
demurrer is revealing. The historian's aim is simply to
contrast the social systems of 1887 and 2000. Julian's long

sleep permitted the historical dimension--what transpired between Bellamy's present and the fictional present of the
twentieth century--to be left out of this historical account.
The citizens of utopia have extirpated the past from their
collective memory, and the professor has no intention of re-
imposing an historical consciousness upon them. Bellamy's
earlier romances had treated the remembered past as an
obstacle to personal freedom. And he had seen the internal-
ized past, the moral values in conscience, as useless and
paralyzing when knowledge of their effects in action was
unreliable. An 1886 short story, "The Blindman's World," had
dramatized the point. A Martian, who can foresee the future,
informs a visitor from Earth: "All your knowledge, all your
affections, all your interests, are rooted in the past, and
on that account as life lengthens, it strengthens its hold on
you, and memory becomes a more precious possession. We, on
the contrary, despise the past, and never dwell upon it.
Memory with us, far from being the morbid and monstrous
growth it is with you, is scarcely more than a rudimentary
faculty. We live wholly in the future and the present." The
Earthling concludes that Martians are "the ideal and normal
type of our race."[31]

Looking Backward relocated the desire for predictability
from the personal sphere back to the social, where it had
originally upset Bellamy's ambitions, and struck a responsive
chord in its readers. Bellamy set the beginning of Julian's
story in an environment in which history was doing uncon-
trollably on its own what Dr. Heidenhoff had done mechanically.
The rapid pace of social change in the 1880's was making the
past irrelevant and the future unpredictable. In the opening
chapters of Looking Backward, Julian describes his contemporaries as living in fear and uncertainty, with "no clear idea
of what was happening" to them. Since 1873, industrial disorders had increased in frequency and intensity, resulting in
predictions of "social cataclysm," with humanity "about to take
a header into chaos." At the very least, all thoughtful men
saw that "society was approaching a critical period." What lay
ahead was unknown. "We felt that society was dragging anchor
and in danger of going adrift. Whither it would drift nobody
could say, but all feared the rocks." Bellamy saw his--and the
Martian's--willingness to give up the freedom conferred by extir-
pation of the past in favor of the certainty that came with knowledge
of the future as matching his readers' desire to find an answer
to the social uncertainties of their own time. The elimination

of the historical dimension from the story indicated an indifference to the pragmatistic forms of action that the New Economists and their allies were then presenting as the only possible mode of reform in an age cast adrift from reliable knowledge. For Bellamy, however, uncertainty was a problem, not an opportunity. Novelty and surprise were not exhilarating to him. It was his mission and Julian's involuntary destiny to relieve "the nervous tension in the public mind" by providing a fictional certainty as compensation for that which seemed to be thoroughly lacking in the world of 1887. Whether he intended it or not, it was also his destiny to rescue a set of traditional values--the Puritan conscience.[32]

In 1880, Bellamy had published serially in the Berkshire Courier a novel about Shays's rebellion entitled The Duke of Stockbridge.[33] Although set in the 1780's, it had two themes that had also pervaded Henry George's Progress and Poverty, first publicly distributed during the same year. One of the themes was that paternalism is an unreliable and dehumanizing form of social system, inevitably replete with injustice and brutality. Inequalities in the distribution of wealth lead not to noblesse oblige, Bellamy argued, but to class-bounded sympathies that only aggravate injustices, prevent their

correction, and ultimately end in revolutionary upheaval.
The other theme was the short-run cruelty and long-run futility of premature revolution, which occurs when the masses
have not yet been educated to see the root cause and cure of
their oppression and therefore attack only its symptoms and
symbols. These two themes posed the social problem for
Bellamy in Looking Backward. The Religion of Solidarity
furnished the structure for the solution.

At the start of the narrative in 1887, Julian West, a
wealthy and educated rentier, is thirty years old. Anxious
about the contemporary social disorders and personally incon-
venienced by them, he shares his class's conservatism. Although men might be politically equal, his peers were saying,
the poverty and toil of some were inevitable. "It was a pity,
but it could not be helped, and philosophy forbade wasting
compassion on what was beyond remedy." The fact that some
rode the coach of humanity, while others pulled it, meant
that the riders were of a higher order. "The effect of such
a delusion in moderating fellow feeling for the sufferings of
the mass of men into a distant and philosophical compassion
is obvious." Compassion, pity, commiseration--passive,
distant, uninvolving emotions--were directed toward the masses.

Sympathy--the extension of being, the feeling of involvement
with something outside oneself--did not extend beyond class
lines.[34]

Because of insomnia, Julian is put to sleep by hypnosis
safe from the vicissitudes of society in a sealed chamber beneath his home in one of the rapidly changing neighborhoods
of Boston. He awakens in the home of a Dr. Leete in the
Boston of 2000 A.D. The rest of the narrative recounts
Dr. Leete's education of Julian into the ways of the new
order, the dialogues between the two serving the historian's
purpose of contrasting the two eras. By the year 2000, the
people have completed the consolidation of capital by nation-
alizing all industry. The "labor problem" has been solved
by applying the principle of universal military service, a
natural corollary of the nation's becoming the sole capitalist. The whole population is organized into one industrial
army, whose organization is identical with that of the government. All citizens, including women, serve to the best of
their ability in a rank and position where their own desires
and talents intersect with the needs of the state. At the
age of forty-five, after twenty-four years of service, they
are retired with full pay and without further obligation.

Each person for his whole life receives an equal share of the national product, regardless of the actual value of his labor. There is thus no need to save (it is not even permitted) and no insecurity. Since incomes are equal and not transferable, there are no class distinctions, no corruption, no conspicuous consumption.

A utopia structured in this way was a logical sequence to the story of Eliot Carson in Bellamy's search for a way of coping with the social chaos around him. His metaphysical Religion of Solidarity had been a full intellectual retreat from the threatening changes in the material world. Cultivating the impersonal, "noumenal" ego was to have been an escape from the uncertainties and challenges that affected only the personality. As a "solution to the problem of life," however, it had one distinctive deficiency. It could not be acted on. Indeed, it rationalized passivity and withdrawal. The true utopia for the Religion of Solidarity was in the hermitage with Eliot Carson, who could provide for his own meager material wants until he met and married a wealthy woman. That solution could not satisfy the characteristic metaphysical demand for universality. Eliot Carson's life was not generalizable. Not even Bellamy dared to imitate it. The utopian system of

of the year 2000 thus generalized and socialized the hermitage.
In utopia, the dual ego is separated into compartments in the
citizen's life. The personal side and the material world
dominate during the social cooperation of the working years,
mobilized by one of the material analogies of Solidarity:
patriotism. Cultivation of the impersonal, the true goal of
utopia, is assigned to the years of retirement, when each
individual seeks fulfillment on his own.

In its broader structure, the utopia is an actualization
of the Religion of Solidarity. It operates by inclusion, by
expanding its circle to take in everyone, by harmonizing interests, rather than by conflict and competition. One becomes
a "communicant" of the system, not by a submissive conversion
experience, but by a liberating educational process, a process
that Julian had to duplicate. The tie that binds the society
is a fact of consciousness, not a faith. In addition, the
citizens are not dependent upon each other, not even children
upon their parents. They are linked only by their separate
connections to the nation, just as in the solitary communion
of Eliot Carson each person was tied individually to the Soul
of Solidarity. Once utopia has been established, sympathy
with other people has as little importance as it had for Eliot

and Edna.

Finally, the structure of utopia imitated Solidarity in its most crucial role, that of ending the threat of change in the material world. Bellamy's metaphysical idealism, actualized as fraternalism, pointed to a rigidly controlled materialism, in the form of absolute egalitarianism. Though this logic by-passed earlier Transcendentalists, for Bellamy a belief in equal participation in a transcendental oversoul could be materialized in social terms only as absolute equality, not as equal opportunity. Equality of condition eliminates the "spectre of Uncertainty" for the individual actor. It also precludes substantive social change entirely. In Bellamy's ideal society, the social world is no longer changing. All subsequent progress is to be in the realm of ideals, the perfection of man into a divinity, "the return of man to 'God who is our home.'"[35]

The contrast that Bellamy expected to impress his readers most was that between the "reason and order," the logic and simplicity, of the twentieth century and the chaos and disorder, the "shocking confusion," of the nineteenth, between a monistic structure and a chaotic reality. Julian expected that an industrial organization such as the utopia's would be vast and complex. He learns, on the contrary, that "nothing could be much simpler." The system "is indeed a vast one," Dr. Leete tells him, "but so logical in its principles and direct and simple in its workings, that it all but runs itself; and nobody but a fool could derange it." It is the very antithesis of complexity. For Bellamy, the answer to chaos and complexity had to be logical unity and simplicity. Consistency and logic, he had noted fifteen years earlier, are the source of all advance. If the structure had not been unitary, it would have had as little appeal as the piece-meal reforms he had always seen as inadequate. "A solution which leaves an unaccounted-for residuum," Dr. Leete notes, "is no solution at all." There are no loose ends in Bellamy's utopia. Its picture is painted with a ruthless deductive logic. Every detail, every mechanism, every social action fits into an absolutely unitary scheme deduced from what was to Bellamy the simplest principle imaginable: equality.[36]

When Bellamy first began writing the book, he later reported, the "idea was of a mere literary fantasy, a fairy tale of social felicity. There was no thought of contriving a house which practical men might live in, but merely of hanging in mid-air, far out of reach of the sordid and material

world of the present, a cloud-palace for an ideal humanity."
It was only the coercive logic of his inspiration, he recalled, that turned the fantasy into "the vehicle of a definite scheme of industrial reorganization." Not every age is
coerced by deductive logic, but Bellamy's appeal to fiction
mirrored Henry George's appeal to science. Though they ap-
proached the social problem from opposite directions, the
alternatives they offered their contemporaries had equivalent
intellectual structures. Scientific statics had its counterpart in fictional statics. Bellamy's standard for the first
draft of his utopia, the pure fantasy, was that it "only required to be consistent with itself to defy criticism."[37]
Five years later, he summarized the approach to literature
that had been evident in his work from the beginning: "Nothing outside of the exact sciences has to be so logical as the
thread of a story, if it is to be acceptable. There is no
such test of a false and absurd idea as trying to fit into a
story."[38]

Henry George offered his disturbed contemporaries theoretical stasis, unity, logic, simplicity, and certainty in
the rescue of the small enterpriser's sense of economic justice. Edward Bellamy was offering the same concepts, willy

nilly, as the salvation of America's other major traditional value, the Puritan conscience. Bellamy's intellectual course had been launched by the conflict between the impulse toward self-fulfillment, made hazardous by the state of the material world, and the impulse toward self-sacrifice, demanded by an out-moded Calvinist conscience. The Religion of Solidarity had attempted to resolve the conflict by making self-fulfillment completely passive and immaterial and then gratuitously and irrelevantly extolling self-sacrifice as a "natural virtue." Calvinism demanded sacrifice without the expectation of a special return; but in the wilderness setting of Solidarity, there was nothing at all to sacrifice. The utopia of the year 2000 reactivated the impulses and made them operative in a social setting. By requiring each person to make his best effort and rewarding each one equally and abundantly for doing so, the two conflicting impulses become one. The natural virtues are translated into "duty." Emulation and merit badges are used only for those industrial soldiers who do not yet automatically follow the natural virtues. The best people in utopia, on the other hand, measure the extent of their duty by the extent of their abilities. And the logic of the system tends to develop such a conscience and calling in

everyone. For, the inexorable unity of the scheme, which was
psychologically compelling for Bellamy and his readers, is
socially coercive in the year 2000: "It [service] is rather
a matter of course than of compulsion. It is regarded as so
absolutely natural and reasonable that the idea of its being
compulsory has ceased to be thought of. He would be thought
to be an incredibly contemptible person who should need compulsion in such a case. Nevertheless, to speak of service
being compulsory would be a weak way to state its absolute
inevitableness. Our entire social order is so wholly based
upon and deduced from it that if it were conceivable that a
man could escape it, he would be left with no possible way to
provide for his existence. He would have excluded himself
from the world, cut himself off from his kind, in a word, committed suicide." There is no special reward in utopia for
doing one's best. There is, rather, extreme punishment for
not doing so. The twentieth-century utopia, then, may ultimately be less an army than the Calvinist family on a national
scale. Bellamy often compared the new society to an extended
family, and in the years after 1888 the analogy became more
important as a defense against the charge of militarism. But
the Calvinist family in particular had a pattern of treating

good behavior as merely normal and not especially laudable,
while severely punishing dereliction, especially by ostra-
cism and a withdrawal of affection.[39]

Thus, Bellamy's intellectual trajectory traced a para-
bola. He had rejected Calvinism and retreated into Solidarity because the Puritan conscience was restrictive and could
not tell a man how to act in a chaotic world, where previous
patterns of behavior were irrelevant and where the effects
of his actions were unpredictable. Translating the Religion
of Solidarity back into social behavior, in the utopian
scheme, restored the direct and dependable correlation between
a man's conscience and the beneficent effects of his actions.
Instead of escaping the Puritan conscience, Bellamy was offering it as a national creed for everyone who, like himself,
had "Calvinism in his blood."

IV

At the end of the novel, when Julian has been sufficiently impressed by the new system, he returns in a dream
to the old Boston, sees the misery and confusion in their
full extent, confronts his wealthy comrades, and is scorned.
He awakens back in utopia, convinced that it would have been

better to have preached reform in 1887 and suffered contempt
than to have tolerated the old order. The dream fulfills
the anonymous historian's preface. It summarizes the book,
compressing the contrasts between perceived chaos and fictional stasis in a compelling way, thus impressing its
readers with the logical ease of reform. Had Bellamy set his
utopia in the year 3000, as he had originally intended, it
would not have had the same effect. It would have been just
another rationalization of passivity. Changing the date to
a thousand years earlier was, as he himself later noted, the
crucial decision that made it into a reform manifesto as
well as a vehicle of social certainty.[40] In fact, the method
of reform was indicated less by the length of Julian's nap
than by the considerably shorter span from 1887 to the institution of the new system. By the year 2000, Dr. Leete points
out, the utopia is already almost a century old. It was only
about a single generation from Julian's hypnosis to the social transformation. With that statement, Bellamy's novel
sought to end his contemporaries' uncertainty about the immediate future of their own society and to indicate that the
stasis he was offering as an end to chaos applied not only
to the final product but to the method of reaching it as well,

a method as effortless as Julian's sleep. As the Martian
had told the Earthling two years before, "No one could have
foresight, or clearly believe that God had it, without
realizing that the future is as incapable of being changed
as the past. And not only this, but to foresee events was to
foresee their logical necessity so clearly that to desire
them different was as impossible as seriously to wish that
two and two made five instead of four."[41]

"The solution came," Dr. Leete says, "as a result of a
process of industrial evolution which could not have terminated otherwise. All that society had to do was to recognize
and cooperate with that evolution when its tendency had become unmistakable." The sole aim of the novel, and of the
unexpected movement that followed from it, was to make that
tendency unmistakable and to arouse society "to complete its
logical evolution."[42] A utopia was incompatible with a truly
porgressive or pragmatistic use of the evolutionary scheme.
Bellamy did not intend his readers to conceive of reform as
a continuous process of conscious experimentation. Nor was
utopia to result from a cumulative process with an interior
logic of its own. Rather, the substitution of stasis for
chaos was to be made by a simple procedural inversion of

what already existed.

Bellamy did seem to appreciate the distinctive modernity of industrial capitalism. The consolidation of wealth had to have reached a certain point before his proposal made sense; and in the year 2000, the perfect society would exist only in the advanced nations. On the other hand, the utopia was deduced from a moral value, not induced from existing conditions. Bellamy seems to have combined two uncongenial concepts: a proposal that was universally and eternally valid because it was deduced from the absolute moral value of equality, and the evolutionary approach that made the proposal fitting only for peculiarly modern conditions. The contradiction was resolved, first, by calling an abrupt halt to social evolution once the principle was embodied in a social system. Absolute equality was not only morally final; it had the effect of producing social stasis whenever instituted. More important, only its ancillary effects were historically, rather than logically, determined. Industrial efficiency made general abundance possible for the first time. Had equality been established earlier, as it could have been, it would have entailed the acceptance of permanent general poverty.[43]

Bellamy thus denied the assumption behind Henry George's

scientific universalism. The natural wealth of the world, Bellamy assumed, was not sufficient to support its population.[44] An economy of abundance was an epoch of history and not a characteristic of the universe. Therefore, whereas modernity and complexity disrupted George's intellectual structure, Bellamy at first found them a useful additional argument for his scheme. Whereas substantive evolution could play no role in George's social science, it had at least an auxiliary role in Bellamy's fiction. Thus, there were enough elements in Looking Backward to have some retrospective appeal to the increasingly pragmatistic reformers of the Progressive Era and the New Deal--though both were repelled by the irrelevance of the very thing Bellamy was trying to sell: its utopianism. For, in the cases of both evolution to a modern age and its complexity, Bellamy parried with an intellectual structure of the same unitary, simple, and deductive character as George's. Complexity was unnatural and illogical and had to be wiped out by unity and simplicity; and there evolution stopped.

Dr. Leete had told Julian that the social transformation had three logical stages. First, the tendency of existing conditions had to become clear. Second, a convincing case had to be made for a logical and simple alternative. "Then the national party arose to carry it out by political methods."[45] Bellamy saw the first two stages completed by the circulation of <u>Looking Backward</u>. The third arose without his help. At first he resisted participation in the Bellamy Clubs and National Party organization, but soon his position expanded until he became its major propagandist, trying to persuade society to vindicate his reputation as a prophet. In becoming an active reformer, Bellamy was for the first time conducting a dialogue with the real world in which he lived. He had made available the moral appeal that could arouse a mass movement, and now he had to spell out what the movement should do. In that process, the proto-progressive and "modern" elements of his scheme were excised, and the stasis and universalism of <u>Looking Backward</u> came once again to the fore, ending the world's part in the dialogue.

The utopia of <u>Looking Backward</u> had resolved the incompatibility of Bellamy's moral philosophy with a changing world. But that resolution was still in 1888 incapable of being acted out. Bellamy then had to create an outline of the simple procedural changes that would bring history to an end. There was only one thing in <u>Looking Backward</u> to guide

reform: the details of the perfect society itself. Having
translated his moral ideals into a utopia, Bellamy simply
rewrote the utopia as a program. The picture of utopia and
the method of attaining it were identical. The perfect society was to be reached by enacting its details, in an order
neither determined by an evolutionary logic nor revised by
experience. Since logic, as Bellamy conceived it, meant
stasis and universalism, there was nothing between the present
and the future except particulars. A pragmatistic theory of
social change was outside Bellamy's ken. And his animosity
toward "German Socialism," for example, was aroused not by its
historical outlook, but by its "moral inadequacy": its economic rather than moral determinism, its denial of the nation
as a moral being, and its use of equity rather than equality
as a moral standard. Its complicated historical model was
simply irrelevant to him.[46]

The program Bellamy devised--the nationalization of railroads and certain industries, municipal ownership of utilities,
enlargement of the civil service--was notable, as he took
pride in asserting, for its lack of radicalism. Indeed, of
all the Nationalist proposals, "it is observable that there
is not one of them which is not demanded by considerations of

humanity and public expediency quite without reference to
Nationalism. A man has no need to be a Nationalist at all
to advocate them." In fact, the program and some of its
personnel had a major impact on the Populist movement in the
early 1890's. Nationalists, he said, were distinguished
only by the absolute certainty conferred by the finality of
utopia, their "clear vision of the glorious end," their
knowledge that "the unprecedented economical disturbances of
the day" were not "a mere chaos of conflicting forces, but
rather a stream of tendencies through ever larger experiments
in concentration and combination" toward the ultimate society.
Nationalists could bide their time and let the "logic of
events" help them prove their case to the people.[47]

As the years passed, this easy assurance gave way to
what C. S. Peirce called "the method of tenacity." The logic
of events seemed to confirm Bellamy's analysis, but the people
at large were not responding to the Nationalist movement as
they had responded to Looking Backward. Other movements and
reformers were adopting pieces of the Nationalist program
without reference to the utopian society. Bellamy regarded
this as an illusory path, for his program could be conceived
only as a logical deduction from its final goal. Reform

could not be haphazard and experimental or a response to immediate and local conditions, as some were beginning to say.
By the mid-nineties, Bellamy was exasperated by the illogical
reformers around him. "Persons whose minds are first directed to Nationalism," he wrote in 1894, "often miss the
point by failing to see that it is inevitable, as the only
alternative of plutocracy, if the latter is not to triumph.
Such persons are wont to regard the nationalization or public
conduct of industry as merely one economic device, among many,
to be compared with the rest as more or less attractive or
ingenious. They fail to perceive that it is the necessary
and only method by which a solution of the economic question
can be secured which shall be democratic in character."[48]

Supplementing his tenacity about the incontrovertible
nature of his scheme, Bellamy turned the Nationalist movement
itself into a religion, just as George had done for the
Single Tax. He might have justified such a turn by taking
an evolutionary view and treating his movement as embodying
a value that was a product of evolution and was just then
struggling to be born. In the light of the biting criticism
that social equality existed only among savages, the tempta-
tion to cite specifically modern conditions as a prerequisite

might have been tempting. Bellamy chose instead to side with the Polynesians and universality. Equality, he argued, was relative to no specific system or constituency. The economy of abundance did not create it; it had always been valid. If it could be had with wealth, all the better; if not, he would take it with poverty. In becoming a religion, Nationalism was not an innovation; it was simply adopting the church's original doctrine, which the church had long since abandoned. When the final society has been achieved, he said, formal religion will come to an end because all historic religious truths will have been fulfilled.[49]

Bellamy's final retreat from ideas of substantive social evolution appeared in the book written to explain the events that Julian slept through. Bellamy worked on Equality from 1893 to 1897. When it was about to be issued, he informed his publisher that he wanted it advertised as follows: "The scene is the same--that is to say, the world of the twentieth century, and the same characters reappear. But while the new book tells us much that is fresh about the institutions of the world of tomorrow, its especial purpose, as distinguished from that of 'Looking Backward,' is to account for those institutions by explaining not only their righteousness and

reason, but likewise the 'course of historical evolution'
by which they were born out of things existing today.   In
this part of his work the author has much to say of the meaning of the events of our own time, which he links with the
future by predictions of changes now close before us."[50]   In
the end, it was "righteousness and reason," not historical
evolution, that was most prominent. The book revealed that
the "course of historical evolution" simply comprised the
events of the "transition period" between the upsurge of
enthusiasm that produced the revolution and the completion
of the new system. It was merely the sequential enactment
of the measures in the Nationalist program. It was evolution
only in the sense that it was not a violent change; it had
nothing to do with the progressive notion of process.

The Great Revolution itself was treated as the culmination not of social evolution, but of what Bellamy liked to
call "political evolution," the triumph of the democratic
idea of the nation. It was in actuality an episode in intellectual history, the story of the popular awakening to
the coercive logic of equality 1900 years after it had first
been revealed. Here the decisive factors were not economic
changes, but the invention of printing and the diffusion of

intelligence among the masses. First expressed politically
as "negative democracy," it required only further public
enlightenment to be logically extended to positive control
of the economic system. Specific economic conditions, such
as the depressions between 1873 and 1896, served only as
object-lessons in the futility of half-measures. Bellamy
took pains to deny substantive distinctions between industrialism and prior forms of society. The consolidation of
wealth that made utopia an obvious necessity would have occurred had the industrial revolution never taken place.
Operating through "landlordism and usury," it would simply
have taken longer. And the revolution waited not for the
consolidation of wealth, but for the Nationalists' completion
of the centuries-old process of public education.[51]

"You see that this last and greatest of revolutions in
the nature of the case absolutely differed from all former
ones in the finality and completeness of its work."[52]
Bellamy could not understand why other reformers in the 1890's
were satisfied with less than this, why, when they accepted
his analysis of the problem, they objected to the finality of
his solution. In his eyes, they could only be practitioners
of futility, conscious or unconscious tools of the current

system.[53] For Bellamy, reform was a conclusive public exercise in deductive logic. Reform was not a dialogue with the
world, but an attempt to render it mute.

PART II

THE PRAGMATIC ROMANCE

CHAPTER IV

INTRODUCTION: UNDERSTANDING TRANSITION

By 1914, when Walter Lippmann dismissed the "panacea
habit of mind" because no "single, neat and absolute line of
procedure" could cope with "our strangely complex world," and
when he attacked visions of future utopias for opening "a
chasm between fact and fancy," for inhibiting effort and intelligence in the "living zone of the present," and for associating perfection with simplicity and stasis rather than
with "change" and "movement,"[1] liberal social thought had
been transformed by an idea that was alien, though contemporary, to the authors of Progress and Poverty and Looking
Backward. Society was patterned after a pluralistic universe,
a purposeless universe of chance, variety, complexity, dynamism, unpredictability, and novelty, analogous to the "tangled
bank" in Darwin's theory of evolution, to the "cosmical
weather" Chauncey Wright saw in the physical world, and to
Charles Peirce's "tychism." This idea and its consequences
underlay the "pragmatism" and "relativism" of the New

Dealers and the Progressives who preceded them.

Its most important consequence was an access of self-conscious ignorance about the "nature of things." The idea that the cosmos lacked inherent design, that nature was genetic or spontaneous rather than teleological or purposive, that complexity was irreducible, that the changing or accidental was no less real than the permanent or predictable, that categories were artificial and represented differences of degree rather than differences of kind, meant that the popular conception of natural laws had to be rethought, that rationalism, which had helped to create the social sciences, had to be abandoned, that purely deductive reasoning could no longer be convincing.

Such consequences might be attractive to those who thought that the alliance between liberalism and rationalism forged during the Enlightenment was being employed for conservative ends in the 1870's and 1880's. William Graham Sumner and other "old liberals" were arguing that the more people learned about society, the more they discovered that they should leave it alone--that the more they knew, the less control they could exercise and the less freedom of action they had. Sumner thus inverted the Enlightenment rationalist's assumption that knowledge was liberating. He argued that actions should be limited to the extent of knowledge, that when people could not predict, they should not act. Sumner adopted Spencer's use of complexity and dynamism only to reinforce the inhibiting effects of ignorance. Henry George and Edward Bellamy, who saw themselves as descendants of the Enlightenment, had responded to that argument--and to the feeling of uncertainty that they felt was unnerving their contemporaries--by going behind complexity and dynamism to find the operation of simple and universal principles, making reform not only possible but easy and certain.

Those who found a pluralistic universe congenial but chafed at the barriers to reform that Spencer and Sumner could deduce from it, had to find a method of accommodation to constant social change that would not result in moral anarchy as unforeseeable things arose to render any accommo-dation outmoded. Social scientists trained in Germany in the seventies and eighties and the specialists they produced in the prestigious new graduate schools had a personal stake in the conviction that social problems were too complex to be understood by ordinary people.[2] The vast influx of immigrants and the resulting heterogeneity of population were objective

examples of social complexity.[3] Some intellectuals as well,
though repelled by the gaudy materialism of the Gilded Age,
still regarded opportunities for self-fulfillment and self-
definition as more numerous and heady in a complicated society.[4] Their problem, then, was to justify acting in relative ignorance and to devise a method for doing so. They
sought not a new method of prediction, but a way of getting
along without it.

By translating the popular conception of science from
the name for a formulated body of truths to a method of approaching the world experimentally, by encompassing within
science what had previously been included in the labels
"policy" and "art," the founders of pragmatism, the New
Economists, and the Dynamic Sociologists of the eighties
were able to turn ignorance and uncertainty to their own
account. Some, like Lester Ward in 1883, still believed
that the consequences of social action were determined by
natural laws that were subject to rational comprehension and
that only the currently accepted body of laws was unscientific. Acting in ignorance, therefore, was the only way to
overcome ignorance. If not everything was known, then a
scientist had to experiment. Others, like the New Economists

and some of the pragmatists, believed that society conformed to the Darwinian model, that the determinative "medium" was not law but the total environment--all facts, actions, institutions, and ideas existing at any given moment. Such a conception, when fully accepted, did deny the possibility of fully predictive social knowledge, but it also made reform possible by finding no obstacle to an experiment's becoming part of the environment it sought to change.

The barrier between the natural and the artificial, which Sumner and the classical economists had exploited, thus came down. If the future would be, as the present had been, the cumulative product of selected novelties, then human creativity and inventiveness could be--in fact always had been--part of the accumulation. If social history was, as Spencer indicated, a process of perpetual transition in which functional and structural adjustments came automatically, naturally, and unconsciously, then all that was needed to eliminate the randomness, inefficiency, and glaring injustices that Spencer admitted were part of the process, was to use Spencer's own knowledge to make functionalism deliberate, artificial, and conscious. For those who thought that the concept of natural law was not applicable to society, it might still be possible to discern trends or tendencies. Some features of the environment were more salient than others; and cumulative causation meant that the past, while increasingly irrelevant, was never totally irrelevant. Predictive certainty was out of the question; but trends or tendencies could serve as a useful compromise between rigid determinism and total disorder. Bounded on one side by possibility and on the other by probability, they were definite enough to suggest accommodations, indefinite enough to allow options. Thus, "working hypotheses," rational goals inferred from experience, became the pragmatistic version of ideals: purposes to be consciously pursued.

Thus, a complex of ideas contained within the popular name "will" came to assert primacy over the complex of ideas contained in the label "reason." Lester Ward remembered that he had read Schopenhauer's Die Welt als Wille und Vorstellung (1819, 1844) in the winter of 1889-90. "It impressed me profoundly," he recalled, "as I saw that Schopenhauer's Wille was the same as my social forces. I also saw that his philosophy gave a subjective trend to human thought. Thenceforward my mind turned largely to psychology, and especially to subjective psychology or the philosophy of the feelings."[5]

Ward's reading of Schopenhauer resulted in The Psychic
Factors of Civilization (1893), in which the intellect or
"objective factors" were systematically made the instruments
of the will. The will intervened in the social process to
substitute art for nature. Nature did not have its own ends
and therefore choices made a difference. Ward's arguments
ten years earlier in Dynamic Sociology, though less psychological, displayed a similar emphasis. He derided the form
of progress he called "passive or negative dynamic," the type
found in Spencer, which was subject to intellectual comprehension but not voluntary control. He offered his own version, which he called "active or positive or applied dynamic,"
in which the social will was the moving force. "Anthropo-
teleology" (as distinguished from "theo-teleology") used
knowledge of unconscious, purposeless, genetic processes in
order to achieve conscious purposes. The method of progress
Ward proposed was the indirect method of "conation," of
effort, of endeavor, of striving after ends, in which the
intellect was the instrument of the will. The will, the
active factor, had to be supreme, because man was reforming
nature, setting himself against it, rather than conforming
to it, in order to control his life and his world. The will

was the source of art, of invention, of creativity, of novelty, and of "dynamic action." It precluded the finality of utopias and panaceas.[6]

Schopenhauer was not a favorite of the pragmatists; and John Dewey criticized Ward's psychology for an unnecessary dualism in its distinction between feeling and function, between consciousness and activity, or, as Ward saw it, between the human and the natural. Ward had tried to make action arise out of passive states of feeling. If one started with action, Dewey argued, rather than with an attempted explanation of action, one could eliminate the dualism and emerge with a psychology embodying what became the idea of "process" --continuous, functional, organic activity. Dewey agreed, however, that the social forces should be identified with "the motive side of mind," rather than with the intellect, and he criticized only the insufficient "activism" of Ward's conception of the will.[7]

William James had given the will a decisive role three years earlier in his treatise on psychology, which, point for point, was the closest thing to what became the progressive model for social action. "The pursuance of future ends and the choice of means for their attainment," James said, in

defining the boundaries of his science, "are . . . the cri-
terion of the presence of mentality in a phenomenon." To
consciousness he assigned a "teleological function." With
its appearance, "real ends"--ideals, of which machines and
automatons knew nothing--"appear for the first time upon the
world stage." The "lower centers" could handle uniform,
invariable functions--rapid, automatic, habitual actions.
Consciousness, most highly developed in humans, had developed to aid action in a complex, variable environment.
It helped humanity adapt to slight and sudden changes in
conditions, and it selected the means for the pursuit of the
ends humanity preferred, the purposes it chose to fulfill.
"This," James said, "is the development of the will; . . ."[8]
Assertion of the will, James had also said, was necessary
to avoid "indecision, plaintiveness and defeat" in the face
of ignorance. Confronted by a choice between opposing positions, neither of which was yet provable, only "men of will,"
those who took a stand, could become the "masters and lords
of life." Those who refused to take risks and live on the
"perilous edge" did not expand the range of human knowledge
and were as useless to science as to the world of practical
affairs. Radical empiricism depended upon the will to act.[9]

In an analogous vein, Charles H. Cooley made the "rise of
social will" the epochal event in the modern overthrow of
formalism.[10]

Henry George in 1880, self-consciously in the rationalist
tradition, and Edward Bellamy, rationalist in spite of himself,
had no need to emphasize the will. "Reason" gave complete and
simple instructions for reform; and once it was obeyed in the
single case, people's ordinary, natural, instinctive actions
would yield progress without planning for it. George, in fact,
criticized Schopenhauer for excessive subjectivism. He dis-
liked Schopenhauer's "philosophy of negation," which regarded
man as caught in "an everlasting trap" set by God, the "icy
devil." He traced Schopenhauer's errors to his acceptance
of Kant's conception of space and time, which had led
Schopenhauer to think that reason was insufficient to handle
antinomies that George believed did not exist. "We may be
wise to distrust our knowledge," George concluded; "and,
unless we have tested them, to distrust what we may call our
reasonings; but never to distrust reason itself."[11]

While the idea of a pluralistic universe was available
even before George and Bellamy had begun their careers, they
achieved their greatest popular successes when they rejected

that idea and responded with monistic intellectual structures
to a perception of social chaos and uncertainty. "Universality" and "economy" indicated that chaos was an illusion,
where pluralism implied that random, unpredictable change
was a permanent feature of society. To the New Economists,
Dynamic Sociologists, and Pragmatists (who had a limited and
specialized audience in the 1880's), pluralism meant novelty
and complexity. It could thus suit a society perceived as
distinctively modern, irreducibly complex, and constantly
changing. In such a society, existing social knowledge
would be continually antiquated; and a method of acting in
ignorance would be needed, a method of working inductively
and tentatively, of "inhabiting reality" (as William James
said of Jane Addams's work[12]), of building up knowledge from
the present forward. Consciously chosen purposes would have
to replace traditional values. Elements of such a perception
began to appear in George's and Bellamy's writings in the
1880's, creating pressures to supplement the monistic modes
with pluralistic modes. George and Bellamy persistently
treated pluralism as unnatural, however; they were most comfortable and creative with a monistic intellectual structure;
and in the 1890's they worked to perfect their monism,

thereby defining themselves out of the "modern" era.

Jane Addams in <u>Twenty Years at Hull House</u> (1910) recalled the 1890's as "a decade of economic discussion." The
Working People's Social Science Club, which gathered at the
settlement on Halsted Street from 1890 to 1897, was the
scene of heated debates about the various social theories
that sought both to explain the new industrial system and to
propose ways of reforming it. Although Jane Addams said that
she often felt vague longings for such a theory, they always
seemed to her unnecessarily complete, and she emerged from
the decade of discussion unbound by ideological ties. From
Jane Addams's perspective of 1910, the significance of the
Club lay in the variety of theories that were presented and
in the freedom with which they were discussed. From the
perspective of 1880, however, two other items in her account
take on significance. First, the theories were judged by
their ability to cure the ills of a distinctively modern society, different in kind from any that had existed before.
Second, apart from the theorists themselves, few people, and
certainly not Jane Addams or Herbert Croly, became committed
to deterministic explanations. Unitary and total theories,
analogous to those of Henry George and Edward Bellamy of the

decade before, attracted only small followings and received
their greatest attention from those who opposed them. They
all seemed, to use George's own term, "superadequate."[13]

The lives of Jane Addams and Herbert Croly span the
years in which American society underwent what came to be
seen as its final transformation into an industrialized society. The first decade of their public careers overlapped
the last decade of George's and Bellamy's; and the end of
both Croly's and Jane Addams's lives overlapped by a decade
or more the early careers of the future New Dealers. Their
different responses to the same stages of social development
are striking. Addams and Croly were both paralyzed during
the social chaos of the eighties, which they experienced in
personal terms. By the mid-nineties, however, when George
and Bellamy were in decline, they had begun the upward
trajectory that made her "the most famous woman in America"
at the height of the progressive crusade and made him the
most influential ideologue of the New Nationalism. They
represented different constituencies--the working poor and
the intellectuals--but they gave the same name--"integrity"
--to the social problem, and their intellectual and personal
influence peaked at the same time and among many of the same

people. Both considered themselves thorough pragmatists, indeed "super-pragmatists," by the nineteen-twenties; and yet they were both increasingly doubtful about a younger group of reformers who took the same name. And so an examination of their intellectual lives can help discover when, in what degrees, and for what purposes the current of ideas loosely designated "pragmatism" was first absorbed into reform thought.

The two or three years surrounding 1893 seem to mark a turning point in the power of both a new perception and a new intellectual structure. A perception of transition that accepted distinctive modernity and substantive complexity superseded the perception of chaos; and a dualistic intellectual structure that accepted elements of pragmatism superseded the structure of monism. Josiah Strong, for example, whose Our Country of 1885 had catered to the sense of extreme crisis of the eighties, published another popular book in 1893, describing The New Era. "It is a common observation," he began, "that we are living in an age of transition." The achievements of the nineteenth century "generally suggest, not finality or completeness, but rather beginnings." In opening his attempt to discern what the coming age would be like, Strong added the caveat that predictions of the future had to be limited to the discernment of possible trends. Society was too complex and unpredictable to allow more than "reasonable inferences concerning the future." Society had undergone radical and profound changes in its economic system in the previous twenty-five or thirty years, Strong claimed, changes in its methods, its extent, its organization, changes in the condition of the worker and in the relation of the country to the city--all changes that he was able to describe in some detail.[14]

This increasing "describability" of society seems to have been the key to the growing use of pragmatism in reform. If a feeling of uncertainty had made the monistic model congenial through the eighties, the pluralistic model seems to have been adopted just in proportion as that feeling declined, as real or assumed knowledge of society increased, as society became increasingly "describable," as the future started to be taken for granted, as the random unpredictable world that pragmatism was designed to handle started to seem orderly and stable. The process would be completed by 1910-14, after the perception changed again, from transition to stasis, making the pressures to accept pragmatism in toto overpowering. In the interim period, the progressives complemented the elements of pragmatism and pluralism, which foreshadowed the intellectual structure of the New Dealers, with forms of moral absolutism and determinism, with idealisms and romantic views of inevitable progress, reminiscent of those found in George and Bellamy. The dualisms were not uncomfortable, since, unlike George and Bellamy, neither Jane Addams nor Herbert Croly was raised in a milieu capable of treating the relation between ideas and activities as fixed and unitary. Neither was brought up to have a stake in the traditional values that the earlier reformers had tried to rescue. Neither had a substitute for the old values, other than "integrity"; but both, unlike Rexford Tugwell and Thurman Arnold, were preoccupied with a search for values, with the necessity to discover in the complexity of existence authentic and authoritative moral knowledge. Thus, the older patterns of thought were as congenial--or uncongenial--to them as the newer, and their characteristic style was to combine both in a dualistic intellectual structure. The older patterns were used in ways that compensated for the uncertainties that the newer patterns tended to reinforce.

The dualism was especially available in the 1890's and early 1900's. It was very easy to confuse the academically fashionable Hegelian view that history was an unfolding, purposive evolution, with the Darwinian picture of a genetic nature, since both involved the conflict or interaction of two processes. It was especially easy, since the popular conception of evolution was less Darwinian than neo-Lamarckian. Similarly, it was easy to confuse the idea of social process, with its inherent functionalism, with the idea of a teleological nature. And both the Hegelians and the Darwinians stressed the epochal importance of the appearance of consciousness. Moreover, there was a general tendency even among those in the pragmatist camp to aid the will's course through the plurality of life by resolving complexity and dynamism into an interaction between change and continuity, with the latter providing the partial fixity and predictability that the pluralistic model, in its purity, lacked. Charles Peirce tempered tychism with synechism; William James, consciousness with habit; Lester Ward, invention with institutions; Charles Cooley, inherited dispositions with communication. John Dewey himself aided the dualism by calling working hypotheses "ideals." (He would ease the final stages of the transformation thirty years later by calling them "plans.")

If these pragmatistic concessions to continuity were still too indeterminate for the 1890's,[15] they did ease the acceptance of an "abolutistic" version that was not. Josiah Royce, for example, who taught Croly cosmology at Harvard, expressed his admiration for Schopenhauer's _Wille_ in his influential _Spirit of Modern Philosophy_ (1892), which Jane Addams read;[16] and Royce placed the will at the center of his own philosophy. He used the pragmatists' own argument for the existence of novelties and their restricted conception of universals to prove the existence of the Absolute, the insufficiency of scientific description, and the necessity for Idealism. But he also stratified the two types of knowledge (moral and scientific) along individual-social lines, with the individual as the pivot of the wider subjective "world of appreciation" or values, and the social as the locus of the narrower objective "world of description" or law. In _The World and the Individual_ (1899-1901), he defined the "inner meaning" of ideas as purposes of the will, or plans of action.[17] In his popular _Philosophy of Loyalty_ (1908), he defined loyalty, the fulfillment of the moral law, as a cause for which one was willing to act, and duty as the individual will brought to self-consciousness. The process of self-consciousness was a conflict between "individual waywardness" or self-will and "social conformity" or conventions, traditions, and ideals. It was a conflict between the inner world and the outer, between the personal and the impersonal. Only loyalty to loyalty could synthesize the conflict and give it "centre, fixity, stability," unity of purpose. Royce regarded the opportunities for loyalty as greater in modern civilization.[18]

Thus, the Hegelian synthesis could serve as well as the Darwinian to contain such dual processes as organization and specialization, innovation and social control, "individuation" and "integration." The Hegelian's advantage of allowing for sudden major changes in the direction of history (and thus distinctive modernity), was balanced among Darwinians by Lester Ward's description of the substitution of telesis for genesis with the epochal appearance of mind and the even more epochal appearance of Dynamic Sociology. Thus elements that played into an acceptance of pragmatism could also play into an acceptance of versions of romantic idealism and moral absolutism. The uses to which they were put, however, were

not easily interchangeable. For what Hegelianism and other
forms of moral absolutism seemed to offer was something "outside" the interaction of the two social processes in which
they could be reconciled or by which they could be judged.
They offered moral authority and the possibility of a
standard of selection more "authentic" than utilitarianism or
functionalism.

When Jane Addams first went to Hull House, she assumed,
like George and Bellamy, that there were certain universal
values to which social life ought to conform. She quickly
realized that that was not fully the case, however, and
through the 1890's, indeed until about 1910, she, like Croly,
combined the two approaches, just as George had begun to
separate his two triads in the 1880's and just as Bellamy's
thought had contained similar options. But while neither
George nor Bellamy was able to sustain the dualism, Croly
and Addams were. Though they ultimately regarded themselves
as pragmatists and pluralists--the progressive crusade of
1912 marked the approximate turning point--the dualisms
were never entirely abandoned. The interplay between the
romantic and the pragmatistic--between the belief that order
in history could be discovered and the belief that it had to

be imposed; between the willing individual dominated by subjective concerns and the necessity to weigh the objective social consequences of actions; between moral ideals and instrumental ideals; between authenticity and objectivity; between creativity and adaptation; between continuity and change; between design and chance--persisted in some degree until the end of their lives and is a distinguishing feature of their thought. Before 1912, their perception of society as in transition, as having made a new beginning and as heading toward increasing complexity, fitted the dualistic structure and kept them from seeing it as dualistic.

It also helped to create a new role for social reformers. In the 1880's, complexity was important to conservative theorists as a defense of the status quo and a bulwark against the assertion of the popular will. To advanced academic liberals, such as Richard Ely, complexity and modernity meant the necessity for rule by experts. George and Bellamy, in contrast, offered simplicity and unity, and thus the possibility of mass movements. They saw the reformer's role as simple advocacy. He was distinguished from the masses only in that he saw something before they did. Once the simple truth was known, anyone could become an

advocate; and once it was spread, the reformer would be
unnecessary. When the perceptions of modernity and increasing complexity became powerful early in the Progressive Era,
reformers sought to keep its consequences democratic by a
permanent stratification of roles. The "people" would be
the source of innovations, and their consent would be the
ultimate "selector"; the reformer would take on the burden of
self-consciousness, which the destruction of traditional
values had created. In the New Deal years, when the perception of transition had passed into a perception of stasis,
the reformer would become the sole actor. There would be no
place for the people save as beneficiaries. The reformer
would be more a hero and less a representative man. Jane
Addams and Herbert Croly represent a halfway stage between
reform as education of the public to engage in collective
action, and reform as persuasion of the public to delegate
its powers. Henry George and Edward Bellamy needed and expected to create mass movements. The New Dealers would regard mass movements as an imposition upon their professional
competency. Though the progressives could participate in a
mass movement that arose spontaneously, they could not create
one of their own because they could not pretend to have

answers. Because the future would be the product of continuous acts of will on the basis of continuous assessment of
the social process, the reformer had to be a perpetual social critic, to "stand inbetween."[19]

The "between-age mood" that Jane Addams referred to in
her memoirs, the sense of "the essential provisionality of
everything,"[20] disappeared after 1912; and by 1930, a younger
group of reformers and planners would have found progressive
dualisms illogical and, worse, unnecessary. But the society
of the progressives stood between the apparent chaos of the
1870's and 1880's and the apparent stasis of the 1920's and
1930's, and the dualistic intellectual structure enabled them
to cope with that peculiar and changing position. Expressing
the dualisms graphically, in many ways John Dewey cannot
stand alone as the symbolic philosopher of the progressive
crusade; Josiah Royce has to be placed beside him.

CHAPTER V

INHABITING REALITY

Jane Addams

Washington Gladden, who had been preaching the Social
Gospel for twenty years, spoke in the late 1890's of a complete revolution in economic life in the preceding half-
century and of the necessity to think out the ethical bear-
ings of "the new system of organized industry." The factory
system had become not only an economic fact, Gladden said,
but a social fact as well. It had divided society into
classes and eliminated personal contact among them. Gladden
wanted employers to live among their employees: "Of all possible social settlements, this is the best, . . ." The
organization of industry was "becoming so extensive and complicated," he wrote, that conduct ought to be guided by the
"solidarity of human interests" and by "social aims." The
specialization of functions in society, the prevalence of
forces that divided and differentiated, had ruptured the integrity of society. "Social integration is the crying need

of the hour."[1]

Simon Patten, also focusing on the need for "integration," saw society in the midst of a transition from a pain to a pleasure economy, a transition that revealed the inadequacy of simpler concepts of natural law. The economic transition could be accommodated in the social order only through use of proper social ideals. Ideals, for Patten, represented "possibilities," "aspirations," not knowledge, and were essential for progress. When the "civic instincts" triumphed over static ideals, he said, a "new era of our development" would begin. "It will mark the beginning of a social integration through which a truly American society can be formed."[2]

One current that fed the perception that society had made a new beginning and therefore had to abandon old absolutes and universals in favor of "relevant and appropriate" social ideals, was the discovery of what had ended. Frederick Jackson Turner, noticing the Census Bureau's abandonment of the frontier line, announced in 1893 that the frontier explained American development and "with its going has closed the first period of American history." Over the next twenty years Turner repeatedly asked whether any of America's historic ideals would prove relevant for new complex conditions. By

1910, the year of his presidential address to the American
Historical Association, he spoke of the previous twenty years
as "two decades of transition" to a new society and spoke of
American history as if it uniquely embodied the notion of process. "Whatever be the truth regarding European history,
American history is chiefly concerned with social forces,
shaping and reshaping under the conditions of a nation changing as it adjusts to its environment. And this environment
progressively reveals new aspects of itself, exerts new influences, and calls out new social organs and functions."[3]

The preoccupation with finding new values for a new age,
with providing, in common Progressive usage, social "integrity" for a society in process, a society that was in its
very basis complex, impersonal, constantly changing, dominated social-reform thought from the mid-nineties until the
outbreak of World War I. But the beginning and the end of
that period were perceived very differently. In the 1890's,
Jane Addams observed that the industrial system was so new
and fluid that conventional patterns of belief and action
were incapable of coping with it. At the time of the progressive crusade of 1912, she complained that the system was
so rigid and static that it seemed as if it had always

existed. Her first and perhaps most important book, Democracy
and Social Ethics (1902), was written at the midpoint of that
transformation. The personal "integrity" and social "integration" that it offered to self-conscious moralists seeking a
new alliance of belief and action derived from its combination of two separate modes of explanation. The book, and
Jane Addams's intellectual career, supported Patten's assumption that "ideals" and "knowledge" were alternatives to each
other, alternatives whose changing relative importance--as
knowledge about society increased, romantic idealism became
less and less necessary and pragmatism more and more attrac-
tive--constituted the modernization of intellectual life.
Her ability to hold onto both modes of thought--her dualistic
intellectual structure--helped bridge that striking intellectual revolution.

I

From her earliest years to the founding of Hull House
in 1889, Jane Addams was forced to deal with conflicting ways
of relating one's beliefs to one's activities: the accepted
standards for a woman's social life and the successful male
life-pattern that she had come to accept as most admirable

during her formative years. Between the ages of two and
eight, she was motherless, and all her significant "earliest
impressions" stemmed from this time when she had her father
to herself.[4] John H. Addams was a respected community leader
in Cedarville, Illinois, a small town on the make since its
frontier days. He appears to have known, and been satisfied,
that it did not have a great future. He staked his life on
good conduct, not outsized ambition, and his local success
allowed him to subsist in the good opinions of his peers.
It was evidence, in a man's world, that his activities automatically embodied a social and moral purpose. When pressed
for religious identification, he called himself a Quaker,
but he made the rounds of the Protestant churches, more out
of indifference than a quest for systematic religious truth;
and he seems to have had an unusual, and well deserved, faith
in his own judgment. His ability to take his moral values
for granted was the thing his daughter most envied in his
life. Whether or not that ability derived from a firm training in his childhood, he apparently never related his judgments to an explicit religious code, and he did not attempt
to inculcate such a code in his daughter. That might have
been considered a mother's function. In any case, Jane

Addams was raised to fit his activist pattern without the
solid grounding in belief that apparently allowed him to act
automatically. Calvinism, for example, did not inhabit the
Addams household. There was to be no fear of eternal damna-
tion, no guilt for improper motives, because there was, apparently, no punishment. There was only a sense of shame
for having acted in violation of her self-image as a projec-
tion of her father, who embodied moral certainty. He never
scolded her and rarely gave advice. Childish opinions were
indulged and respected. Confessions of sin were turned back
to create a respect for honesty. Expressions of moral dilemma
or self-doubt were turned into experiences in self-dependence.
Supporting all this, in lieu of formal religious training,
was an assurance of affection and place that seems to have
made God unnecessary to her.

The other possible source of her father's self-assurance--
an accepted life-pattern that exemplified purposive action,
with the purpose taken for granted--was denied Jane Addams
by the lack of occupational channels acceptable for a middle-
class woman. Her father's example imposed one set of expectations upon her; society, another; and society's claims were
reinforced by a strong-willed step-mother, who not only

challenged her security of place, but who held to a Victorian woman's ideal--perhaps the most unproductive relationship between belief and activity--that woman at her best was a passive embodiment of permanent cultural values.

The search for surrogates for these two sources of automatic action dominated Jane Addams's early maturity. Four years at Rockford Female Seminary brought clearly to the surface her lack of the genuine religious beliefs that could enable her to act without thinking. Her father's church-hopping and demand for "mental integrity" might have dove-tailed nicely with a systematic pragmatism or a self-conscious agnosticism; but neither of those were live options at Rockford. The school's insistent evangelism simply made clear to her that the freedom of action she desired, if it could not be based on coherent goals, had to be underwritten by a certainty of belief that she had not arrived with.

Religion was something she would rather take for granted, she wrote her friend Ellen Starr from Rockford, especially the finer points: "as a general thing I regard it with indifference." But the necessity for certainty plagued her, and she complained that in her constant exploration of different creeds she found no answers she could regard as final. "I am

not <u>un</u>settled, as I <u>re</u>settle so often, but my creed is ever
<u>be sincere</u> and don't fuss." She complained of being able to
settle such questions only intellectually, without the emotional commitment that would turn the solutions into habits
of mind. Religion was not to be an obsession forever, she
noted; it was a problem to be settled so that she could turn
her energies to action. "I only feel that I need religion
in a practical sense," she wrote in her third year at the
Seminary, "that if I could fix myself with my relations to
God and the universe,and so be in harmony with nature and
deity, I could use my faculties and energy and could do almost anything."[5] As long as she did not have this solid
grounding in belief, she felt she would be passive and undirected, though this need not be devastating so long as she
was a child and her father's example was vital.

Her father died shortly after she was graduated in the
summer of 1881. The mental depression and physical breakdown
that had begun that summer continued intermittently for the
next eight years. Whether her father's continued presence
would have allowed her to settle earlier than she did the
dilemmas posed by conflicting demands is impossible to say.
She had lost the integrating forces in her life--her father's

presence and the pursuit of a liberating education--at just
the point when she most required some directing purpose or
some sustaining creed to put form into her future. She had
been raised, if not to succeed, at least to work. She found
at twenty-one, however, that she had been prepared to be
someone, but not to do anything, and that there was nothing
that could channel her, willy nilly, as it might a man, into
action that would affirm by its very existence a moral purpose. Her stepmother's insistence on a "finishing" tour of
Europe only emphasized the opposition between the passivity
expected of her and the activity that she had come to regard
as the expression of purpose--and, as a corollary, the opposition between art, which had always been "rather out of my
line," and life. Art could not give form to life, she felt;
only action could. But to act effectively seemed to require
the ability to take one's mental life for granted. "I quite
feel as if I were not 'following the call of my genius,'"
she wrote Ellen Starr before embarking, "when I propose to
devote a year[']s time to travel in search of a good time
and this general idea of culture which some way never commanded my full respect. People complain of losing spiritual
life when abroad. I imagine it will be quite as hard to hold

to full earnestness of purpose." It was hard, indeed, as it was hard to find that solid grounding in belief, those "habits of mind" upon which "so much is dependent."[6] Her baptism in the Presbyterian church in 1888, when she was twenty-eight, was a purely passive acceptance, she recalled, of "an outward symbol of fellowship, some bond of peace, some blessed spot where unity of spirit might claim right of way over all differences."[7] Her interest in Positivism during these years flowed from a similar impulse to find something that could be taken for granted and thus leave the mind free to concentrate on specific problems.

As Jane Addams had experienced it at home and as she used the term later on, "mental integrity" seemed to demand that a person combine within her own intellectual structure ideas that were mutually exclusive. On the one hand, it offered spontaneity and self-expression; on the other, it demanded discipline and self-control. It promised both order and fulfillment, security and possibility. It impelled purposive action, rather than guilt-ridden inertia; self-realization, rather than a preoccupation with material rewards. At college and during the eighties, when the disorder of her own life seemed to match the chaotic state

of society at large, Jane Addams wrestled with her own assumption, as her correspondence with Ellen Starr revealed,
that a monistic intellectual structure, as William James
later characterized it, was the only acceptable one. She
assumed that solid "habits of mind" had to precede activity,
that theory had to precede practice, that critical standards
had to precede creativity; and yet those assumptions produced only paralyzing self-consciousness. It had not yet
occurred to her that the process could be reversed or that
"integrity" could hold its contradictory parts in a perpetual,
if tense, balance. Thus, her pursuit of culture and her
search for a final relgious creed reflected an older approach
to the world that was out of line with both her circumstances
and her character; and they only aggravated, with their
fruitlessness and passivity, the feeling of disintegration.

Edna Damon, in Edward Bellamy's "Story of Eliot Carson,"
had been a religious personality who could find no satisfaction in unself-conscious activity. She had required a faith
that rationalized inaction and passive acceptance of one's
own perfection. Jane Addams's crisis came from an opposite
source. Her father's example indicated that the meaning of
life was not in what one believed about it, but what one did

in it, and that the doing itself had to embody purpose.
Since there were no conventional ways to provide that for the
new situation of the college women of the 1880's, Jane Addams,
trying to follow the monistic mode, decided that the active
life required that a set of values be explicitly fixed upon
and that ways then be consciously devised to act them out.
The premise of a settlement house seemed to offer a solution.
Initially at least, it was an ingenious way to satisfy both
the female model--life as embodying permanent cultural values
--and the male--life as automatically purposive action.

II

From the perspective of society at large, the two major
functions of the "social settlement" were contained within
its name. When Hull-House was opened on South Halsted
Street, Chicago, in 1889, Jane Addams saw the "social problem"
as the "disintegration" of society into classes that were increasingly unaware of each other's existence because they
lived apart. The physical separation of the classes belied
the real unity of society by breaking channels of communication between the two "ends of the city."[8] Like C. H. Cooley
a decade later, Jane Addams believed that the "imaginations"

people had of each other were the solid facts of society, that a person was not "socially real" unless he was sympathetically imagined, unless he affected the minds and conduct of others; and that could not happen, she believed, without personal contact.

The solution to the social problem thus seemed to be to infiltrate the poor, to "settle" among them without giving up one's own identity, and to carry on regular social intercourse as had been done before the city had become so large. The charity organization societies had developed a similar analysis of social fragmentation, but the settlements rejected both the role of lady bountiful and the institutional bias. "There is to be no 'organization' and no 'institution' about it," Ellen Starr said, reporting her friend's plan. "The world is overstocked with institutions and organizations: and after all a personality is the only thing that ever touches anybody. . . . People are coming to the conclusion that if anything is to be done toward tearing down these walls--half imaginary [--] between classes, that are making anarchists and strikers the order of the day, it must be done by actual contact and voluntarily from the top. . . . [We said] that Miss Addams & Miss Starr simply intended to <u>live</u>

there and get acquainted with the people & ask their friends
of both classes to visit them, . . ."[9] Simply by being open
and accessible as a meeting place for both ends of society,
Hull-House would be an instrument of social unity. Social
in the sense of "sociable" was Jane Addams's meaning when
she first observed that settlement residents "claim to have
added the social function to Democracy."[10]

In settling and socializing, the social settlements thus
claimed to fill a need, but they did not claim that they constituted reform. The problem of reconstruction was outside
Jane Addams's purview in the first years. In the beginning,
the settlement movement was, at its most reformist, an extension of the method of utopian colonies founded not simply as
models for society but as spores that were to proliferate,
grow, and ultimately coalesce to become the whole society
itself. Hull-House, Jane Addams reported, was in the vanguard
of a movement toward an ultimate physical integration of the
city. "It is to be hoped," she said in 1892, "that this
moving and living will at length be universal and need no
name. The Settlement movement is from its nature a provisional
one." She later dismissed this view of the movement as "geographical salvation," but both settling and socializing were

attempts to embody in a new form the monistic pattern that
Jane Addams had been told was natural--the conscious founding
of action on the basis of standards accepted as universal and
absolute. They operated on the assumption that there was a
fundamental unity in the world, both in the realm of ideals
and in the material basis of society, and that this theoretical
unity simply had to be restored to the conduct of social life.
The segregation of the classes, she wrote, was a violation of
the Christian and democratic ideal of the "solidarity of the
human race," which Hull-House would affirm. In more material
terms, "Hull-House endeavors to make social intercourse express the growing sense of the economic unity of society."
With this underpinning of ideal and real fixity, settling
and socializing would offer undirected young people an instrument for "putting theory into practice," for automatically purposive action. Settling and sociability had to be acted out in
order to exist at all.[11]

The same pattern defined the settlement's third major
function, the integration of the neighborhood itself. For
the neighborhood, initially conceived as passive and unformed,
the settlement was to be the functional equivalent of the
female finishing tour. The permanent values that the

settlement residents represented would confer order and unity upon the area. The first requirement Jane Addams and Ellen Starr had when searching for a house was that it have "one large room" where classes and discussions could be held. Their first projects upon moving in were classes in literature and displays of reproductions of great art. As agents of culture, the residents would bring the poor into the fellowship of the educated and mold their behavior to conform to the permanent values of civilization. The settlement aimed, Jane Addams noted, "to focus and give form" to the social life of the neighborhood and "to bring to bear upon it the results of cultivation and training." Of London's Toynbee Hall, the first settlement, she noted approvingly that it stood for "the fittings of a cultivated, well-ordered life, and the surroundings which are suggestive of a participation in the best of the past."[12]

It was not to be expected that this static relationship between permanent ideals and activity, between "a really living world" and "a shadowy intellectual or aesthetic reflection of it," would be sufficient for the poor any more than it had been for Jane Addams in the 1880's.[13] Almost from the beginning, the settlement residents discovered that

life in the industrial districts was more complicated than
they had expected, and that the "social statics" that they
had brought in with them from the outside and expected to
impose onto the area had to be supplemented by an understanding of the "social dynamics" of the neighborhood itself and
by a flexible response to changing needs.[14] Jane Addams
found that some of the best suggestions for projects came
from the neighbors and that the major lines of the settlement's
activity resulted from demand and not from preconceived notions. She found among the residents "a constantly increasing tendency to consult their neighbors on the advisability
of each new undertaking."[15] Indeed, acting "deductively"
from the residents' own theories produced some eye-opening
failures.[16] This gradual realization that there were two
legitimate ways of approaching the social problem--a static
or monistic one on the basis of preconceptions, accepted
knowledge, and permanent ideals, and another, dynamic or
pluralistic one, carried out in ignorance and in response
to conditions and to demands--was accelerated by a rapid
series of social events in 1893-94, which brought to consciousness a new perception of the nature of society and its
relationships to the past and the future.

For Jane Addams in 1889 and the early 1890's, the problem of "industrialism" had been the problem of the manufacturing quarters of the great American cities. She displayed no feeling that society had changed in a radical way or that anything more than spreading the values of traditional society was required. The industrial revolution seemed a long way in the past; it had produced the slow growth of factories and cities, which had isolated the poor physically and socially; and that isolation had to be brought to an end. But the question of distinctive modernity soon became pressing: when does it aid understanding and conduct to regard a difference in degree as a difference in kind?

Robert A. Woods, head of Andover House in Boston, in an address at a conference that Jane Addams attended in 1892, analyzed the social situation in much the same way as she and observed: "This situation, while it has always existed to a degree, is yet distinctly the product of the present time. Not until now could we fairly have appreciated it. Only now have we means adapted to meet it. Only modern civilization could have brought about the difficulty; only modern civilization could have understood it; only modern civilization can overcome it."[17]

Jane Addams's public writings began to reflect such a perception of distinctive modernity during the events of 1893-94, the Columbian Exposition, the great depression that immediately followed, and the Pullman Strike less than a year later. She had not gone to Halsted Street because of the ills of "modern industrial society"; such a conception was outside her consciousness in 1889. After 1893, however, it seemed as if the whole moral universe might have to be rethought and remade for a new era.

III

The events of 1893-94 did not cause Jane Addams to abandon the conceptions and techniques that she had been using since 1889. Rather, they planted seeds around which slowly crystallized new approaches that occasionally supplemented, often complemented, usually competed with, but in all cases coexisted with the old. In a search for new justifications for settlements, her articles and speeches during the decade after 1893 reveal that she was analyzing society from two distinct points of view. She was heading toward a pattern of understanding and coping with social changes that was an extension of the literal "dialectic" that had begun to arise soon after

1889: the dialogue between residents and neighbors, outside and inside, deduction from permanent values and induction from particular circumstances, imposition of order and unity and response to the unexpected and complex--the articulation of the dualistic intellectual structure that, if she and Herbert Croly are salient examples, is characteristic of liberal thinking in the Progressive Era.

The two most prominent examples of this interweaving in the decade after 1893 were the addition of reform to the settlement's role of philanthropy and an extension of the meaning of "social" from "sociable" to "collective." The additions reflected the new perception of society, the grafting of the idea that "industrialism" was different in kind from the previous era onto the idea that it was different only in degree, the growing consciousness that novelty and complexity had to be accepted along with permanence and unity.

The depression of 1893 "resulted at times," Jane Addams later recalled, "in a curious reaction against all the educational and philanthropic activities in which I had been engaged. In the face of the desperate hunger and need, these could not but seem futile and superficial."[18] The crisis showed that "solidarity," when acted out as sociability, was no

solution to the novel problems facing industrial workers,
and so Hull-House became a campaign headquarters for concrete
legislative and administrative reforms. These measures were
attempts at functional adjustment at the nether end of the
industrial process to make the lives of the neighbors more
bearable, to increase their security, to protect them from
injustice, and to keep open channels for individual mobility.

Hull-House did not give up its older methods. In fact,
the number of plays, clubs, outings, classes, discussions,
exhibitions, and other "social" activities increased. New
types of group activities were tried and the older ones were
expanded. Nor did Jane Addams believe that the simple
religio-philosophical ideal of solidarity had to be sacrificed
to an articulated social theory when reform was added to sociability. The reforms she favored were responses to immediate conditions. As measures of welfare and relief, rather
than measures of reconstruction, they did not have to be
deduced from any social theory. Solidarity could continue
to be expressed in educational and philanthropic activities;
reforms could be induced from particular needs. Indeed, she
confessed her perplexity in the face of the proliferation of
social theories in the 1890's, and she remained continually,

if uncertainly, aloof from them. At one point, she earnestly tried to convert to socialism, accepted its statement of the relationship between distinctively modern forms of production and distinctively modern problems, but she was repelled by its use of the same determinism to treat "principles, ideas, and categories as merely historical and transitory products."[19] She was satisfied with keeping to a universal ideal in one set of activities and responding pragmatistically to particulars in another, with acting out social unity in one sphere and flexibly responding to the new, the complex, and the unexpected without the encumbrance of theory in another.

The grafting of a new definition onto "social"[20] paralleled the grafting of reform onto sociability. The earlier activities of Hull-House, as Jane Addams looked back on them after 1893, were distinguished by their individualism. Although she had preferred to call them "good citizenship" rather than philanthropy, she did come to see them all as essentially philanthropic, as simply services given on a local and individual basis. The house itself, as a place, seemed no more than a symbol; and often the settlement resident intended only to set herself up as an example. After 1893, the exemplary function was partially directed elsewhere:

the services themselves were to be examples to the state.
And there began to be added to the romantic idealism that put
the subjective individual and his personal contacts at the
center of concern, a more pragmatic emphasis on an external
and objectively "real" thing called society.

Her reflections on the Pullman Strike of 1894 brought to
the surface this new conception of social as "collective."
The strike showed her that the personal relationships of sociability were an insufficient expression of what she had
called the "social compunction." The behavior of labor union-
ists during the strike demonstrated that personal contact was
not a prerequisite for the sympathetic imagination of others.
It demonstrated that people could feel and act on solidarity
with other people whom they had never seen, never communi-
cated with, and could not identify in any personal, individual-
ized way.[21] The achievement of social integrity through collective action and collective consciousness was thus added
to the method of personal sociability.

As scientific discoveries occasionally decrease rather
than increase the store of accepted knowledge, so the discovery of the collective consciousness created a sudden
access of ignorance about society where before there had been

easy assurance. The authenticity of the new phenomenon was beyond doubt for Jane Addams because it had been objectively exhibited. For the very reason, however, that it had been induced from experience, it had no clear relationship to the ethical ideals and conceptions of society that had informed the personal neighborliness of the settlement. Indeed, collectivism had two characteristics that seemed to imply that the earlier ideals were archaic. It was new. It had not been seen before, as far as Jane Addams could tell, and therefore the social setting in which it arose might be substantially novel as well. In addition, it was impersonal and exclusive and thereby implied a society that was diffuse and complex. There was nothing in Jane Addams's original conception of her role that could absorb these ideas. The residents had settled in the neighborhood to make it conform to the state of society at large, which they saw as materially unitary and as embodying universal and permanent values endorsed both by religion and by "the best speculative philosophy."[22] Since, after 1894, society as a whole seemed to resemble the neighborhood in its dynamism, its complexity, and its impersonality, those traits could no longer be "cured." The Pullman strike forced Jane Addams to acknowledge that the course of history had taken a turn and that a new intellectual style might be required.[23]

Graham Taylor, who headed a settlement with a greater religious emphasis than Hull-House, also experienced the Pullman strike as a turning point in his perception of society. "The insight it opened into the sphere of industrial relations between employing capital and employed labor was so sudden and startling," he wrote in his memoirs, "that it has always seemed to have been brought to sight by the glare of a bursting bomb rather than by the dawning of a new experience." Taylor wrote that it caused him to change his pattern of action, to reject the dogmatic imposition of known standards and to place himself where he could examine events and communicate, without judging, the conflict of values they involved. "It was a trumpet call to refuse to be classified and to stand inbetween, . . ."[24]

Others in Chicago had analogous experiences during those two years. Clarence Darrow was a railroad attorney in 1894, when the outbreak of the strike changed his intellectual approach to social problems from the monistic pattern of Henry George, of whom he had been a "pronounced disciple," to the pluralistic pattern being explored by the pragmatists.

He came to doubt George's philosophy because of "its cock-sureness, its simplicity," its ignorance of the selfishness in men, and its doctrine of natural rights. Socialism, on the other hand, was too coercive; anarchism, too utopian. Society, he discovered, was complex and dynamic, "always in motion," always changing, too unpredictable and inconsistent to be the subject of an exact science.[25] Brand Whitlock similarly recalled that the events of 1893-94 helped alter his conception of what was "fundamental."[26]

Henry George, writing <u>Progress and Poverty</u> in a period of transition, had a consciousness not of transition, but of social chaos or disruption. Jane Addams in 1894 had a sense of what had ended and what had begun, but the fact that she could spell out in detail neither the characteristics of the new society nor the ethic that embodied its proper social relations meant that the transition had not ended. The future was still in the making and, beyond the broad out-lines, uncertain. The attractive aspects of a transitional period--its exhilarating sense of possibility--would pervade her writings until her death in 1935, though their realm would change when she perceived, after 1907, that the indus-trial transition had ended and that society had moved into an

era of stasis. In the 1890's, however, transition meant ignorance of the future, an uncomfortable position for one
actively engaged in social reform. Throughout the decade,
as if to compensate for the uncertainty created by the new
beginning, she wavered in her acceptance of it. Sometimes
she treated it as a real break with the past; sometimes,
simply as an extension of the past. Sometimes the new society seemed different in kind from what had gone before; at
other times, different only in degree.

The Hull-House Labor Museum of the nineties, for example, had two purposes. On the one hand, it was intended
to bridge the gap between the first and second generations
of immigrant families. It was intended to show the modernized
and Americanized youngsters, who had never known anything but
cities and factories, that the archaic skills of their parents
had a dignity and worth in their own time and place and that
the elders' inability to adjust to the new conditions resulted
not from incompetence but from the shock of transition. On
the other hand, the Museum would overcome the alienation of
the industrial worker himself by giving him a "consciousness
of historic continuity and human interest" in his labor, so
that the feeling of detachment from the past would be

revealed as an illusion. "Workers are brought in contact
with existing machinery," Jane Addams complained, "quite as
abruptly as if the present set of industrial implements had
been newly created."[27] Although a decade later her complaint
would be significantly different--that the industrial system
was wrongly regarded as if it had always existed--elements
of that position were already present. Current industrial
technology may have been the product of the slow accretions
of history (she saw no sudden acceleration in the recent
past); but a class of permanent industrial workers was, she
acknowledged, a new thing.

To the extent that the new society was different only
in degree from the previous one, Jane Addams could maintain
her older values and roles alongside her newer ones. The
definiteness of the older could compensate for the vagueness
of the newer. They did, however, represent opposite approaches to the world. Deduced from the residents' conception of universals, settling and sociability embodied certainty, predictability, unity, and continuity. Reform and
collectivism were inferences from particular circumstances,
and embodied ignorance, chance, complexity, and distinctive
modernity. In the earlier roles, the resident was the most

significant participant in a completable solution to the social problem. The newer function of reform, as a response to
constantly changing conditions, could never be completed, and
it made the resident an outsider, at best a mediator between
the neighborhood and the state. The loss of the dominant
historical role could only seem definitive when, in the case
of reform, the residents were continually called upon to
serve on investigatory commissions and, in cases of conflict,
boards of arbitration. The publication of Democracy and
Social Ethics in 1902 indicated that the posture of "bystander,"
of "standing inbetween," as Graham Taylor had put it, did not
consign the resident to the dustbin of history; but until
then, Jane Addams was unable to find a stable justification
for the settlement's existence. She was not so unsettled,
as she resettled so often.[29]

IV

"Of what use," John Dewey, Addams's friend, wrote in
1902, "educationally speaking, is it to be able to see the
end in the beginning? How does it assist us in dealing with
the early stages of growth to be able to anticipate its later
phases?" The question, he said, suggested its own answer.

The end, no matter how distant, defined the direction of movement. Knowledge of the end--the curriculum, the educated
adult--was useful in "interpreting the child's life as it immediately shows itself, and in passing on to guidance or direction." It affirmed the perception that the present was
always transitional. It allowed the teacher to select for
encouragement those parts of the child's experiences that
were "prophetic" and to select for discouragement those that
were "symptoms of a waning tendency." By such discrimination,
the process of education was "economized." Aimless, haphazard action was avoided, and the desired result reached
quickly and certainly.[29]

For the reformer, the problem was whether social action
could be similarly economized. In 1902, Jane Addams knew the
beginning, but its apparent recency precluded knowledge of
the "end." The settlement, she had noted in 1899, sought to
"hold a clue as to what to select and what to eliminate in
the business of living." But a standard of selection was
not as readily available to the reformer in a transitional
era as it was to the teacher who could define an educated
adult. "The obvious fact is," Dewey had observed in the
same year, "that our social life has undergone a thorough and

radical change." The new beginning had subverted the authenticity of existing values and had outdated determinisms based
on inferences from the past. Albion Small, with whom both
Dewey and Addams had intellectual contacts, observed this
"ethical bankruptcy" in 1902 and, by tracing it to the "frag-
mentary and incoherent sociology in our minds," the lack of
complete knowledge of modern society, gave a clue to a potential solution. Dewey gave similar indications a few years
later. "The conscious articulation of genuinely modern
tendencies has yet to come," he wrote in 1908, "and till it
comes the ethic of our own life must remain undescribed." The
destruction of "authentic" social standards, it was implied,
might be compensated for by the accumulation of "objective"
social knowledge; and therefore the key role in the transition would have to be played by the social scientist. The
fact that "social ethics" was often used as a synonym for
sociology and therefore had both normative and descriptive
connotations--describing appropriate social relations for
given social conditions--made it the "relevant science" for
the new age.[30]

E. A. Ross, for example, observed in <u>Social Control</u> (1901)
that the "increasing complexity of social relations" required

greater reliance on a Mandarinate. A simple and open society
could get along without an elite. "But when population thick-
ens, interests clash, and the difficult problems of mutual
adjustment become pressing, it is foolish and dangerous not
to follow the lead of superior men." The rude beginnings of
a social ethos, he argued, might arise in the unconscious
process of folk-evolution; but any higher ethical development
required an inventive genius, a person with superior insight
into his own society. Ross's major examples of ethical genius were the ancient prophets; but for modern society, he gave
the role of "prophet of the new social ethics" to the soci-
ologist, the disinterested observer of social conflict, whom
he called the "bystander."[31]

For Dewey, Ross, and Small, then, the social transition
had set authenticity and objectivity against each other. Jane
Addams, however, as an active reformer, could not wait for sociology to finish its job. She needed a standard of selection
that had not only sufficient objectivity to guide solutions
to current problems, but also sufficient authenticity to command public loyalties and impel reform in the absence of
complete knowledge. Thus, Democracy and Social Ethics, while
ostensibly a sociological treatise, was in fact written from

two points of view. One, relativistic, inductive, descriptive,
pragmatistic, reflected what she knew about the new society
and was an attempt at an objective sociology, a conscious
articulation of currently unconscious trends. The other
viewpoint, universalistic, deductive, normative, "authentic,"
sought to compensate for the remaining ignorance by establishing the authority of her standard of selection, her social
ethic, in more traditional ways.

The dualities extended to every aspect of the book. She
found the cause and potential cure of the social "mal-adjustment"
--the divergence between conscience and conduct--in two separate processes. First, many sensitive and educated people
were trying to practice a code of morality that they had consciously conceived as a logical extension of the authentic
ideal of Democracy. And second, social evolution was pushing
behavior into patterns in which the new ethic was objectified
by being acted out unconsciously by the inarticulate masses.
The case studies in Democracy and Social Ethics analyzed
social conflicts as struggles between "sociologies," between
older patterns of behavior and either a conscious conception
or an unconscious practice of a new kind of democracy. In
philanthropy, the aristocratic and paternalistic methods and

motives of the charity organization contradicted the daily experiences of instinctive democracy among the poor. In the home, the conflict between the family claim and the social claim disrupted relations between parent and child and between mistress and servant. In municipal politics, democracy conceived as either a "mere governmental contrivance" or a source of private benefits was in conflict with a reformer's ideal of political democracy as the expression of a democratic moral and social life. In industrial relations, the individualistic profit motive conflicted with the social organization of industry and with the appropriate ethic for industrial democracy, which the unions embodied. In education, the standard forms of "culture" were being challenged by a pedagogy that stressed the child's ultimate membership in an interdependent society and his likely status as a factory worker.

In each case, Jane Addams characterized the older ways as static, stilted, dogmatic, a priori, artificial, deductive, individual, as unconnected to the emerging life of modern society. She characterized the newer as dynamic, vital, responsive to conditions, natural, experimental, and social. In each case study, she thus identified the future with the

new, with the challenging force, with those whose ideas or
behavior were geared to a diffuse and impersonal society.
Predicting the future by discerning the new was not an obvious exercise. Henry George, for instance, would have argued
strenuously that it was not the way a social science made
predictions. But it led Jane Addams to conclude that the
older personal ethic was not a sufficient guide to the "complicated life of to-day" and had to give way to the "moral
dynamic" appropriate to distinctively modern conditions.[32]

The persuasiveness of that moral dynamic, however,
had derived from two separate logics, which their coincident
production of the same ideal naturally concealed. Jane
Addams used each of the logics to deal with that component
of her perception of transition--society as both made and in
the making--with which it was polar. As a pragmatist's working hypothesis, for example, as an outsider's attempt to explain cogently the pattern of actions of people who were
unaware of its existence, the ideal was verifiable only where
Jane Addams could use it as a measure of what she already
knew about modern society, rather than as a method of increasing knowledge where she felt uncertain, as the pragmatists intended. Her case studies of charity, unionism, and

the master-servant problem verified the ideal-as-hypothesis, showing it to be "rational," "natural," and "objective," or, as Herbert Croly would put it, "relevant and appropriate" to modern society. The argument was to a degree self-fulfilling, as in a pluralistic universe it ought to have been. From the vast welter of facts, it automatically selected those things it explained best and then used them as evidence of its own scientific validity. She thus could call a hypothetical collection of facts a social ideal. Dewey himself often used "ideal" as synonymous with hypothesis.

Conversely, where knowledge of modern life was lacking, where uncertainty troubled her, she identified the social ethic with a more traditional romantic idealism and with a form of evolutionary determinism. As a reformer, she had to act as if she knew the future. Pure pragmatism, such as G. H. Mead called for in reform, would have meant accepting a large degree of permanent ignorance. "It is always the unexpected that happens," Mead noted in advocating the working hypothesis as the only scientific reform instrument.[33] Albion Small and Lester Ward themselves, however, had, like Addams, paradoxically tied the acceptance of pluralism to a growing sense of order, certainty, knowledge, and continuity,

rather than to their opposites. Small, for instance, tied the
"rationality" of a "social teleology"--a hypothetical reconstruction of society--to the amount of knowledge available
about society. Retaining considerable residues of positivism,
he saw experimentation as only a temporary expedient, a means
of building up "a quasi-absolute standard, which is the nearest
practicable approach to finality," which would ultimately make
trial and error obsolete.[34]

Thus, those most engaged by social problems adopted pragmatism where the philosophers conceived it as least necessary;
and, where the philosophers considered it most appropriate,
the reformers found it unattractive. Feeling a need to know
the consequences of reforms, Jane Addams required a convincing
means of overcoming the uncertainty that the future still contained, not an affirmation of permanent uncertainty. She thus
complemented her conception of the new ideal as a hypothesis,
as a possibility within the modern social process, as a trend
or a tendency, with its conception as a logical deduction
from "Democracy" or "Solidarity," the moral absolute that,
she had said when founding Hull-House, was authenticated by
both Christianity and the "best speculative philosophy."
As the case studies of reform, pedagogy, and the family claim

indicated, its universality had not in fact been negated by
distinctively modern conditions. In addition, the fact that
the majority of its bearers were unconscious of their role
in moral progress meant to her that the ethic was an objective
force in history. Unconscious behavior, she assumed, was the
closest approximation of determined behavior. If there was
inherent natural order anywhere, it would be seen among those
who did not artificially impose order on their own actions.
The ethic thus had additional authenticity as a natural product of evolution.

The two sets of studies in Democracy and Social Ethics,
the modes of thought reminiscent of monism and those antici-
pating pluralism, supplemented each other. Jane Addams saw
the polarities and recognized the attractiveness of the
monistic modes as compensation for the areas of ignorance
inherent in a transitional era. As she began the volume by
equating ethics with "righteousness," she concluded it with
an expression of faith in Democracy as an antidote for
"partial experience" and "limited intelligence."[35]

The sense that the pragmatistic mode was the mode of the
future did, however, point toward the end of Jane Addams's
search for a role for the settlement resident in the new age.

While still identifying herself and others who felt the
"social compunction" as ethical pioneers, pushing the boundaries of morality from the personal to the social realm, the
implications of Democracy and Social Ethics as a sociological
treatise argued that progress occurred in a different way and
that the extraordinary individual had a different role. The
"quite unlooked-for result of the studies," she noted, "would
seem to indicate that while the strain and perplexity of the
situation is felt most keenly by the educated and self-
conscious members of the community, the tentative and actual
attempts at adjustment are largely coming through those who
are simpler and less analytical." The pioneering was being
done not consciously by exceptional individuals acting on a
deductively derived ideal as in the first days of Hull-House,
but unconsciously by the masses of "cruder men, whose sole
virtue may be social effort, and even that not untainted by
self-seeking, who are indeed pushing forward social morality,
but who are doing it irrationally and emotionally, and often
at the expense of the well-settled standards of morality."
The role of the exceptional person, therefore, was not to
lead; it was to channel the "forward intuitive movement of
the mass." It was his or her job, as social critic or

ethical scientist, to make the movement conscious--make a

hypothetical picture of it--and thereby economize its effort.

Like Dewey's teacher, she would first interpret and then

establish channels for guidance and direction.[36]

The new role meant that Jane Addams could cease worry-

ing about the sensitive young moralists who had felt out of

place in the society of the 1890's. Their self-consciousness

had mirrored the self-consciousness of a society without

reliable standards, producing either paralysis or frenetic

activity. Self-conscious adaptation and adjustment were,

she had noted, impossible.[37] And yet self-consciousness was

inevitable once accepted values were perceived as outdated.

The solution implicit in Democracy and Social Ethics was to

separate consciousness as a function from activity as a func-

tion, as Herbert Croly was then advocating in the realm of

architecture. The sensitive young moralists could lose their

self-consciousness by sharing the instinctively collective

activities of the mass, thus building up habits of collec-

tivism untainted by the assertion of their individual wills.

The few critical intelligences, such as Jane Addams, would

act much as pragmatists believed scientists acted in the

laboratory. Self-consciousness would be transformed into a

social "reflective consciousness," as it was often called, humanity's unique ability to evaluate its surroundings, delay its responses until alternatives were examined, and select its course of action on the basis of its likely consequences. The critical intelligences, or sociologists, would take it upon themselves to be the reflective consciousness of society at large.

The advantage of this stratification of roles lay in its offer of a dynamic social integrity much like the "mental integrity" that had been the model of Jane Addams's youth, a pattern perfectly suited to an age of perceived transition. It provided a place for uncertainty, novelty, innovation, growth, variation, and complexity in the unconscious actions of the mass. The critic was to observe this dynamism and try to discern trends within it. She would then, as society's agent, use these "syntheses" or hypoteses to create channels for adjustment, selection, guidance, and control, "and thus by indirection to direct." Together there would be social integrity: order and possibility, discipline and spontaneity, control and freedom.[38]

Before 1893, Jane Addams had idealized traditional civic duties. In 1902, by adding an idealization of

distinctively modern social trends, she was doubly validating
a social prupose whose acceptance could both integrate and reform an "incredibly complex and interdependent" society.[39]
And in creating this dualism, she was foreswearing both the
laissez-faire fatalism of the conservative social Darwinists
and the utopia and panacea that had been so attractive fifteen
and twenty years earlier. The expectation of continual variations and innovations precluded the finality of a utopia on
the Bellamy model; and the necessity for continuous scrutiny
and selection precluded a panacea like Henry George's. The
same two factors precluded as well the long-range planning
and direct manipulation that Ward foresaw as "sociocracy"
and that were later to be called the collectivist state.

V

Charles H. Cooley, an admirer of Jane Addams on the
periphery of the Chicago circle, and the man most closely
identified with the idea of "process" in sociology, remarked,
also in 1902, "In these days we no longer look for final explanations, but are well content if we can get a glimpse of
things in process, not expecting to know how they began or
where they are to end."[40] In the years after 1902, it became

increasingly easy for Jane Addams to pinpoint the beginning:
"the past hundred years," "a generation ago," and, by 1910,
"forty years ago." By the outset of the national progressive
crusade, progressives seemed automatically to locate the beginning of modern times in 1870 and to characterize the new
era as complex, impersonal, and dynamic. In August 1910, in
one of numerous examples, Theodore Roosevelt, in launching
the New Nationalism, which Addams ultimately supported, noted
that government had not kept pace "during the last forty
years with the extraordinarily complex industrial development. We have changed from what was predominantly an agricultural people, where all were on planes of livelihood not
far apart, and where business was simple, into a complex
industrial community with a great development of corporations,
and with conditions such that by steam and electricity the
business of the nation has been completely nationalized.
In consequence, the needs have wholly changed."[41]

By the end of the first decade of the century, Jane
Addams was using the phrase "industrial society" to describe
the new social setting. Until at least 1902, "industrial"
meant to her "pertaining to production." She referred to
the "industrial organization," the "industrial basis of

society" with no hint that the terms described something distinctively modern or a determinative fact. Indeed, "industrial virtues" continued to be the label for traditional morality. By 1907, however, she was referring to an "industrial and cosmopolitan era," "this industrial age," "this industrial society of ours." Radicals could not ignore, she noted, "the fact that our present civilization is most emphatically an industrial one." People in power could no longer act, she said, as if the current situation had always existed, for historical development had, quite unexpectedly, made the situation "novel." Jurists especially had to realize "that a difference in degree may make a difference in kind."[42]

The ability to give the new era a name indicated the achievement of that apparently final knowledge about society that Jane Addams had earlier lacked. It meant the close of the period of perceived transition. With the pinpointing of the beginning thus came the realization of the "end," of the final emergence of a mature society, even of a rigid and static one. The first hint came in 1904. In assessing the special virulence of recent labor troubles, Jane Addams noted that "America is only now beginning to realize, and has not yet formulated, all the implications of the factory system, and the conditions which the well-established system imposes upon the workers. As we feel it closing down upon us, moments of restlessness seize us all." By 1907, she was speculating that a technological frontier had been crossed, marking the last phase of industrial evolution, one of several frontiers whose apparent closing supported the perception of social stasis among New Dealers twenty-five years later.[43]

Since she, like Albion Small, had hinged the acceptability of pragmatism on the growth of knowledge about society (rather than conversely), the new certainty created major pressures to resolve the dualisms that had suited the perception of transition, to abandon the concern for authenticity evident in both her romantic idealism and her evolutionary determinism, and to let their functions be taken over by knowledge. The new perception of social stasis did apparently make the picture of a pluralistic universe irresistible. She began, for example, to attribute to society in toto the characteristics of such a universe--dynamic, open, varied, uncertain-- at just this moment when she was describing its reality as static and rigid. She began demanding self-conscious ignorance about the future when she had finally acquired the sense of certainty she had sought. In Newer Ideals of Peace

(1907), where the description of a fully defined and static
society bulked large, she rejected "idealistic" pacifism and
argued that only a "dynamic" version was natural or rational
for the modern world. She similarly rejected all a priori,
artificial, idealistic, and deterministic accounts of human
nature as static, and she demanded that the personality be
regarded as "incalculable." In reform, her program changed
from relief to "nurture," an emphasis on "life and its possibilities." She called for a "genuine evolutionary democracy" that would expand to meet the constant growth of human
needs and relationships. She contrasted social orders founded
upon "law enforced by authority" with social orders founded
upon "liberty of individual action and complexity of group
development," and she stated her preference for the latter.[44]
She attacked modern society for repressing self-expression
and free development; and she advocated with great urgency--
and devoted a whole volume to the theme two years later[45]--a
creative individualism, an individualism of the artistic,
rather than of the economic, man, even--especially--for
factory workers. Where she had previously wanted education
to "offset" the "overspecialization" of the factory system
with a sense of social and moral unity, she now wanted schools

to cultivate the "play instinct" and the "art impulse" so that the variety of human nature would itself be an instrument of reform.[46]

In the early 1890's, Jane Addams had sought to cure social disintegration with a consciousness of philosophical unity. Now that philosophical unity had been realized as material rigidity, she was seeking to offset it in turn with the cultivation of disintegration, of individuality and spontaneity. "Specialization" became "variety"; "disintegration" became "pluralism." The problem she had been trying to solve in 1889 itself became the solution of the new problem of social stasis.

The new perception also meant that her earlier preoccupation with the "intellect," with the effort to overcome uncertainty and find some "basis" that could be taken for granted, could cease. The cutting edge of her thought could become the "will," the active faculty. Reform had been reactive and adjusting; it now became creative and controlling. In a pluralistic universe, it was possible and necessary to impose one's own order on the future, rather than to discover, adjust to, and at best economize the order that was already there. The polarity between perception of society and ideal of natural order persisted, but the poles were reversed.

Jane Addams's social ethic faced similar transforming pressures from the change in perception. In Democracy and Social Ethics, she had pinned a great deal on the ethic's status as a prediction, as an actual description of the social relations of the emerging society. It had not yet become a domineering force in 1902 because it had not yet been brought to public consciousness--that was to have been her contribution--and because it could not be fully articulated until the transition had ended. That point seemed to have been reached when she published Newer Ideals of Peace in 1907, in which she assumed the ideal's full articulation as she assumed the end of transition and the maturity of the social order. The definitions she used there, in fact, were never subsequently abandoned or expanded. The book only explained their relevance to international trends as she had earlier discovered their relevance to domestic ones. The ideal thus took on a quality of definiteness and finality that it had earlier lacked. That by itself had a transforming impact on the role of the reformer. Because the future would be like the present, it was no longer necessary to search for trends, and thus the neighborhood and the masses were no longer

intellectually useful. The separation between consciousness
and activity could be discarded and the two functions performed by a single individual. Reform could be a professional
concern, dealing in persuasion and control, rather than in insight and mediation. There was no longer a reason to wait
for events. The reformer could be a leader or, perhaps more
accurately, a hero. She could be, as she had tried to be
before 1894, the representative of articulated values to
which society should conform.

But there were substantial differences between the articulated values of 1907-12 and those of 1889-94. While the ethic
had acquired definiteness, it had also turned out to be a predictive failure. Jane Addams analyzed social relations in the
two years after Newer Ideals as even more inequitable than in
the 1890's, and worse, they seemed to be locked into their
inequities by the end of transition. That reinforced the
need to abandon both the remnants of moral absolutism and
the evolutionary determinism--the two residual sources of
authenticity in 1902--because they did not suit the pluralism
that she wanted to use to break the rigidity of society. Thus
the ideal after 1907 began to look arbitrary. Since it no
longer described an emerging society and needed no

ratification by the mass, it had to be her own selection from among a number of possibilities, her own choice of what was best from what was possible. The fact that it was still a possibility, that it bore some "rational" or "natural" connection to life, precluded what she regarded as futile utopianism.[47] But that it was only a possibility made it a deliberate and artificial "teleology"--a pragmatist's working hypothesis, or plan. It fitted her use of pluralism to counter the perceived stasis, because it implied that society could, within the limits of "rationality," freely choose the future it wanted--including a radically reconstructed one--by choosing the ethic or plan that it would act on. Freedom and "planning" thus went together. But it also put the reformer in the difficult position of dictating to the public on the basis of values whose authenticity she was denying.

In the two or three years leading up to the national progressive crusade, these intimations of the historical and moral relativism that would flourish during the New Deal years and the consequent shift of emphasis to leadership and "planning" became increasingly prominent.[48] She began her first attempt to trace the origins of her social views, for example, Twenty Years at Hull-House (1910), by using history

as an explanation ("the compulsion of origins," she had once
called it); but she discarded the attempt as unwieldy and
inappropriate a third of the way through the book, since
history had taken such a turn after 1894. She switched instead to a topical organization, suitable to the assumptions
that social things were too complicated to permit a search
for implicit order, that novelties could not be explained
historically, and that progress was made consciously, with a
free hand, and with a "teleology" of one's own choosing. She
stressed the foreignness of the pre- and early Hull-House days
and the importance of discarding their relics as archaic and
irrelevant.[49]

Yet some discomfort with this new position was also apparent, keeping her from adopting pluralism unalloyed. The
dualistic intellectual structure that had made her a resonant
critic for a period of transition remained, resisting to some
degree the pressures to relativism. She was never able to
assert the arbitrariness of ideals as hypotheses or plans (as
Rexford Tugwell and Thurman Arnold were later able to do)
without some echo of the 1889-94 pattern, just as she had
sought a degree of authenticity in Democracy and Social Ethics.
Evolutionary determinism--authentication by an emerging order--

was no longer available to her, but she apparently could not

accept the idea that the values or ideals, the hypotheses or

plans that would make the future, could be totally arbitrary.

And so her immediate reaction to her own use of that idea was

to reestablish a connection with the authenticating power of

historic religions and to identify a call for reform enthusi-

asm with a call for religious revival.[50]

Arising at this time, Theodore Roosevelt's popular, al-

most evangelical challenge to the Republican Party served as

an intellectual decompression chamber, just as it did for

Herbert Croly, crystallizing the shift in emphasis toward

pluralism, while allowing Croly and Addams to hold on, if

briefly and less firmly, to their older concern for authen-

ticity. The spontaneous appearance of a movement dedicated

to the social ethic gave some credence to Jane Addams's old

faith in collective action, in the forward intuitive movement

of the mass; and it revived the possibility that her social

ideal really had been connected to ongoing trends in society,

that it was a real prediction of the coming order, and that

the elitism of her new position and the arbitrariness of her

ideals were not as inevitable as they come to seem. She

spoke of "that remarkable convention where, for the moment,

individual isolation was dissolved into a larger consciousness
and where we have caught a hint of the action of 'the collective mind,' so often spoken of and so seldom apprehended,
. . ." "[P]erhaps never before on this continent were the
wills and hearts of the people so merged in one another as
they were in the convention in Chicago." She praised Roosevelt as if he were the settlement resident of 1902, as "one
endowed with the power to interpret the common man to himself
and to identify with the common lot," "to put the longing of
the multitude into words that they do not forget." She saw
the movement as an objectification of the social ethic, an
indication that "a new order of things is coming about," a
catching up of ethical evolution with industrial, "the inevitable emergence of a new position." The Armageddon
rhetoric of the Progressive Convention, which later seemed
an embarrassment, may thus have reflected a significant intellectual need.[51]

On the other hand, reflecting the recent turns in her
thinking--those that would dominate subsequently--Jane Addams
also saw the party as if it were the special vehicle of the
social critics, as if its convention existed in order to
synthesize the isolated facts, knowledge, and experience of

individual experts into working hypotheses and in order to
organize their efforts at gaining the "inner consent" of the
masses to their proposals, rather than the masses' active
participation. In taking to political agitation, reformers
were no longer just an embodiment of consciousness. Their
function now was persuasion. They were leaders and experts,
people with special and conclusive knowledge seeking public
acquiescence in the measures they wanted to execute and public support for the kind of society they thought it was possible to make. In the year or two after 1912, when Jane
Addams was still optimistic about the movement, she made increasing demands on reformers as leaders to build its momentum.[52]

After 1914, when it became clear that the organized
progressive movement had collapsed, this leader or hero
posture became even stronger, rather than weaker, indicating
that it was not the movement itself that had caused the shift.
In prospect, 1912 had seemed to Jane Addams an act of collective will and a validation of the social ethic as a description of modern society. In retrospect, it was an occasion
for individual will, for some people who held certain
articulated values to try to persuade others to act on them,

because the values could have predictive success only if
people acted as if they were true. They were now less predictions, or statements of tendency, than programs, or statements of opportunity. The unexpected outbreak of war in 1914
only increased the intellectual pressures in this direction,
and American entrance confirmed them. The newer ideals of
peace could not be treated as real predictions in the midst
of war. It took some time for Jane Addams to reconcile herself to this, but the programmatic character of the ideals
did finally drive out their remaining predictive character
soon after the first shots were fired; and the inadequacy of
the unrestricted collective will, which had been demonstrated
by the progressive collapse, was fully confirmed when popular
hysteria began to dominate the home front.

VI

The pluralistic universe was a particularly attractive
concept in these years because war and domestic repression
were extreme and graphic analogies of social stasis itself.
War, Jane Addams argued during the European phase, was
unnatural, antiprogressive, and immoral. It precluded spontaneity; it was a throwback to an archaic stage of social

history; it had interrupted the growth of a vital new internationalism based on cultural pluralism; and it was being
fought to maintain the balance of power, a concept that
glorified stasis and left no room for innovation.[53] After
America entered the war, she used pragmatism against the war-
supporting pragmatists themselves, showing in effect that
they were retrogressing to pre-modern modes when they justified the war with idealistic language. Modern ideals, she
reminded them, were only descriptions of the outcomes of experimental processes--hypotheses--and therefore no action
could be moral whose aim and method were contradictory. The
belligerents, she predicted, would find their idealistic war
aims gradually reduced until they matched the methods of war
itself--unconditional destruction of the enemy. The divergence
between method and aim, the unnatural or irrational character
of idealistic war aims, was an especially trenchant criticism
of Woodrow Wilson and a painful reproach to John Dewey, whose
support of the war rested on grounds similar to her opposition
to it.[54]

Jane Addams did see that her own pacifism could be subject to a reverse attack, since war deprived it of that
natural "connection to life as it is lived," that verification

in action that a hypothesis required. Although she could
support pacifism's validity with "bookish" reasons--historical,
anthropological, and bio-evolutionary arguments--such reasoning could not be as persuasive as the ability to show its
functional relevance and propriety. "That, perhaps, was the
crux of the situation. We [pacifists] slowly became aware
that our affirmation was regarded as pure dogma," while they
were "no longer living in a period of dogma." Worse, she
lacked a constituency, which had been some validation of her
ideas during earlier attacks. In this case, she and the few
other outspoken pacifists seemed almost completely isolated.[55]

Her response to the isolation was at first an uncertain
and then a resounding affirmation of individual will. She
challenged her own fundamentalist democratic faith of 1902
in "popular impulses as possessing in their general tendency
a valuable capacity for evolutionary development," and she
finally rejected, along with the war enthusiasm, the collective will and the collective mind as the sources of progress.
She was, she later recalled, "forced to the conclusion that
none save those interested in the realization of an idea are
in a position to bring it about." Since she would no longer
seek verification or authentication in any way incompatible

with a pluralistic universe, her steadfastness in maintaining her position was at bottom supported by the intellectual
consequences of the perception of stasis. The full articulation of the modern ideal of peace in 1907 as the label for
the appropriate social relations of modern industrial society
had given it a power and certainty independent of any further
proof. Its validity would only be affirmed, not tested, by
the efforts of those who heroically insisted that it was an
order that could be consciously imposed on society. The perception of stasis had made persuasive both an uncertain universe and certain ideals. Addams's retrospective examination of the progressive crusade itself showed it to have
been neither a testing of values in action nor the finding
of them in experience--it was not a movement, she decided,
in that instrumentalist sense--but a survey of public opinion
and an attempt at persuasion. Its failure could no longer
imply, as it might have implied at the turn of the century,
that the people were right and she wrong, but only that there
was a disjunction in views and experience that mere enthusiasm
could not cover up. With the perception of social stasis,
collective ideas had lost their evolutionary role; they no
longer had a greater validity than the untested ideas held

by individuals alone.[56]

The outcome of the war thus required of Jane Addams no great intellectual adjustment. The major transformation in her thinking had occurred in the years of the national progressive movement. Indeed, the outcome simply confirmed her tenacity because, for perhaps the first time in her intellectual career, one of her predictions had proved correct. She found, unfortunately, that prophets of disaster are not rewarded for accuracy.

VII

The heroic role, that of an individual standing for her own order in a universe of "flux and complexity,"[57] served Jane Addams's personal needs in the twenties, when her preoccupation with international peace movements kept her isolated from mass support; and it gave her some resonance among the younger liberals who would later make their mark during the New Deal. But there were reservations and ambivalences in her version of that role that detached her from the new reformers and marked her, to them, as belonging to an earlier era. Even during the progressive movement and the war, her affirmation of individual will had not been the whole of the reform process, which was the reason her isolation had been especially painful. She had never abandoned the idea that had suited transition, that reform was a continual process and that the process was a double one of variation and selection. The roles had become reversed--from mass variation and re- form guidance to reform innovation and mass ratification--but the dualism remained. Reform was an exercise in persuasion-- rather than, as for George and Bellamy, an exercise in educa- tion to the single truth--but it was not, as it seemed to be to the younger reformers, only an attempt to persuade the public to delegate its powers. Rather, it was a continuous search for the "inner consent"--a phrase she used with in- creasing frequency after 1912--of the people to each of the experiments that reformers would propose.

She was thus ambivalent about the new dominance of the experts. She had prepared their way herself; she had turned intellectually to individual leadership; and she voted for LaFollette in 1924 partly because he seemed to embody both expertise and statesmanship. But she had derided the "cold expert" in 1902, and she now looked nostalgically to the emotional fervor and enthusiasm of the nineties, even though, and partly because, she admitted, none of the would-be social workers had been quite sure they knew what they were doing.[58]

Acting in ignorance had been a problem to overcome in
the 1890's. In the 1920's, when a sense of certainty had
been achieved, she relished her memories of it. Transition
had been the context in which she had functioned best, and
it was the feeling of transition with its sense of possibilities which she hoped to use pluralism to restore. She
saw social work becoming commonplace and flat, profession-
alized and routine. Social workers were becoming functionaries, bureaucrats, agents of adjustment, not of innovation.
She wanted them to be social pioneers, to push experiments
into outlying areas of social concern, and then, when
government or some other agency took over, to push on to
new problems and new solutions.[59]

The perception of social stasis, however, could make
Jane Addams's particular use of pragmatism seem suited to
a different social context. The logic of stasis could in
fact demand relief and collective adjustment rather than
pioneering and individual creativity. It could make the
routinization of social work seem not only possible, but
reasonable. The possibility that knowledge of society could
be reliable, that it would not be outdated by novelties and

unexpected turns in social evolution, could encourage professionalization and reliance on experts, on those who had

the greatest stores of such knowledge. It could make reason-

able a redefinition by social workers of the scientific

method as dependence upon accumulated expertise rather

than as experimentation. Jane Addams herself wondered

whether the enthusiastic experimentation of the early years

had been worth all the effort.[60] If the social ideals were

indeed final, if the masses were no longer the source of

forward movement and were therefore intellectually unneces-

sary, then social workers might reasonably believe that it

was right and proper for them to dictate to the social pro-

cess, to manipulate it and the people who composed it. And

if adjustment was required, if routinization was legitimate,

if knowledge was reliable, if expertise, therefore, could be

sufficient, then talking of "ideals" might seem archaic.

Jane Addams could find some intellectual comfort, though

none of the satisfaction of success, in her antiwar activi-

ties, in which she could combine some of the attractive as-

pects of her earlier intellectual patterns with the patterns

demanded by the new social context. As president of the

Women's International League for Peace and Freedom in the

twenties, she promoted its attempt to create a world consciousness that would overcome the fragmentation resulting
from hysterical nationalism, and she supported its advocacy
of "nurture" as the only moral equivalent of war.[61] The
group's activities recalled various eras of the settlement's
history, with the world consciousness intended to play the
role of the earlier social consciousness is both a source
of unity and an affirmation of diversity, as both a director
and selector of the actions that would make progress. Although the League lacked the settlement's ability to perform concrete experiments, the fact that it was limited to
propaganda was consonant with Jane Addams's recent intellectual position. She no longer regarded action as a means
of finding or of testing values--that was no longer necessary
--but only as a medium of propaganda for them.[62] She saw the
ideals of the W.I.L. as simply the social ethic in the
"cosmopolitan" version that she had discovered in 1907 and
had stood for even after it had become disconnected from experience. Since she no longer believed that there was any
implicit moral order in history, moral order would have to
be imposed. In that effort, she would be a leader. Unlike
the newer generation of professional social workers, however,

she did not envision success unless she acquired a mass following.

Jane Addams saw that the magnitude of the Great Depression
would shift the center of relief, reform, and reconstruction
to Washington. There was little the trained or untrained social worker could do in those fields on her own. With the
advent of the New Deal, some commentators noted with hope
and some with disdain that social workers were taking over
the government and injecting into national policy two of
their own styles of action--the apparently random attack on
symptoms and the expert manipulation of systems for the purpose of adjustment. Jane Addams was once again a public
heroine. She had consistently striven to view society from
the perspective of its victims, and so in the advocacy of
specific reforms she was as advanced as any of her younger
colleagues. Her residual use of some of the language of
idealism; her objections to a method of reform that did not
include the continuous attempt to seek the inner consent,
rather than passive acquiescence, of the people affected; her
emphasis on the primacy of individual freedom, spontaneity,
and creativity; her adherence to a double-edged progress, a
process of variation first, and then of selection--these

were generally ignored. "Idealism" implied a lack of sophistication that American liberalism felt it had outgrown. Self-
assertion smacked of rugged individualism, save when practiced
by collectivists in power. Problems could be more easily
treated, and the individual still protected, if people were
statistically defined. And all the frontiers had closed;
novel significant variations were not to be expected.

As if in response, Jane Addams, a hundred days after the
Hundred Days, called upon social workers to fulfill the original promise of the settlement.[63] The government could
take over relief and reform, mass things; but it was important,
she said, to give the victims of the depression a sense of
belonging, an assurance of place and affection and purpose
that alone were sufficient to maintain their humanity. She
exhorted social workers to restore their contacts with the
poor, as if bearing witness to the personal inadequacy (or
impersonal adequacy) of the newer style of reform.

CHAPTER VI

GERMAN DARWINISM

Herbert Croly

"There is one great basic fact which underlies all the
questions that are discussed on the political platform at
the present moment," Woodrow Wilson observed during the 1912
campaign. "That singular fact is that nothing is done in
this country as it was done twenty years ago. We are in the
presence of a new organization of society. Our life has
broken away from the past." Life had become "so complicated
that we are not dealing with the old conditions." On the
face of it, random pragmatic functionalism or experimentalism
would seem to be tailor-made for reform in a radically new,
complex, constantly changing society. But change, movement,
and variety were not yet acceptable without the counterweight
of some sense of fixity and certainty. "Most of our calcu-
lations in life," Wilson observed, "are dependent upon things
staying the way they are."[1]

The social psychologist and instrumentalist George
Herbert Mead dismissed this need when he analyzed the "basis
and function" of the social settlement in 1908. He regarded
the modern reform movement, which the settlement exemplified,
as purely intellectual. It was necessary, he said, to discover what the new social problems were and what new moral
values were relevant and appropriate to their solution. Both
questions were to be answered scientifically, the connection
between them illustrating the "identification of moral consciousness with our modern scientific consciousness." He
saw the settlement's residents as motivated solely by an
"interest in an intellectually interesting problem" and not
by a sense of duty or obligation.[2]

Like some other academic liberals, Mead was too consistent
and saw only half the problem of social reform in the first
decade of the century. It was not sufficient just to ferret
out moral values opportunistically or pragmatically for each
problem. A more "authentic" standard of selection was necessary to compensate for the uncertainty that society still
contained and to resist the increasing "disintegration" that
Veblen had said was the inevitable cultural result of the
machine process. Veblen had associated "authenticity" with

pre-modern "standards of certainty": "arguments from conventional precedent or dialectically sufficient reason,"
"anthropomorphism," the belief that something was "an in-
tegral factor in the order of things." He contrasted these
"tests of authenticity" with specifically modern tests
geared to technology, complexity, and process: "tests of
sense perception," of efficiency, of causal sequence, of
functionality and relativity. Modern empirical and pragmatic reasoning was "de facto"; pre-modern romantic or
rationalistic reasoning was "de jure." The two were incompatible, Veblen said; and in the modernization of culture
caused by the dominance of the machine, "matter-of-fact
ideals are superseding ideals of conventional authenticity."[3]
But the process had not yet been completed, he noted; and
not everyone shared Mead's opinion that it was a beneficent
substitution of pragmatism for romanticism. Josiah Royce,
for example, one of Herbert Croly's teachers at Harvard, was
aware of the intellectual options and argued for the "pre-
modern" conception of ideals and values, for ideals that were
not mere personal preferences and hypotheses, but were the
"abiding and satisfactory truth" and were therefore entitled
to general loyalty.[4]

The fact that Jane Addams and Herbert Croly wavered between "authentic," "inherent," "dialectically sufficient," "abiding" standards, on the one hand, and hypotheses, personal preconceptions, and functional standards, on the other, would have been another proof, in Veblen's eyes, that culture was still in transition. To the extent that social reformers still acted out of authentic values, they were still amateurs, advocates, and participants, not simply, as Mead supposed, scientists. And thus duty, obligation, and self-sacrifice were still effective motives.[5]

Walter Rauschenbusch's Christianity and the Social Crisis (1907) resounded with the theme. Society required not the discovery of new functional values, but a reinfusion of authentic, Christian values; and the instruments of the infusion were not people who wrote books and articles, but "evangels" or saints, who combined "religious faith, moral enthusiasm, and economic information." Rauschenbusch wanted heroes as well, men who in pursuing their own interests could redeem society. For Rauschenbusch, the heroes were the working class. For John Jay Chapman, whom Herbert Croly read and admired, the heroes were artists. Chapman, too, decried the disintegration of authentic values. "Indeed," he wrote, "you may gauge the degradation of an age by the multiplicity of its standards."[6]

Mead had, however, caught what was new in social reform. Reformers were beginning to identify themselves as professional social critics, who continuously scrutinized the complex social process and who mediated between the saints and heroes and society at large. In The Promise of American Life (1909), Herbert Croly praised the saints and heroes and hoped the American people would take on some qualities of each. But he made the critics--the equivalent in his thought of the settlement residents--the pivot of social progress. They were not "manipulators,"[7] but mediators. They sought not to dictate to the social process, but to eliminate its friction. Only by stratifying roles in that way could reform be carried out for a society in the midst of a transition without sacrificing creative freedom.

I

By the time Herbert Croly was born in New York City in 1869,[8] both of his parents were well-established journalists and reformers caught up in the possibilities for the future that the social and political ferment of the preceding decade

had created. Both seem to have been early Greenwich-Village
types, striving, apparently successfully, to live in two contradictory milieus: that of the establishment and that of
the avant-garde. In their daily work, they were technicians
who performed their jobs with dedication and loyalty to the
interests who paid them. On their own time, they were self-
consciously free spirits, intensely seeking and therefore
finding schemas that could account for everything they knew
and yet leave them free to adopt the latest reform cause.
They were a half-step ahead of their younger contemporaries,
Edward Bellamy and Henry George. The social order was not
yet in such disarray as to make the demand for certainty
feverishly insistent, but there was just enough leaven to
make millennial theories attractive to some people.

Jane Cunningham Croly was one of the first "new women"
of the nineteenth century. She became a newspaperwoman in
1855, writing a column on women's fashions; and journalism
remained her career through five children. She seems to
have been strong-willed, independent, and persistent, caught
by the practical side of life--and, like many such people in
a speculative age, easily caught up in romantic visions of
the cosmic value of mundane things. "Work is the best thing

we have in this world; and we should be thankful for it--"
she wrote in 1863, "as for that which more than ought else
makes us part of the great order and ministry of the universe."[9]

Her cause was herself universalized. She helped found the
first important general women's club in 1868 and played a large
part in the women's club movement, which culminated in the
General Federation of 1889. The unity of women, she argued,
would bring the millennium. Since world history was progressive in the direction of emancipation, the emancipation of
women would be the last stage in the "moral awakening" of the
nineteenth century. The role of the women's club movement
was to create the freedom of women simply by recognizing it.
It did this by being founded for no purpose at all. That
was Jane Croly's major contribution. People had always expected clubs to be founded for a specific purpose, and men
believed that women could not work together except temporarily and for some cause. Organized simply around woman's
spirit and humanity, the general women's club constituted a
recognition of woman's freedom and dignity and gave her an
open field for its exercise. It proved she was clubbable.

By 1890, with the founding of the General Federation,
Jane Croly urged the clubs to enlarge their field from

individual to social fulfillment. Men were iconoclasts, she said; women were affirmers, and affirmation was the condition most favorable to "true development." Woman, the reconciler and humanizer, would bring about "a more complete realization of the eternal ideal, the fatherhood of God, the motherhood of woman, the brotherhood of man."[10]

The occasional mysticism in Jane Croly's devotion to the women's movement may have been reinforced by her husband's Positivism. David Goodman Croly, like his wife an important journalist and editor, helped bring Positivism into America at its woman-worshipping stage, when August Comte and his followers had added to their proposed science of society a Religion of Humanity to attract the irrational side of human nature to their rationalistic movement. The concrete aspects of Comte's teachings--the dislike of popular rule, the distrust of capitalistic individualism, the desire to moralize power and enforce personal responsibility through an organized intellectual and spiritual elite--fitted the genteel liberalism of the 1860's and 1870's to which David Croly, "a conservative democrat of the strictest sort,"[11] seems to have subscribed. But Positivism's main appeal to him lay in the fact that its "social physics" did not challenge, but reinforced, the authenticity of the traditional values of duty and self-sacrifice, which had previously been dependent upon the authority of religion. For David Croly, Comte's contribution was his assertion, modeled on Newtonian physics, that natural laws of society could be induced from historical data and used to predict the future. The predictions would then constitute people's duties in the present. "We insist," David Croly wrote, "that society is ruled by laws as invariable as those which control the heavenly bodies,--that it is our business to seek and discover those laws, and then to conform to them." Thus, for the Positivist, the limits of action stood in an inverse relationship to the extent of knowledge. Knowledge conferred freedom; but the more people knew, the more restricted was the range of their moral actions. True freedom was conformity to the dictates of science. True freedom was total awareness, not unlimited action.[12]

The Religion of Humanity was invented to serve as interim sanction for duty and self-sacrifice while the technique of prediction was being perfected. As long as knowledge was still tentative, the Positivists' prescriptions for action were provisional at best, and current behavior had to be enforced by a higher loyalty. On the grounds that nothing

unknowable was true, that nothing undemonstrable existed,
and that all conceptions of God and nature were antropomor-
phic, the Positivists asserted that Humanity--relative,
demonstrable, imperfect--was the only god people could
really know. The symbol of Humanity was woman; man incar-
nated Human Providence; and rituals were devised to provide
the emotional gratification of older religions.[13] (Herbert
Croly as an infant was baptized in the new faith.) While
this was partly just a metaphorical way of putting human
consciousness at the center of the universe and mankind in
charge of its own destiny, it was also an admittedly manipulative attempt to imitate artificially the traditional ways
of giving authenticity to values. Such apparent authenticity was needed, David Croly suggested, only to compensate
for current ignorance. As certainty increased, outside
authentication would become superfluous.

There are hints in David Croly's own writings of an
incipient conflict between social physics and the later
Darwinian and pragmatistic model of progress. While David
Croly took "social physics" to mean that the course of progress was predetermined, Darwinism and pragmatism implied
that the future was the result of novel increments of reality

added to the past and present as time went on. David Croly
absorbed this conception in his belief that the major social
changes result from technological novelties and that most of
these are accidental.[14] But if progress thus meant the appearance of real novelties, then part of the future would
always be unknown, and the final triumph of intellect, the
replacement of traditional sources of authenticity with
authentic knowledge, could never come about. By forcing
conformity to certain arbitrary standards of behavior,
Positivism would deny freedom of action in the present in
anticipation of a new kind of freedom for the future, while
justifying this sacrifice on the basis of its ability to predict the future. But David Croly's technological determinism
raised the possibility that the Positivist's vision of freedom might never be realized, that certainty might never fully
replace ignorance, and that the values of duty and self-
sacrifice might always require real, rather than counterfeit,
authentication. These possibilities dominated his son's attempts to deal with a period of apparently continual novelty,
the period of transition to modern industrial society.

This, then, was the launching of Herbert Croly. His
mother, for most of her life, was a standard believer (she

was the daughter of a Unitarian minister); his father, a staunch anti-Christian and rationalist. His mother saw social groupings as a means of individual fulfillment and was not at all ascetic; his father regarded the individual as an instrument of social salvation and preached self-sacrifice and living for others. Jane Croly saw freedom as an ever increasing field for activity; David Croly saw it as a contraction of action--a willing submission to the inevitable-- and an expansion of knowledge. But each, in those different ways, saw freedom as a function of increasing consciousness.

Both parents were strong-minded, and Herbert Croly as a child was apparently treated as a small adult, someone to be argued with and persuaded about the rightness and wrongness of philosophical doctrines.[15] He was put in a position of having to judge his parents' beliefs and find a standard to choose between them. Like Jane Addams, who was faced with similarly conflicting assumptions about knowledge and action, Croly found that interweaving, rather than choosing between, the two positions, was most useful to him; and, like hers, Croly's dualistic cognitive style was expressed in his concern with "integrity" to encapsulate the problem of right action in a transitional era.

II

Croly remembered his college years—scattered from the late 1880's to the late 1890's—as partly devoted to thinking through the implications of his father's positions and their conflicts with the new learning he was exposed to. "While retaining everything that was positive and constructive in his teaching," he wrote of David Croly, "I dropped the negative cloth in which it was shrouded."[16] Since he was exposed to James, Royce, Palmer, and Santayana, the "negative cloth" was probably David Croly's belief in the mechanistic determinism of events and personality, his extreme rationalism, his distrust of values whose authenticity derived from nonscientific sources, and his depreciation of humanity's ability to alter social conditions at will without reference to scientific laws. A familiarity with Darwinism, the New Economics, and Dynamic Sociology might have produced some of the same results. Croly would still have been left with the Positivist method of examining the past and present, its search for a synthesis of emotion, belief, and the practical life, its organic picture of society, its reliance on intellectual and spiritual elites, and its recognition that men need something "higher" to live by,

though it need not be as artificial as his father admitted the
Religion of Humanity to be.

Robert Morss Lovett recalled that "in the Harvard of the
early nineties Herbert Croly was alone as an example of an
intellectual making politics his chief preoccupation," while
everyone else focused on the general problems of culture.[17]
In fact, Croly defined politics very broadly throughout his
career, as the problem of finding a synthesis of ideas and
activities appropriate to the particular social setting of
his age. His earliest published writings, from his first
in 1889 until the publication of The Promise of American Life
in 1909, looked at the problem through the medium of cultural
criticism, primarily in the pages of the Architectural Record,
a journal that, during his editorship, was interested in the
emergence of a modern American architecture. The medium was
an especially effective one because it could allow a perceptive and thoughtful generalist like Croly to deal explicitly
with the connection between standards of belief and action
and a particular perception of society. There were few callings that demanded artistic insight, objective criticism,
sensitivity to immediate practical demands, and awareness of
social conditions in as close a combination as did architecture.

The pure estheticism and eclecticism of architects like McKim, Mead, and White could ignore the extra-formal connections, but Croly and the Architectural Record were seeking an architecture that was "relevant" and "appropriate." That added a social and moral dimension to what might otherwise have been merely a cognitive question. Thus, the problem that the Eclectics seemed to solve so easily became very complicated for Croly: how do we know what to do and how do we go about doing it, on the one hand, and, on the other, how do we know how to judge what has been done?

The social dimension was the key to the problem's complexity. In 1897, when Croly was still at Harvard, Josiah Royce, with whom Croly took three courses on the philosophy of nature and one on the modes of literary expression,[18] had written in a student magazine that "one of the most powerful enemies of effective originality, in conduct, and in artistic production, is the conscious wish and intent to be original."[19] Croly accepted that as one cause of the anarchic cultural climate of the turn of the century--a self-consciousness that yielded either paralysis or feverish and unproductive activity, both justified by intellectual rationalization where the intellect had no business. As an antidote, Royce had advised

"self-conquest"--a studied unconsciousness, an abandonment
of the desire to be original, and a devotion to serious work.
Whatever originality an artist had would then appear on its
own as "a happy accident." Croly in the Architectural Record
similarly advised architects to focus on the requirements of
the specific problem. Since all problems were different,
particular, and local, their solutions would give the distinctive originality the artists craved.[20]

But Croly also saw what Royce omitted. The wavering between artistic paralysis and artistic anarchy came not alone
from the desire to be original, but from the desire to be
original in a specific social as well as artistic setting.
Looking at architectural history, Croly discovered that pure
functionalism (the appropriate solutions of particular problems) had been most fruitful and abundant during ages with
accepted values and stable social forms. For Croly, artistic
creation, like ordinary social action, was best performed
automatically, when the artist could take his values for
granted and neither have to search for them nor justify the
ones he found, when, in fact, the limits of freedom were
very narrowly prescribed, either by a tradition or by accepted
conventions.[21] Unlike the estheticians of the Jacksonian

period, for example, who exulted in the self-indulgence that the Gothic allowed the craftsman, Croly admired Greek and Gothic architecture because their "noblest monuments were almost literally the work of communities" and because "certain particular, although flexible, forms were absolutely imposed upon the architect." Renaissance artists, he declared, had consciously imitated classical models in order to break the communal restraint on originality, a phenomenon that, lacking limits, had finally resulted in the "degeneracy" of nineteenth-century architecture.[22]

The problem was especially acute in America, Croly noted, because the country had never had any authoritative tradition of its own to limit and correct artistic, or social, extravagance and disintegration. More important, the current American social environment was such that the modern architect could "never regain the comparative unconsciousness and single-mindedness of his Greek and Gothic predecessors." Like Jane Addams, Croly perceived America to have recently entered a new stage of its history, which had suddenly antiquated whatever values and conventions there were, but which had not yet developed to the point at which new ones had taken their places.[23]

It was thus the shock of social transition, not the desire to be original, that had produced the current self-consciousness. In Croly's view, the years 1865 to 1885 had witnessed the beginning of the "modern" period, and the late 1890's and early 1900's, the attainment of "comparative economic maturity." "Taste," "conventions," and "social forms," however, had not matured as much as the economy. American life was still amorphous, unfinished, "in the making." "Its social forms are confused and indefinite," Croly wrote; "its social types either local or evasive, or impermanent."[24] The sense of transition, of having made a new beginning but of not having reached an end, was reinforced by the very definition of economic maturity. Croly defined it not as the full growth or perfection of prior forms, but rather as a relatively sudden move into a new type of society, one that was fragmented, heterogeneous, and complex, and that tended to become more so as time went on. The contemporary self-consciousness therefore had social roots; it was virtually inevitable in a period of transition, when little could be taken for granted.[25]

While there are few people more self-conscious than artists and critics in an age of sudden valuelessness, Jane

Addams, for one, had found a similar self-consciousness nearly
universal among her contemporaries during the 1890's. Thus,
the problem of finding a way to re-synthesize ideas and activities for a period of transition was significant beyond
the realm of high culture. Since, in a changing environment,
each act of adaptation was also an innovation, a creative
act, the problem of the artist would be only a heightened expression of the problem of the ordinary person at that moment
of social history. The artist's problem at the turn of the
century was thus not simply the usual complaint that America's
preoccupation with commerce was riding roughshod over artistic
sensibilities, though that was true.[26] It was, more significantly, the challenge to "integrity" caused by being aware
of the irrelevance of existing standards and yet feeling a
need for standards; the problem of finding something that
would hold things together, maintain cohesiveness, avoid
disintegration, and still allow the freedom of adaptation
to new particular needs. The ability "to take a great deal
for granted," Croly observed, "is one indispensable condition
of economical and progressive human achievement."[27] In addition, the artist, like the ordinary person, could not find
artistic consummation outside society; and if he tried, his

work would at best be restricted, special, displaying only
technical brilliance and perfection of form.[28] It followed
that the problems of the individual artist and citizen and
those of society at large had to be solved together.

The studied unconsciousness that Royce advised thus
could not be the solution. It was impossible in the current
setting and insufficient even if it could have been achieved.
The problem was to satisfy not just the artist's desire for
originality, but society's ability to define good work.
And that was possible, according to Croly, only in a culture
with coherence and integrity, which were most easily
achieved in static societies that had authoritative conventions and values available to critics. Those were lacking
in America, and both Croly's concrete analysis of society
and the intellectual models he adopted raised the possibility that they might never be acquired. They implied that
transition, which he accepted as the salient feature of his
own era, might never end, stranding artists in a perpetual
combination of knowledge and ignorance, certainty and
uncertainty.[29]

How was the critic, as society's agent in the creative
process, to act in such a context? How could he make action

both "economical and progressive" in the absence of things that could be taken for granted? One possible answer was pragmatistic: treat standards as only hypotheses in an experimental process by examining the welter of created things, trying to discern a trend within them, and then publicizing that trend as a directive to future work. Croly could accept that solution, but only to a degree. Like Jane Addams in Democracy and Social Ethics, he was comfortable applying it only to those areas where the need was less urgent, those areas where some order already existed-- where the previous generation of architects had already narrowed the limits by accepting certain conventions, so that current architects could work within them with a fair degree of certainty and self-confidence. In those areas, technical criticism was sufficient; the architects were best equipped to handle that task themselves; and critics served merely as publicity agents.[30]

Where he saw artistic anarchy as most rampant, however, where he treated social conditions as least integrated, most transitional, Croly urgently pressed for a more authentic and powerful limiting force than a hypothesis. In those areas, pure functionalism was least acceptable, since it could

not create authority while the problems it was intended to
solve kept changing. It was in those places that Croly looked
to the development of a "sound national culture" to match the
increasing nationalization of American industry and politics,
and it was those times that Croly expressed the hope that the
transition would in fact come to an end, that American society
would emerge as mature. In a mature society the work of the
critic was easiest, his authority most powerful, his standards
most apparently authentic, and the process of innovation and
control most "integrated."[31]

If Croly was to supplement functionalism with authoritative ideals, if he was going to satisfy this residual need
for authenticity in architecture, he would have to look outside the immediate field itself. Otherwise his standard might
appear to be merely arbitrary. He would also be attracted to
an area where consciousness seemed less of a problem than it
did in a social art: social science. Since in his esthetic,
social conditions were determinative--solidly authentic
standards existed in periods of social stasis; only technical
ones, in periods of uncertainty--and since his search was for
products that were "relevant" and "appropriate" to his era,
his natural recourse was to an analysis of American society

and its history. American history might reveal an authentic
tradition; a study of contemporary life might reveal a trend
that would outline the character of a future, mature America.
History and current reality had, in fact, been the testing
grounds for authenticity in his father's Positivism. But
Herbert Croly, unlike his father, saw the two as detached
from each other, and so his resort to both would reveal even
more starkly than his writings on architecture the dualistic
intellectual structure useful in comprehending social transition.

III

Croly had once noted with regret that the decline of the
romance and the rise of scientific history had separated the
rendering of the past from the expression of personal vision,
dramatic appeal to the imagination, and commentary on contemporary life.[32] The Promise of American Life,[33] which he
began in 1905 and published in 1909, attempted to restore
the combination. Recommended to Theodore Roosevelt by
Learned Hand, the book helped crystallize the ideas that became Roosevelt's New Nationalism campaign of 1910-12. The
structure of the volume reflected the interweaving of

conflicting modes of thought that Croly had displayed in his
architectural criticism. The cogency of the structure, and
the invisibility of the conflict, are most easily understood
in the light of Croly's perception of society, the context
for which the book was written.

Croly's two approaches--an examination of American
history and an analysis of contemporary American problems--
were not necessarily mutually exclusive; but, as his contemporaries in the social sciences were discovering in their
reconsideration of Positivism, they did involve different
conceptions of what constituted "understanding." The cogency
of such a combination to his own contemporaries was likely
to depend upon where an author chose to make the past end
and the present begin. Croly's choice, like that of Jane
Addams, Walter Weyl, Theodore Roosevelt, and other progressives, was 1870, almost forty years before.[34] "Although
nobody in 1870 suspected it," he observed (an accurate observation if Henry George's experience is evidence), "the
United States was entering upon a new phase of its economic
career; and the new economy was bringing with it radical
social changes." Of the period before 1870, Croly provided
an historical synthesis; of the period after, a topical

analysis. The topical analyses continually declare the irrelevance of the American past; the historical dimension is
largely absent from his analyses of the 1870-1909 era; and
Croly saw himself as a member of the first post-war generation. The two parts of the book were therefore held together
only by the pivotal term "national democracy." The single
term, however, concealed a dual origin, a dual nature, and
a dual function to serve the two modes of explanation Croly
used. His perception of society as in transition, as partly
but not yet fully ordered, made the dualism appealing.[35]

The double nature of "national democracy" reflected
Croly's acceptance of competing philosophies of history.
On the one hand, he treated the ideal as actively present in
the American past, as a "formative principle" with objective
historical force. His historical chapters, in a quasi-
Hegelian mode, traced a conflict between democracy, economic
individualism, and equality, on one side, and nationalism,
order, and liberty, on the other, through the Jefferson-
Hamilton, Jackson-Whig, and abolitionist-slaveholder controversies, finally "synthesizing" in the Republican Party,
the first national democratic party (favoring union and opposing slavery), and in Abraham Lincoln, the first national

democrat, who showed that "living Americans were responsible
for their national integrity." With Lincoln, not only were
the competing ideas of nationalism and democracy in synthesis;
they were also in synchrony with the material development of
society; and, more significantly, Lincoln was unconscious of
his historic role. With that culmination, history came to
an end for Croly, and he found it appropriate to turn to an
analysis of contemporary life. The 1860's, he argued, were
the last decade in which unconsciousness could result in
social integrity. The epochal event of the modern era was
thus the ideal's appearance in consciousness, the sudden
awareness on the part of the critic--Croly himself--that the
past contained an implicit order and direction that the
present had to fulfill. The fact that this happened almost
forty years after it was first appropriate, was not a problem for Croly, not because he wanted to exaggerate his own
role, but because the period since 1870 was part of the historical present to him. There had, in effect, been no
delay.[36]

On the other hand, Croly gave an opposite account of
national democracy. He introduced his history with a renunciation of the romantic conception of progressive history and

adopted instead the view of the pragmatist and historical
relativist. He announced that the concept was not an objective force in history, not even an American tradition, but
his own "preconceived ideal," or hypothesis, chosen because
it reflected current needs. The epochal year thus marked
the crystallization of a set of distinctively new material
conditions that rendered the past, ordered or not, irrelevant. American society since 1870 had been novel and complex
--marked by the "disintegration of [its] early national consistency"--and it tended to become more and more complicated
as time went on. From this point of view, Croly's ideal of
national democracy was not "authentic," but instrumental.
It was a program, a hypothetical solution to modern problems
to be validated by its future success, rather than by its
dialectical sufficiency (in Veblen's phrase) or its presence
in history. As an <u>historical</u> hypothesis, it produced not an
objective reconstruction of the past, but an almost fictional
account illustrating how history could be made useful for
present purposes.[37]

While Croly's two accounts of national democracy did
have an important element in common--both made the contemporary self-consciousness into an opportunity--they were modes

of thought that someone concerned with thorough consistency would have been forced to choose between. They did in fact gently abrade each other in Croly's work. In the same paragraph in which he proclaimed the instrumental character of national democracy, he also noted that he had "sensibly modified" it in order to make it conform to his historical discoveries.[38] A thoroughly relativistic stance--such as that taken by some leading historians in the 1920's and 1930's and by Croly himself after 1912--would have reversed the process. The problem, however, is not to try to rationalize the conflicts in Croly's arguments, nor, of course, to dismiss his ideas because of them, but to try to explain why they were attractive and useful, if not invisible, to him.

"Integrity," Croly's ultimate goal for both individuals and society, was not a label for rigidity and stasis, or even for consolidation. Rather, as his cultural criticism indicated, it embodied what it did for Jane Addams--a very dynamic process of variation and selection, containing both possibility and order, novelty and uniformity, spontaneity and discipline, freedom and control. When Croly used phrases like "economical and progressive human achievement,"[39] he was juxtaposing competing and complementary, not supplementary,

adjectives, something he did countless times, and he was thus
expressing that dynamic process in his choice of language.
The alternatives to the process were paralysis or haphazard
creativity in the artistic realm and fatalism or fruitless
utopianism in the social. Treating national democracy as a
real novelty, as his own preconception, made it similar to the
artificial teleology of Lester Ward and Albion Small, which
made thorough freedom of action and therefore radical reconstruction of society intellectually possible. It identified
the concept only with that part of the promise of American
life (the promise of continuous improvement) which had not
yet been achieved, which had not even been foreseen, and
which was not simply an expansion of existing benefits but
was substantially different from them.[40] Josiah Royce himself had defined "ideal" precisely in that way. Only as
something "indescribable" and "unverifiable" could an ideal
serve as an innovating force.[41] On the other hand, in its
"authentic" guise, as immanent in American history, it could
serve the function of the traditions that had been missing in
architecture, the authoritative director and selector of appropriate actions. In fact, Croly occasionally referred to
it as the single authentic American tradition. The dual

nature of "national democracy" thus enabled Croly to subsume
both halves of the economical and progressive process in a
concept that itself synthesized two conflicting ideas.

While working on The Promise of American Life, Croly had
observed that "an adequate and fruitful idea" could replace a
tradition as "the really formative influence" on the future
where there was no past.[42] He often interchanged the words
"idea" and "ideal"--one with the flavor of authenticity,
the other with the flavor of hypothesis--and the phrase
"adequate and fruitful ideal" occurs in his book.[43] "National
democracy" with his submission to fit the bill. Thus, the
key to its dual nature lay in the question of continuity or
discontinuity among past, present, and future. The cogency
of a concept that was both idea and ideal, hypothetical and
authentic, pragmatistic and Hegelian, therefore lay in
Croly's perception of society as in a period of transition--
made and in the making, detached from and attached to the
past, its future partly certain and partly uncertain.[44]

Here the polarities between his perception and his intellectual structure emerged very clearly. He may have been
drawn to the pluralistic universe as an accurate model of a
society in flux, and to the hypothetical nature of national

democracy as a way of threading through complexity and dynamism
and of functioning with a degree of perpetual ignorance and
uncertainty. But he in fact used this instrumental version
in the topical chapters--only where he had knowledge, where
he was able to describe his society, where he could count on
its complete development, where he regarded the transition
as having ended. Only to the extent that society was "describable," could his hypothesis be "verifiable." He was
not using the hypothetical national democracy as a device
to find information in practice or to encourage experimental
attempts at problem-solving with limited information, as the
pragmatistic New Dealers would feel they were doing. Rather,
he was using it as a way of organizing existing knowledge of
modern life, testing and verifying the hypothesis by whether
it made a convincing book.

Conversely, he may have assumed the validity of the
quasi-Hegelian approach because American history seemed to
contain an unfolding order. Yet he appealed to the authenticity of the ideal only where he saw society as comprising
real disorder, flux, and complexity. Disintegration, not
simply poverty, was the modern social problem: the existence
of "fundamental differences among the members of society of

interests and of intellectual and moral standards. In its
deepest aspect, consequently, the social problem is the problem of preventing such divisions from dissolving the society
into which they enter--of keeping a highly differentiated
society fundamentally sound and whole." Loyalty to the
authentic ideal of national democracy would provide social
integrity for a complex society by substituting for the instinctively shared values and actual homogeneity of the
earlier period.[45]

The polarity between perception and structure was crucial in redefining the role of the intellectual in politics.
To handle the disorienting incompleteness in intellectual
life Croly urged the talented person to confine himself to
the solution of particular problems, which would be judged
only on technical grounds, thereby building up a body of technical knowledge. Eventually he might be more a scientist than
an artist; his knowledge might be greater than his ignorance;
his expertise might be more reliable than his instincts;
authoritative standards might develop. But they might not,
because the process was not self-resolving. It awaited the
end of social transition. In the interim, therefore, the
critic was pivotal and had a dual role. Where knowledge was

available, and as it accumulated, he was the guiding pragmatist, discerning trends or tendencies within it to build
up a temporary "creed" that "illuminate[d] the path" the way
a hypothesis did. Where knowledge was least available, however, he was not the pragmatist, but the discoverer of a
"theory" to which he was to cling with heroic tenacity, insisting that it be accepted as authentic. If he convinced
his readers that national democracy was sufficiently authentic, Croly could see the critic--himself--finally performing
the second role as well as the first, to which he had been
limited in the Architectural Record. While knowledge was
accumulating, national democracy, Croly's theory and his
creed, would, as an "authoritative and edifying" ideal,
compensate for current ignorance and limit haphazard activity. "An authentic standard," Croly noted, "must be based
either upon acquired knowledge or an accepted ideal."[46]

Croly thus tied the future displacement of rationalism,
moral absolutism, and romantic idealism by automatic problem-
solving and reliable criticism--the modernization of intellectual life as Veblen had described it--to the end of
transition and uncertainty, to the growth of knowledge about
modern society, to its complete "describability." It was a

prospect to which Croly looked forward and yet one that he
had a tremendous stake in seeing not come about. Like Jane
Addams, he wanted a creative individualism to replace economic
individualism; and, like so many of their contemporaries, he
at first felt that an increasingly complicated society was
the modern substitute for social mobility, offering the sort
of freedom that was identical with personal development.[47]
But to the extent that Croly retained elements of the Positivists' rationalism--looking forward to final and complete
knowledge when social stasis was achieved--intellectual and
moral freedom could bring about their own negation. He had
tied a person's fulfillment to increasing specialization.
He had made freedom consist, like Positivist freedom, of an
ever narrowing range of activity and an ever expanding amount
of technical knowledge about it. At some point, knowledge
might be complete, freedom of action nil; and the innovator
might become at best the expert and at worst the functionary.
Similarly, the critic's usefulness as a "free lance" depended
on the lack of authentic standards, which his own actions
might ultimately overcome. Thus freedom, the "unscrupulous"
pursuit of personal excellence,[48] depended on the continued
existence of some areas of ignorance and uncertainty in moral

and intellectual life, on continued transition.

To preserve this possibility in 1909, as in his earlier
cultural criticism, Croly affirmed pluralism as a picture of
society not where transition was disconcerting, where it
would have "matched" his perception, but where he felt the
necessity to counterweigh the restrictions posed by the prospect of finality, to affirm continuous transition, permanent
incompleteness, and therefore the freedom of the individual
and social wills. It was pragmatism in this form that would
dominate after 1912. Croly would then thoroughly replace the
social transition that he would then perceive to have ended
with the theoretical or fictional transition that he found
in pragmatism. For by then, he would have become convinced
that the free will was restricted by the nature of society
far more than he himself had tried to restrict it by a tradition ten years before.

IV

Croly did not anticipate the emergence of a mass movement
dedicated to his ideal, since he had included such things in
the category of spontaneous religious revivals. He did, however, make his services available to Theodore Roosevelt in

1910; and when the progressive movement became a national enthusiasm, he saw that Roosevelt's campaign in particular could
be an instrument of integration, of the individual connection
to social purposes--the acceptance of national democracy as
an ideal--that he had not hoped to attain so easily or so
soon. By selfless participation, professional intellectuals
could also retain some of the attractive features of their
disappearing amateur status. Only disinterested and dedicated
work, Croly said, and "unusually costly personal sacrifices"
could justify progressives' pretensions to being a unique
political force representing social rather than special interests. To seal the identification, Croly wrote T.R. that
he hoped the new party would be called "The National
Democracy."[49]

While thus shifting Croly's concern from personal distinction and intellectual authority to individual subordination and the authority of the collective will, the movement
also signaled a shift in the balance between pragmatism and
romantic idealism that had dominated The Promise of American
Life, just as it did for Jane Addams. The balance had
stemmed in part from Croly's treatment of the forty-year
period between 1870 and 1909 outside the realm of history.

His new role as the Progressive Party's unofficial theoreti-
cian[50] made him see the usefulness of rewriting history so
that it ended in 1912. "[W]hile fully admitting that the
transition is not so abrupt as it seems," he wrote in 1914,
"we have apparently been witnessing during the past year or
two the end of one epoch and the beginning of another."[51]
Taking 1912 as the epochal year meant that history could be
examined for the new conflict between conservatives, who
wanted to hold onto a disconnected past, and progressives,
who knew that the history of the future would extend no
further back than the present moment and therefore was open
to be made. Croly associated conservatism with ideas that
had appeared in his own work of 1909 as elements of romantic
idealism, as remnants of Positivism and rationalism, and as
surrogates for the restrictive role he had earlier assigned
to tradition. The polarization of politics thus helped push
him more fully into the camp of pragmatism. Progressive
Democracy, his manifesto of 1914, was the work of a radical
empiricist.[52]

The pressures to pragmatism were powerful and permeated
every aspect of the book. Croly grounded his argument on
the attribution to society of an extreme version of the

pluralistic universe: capricious and unordered, replete with
the novelties, irregularities, and uncertainties that made
any "formulation of authoritative political and social
truth" impossible. The social process was "too complicated
and too wilful" to be predicted or dictated to. Even attempts
at finding trends, which exalted some parts of reality over
others, had to be rejected. Positivists, who believed that
there were natural laws of society, and conservative lawyers,
who believed that permanent political principles were enshrined in the Federal Constitution, stood for "codified
reason," which, Croly said, restricted the will and therefore
precluded progress. He thus transformed the progressives'
attack on the courts into a conflict between politics and
law, between freedom and restriction, between activism and
passivity, and, most generally, between will and reason.
The elements that had complemented each other in Promise
were set against each other in Progressive Democracy. He had
come to regard his task as an historian and social critic as
neither seeking an authentic tradition, as in his architectural criticism, nor building up a directing "creed," as
in The Promise of American Life, but as, on the contrary,
liberating the nation from the rule of "a rigid and authoritative

traditional creed."[53]

Since he was now rejecting all the restrictiveness inherent in claims to authenticity, his tactic as an historian was to undermine tradition by showing that history was indeterminate, accidental, and irregular. Consequently, the historical chapters of the volume, while a persuasive reconstruction of the past, were an exercise in thorough historical relativism. Following (and correcting) J. Allen Smith and Charles Beard, he argued that the Constitution reflected the limited wisdom and conflicting interests of a particular time and place and that the illusion of finality had been accidentally maintained by the special circumstances of each succeeding period. The institutional history, which he paralleled to the intellectual, similarly revealed no progressive pattern. It was the story of the failure of successive economic systems, the last of which was demonstrating its inadequacy in his own time.

Croly's argument[54] was relativistic not because he was searching for the origins of a contemporary problem--an enterprise anti-relativists could regard as legitimate--but because his analytical categories would have been of no use to him if he had not carried his history right up to the present and then cut it adrift. He was not reconstructing the past; he was seeking to show what had been missing from it that the progressive movement was supplying. The conflict between reason and will, which was his new concern and which had also become his historical framework, could not have existed before precisely because Americans had not conceived of a "positively socialized will," a collective willingness to make the future. The past became manipulable for Croly the moment he decided that the future was totally undetermined.

The same decision radically altered his attitude toward social ideals, including his own national democracy, whose duality had answered his concern for a balance of freedom and discipline. He now wanted to preclude discipline entirely, either the indirect discipline of accumulated knowledge or the direct control of an authentic ideal, both of which, as The Law, were stifling reform. He therefore denied ideals all authority and all content and called only for a belief in progress itself. Since his goal was to liberate the Will from Reason and Law, he did find it easy to call this belief Faith and to offer it as "sufficient compensation" for the permanent absence of prescriptive and predictive knowledge, as the Hegelian national democracy had been compensation for current ignorance. The resort to Faith and the use of a long mystical allegory to describe it were--like his resort to the history he was discarding--portents of future intellectual problems arising from the resistance of his dualistic structure to the pressures toward pragmatism. At the same time, they showed the overwhelming power of those pressures. For, like Royce's loyalty to loyalty, Croly's Faith turned out to be only "faith in the power of faith." And the allegory only illustrated the experimental method in a progressive society. The community, consecrated to progress as an "ideal," willed to act; and, from the resulting experience, it built up a store of knowledge sufficient to design only temporary programs (hypotheses), whose enactment would yield further knowledge for further temporary programs. All knowledge was relevant only to further action. It had no permanent authority, and so the process of reform could never be completed. In a progressive society, no "fund of really authoritative social reason can be held to exist." The only knowledge Croly would accept was the transitory technical expertise needed for immediate adjustments, knowledge that, in "the more complex, the more fluid, and the more highly energized, equipped, and differentiated society of today," would always be quickly outdated. This was at best

"relatively authentic knowledge, the authority of which a
free man may accept without any compromise of his freedom."
The "sufficient compensation" for the absence of prescriptive
and predictive knowledge was thus precisely the assertion of
the absence of prescriptive and predictive knowledge. The
counterpoint between the critic as the seeker of authoritative standards and the architect or innovator as the
builder of technique, thus disappeared. Whether progress was
made individually or collectively, the separation between consciousness and activity was no longer necessary or appropriate.
The kind of freedom Jennie Croly had sought in the women's
movement fully replaced the kind David Croly had found in
Positivism.[55]

While Croly's new belief in collective action may be
readily traced to the rise of the Progressive Party (the book
was written before the disastrous elections of 1914), the
source of the pressures toward pragmatism and relativism must
lie elsewhere. The progressive crusade of 1912 might logically have reinforced the authenticity of national democracy,
since there could be no better verification of a Hegelian
ideal than the spontaneous emergence of a mass movement prepared to fulfill it. Instead of building on this verification,

however, Croly abandoned the romantic progressivism and the
positivism it could have supported in favor of radical
empiricism.

The key seems to lie in a changed perception. It was
only in static societies, Croly had said ten years before,
that the conflict between consciousness and activity was
avoided. And it had been only to the extent that he could
describe society in 1909 that he had used national democracy
as an ideal in the instrumental sense, as a hypothetical
method of resolving modern problems. Only to that extent
could the hypothesis be verifiable. Description and verification went together. He had used its "authenticity" in the
areas of ignorance and uncertainty, where flux was still a
problem. By 1914, his growing certainty about the material
state of society had become virtually absolute. _Progressive
Democracy_ assumed the existence of a fully built economy and
a fully articulated social structure. Croly began to refer,
for example, to the vital characteristics of modern industrial
society as "ultimate" facts and conditions, and his rejection
of Woodrow Wilson's New Freedom was based on the observation
that more than just the geographical frontier had disappeared.
The perception of transition had become a perception of

stasis.[56]

In the face of this new certainty, Croly's romantic idealism no longer had a role to perform, and the pragmatism that was left denied the very possibility of certainty. The polarity between static social perception and pluralistic ideal of natural order was useful to Croly in breaking a static world open to reform by affirming that transition, and therefore freedom, was society's natural state. It also determined the concrete content of reform itself--the discretionary powers that had to be delegated to an administration, for example, in order to cope with unexpected changes in conditions.

Croly's conversion to the will as the dynamic factor in history, his demand for unbridled creativity and spontaneity, his picture of society as thoroughly dynamic, and his remerger of consciousness and activity, matched the changes in Jane Addams's thinking at the same time. Both were pushed to embrace pragmatism just when they saw society as fully developed and articulated. The underlying certainty they had about the future--that the basic structure was final--accompanied their denial of the need for certainty and predictability and pressured them to abandon the residues of rationalism, moral absolutism, and Positivism in their thinking.

Walter Lippmann, Croly's future colleague on The New Republic, was probably too young to worry about extricating himself from nineteenth-century rationalism, but he did take on the task of freeing society from it. His two contemporary tracts--A Preface to Politics, written during the 1912 campaign and published the following year, and Drift and Mastery, published in 1914--so closely paralleled Croly's arguments in Progressive Democracy that they could have been collaborative efforts. Though Lippmann put more emphasis on the irrational elements in the personality, his anti-rationalism was, like Croly's, an attempt to shift the pre-occupation of critics from the imposition of systems to the breaking of forms, from "pretensions to finality" to creativity. To the extent that the future could be made--"we have begun to speak of our age as a transition"--the will had to be the "dynamic" factor. Rationalism had depended upon predict-ability and thus denied real novelty, Lippmann complained; but "man when he is most creative is not a rational, but a wilful animal."[57]

In Drift and Mastery, the sense that the free will could be an agent not simply of adjustment, but of control, was more

pronounced. Like Croly's, Lippmann's statement of the modern
problem--combining democracy with the freedom of centralizing
agencies to cope with a world that was "brainsplitting in its
complexity"--was in some ways an artificial one, an example
of the polarity between perception of stasis and the attribution of pluralism, which alone required the problematic "administrative power." After devoting seven chapters to describing in detail the essential features of the modern age,
pinpointing its determining characteristics, and even predicting its future, Lippmann adopted pragmatism as the only
posture capable of coping with an indescribable, indeterminate,
unpredictable society. There was no "surer key to the complexity of life."[58]

Like Croly as well, Lippmann felt a residual social need
for a higher loyalty to hold the progressive society together.
For both Croly and Lippmann, not traditionally authentic
ideals, but science "rightly understood" (though presented
in religious language and performing a religious function)
could be the object of that loyalty in an impersonal world.
Science, as twentieth-century pragmatism rather than as
nineteenth-century rationalism, would affirm, rather than
deny, the variety, spontaneity, and fertility of life.

Croly called it Faith; Lippmann, the Modern Communion.[59]

V

The new form of political and cultural journalism that
Croly began when he launched The New Republic in 1914 resulted from the effects of his new intellectual position on
the role of the critic. With settled social forms, the
critic finally had the ability to judge relevant and appropriate work. The journal would be a forum for critics to
present the results of their syntheses of the facts of social life into possibilities (hypotheses) worthy of realization and then to synthesize new hypotheses from the new
facts created by attempts at realization. The merger of
consciousness and activity thus moved the intellectual into
the central, responsible, and professional role in the reform process. "It will be the function of the critic,"
Croly wrote Willard and Dorothy Straight, his financial
backers, "to transmute the experience which the American
people will obtain in the pursuit of their national purpose
into socially formative knowledge."[60] Walter Lippmann and
Walter Weyl joined Croly on the editorial board.

By the time the first issue appeared in November 1914,

the Progressive Party was already in disarray and war had
broken out in Europe. Croly faced down the two events--and
American entrance two and a half years later--without intellectual trauma. The test of his faith had been not only the
creativity it inspired, but also whether it could hold a
progressive society together. Loyalty to the progressive
society itself had become the requisite for reform. Although
the fragmentation of the movement might dampen his optimism,
war mobilization could easily take its place. Thus the war
became, for a time, the functional equivalent of reform.

As Croly promoted it, preparedness would serve as an
incentive for national self-examination, it would promote
governmental reorganization, and it would be an exhilarating
test of Americans' willingness to sacrifice for the democratic process--precisely the kind of test that the progressive movement, by disintegrating so quickly, had failed
to provide. He switched his support to Wilson when the latter abandoned the New Freedom and undertook military preparedness, and Croly become a strong supporter of a league
of nations analogous to his proposed reorganization of
domestic politics. A league would give nations the beginning
of the international community they required to achieve their

purposes, just as artists required society; it would subject
national policies to public scrutiny; it would put disinterested parties (the neutrals) in pivotal positions; and it
would stand for "the conscious recognition of the community
of nations as an ideal and a systematic attempt on the part
of individual nations to adjust national policies to the
development of such a community."[61]

Once America entered the war, however, its prosecution
on the home front radically altered Croly's mood from the
alacrity of _Progressive Democracy_ to a crushing distress
that persisted through the 1920's. Nevertheless, the experience confirmed, rather than negated, the attractions of the
pragmatism, pluralism, and relativism that he had adopted
in the happier years of the progressive movement, an indication that the pressures to adopt that posture came from
sources separate from the shattering foreign events of 1914-
1919. In fact, Croly interpreted those events in such a way
as to confirm the perception of social stasis that had first
prompted the dominance of pragmatism in 1910-1914.

Watching the enforced loyalty and conformism of the war
effort, Croly worried that social rigidity was destroying the
symbiotic relationship between democracy and the pragmatistic

conception of science that he had elaborated in <u>Progressive</u>
<u>Democracy</u>. He blamed both an inadequately pluralistic con-
ception of democracy and the residues of rationalism in science. From Croly's point of view, faith in a democratic
society, which in <u>Progressive Democracy</u> he had tied to pragmatism, was being used by the war machine to suppress the
very things it was supposed to liberate--creativity, experimentation, openness, tolerance. Although he had himself declared in 1914 that "constraint which is justified by expediency" was "tolerable because it is temporary," he had
expected to constrain irresponsible businessmen and corrupt
politicians, not creative and inventive people. Without
variations, social selection was meaningless. But, as Jane
Addams observed of Wilson's prosecution of conscientious ob-
jectors, "The reformer in politics knew only too well how to
deal with the reformer out of politics."[62]

In reaction, Croly sought a concrete method of limiting
the use of political power to suppress inventiveness and dissent and of restoring to American democracy its "tentative,
experimental, and chiefly educative character." He proposed
the cultivation of groups and associations that would compete
with the state for the loyalties of their members and thus

force the state to earn, rather than conscript, the allegiance
of its citizens. The idea had been adumbrated in Royce's
Philosophy of Loyalty of 1908 and had been proposed by the
antiwar polemicist Randolph Bourne. For Croly, as for many
social critics during the war and the twenties, the "group"
provided an attractive escape from the historic opposition
between the individual and society; and it seemed to be a
remedy for a peculiarly democratic vacillation between "individualism and indivisibility," which Croly, like several other
critics, blamed on Rousseau.[63]

If existing democracies were misnamed, so, in Croly's
eyes, was the popular conception of science. He joined
John Dewey, also writing in The New Republic, in the continuing effort to liberate science from rigid positivism and
rationalism, which encouraged the masses to passively "obey"
science while the clever ruling classes used it for their
own purposes. Social change had to be seen as "complex and
fluid"; social data, as "elusive"; social science, as unend-
ingly experimental; social reform, as the realm of will as
well as intelligence.[64]

These two pluralistic remedies began to seem intellectually insufficient, however, as Croly observed the peace

conference and the worldwide reaction with a distaste that finally turned to disgust. The lesson he drew from the home front was that there was nothing available with which to make a convincing judgment between competing moral authorities--that of the state and that of the individual resisting the state--and the result was a cycle of force, protest, and repression. The lesson he drew from Versailles--the power of capitalist states to sidetrack social democratic aspirations--reinforced his conclusion from the prosecutions at home, that a democratic relationship between knowledge and will, between science and politics, even when properly conceived, could not be maintained without an external incentive, such as the tradition he had missed twenty years earlier. Politics, the special realm of the will, had failed, he decided, because there had been no authentic morality to direct it. [65]

It was perfectly natural, then, for Croly to reopen his early quest for authentic and authoritative standards. His intellectual structure had been fundamentally dualistic; he had had his greatest resonance when he had been able to comprehend social transition by counterpointing the competing monistic and pluralistic modes of thought and action. The

progressive crusade and the early war effort had served as
surrogates for the elements of monism in one of their func-
tions--that of tying pragmatic forms of action to a convinc-
ingly authentic social purpose. But both surrogates had
failed him badly, and he discovered that pragmatism unlimited
could serve as a cover for the crude and repressive opportunism of corporate capitalism and for the rigid social planning
of the engineers, which, however humane in intent, would restrict personal creativity.

His first recourse was thus to revive the counterpoint
of 1909 with a source of moral absolutism that his postwar
audience might find convincing--Christianity. The effort
would ultimately prove futile and mark him as a rearguard,
as fighting, while inexorably yielding to pragmatism. He
did not need Christianity, it would turn out. The real
surrogate for his earlier search for authenticity in its
most basic function had been not progressivism or preparedness, but the coincident change in his perception of society
from transition to stasis in the 1910-14 period. In his
architectural criticism, Croly had himself tied the triumph
of pragmatism to the growth of certainty about society,
and he had looked to the maturation of modern industrial

society to end the artists' and critics' need to authenticate
the "relevance" and "appropriateness" of their work in arbitrary and artificial ways. That had been achieved by 1914.
In the postwar years, the perception of maturity and stasis
would only be reinforced by American political and economic
life, and the rigidities of Normalcy would only make "pluralism" as a way to theoretically break stasis down and restore
the advantages of transition virtually irresistible. At the
same time, Croly's dualistic intellectual structure, his penchant for balancing restriction against liberation, would
cause him to submit to pluralism in a way that would separate
him from the younger liberals who felt more comfortable with
both stasis and pragmatism and who would come to power in
1933.[66]

VI

Croly's attempt in the postwar decade (he stopped publishing in 1928 and died in 1930) to rethink for a static
society the relationships he had handled so well for a
transitional one--the relationships among knowledge, moral
authority, and power, or, more concretely, among social science,
religion, and politics--was complicated by the fact that he

was fighting on three fronts. Besides the internecine warfare among older liberals themselves in the twenties, Croly
had to contend with both the conservatives in power and a
rising generation of social scientists and reformers whose
self-confidence he could not abide and who, it turned out,
could not understand the source of his doubts. While he
continued to submit to the usefulness of pragmatism, he was
never comfortable with the managerial liberals' lack of concern for the restrictive and "authentic" sort of knowledge
(a tradition, a national culture, a Hegelian ideal, the
coercive effects of a mass movement) that he had always
counterpointed to the liberating and empirical sort.

"Progressivism or liberalism," Croly wrote in the fall
of 1920, "is fundamentally the attempt to mould social life
in the light of the best available knowledge and in the
interest of a humane ideal. It lives by the definite formulation of convictions, by the initiation of specific programs
and by the creation of opportunities to try them out. It is
necessarily aggressive. In order to be successfully aggressive it must know what it wants; and it must be willing to
make the sacrifices which are necessary for the success of
its aspirations and plans. The various progressive groups

are no longer sure or clear about what they want. They do
not know how to get what they want; nor are they willing to
pay the price. Their political futility is born of the
equivocal meaning of American liberalism, its failure to
keep abreast of the best available social knowledge and its
inability to interpret candidly the lessons of its own
checkered career."[67] To remedy these deficiencies, Croly
devoted himself to three closely related questions in the
postwar decade. First, and most concretely, what was to be
the role of the progressive--the liberal in politics--in
creating the "realistic technique" for democracy that he had
found lacking, now that progressives were out of power?
Second, if Christianity was to give authority to the liberal
search for liberating knowledge, what, in the anarchy of
Christian opinion, was to give Christianity authority?
And finally, considering liberalism as an intellectual
posture, what kind of knowledge was to be sought, how was it
to be acquired, and what was to be the relationship among the
seeker, the knowledge, and society at large? In each of
these areas, the pressures to accept pragmatism in toto ran
up against Croly's inclination to rescue the dualisms that
had been so useful in the first decade of the century.

The first question, that of political progressivism,
was raised by the need for a democratic strategy specifically
geared to a static society. The settled social forms Croly
had missed in 1903 had materialized to repress, rather than
facilitate, individual creativity. If there was one concept
that did not fit a pragmatistic view of the universe, it was
Normalcy. To create a pluralistic polity to match the
pluralistic natural world, Croly expanded his wartime plea
for competing loyalties to a more materialistic cultivation among excluded economic groups of "an aggressive consciousness of their group activities and interests." He
also called for a creative federalism based upon a reconstruction of the local unit, which had been left behind on
the centralizing "path of conscious progress" between 1890
and the war.[68]

The attempt to match political pluralism to theoretical,
however, disrupted Croly's stand on activism. In the early
years of the decade, he was attracted to a temporary liberal-
labor alliance to resist "capitalist domination" and to
connect political progressivism to the groups it hoped to
benefit. After supporting the third-party candidacies of
Christenson and LaFollette in 1920 and 1924, he proposed a

radical farmer-labor party to polarize politics and force liberals to make a political commitment.[69] But over and over again, he argued that liberals were not a viable alternative to conservative rule because they did not have sufficient knowledge to construct feasible programs. Croly had celebrated that lack in 1914, claiming that progressives, by their willingness to operate without complete certainty, were the only group that could be trusted with power. In the twenties, however, Croly increasingly gave it as a reason to remove liberalism from politics entirely and make it purely an intellectual profession. A commitment to "programs," he came to fear, would only reinforce, rather than counterweigh, social rigidity. Thus, by 1928, when another third force was being organized, he had decided that the liberal had to be a disinterested critic, not an active partisan. The necessity to recruit a majority, discipline it, and formulate and enact a program would force liberals to hide their pragmatic knowledge of "processes" in favor of the "romantic" myth that conclusive knowledge was possible.[70]

The pressures of pragmatism wrought similar havoc in Croly's second concern in the 1920's, his attempt to use Christianity as a source of moral authority. Since he

blamed the war and the failure of the peace on the lack of
moral ideas powerful enough to overcome material demands, and
since he blamed the collapse of the progressive movement on
the insufficient vitality of the faith in progress to overcome temporary failures, he was attracted to Christianity
by its apparent staying power. He found, however, that the
churches were in much the same boat as liberalism. They had
failed to provide a moral alternative to war, and they had
been able to do nothing to stop the secularization of knowledge, which had allowed science to be captured by the capitalists and their governments. In so far as it tried, in
its several modernisms, to aid fulfillment in the modern
world, Christianity lost out to science, which had better instruments for the job. In so far as it rejected science, as
in Fundamentalism, it lost its authority, since scientific
knowledge seemed the only kind that had authority in the
twentieth century. If Christianity were to become a partner
in liberation, Croly discovered, he would have to contrive his
own version.[71]

Christianity had to perform a dual role for Croly,
reminiscent of the one assigned to national democracy: to
affirm the possibility of continuous fulfillment and thus

justify research into human nature, and to serve as a
standard to select only those findings that were liberating.
Since he conceived of personal, social, and natural processes as in the making, as becoming, Christianity, by affirming "as an actuality" the future regeneracy of mankind,
could inspire continuous scientific exploration. "Increasing knowledge and experience," he wrote, "can never entirely
vindicate this affirmative faith. The needed affirmation in
advance of experience is what men mean by religion." In
addition, since science was instrumental and could be used
to suppress rather than liberate, Christianity would serve
as authenticator of only those facts that led to fulfillment. [72]

In the wake of the war, however, Christian opponents
of social reform seemed to be in the ascendancy, and some
of the most prominent attempts at a humanistic reconciliation of religion and science were made by recent converts
to conservatism and long-time reactionaries. Croly was in
the wrong company, and he gradually defined himself out of
it. Just as he had sought to overturn deterministic conceptions of science, and just as he was seeking to break
open rigid social forms, so he seemed to realize that

Christianity might only reinforce stasis by reviving the notion of a "Divine imperialism in the universe."[73] And so he came to deny that Christianity had the authenticity and authority that he had originally sought in it.

In 1924, for example, while insisting that he was talking about religion, he admitted that Christianity had little to do with his argument. As social science should not make even temporary rules for human conduct, neither, he said, should religion. Truth was not prior to life and therefore could not dictate to it. The simple assertion that people were able to find their own way to fulfillment by examining their own experience became his definition of religion. The Christian appeal to the imagination through the example of Jesus might serve as an incentive, he wrote, but the churches could not be the purveyors of the method. It was an art, not a science or a religion, and was completely individual.[74] By 1925, religion to Croly was simply "the choice by individuals to govern their lives by the truth, no matter what it is, and the willingness on their part to discover what the truth is by means of conscious methodical experience."[75]

Finally, in 1926, he deprived religion of even the right to formulate "the ultimate purposes whose realization

would fulfill the nature of man," for that stressed finality,
not process. He still tried to keep the realms of science
and religion separate and thus rescue the dualism that had
served so well in transition. "Scientific inquiry must
posit the existence of a world which the human mind is capable, after a fashion, of understanding," he wrote. "The
religious life must posit the existence of a world in which
human purposes can, after a fashion, get themselves realized."[76]
Croly's own pragmatism, however, like his earlier Faith in
Progress, contained both those assumptions. He had turned
to religion to ensure that the search for knowledge of human
nature would not be used for any purpose but liberation. The
necessity to counter the social stasis that obstructed liberation forced him to turn religion into that search. His
conception of "art" and of "science" as methods had been sufficiently similar to allow him to interchange the two. By
the mid-twenties, he had shaped "religion" to fit into the
same pragmatistic mould. Like the Hegelian ideal and the
tradition, Christianity came to seem inauthentic because of
his fear that it would reinforce, rather than counterbalance,
a static society.

The third of Croly's major concerns in the twenties--

the nature of a liberal behavioral science--was most crucial
to his sense of dissociation from the younger generation of
reformers, who also thought of themselves as pragmatists.
He had decided by 1920 that social psychology could be the
source of "a valid moral and psychological substitute for
war" and of the knowledge useful to fulfillment. But the
propaganda machine during the war and the growth of adver-
tising afterwards showed that knowledge of human nature could
be used two ways. And certain kinds of social knowledge,
such as traditional religion, conservative legalism, and
positivistic social laws, implicitly recommended passive
acquiescence in the rigidity of society. Even the "dynamic
sociologists," like Lester Ward, who conceived of society
as a continuously developing set of activities determined by
human purposes, had not broken away completely enough to
satisfy Croly. They "lacked the sceptical modesty of science," he wrote; and the "social engineer" whom they envi-
sioned still contained a strong inclination towards "presumption" or manipulation. They sought to dictate to social
processes, and they thus seemed only the obverse of the conservative formalists.[77]

The closed state of society thus aroused Croly's hostility

not only to the conservatives, but to the group of reformers-
as-experts whose precursors' way to power he had earlier
tried to clear. The rising Positivist elite, with the
new techniques of behaviorism, had to be circumscribed.
Croly wanted to break forms, to make the social universe
match the open, spontaneous, pluralistic universe that had
dominated his thought since he had first perceived society
to be fully developed and which now seemed so urgent. Like
Jane Addams in the twenties, Croly wanted to restore the
primacy and freedom of the individual in opposition not only
to official conformism, but also to a growing tendency among
their own allies to treat persons as statistical averages
and to treat society as a mass rather than as a collection
of distinct people. Croly wanted to increase the freedom-
giving aspects of knowledge and at the same time restrict
the power of the knowers.

This concern was reflected in his changed attitude toward self-consciousness. In the first decade of the century,
he had seen it as an obstacle to creativity, and he had
traced it to the fluid and undeveloped social forms of a
society in transition. In early 1912, just before the progressive movement had been "objectified" in Roosevelt's

campaign, Croly had published a major biography of Mark
Hanna, who, Croly indicated, was the best of what he was because he was unconscious of it. Hanna had not had to create
himself. He had been an unconscious part of a vital American
tradition, that of the pioneer, which had allowed him to be
successful, even original, by acting automatically. The
biography was written in 1912, however; and Croly was seeing
infirmities in such a posture. Because unself-consciousness
was Hanna's lifestyle, he was unconscious of his own limitations and he was unaware that he was out of date.[78]

In the twenties, individual self-consciousness became
a liberating force for Croly, rather than a paralyzing one.
"Consciousness," he wrote, "is the only agency which human
beings may invoke to prepare themselves for novel specific
responses to the demands of specific situations."[79] In 1924,
he used the life of Willard Straight to illustrate a method
of conscious, progressive self-education, a personal version
of his description of the progressive society in 1914. The
early chapters, dealing with Straight's pre-China years,
treated the interplay between Straight's intelligence,
imagination, and will, on the one hand, and the real world
with its risks, its discipline, and its restrictions, on the

other. Straight's mother had tried to create an integrated
human being out of an unruly, wilful child by encouraging
his impulsiveness while forcing him to consider its effects
on others. Later, at a military academy, his club activities channeled his will and gave it social expression by
"'finding a proper ground for discipline in the joint acceptance of a common code by a group of human beings of his
own age and interests.'" The result was an ideal progressive.
Straight acted out of loyalty to social ideals. He embodied
them in programs that were constantly adjusted to the real
world, never forcibly imposed, and never left unscrutinized.
Once the meaning of an experience was fully articulated, he
moved on to something else. His life was a work of art. He
used his imagination to prompt experience and his intelligence
and his will to put form into it.[80]

To keep this process free of outside engineering,
Croly used pluralism and relativism to construct a barrier
between the critic and the artist, between the psychological
researcher and the individuals who were the subjects of their
research. Knowledge of human nature, he said, had to be
acquired by the individual himself to be used by himself for
his own fulfillment. The exercise was the "methodical

exploitation of consciousness," and it implied continuous growth, constant seeking, perpetual incompleteness. Psychologists and educators were limited to discovering the method and its limits and possibilities. The method, Croly said over and over again, would be an art, not a science.[81]

The easy passage from "art" to "science" that Croly had made twenty years earlier was thus reversed. Although his conceptions of the scientific method and the process of artistic creation were both versions of pragmatism, art had the advantage for his concerns in the twenties, just as science had had the advantage from 1909 to 1914. For the knowledge that resulted from the practice of an art lacked the cardinal qualities Royce had attributed to scientific knowledge--describability and verifiability by others--and thus it was not transferable. In the art of self-consciousness, the distinctiveness of each individual would thus prevent the intellectual dictation that Croly feared. Consciousness would yield self-control, self-direction, and self-fulfillment--a position he had not thought possible in the context of transition at the turn of the century. The artist would be his own critic.

The process of social research was to be analogous to that of psychology. Postulating a society composed of a plurality of groups, Croly argued that social science should consist only of "a perpetual audit of social activities by participating agents who were also observers." The insights would be only "partial," and the distinctiveness of each group would preclude the transfer of the knowledge acquired so that it could not be used for dictation. Social science would be taught as a method, as an art, not as a body of knowledge or of laws. When social observers talked of action, Croly noted, it always had to be in the form of alternatives. They had to avoid speaking of a social consummation, and they had to resist all those who thought that some final knowledge, "some final form," was possible. Croly thus recommended a version of pure functionalist sociology that called itself "super-pragmatism."[82]

Croly's desire for knowledge for understanding social processes, but not for dictating to them--even the mildest form of dictation, prediction--his desire to keep the experts out of other people's lives, brought him perilously close to the conservative fatalism that as much his enemy as "presumptuous" social engineering. Croly was still a reformer, and he had a reform test of knowledge-- only that was true which contributed to fulfillment. But he had restricted knowledge so much that it might not be possible to use it at all.

To cover these difficulties, he turned, as he had occasionally done before, to metaphor. Liberals, he wrote in 1927, had regarded "the creative process" as engineering, "born of an alliance among expert knowledge, definite purpose and good will." That metaphor, he said, gave too much credit to the intellect, relied too much on the predictability of unpredictable processes. To replace "engineering," Croly proposed the "catalyst," an agent that "by its presence will modify unexpectedly, but not arbitrarily, customary behavior, without itself planning or insisting what form the modification will take, and without becoming identified with the success or failure of the new synthesis."[83] Croly was trying to use pragmatism, pluralism, and relativism to make what he had come to see as a static, rigid, and repressive society, dynamic, fluid, and free. In that process, he managed, by 1928, to take the progressive out of politics, doctrine out of religion, and now the reformer out of reform.

Croly had begun the postwar period with the task of making progressivism "successfully aggressive." By the end of the decade, he had rendered it thoroughly passive and

detached, defenseless against both the conservatives in power
and the self-confident new liberals waiting in the wings. He
had turned to Christianity in the early twenties because the
postwar crises, initially seen as the product of the breakdown of moral authority, had resurrected his penchant for resolving a complex, dynamic world into a dual process of variation and selection and consequently for stratifying the
roles of participant and observer, artist and critic.
Christianity was to replace the romantic ideal as a standard
of selection whose independence of a pluralistic world would
permit it to control that world. Such dualisms, however,
though perfectly tailored for reform of a society in perpetual transition, were no longer relevant once the transition was perceived to have ended. Croly's concern in the
twenties could no longer be to limit and direct, but to
liberate and impel, the creativity, variety, and spontaneity
that a static world lacked. And for that task, a consistent
pragmatism should have been sufficient. That Croly was
uncomfortable with such a conclusion and turned to religion
for aid, as he had earlier turned to tradition and romantic
idealism, set him apart from the experimentalists and func-
tionalists who would help give the New Deal its distinctive

flavor.

Similarly, his attempt to defend the individual against the "presumption" of the rising social planners was self-defeating. His declarations of the unpredictability of the future and of the futility of plans were useful in reaction to the perception of social stasis, but the perception in fact allowed the future of society to be taken for granted, the very thing Croly had earlier sought. It also allowed the new tool of liberal economists--probability theory--to override the declared untransferability of knowledge and to relegate the problem of individual freedom to a back burner.[84] Free individual choices could now be synthesized into statistical trends; and his own developing relativism could allow an arbitrary and artificial order to be imposed on recalcitrant facts.

Finally, Croly had sought to take liberals out of politics because they did not have enough knowledge to formulate constructive programs. Such reasoning would be less than persuasive to both the experimentalists and the planners. If the social order was in fact fully developed, if the underlying industrial structure of society would not be altered by current actions, then nothing would be risked by a

collective version of the random, pragmatic functionalism
that Croly himself had been proposing for individuals and
groups and which he had proposed for society in 1914. On
the same grounds, planners could identify the scientific
method not with humility in the face of ignorance, as Croly
was now advocating, but with Taylorism: the construction of
programs on the basis of however much information happened
to be available at a given time. In order to be successfully aggressive, Croly had said in 1920, liberalism would
have to be sure of what it wanted, it would have to learn
how to get it, and it would have to be willing to make
sacrifices. His position was outmoded in the eyes of those
who knew what had to be done, were sure that methods could
easily be devised, and found sacrifice an alien concept.
All they required was power.

PART III

THE FORESEEABLE PRESENT

CHAPTER VII

INTRODUCTION: THE PRAGMATIC METHOD

IN THE MATURE SOCIETY

While Jane Addams and Herbert Croly differed in important respects, their intellectual structures and social perceptions were nearly identical and, more important, underwent
the same transformations at the same times. If they can be
taken as exemplars of the varieties of American liberalism
in the Progressive Era, then a dualistic intellectual structure characterized progressivism, and the years from about
1910 to 1914 can be fairly precisely identified as a major
inflection point. It was during that brief period that
pragmatism--the attribution to society of the pluralism of
the universe and the modes of thought and action appropriate
to it--clearly emerged as the dominant mode of reform thinking. The same period witnessed the culmination in national
politics of the progressive movement itself, and several
shifts in Addams's and Croly's thinking may be attributable
to that fact alone. Most notably, attitudes toward collective

consciousness, mass politics, individual subordination, and even leadership may have been affected by the rise and fall of the enthusiasms surrounding the campaign of 1912. But the epochal shift in cognitive style, at least, seems more closely correlated with the shift in perception from social transition to social stasis.

The two progressives had dealt creatively with the decades of perceived transition, when their own intellectual needs and dispositions had neatly intersected the needs of society at large. The conflicting modes of thought in their backgrounds had left them with a need to take things for granted and an inability to do so. They had emerged, in response, with a dualistic intellectual structure, one that ultimately allowed them to combine monistic modes of thought and pluralistic modes and thereby to handle in an ingenious way the combination of knowledge and ignorance, certainty and uncertainty, adjustment and innovation that characterized a transitional era. Their private concerns became a social concern in the mid-nineties when the outlines of a new age began to emerge from the apparent chaos of the previous two decades. People living in a distinctively modern era still only partly understood, and feeling that conventional patterns

of belief and action were outdated, would face the same problem of self-consciousness that was privately faced by Jane
Addams and Herbert Croly, who had never shared those conventions. Thus, a particular stratification of roles between
artist and critic, neighbor and settlement resident, society
and reformer, offered the possibility of interweaving spontaneity and control, change and continuity, progress and
order, in a society still believed to be in some flux. The
"mental integrity" of the reformers' own lives--the combination of two opposing intellectual traditions, neither of
which by itself was useful to them--thus became an attractive
reform philosophy for that particular social perception.

It proved to be less congenial when the perception
changed from transition to stasis and the pressures to adopt
pragmatism undiluted became coercive. The distance between
the progressives and the future New Dealers during their
period of contemporaniety in the 1920's can thus be measured
by differences in the intellectual structures they found most
congenial and in the perceptions to which those structures
were most appropriate. While those who lionized Jane Addams
in the thirties and memorialized Herbert Croly were intellectually embarrassed by the residues of monism that the

progressives seemed unable to abandon, their major differences centered on the uses to which the pragmatic method could be put. During the era of perceived transition, the progressives had been attracted to it as a method of adjustment rather than of creation. It had been useful in handling "particular" and technical problems, those that arose in areas where the future could be taken for granted, where the emerging society was "describable" and the results of actions "verifiable" in advance. Elsewhere, where uncertainty created paralyzing or undirected self-consciousness, they had relied on the guidance of principles or methods of traditional authenticity. When the "between-age mood" appeared to have ended, and the knowledge encapsulated by the name "modern industrial society" finally gave a sense of assurance about the future, the pragmatic mode could triumph as a method of experimental control. Yet the progressives at that point made a turn. The pluralistic universe, which would only have increased their uncertainty in the 1890's, became useful as a way of breaking open the "ultimate" social system to restore the sense of possibility and uncertainty inherent in social transition, the context in which they had been most intellectually creative. In a sense, it was left to intellectuals who had no stake in recapturing the virtues of transition and whose intellectual structures were thoroughly pluralistic to carry on the pragmatic method of experimental control without the inhibiting residues of the progressives' intellectual dualisms.

The younger reformers themselves, both in their pre-New Deal writings and in their work during the 1930's, verified the progressives' perception of the shift by regarding the period since 1870, which the progressives had taken as the beginning of modern times, as a period of development that had not concluded until four and a half decades later. A Second Industrial Revolution was seen to have begun in 1870 and to have culminated by 1914. From that date on, the future would be identical with the present. Theodore Roosevelt's New Nationalism campaign of 1912 seemed to mark the first noticeable injection into national politics of the idea that the United States had to face the future as a "modern industrial society"; and yet the concept of national interest chosen for the new age (that it was different from the sum total of individual interests) and the method chosen to effectuate it (the creation of elites) were analogized to seventeenth- and eighteenth-century mercantilism. The concepts were democratized for the twentieth century (the elites were to revolve, they were to be temporary, and they were to be closely watched; and the national interest was the public's or the consumer's interest rather than the state's); but neo-mercantilism was considered appropriate to the distinctively modern era because the two periods were seen as alike in their presumed stasis, the presumed end of substantive change in the nature of society. It suddenly became clear that what the United States had been doing in the forty or so years before 1914 was "industrializing" and "urbanizing" and that the meaning of that experience was the emergence of a rigid economic system and a static and interdependent society, one without fluidity, mobility, or expansiveness. It meant the end of the factor that was presumed to cause economic change (the perpetual excess of demand over supply) and the emergence out of national adolescence into economic and social maturity. Industrialism was the last, not just the latest, stage in social evolution.

Before 1910, and particularly in the 1890's, some of the same trends had been interpreted as symptomatic of something else: the fragmentation of society, rather than its consolidation. The physical or geographical separation of classes in

the cities, the ethnic breakdown of American nationality, the
cultural distinctions implied by the rise of popular media,
were taken as symptoms of a disintegration that might be
overcome by settlement houses, Americanization campaigns, the
creation of national metropolises, or the mobilization of the
people by some common identity such as the "consumer," the
"public," or the "nation." For Jane Addams and Herbert Croly,
this perception of the problem had clearly disappeared by
1912; and the sudden collapse of the progressive enthusiasm
and the experience of the war could only serve to ratify the
change. Wilson's attempt to overcome social fragmentation by
mobilizing the war effort on the basis of abstract ideals,
rather than on divisive questions of national interest, and
by suppressing civil liberties marked him as outdated,
caught by an earlier perception. It shocked Addams and Croly
into intensifying their insistence that the social problem
be redefined in order to rescue the variety, fluidity, and
spontaneity that had seemed problems twenty years earlier.
As "cultural pluralism," fragmentation became itself a solution to the problem of social stasis, and the cultivation of
competing loyalties would serve to counteract the excessive
power of the state.

Similarly, the problem of economic mobilization for the war effort--the failure of voluntary cooperation and the evident inefficiency of a competitive system that had evolved for an expanding society--seemed to force even Wilson himself to finally adopt the neo-mercantilist viewpoint, to face the irreversibility of a mature industrialism as the determinative modern condition, and to acknowledge the consolidation of the economy as the factual state of society. The experience of the war on these two counts of loyalty and mobilization ratified the perception of stasis and the techniques of pragmatism as the modern synthesis. By the beginning of the 1920's, reformers shared a generally uniform conception of what American society was like and what had been happening to it in the period since 1870.

There were three primary factors that observers like Rexford Tugwell and his colleagues pointed to after the war as evidence that the modern era meant the end of substantive change. The first was a noticeable decline in the rate of population growth. They found that from 1910 to 1920, American population had increased by the smallest percentage in its history, less than half the average percentage increase in every census since 1790. Between 1920 and 1930 it

would be similarly small; and between 1930 and 1940 it would
be cut in half again. Since increases in population had been
taken as the clearest sign of American vitality throughout
the nineteenth century, the leveling off was, Stuart Chase
noted, a "shattering fact." The rising social sciences of
human ecology and urban sociology attributed declines in the
rates of population growth to crowded and static conditions,
leading to the conclusion that when America became an urban
industrial society, it also became a static one. The passage
of immigration restriction legislation was one of a number of
extreme phenomena during the twenties that ratified on the
popular level the notion that the country had no more room.[1]

The same causal connection pointed to the second evidence
of stasis, the declining attractiveness of technological
progress. Population decline reflected a labor surplus,
attributable to excess technology; and despite spectacular
innovations during the 1920's, especially in communications,
power, and transportation, there seems to have been a growing
agreement among economists that the economy had been mechanized as much as it possibly could be without causing an intolerable amount of unemployment, thus further reducing the
purchasing power that had once supported expansion.

Dexter S. Kimball, for example, in a study for the President's Committee on Recent Economic Changes, connected the passing of a technological frontier, which the progressives had first noted twenty years before, to the end of the age of substantive economic expansion. Wesley Mitchell, in summarizing the committee's findings, acknowledged that as "matters stand in the spring of 1929," it was reasonable to expect that the pace of technological progress would "slacken presently, and that many years may pass before we see another well-maintained advance."[2]

That was an epoch-shattering statement in the context of the widespread belief in technological, if not economic, determinism evident in the renewed impact of Veblen's Theory of Business Enterprise of 1904 and particularly in the influence of William Fielding Ogburn, a colleague of Rexford Tugwell's. In 1922, Ogburn had revised the language of social analysis by expounding the theory of cultural lag and putting technology at the center of social change. Ogburn's thesis--that "the various parts of modern culture are not changing at the same rate" and that there was a "more or less definite sequence" that began with technological changes and progressed through other social realms in

proportion to their distance from technology (the last
changes were those in social philosophy and codes of behavior)
--received increasingly wide currency, culminating in the
official stamp of the President's Research Committee on
Social Trends, whose staff Ogburn headed.[3]

The third factor defining the perception of stasis--the
"economy of abundance"--had been first proposed by Tugwell's
mentor, Simon Patten, in 1907. He had defined the coming
modern age as one that would have solved the problem of production. The American problem would no longer be how to al-
locate scarcity, but how to handle surpluses, and that would
require economic and social sciences and institutions of a
sort different from any that had yet been conceived of. The
economy had passed, the President's Committee noted in 1929,
from a seller's market to a buyer's market (demand no longer
exceeded supply), and any future growth would have to result
from unknown factors substantively different from those that
had prompted the great productive expansion of the 19th
century. Apparent increases in consumer demand in the
twenties, particularly for certain new products, kept this
possibility from being a major concern, but it was conceivable to Tugwell, among other future New Dealers, that

America's productive capacity was permanently excessive, that the country could produce too much for its needs (if not for its wants), and that part of its machinery would always be idle. In early 1929, when Wesley Mitchell synthesized the findings of Recent Economic Changes, he cut beneath the official optimism of the report to point out the dangers ahead and the necessity to counter them with an active policy of coordination.[4]

During the early years of the Great Depression, the analysis became compelling and was reinforced by overproduction-underconsumption theories of the business cycle. From extreme left to extreme right, the depression became symptomatic of a mature, indeed senescent, capitalism that had outlived its usefulness. The young independent Marxist John Chamberlain chastised liberalism for its failure to follow through on the perception that "however we look at it, eventual constriction stares us in the face" to the conclusion that America was ripe for revolution. The communists Anna Rochester and Lewis Corey made a similar analysis, as did the fascist Lawrence Dennis. Liberalism could be "logical, effective, and successful," Dennis argued, only so long as capitalism was "a system in expansion or prosperous."

Stuart Chase and George Soule, the influential popularizers
of the newer institutional economics, both concluded that an
end to laissez-faire and the beginning of national planning
were required, because "we have," in Chase's words, "to deal
with a roughly static rather than an expanding structure," a
fact that was not attributable to the Depression alone.[5]

These three evidences of apparent stasis reinforced a
fourth factor, possibly more symbolic than real, but psychi-
cally perhaps more compelling, that set the era of substantive change off from the modern era. The closing of the
frontier marked both the loss of a supposed safety valve for
society's mistakes and the end of the sense of adventure that
had accompanied the era of development. The theme was pervasive in the social and economic literature of the thirties
and was most useful to those who called for a shift in values
away from the rugged individualism that had characterized
both the frontier and the laissez-faire economic theories
of expanding capitalism. The Turner thesis reinforced the
sense of detachment from the past by dividing American
history into two distinct phases, each with its own determining fact. In the first phase, free land had produced an age
of expansion, change, scarcity, and individualism. In the

second, advanced technology had produced an age of stasis,

crowding, abundance, and interdependence.[6]

The concrete aspects of the shift may have been enough

to justify new departures in the government's relationship

to the economy: the welfare state would substitute for the

safety valve of westward migration. But the modes of thought,

the use of language, the methods of phrasing and solving

problems, were more affected by the differences in contours

between the phases, by "metaphysical" differences between

the eras. "The factor of time in American history,"

Frederick Jackson Turner asserted, "is insignificant when

compared with the factors of space and social evolution."

Indeed, the "metaphysical" effect of the frontier was to make

space seem boundless to Americans, while time was collapsed

into insignificance.[7] The perception of stasis had just the

opposite impact. By making the future identical with the

present in all fundamentals, it created a sense of boundless

time in which to act, despite emergency conditions. Freedom

had not disappeared; it would only operate in a new dimension.

The Depression may have created the urgency to act immediately

on relief, but the perception of stasis conferred the time

needed to work out the best arrangements for reconstruction

experimentally. Space had once allowed American society to exile its mistakes; now time would allow it to correct them.

The perception of stasis could thus underwrite both planning and random experimentalism, which the reformers of the New Deal took as the two pragmatistic techniques, allowing a recasting of pragmatism so that it blended with a variety of neo-rationalism emerging out of the scientific-management movement. The perception made the work of social scientists reliable and useful. Some of the early Pragmatists, New Economists, and Dynamic Sociologists had seen experimental reform as a method in which any action inevitably changed the context into which it was injected, affecting that context in unpredictable ways, a theory that reinforced the sense of transition in society. The experimentalists of the New Deal, in contrast, could rely on a solid, dependable reality--modern industrial society--that would not change. Stasis gave the freedom to conduct experiments in a random or arbitrary order because the knowledge that was accumulated would be reliable, transferable, and reusable until satisfactory measures were found. Thus the ability to rely on the "fundamentals" of society allowed the triumph of research, rather than theory, as the social-science pattern of reform.

John Dewey observed in 1929 that modern humanity had abandoned the quest for certainty. As far as the nature of society was concerned, modern reformers had the certainty they needed. The perception of stasis meant that, unlike Edward Bellamy, they knew "factually," rather than imaginatively or fictionally, what the future would be like. It perhaps gave them their characteristic willingness to leave questions of traditional significance unanswered--the pragmatic attitude, as James had characterized it--their apparent lack of concern for "moral values," which was often criticized during the 1930's. Edgar Kemler, looking back at the decade, noted that the New Deal had "deflated" progressivism, that it had reduced progressive ideals to statistical terms, that it took the "poetry and moral content" out of reform. Tugwell, Arnold, and their colleagues, however, were not bothered by such an attack. They were comfortable without "authentic" values; they rejected and were embarrassed by "idealistic" language; and while claiming to have been set free from all intellectual moorings, they did operate with a wonderful self-assurance that implied that they were able to take something very basic for granted.[8] Since the

Progressives had turned to "idealism" as compensation for uncertainty, it had become extraneous after 1912, when the perception changed from transition to stasis. A perceptual certainty had then made a theoretical or fictional certainty unnecessary. The resonant intellectuals for the twenties and thirties would therefore be those who felt no need to search for authentic knowledge or "moral absolutes," who had no residual desire for "logic," who were self-dependent and immune to "disillusionment" when politics or diplomary deflated ideals. As the progressives' early separation between consciousness and activity had been geared to transition, stasis could allow reformers to be both professional intellectuals and wielders of power. There had still been elements of the amateur in the progressives' early careers; and the motive of sacrifice had helped prompt a self-effacing, though crucial, role as mediators. It had also served as a bulwark of their disinterest. When stasis allowed reformers to presume real social knowledge, they could be profession-ally disinterested, and they could seek a controlling role without the modesty that both sacrifice and transition re-quired. Reform was their job. They would be comfortable wandering through remote and related disciplines, using what they needed without concern for consistency. The resonant intellectuals of the twenties and thirties, therefore, would be those who had a naturally pluralistic intellectual structure. And that personal pattern would fit the needs of a society that perceived itself to have reached the end of its road.

The pluralistic intellectual structure gave society the freedom to control its future. It was the theoretical basis of both social planning (for Tugwell) and random experimentalism (for Arnold), since both techniques meant the reordering of facts. However much Edward Bellamy's widow may have seen the New Deal as a "vindication" of her husband's philosophy,[9] in his utopianism there had been only one logical future. For Tugwell and his allies, planning meant the ability to select arbitrarily--that is, freely--from among any number of possible futures. Similarly, in whatever ways the income from the Single Tax might ultimately have been used, there was for Henry George only one sovereign reform. For Thurman Arnold and New Deal "activism," reform had no inherent priorities. It was a process of attacking problems as one got to them, in any order that was expedient, that satisfied any arbitrarily, or freely, selected factual

criteria, from building a coalition, to alleviating salient
miseries, to altering the governing system entirely. Pri-
ority was a question of selecting facts, not of metaphysics,
logic, or natural order.

The pervasive historical relativism among reformers of
the 1930's was the primary abstract expression of these ideas.
Beyond the subjectivism that assumed inevitable bias in historians and beyond the propagandism that ransacked the past
to legitimize current policies, there was a genuine historical relativism that reoriented attitudes toward time itself
and neatly satisfied the reform needs of the New Dealers.
According to George Herbert Mead, pragmatism in the realm
of history meant the legitimacy, indeed necessity, of reconstructing the past to account for each novelty. As different
facts acquired salience, the past was automatically reordered
in people's perspectives to give these "emergents" continuity.
"We speak of the past as final and irrevocable," Mead wrote.
"There is nothing that is less so, if we take it as the pic-
tured extension which each generation has spread behind itself." Such relativism was the obverse of planning and experimentalism. If there was no necessary order in what had
already happened, if the past could be reordered, then there

also existed the ability to reorder what had not happened
yet. "It is the relativity of time, that is, an indefinite
number of possible orders of events," Mead observed, "that
introduces possibility in nature. When there was but one
recognized order of nature, possibility had no other place
than in the mental construction of the future or the incom-
pletely known past." The intellectual revolution begun by
the Progressives was thus completed. Edward Bellamy had said
that the future was as incapable of being changed as the past.
Historical relativism argued that the past was as changeable
as the future.

As the sense of boundless time that was the obverse of
the Turner thesis coexisted with, and possibly helped to sustain, the relativity of time in Mead's historical pragmatism,
the polarity between the perception of stasis and the pluralistic intellectual structure was similarly useful, as the
polarities had been during the earlier eras of reform. Both
the perception and the intellectual structure helped break
the shackles of the conservative argument that reform was
impossible or dangerous: the structure by affirming possibility as inherent in the universe; the perception by removing
the risk of uncorrectable consequences and by precluding the

idea that problems could solve themselves. The polarity may
explain such statements as George Soule's apparently contradictory remark that planning was "to serve certain ends that
either arise out of brute necessity, or are assumed to be
good."[11] The pluralistic universe gave the freedom to assume
"good" arbitrarily. Since facts took on significance with
respect to plans or hypotheses, society or its leaders could
will its own ends. The perception gave the primary working
tool (the reliability and reapplicability of acquired knowledge) and the basic faith that whatever end was chosen, one
best way could ultimately be found to fulfill it. The polarity allowed reform to be a professional occupation. The flux
and complexity of a pluralistic universe required the delega-
tion of power, while ultimate responsibility could be delegated to "brute necessity." The perception said that the
facts rule, and therefore government-of-men was not arbitrary;
the intellectual structure said that humanity rules the facts,
and therefore government-of-men was both necessary and free.

Rexford Tugwell and Thurman Arnold represent the most
clear-cut positions in the congeries of personalities and
ideas swirling through the New Deal. If there were two New
Deals, they have served as their archetypes. Tugwell was the

most visible and articulate member of the economist-flavored first New Deal, the clearest representative of the liberal reformism that found its solution to the social problem in planning. An original member of the Brain Trust, his presence was, for many reformers, a touchstone of Roosevelt's liberalism. When he was forced out of the administration in late 1936, it was taken as a sign of Roosevelt's shift to a different set of policies--Brandeisian or Wilsonian in emphasis, featuring enlarged antitrust activity, and dominated by lawyers. Thurman Arnold, who had already written two books that seemed the epitome of the New Dealers' universe of discourse, took over the antitrust division of the Justice Department and became the visible symbol of that shift. From that point on, Tugwell and Arnold accepted each other as the personifications of two different strategies of modern liberalism on the issue of government and business, and historians and critics have generally accepted that characterization.

Both began their adult lives when Progressivism had reached its national peak and when the perception of stasis had taken over the progressives' thinking, creating intense pressures to adopt a pluralistic intellectual structure.

And both responded to those pressures easily and creatively until they became the most articulate completers of the modernization of American liberalism. They also lived to see that liberalism challenged three decades later on the startling grounds that the modern era had ended.

CHAPTER VIII

THE VIRTUES OF NECESSITY

Rexford Tugwell

"A declared part of the philosophy of those who object
to our American system," Herbert Hoover complained of the
New Dealers, "is the notion that America has reached the end
of the road of economic development--the end of the road of
progress. We have been told that our industrial plant is
built, that our last frontier has long since been reached,
and that our task is now not discovery or necessarily the
production of more goods, but the sober, less dramatic business of administering the resources and plants already in
hand." He called this perception "the counsel of despair"
when it had appeared in a 1932 campaign speech drafted for
Franklin Roosevelt by Rexford Tugwell.[1]

"Gloom and despair; the end of the world? Not at all,"
Stuart Chase, a Tugwell ally, noted; "at least not necessarily."
It depended on who was put in charge and how they conceived
their task. The managers of such an age, Tugwell remarked,

had to accept the requirements of an era of stasis and learn
"to make virtue of necessity." They had to be "conscious of
modernity and skilled in its pragmatic way of thought." Pre-
modern habits of mind had to be abandoned. He told social
workers that if they wanted to be effective in modern life,
they would have to give up the remaining "romance" in their
approach to society, which was reminiscent of an earlier era
of amateurishness and improvisation. He looked further back,
at the philosophy of Henry George, and found the source of
its popularity and its futility in its offer of "a simple
program of reform to a harassed world." That a simple program
could not have a similar appeal in the harassed world of the
Great Depression, Tugwell could lay to the increased level of
sophistication reached in the interim. He might also have
laid it to the changed context of the harassment and so have been
receptive to a later context, in which sophistication itself
would seem old-fashioned.[2]

I

In The Light of Other Days, the autobiography he published in 1962, Rexford Tugwell could find little but irrelevance in the environment and training of his childhood. He

was born in 1891 and spent his early years in Sinclairville, New York, a small rural community where his father engaged in businesses tied closely to agriculture. The things Tugwell recalled as part of community life in the 1890's—the small scale of enterprises, the sense of security and confidence in the future, the belief that personal contact was the whole of social life, the assumption that the common good resulted from the pursuit of individual interests—were the things Jane Addams was just then finding outdated in Chicago. Tugwell himself looked back upon them as "dangerously anachronistic." America was turning into a modern urban and industrial society, and the children who were being raised in an outmoded environment would become a drag on evolution, obstacles to the attempt to make a rational institutional adjustment to the new social and economic conditions.[3]

Intellectual autobiographies usually aim to give the sources of their subjects' interests in the field for which they are celebrated. The end selects the appropriate beginning. In Tugwell's case, the end and the beginning were mutually exclusive. He ended as a planner, and thus the theme of his autobiography, which concludes with his departure for college and his journey into modern industrial

America, is his exceptional escape from an unplanned rural
environment and its values. Yet an important aspect of modern
urban and industrial liberalism, of which Tugwell became an
exponent, could have developed just as easily in Sinclairville
as in any other place, though it would require a modern context to give it resonance. That was a special self-assurance,
a freedom from traditionally authentic values, which can be
seen as the final product of the emphasis on will and leadership that the progressives had displayed after 1912. In contrast with George and Bellamy, for example, and even Addams
and Croly, Tugwell was brought up with a strong sense of
detachment from restrictive values. As the only surviving
son of parents who experienced the deaths of two other boys
in infancy, he assumed a central position in the family that
exempted him from many of the demands children ordinarily
face. He recalled only rare punishment; and whatever
troubles he caused in the community were straightened out
for him by his father, so their consequences never reached
him. There were thus none of the inhibitions on experimental
forays into the world such as might have been created by a
fear of bad results; and the impulse toward self-sacrifice,
so intimately connected to the motivation of the amateur

social activist, was not prized. The interior dialogue between spontaneity and control that had been prominent in
Addams and Croly was decidedly mute in the case of Tugwell.
Just as important, he received no conflicting impulses. Like
Croly and Addams, he seems to have enjoyed a healthy relationship with his father. In their case, however, their fathers'
attitudes were counterbalanced by their mothers'. Tugwell's
mother seems only to have reinforced her husband's doting.
Tugwell remembered that whatever freedom and independence he
enjoyed were in fact within a very protected environment--a
stable village community in which his parents were respected
but independent figures.[4]

Tugwells, he recalled, had a historic propensity for
leadership, even bossiness, and as a boy he liked to be the
head of any group he belonged to. In his summer jobs in
his father's canning factory, he displayed a predisposition
for order and rationality. Though he professed a healthy
respect for individuals as the irreducible units of society,
he also displayed a leader's distaste for capricious people
and an engineer's dislike of recalcitrant parts. He developed, he said, a sensitivity to "rattles anywhere in the
machinery." Self-assertion by any one but the leader

destroyed groups the way ill-fitting pieces destroyed machinery, and so disorder, irrationality, and individualism became
linked in his mind. This attitude was evident even in family
life. A tacit alliance developed between Tugwell and his
father in the subtle management and protection of the moody,
unpredictable, and sometimes willful person who was his
mother. It was individualism in other people and randomness
in mechanical systems that Tugwell associated with irrationality and disorder. His own individualism or self-assertion,
as an instrument of control, was exempted from condemnation.
He spent two high-school years in Buffalo, where he discovered
regularity behind the acts of capricious individuals, and he
concluded that the regularity existed not because of an invisible hand but because somewhere there were people who specialized in maintaining it. "These would be individuals,
too. But they would be different. . . ."[5]

The sense of certainty and self-confidence with which
Tugwell operated as a child in a stable and circumscribed
world did not desert him as his world was gradually expanded
during his adolescent years. The family's moves and his college preparatory years in Buffalo made him familiar with
successively larger communities, and his father's business

career was a highly visible example of the transition to modern industrial society.[6] When, at age twenty, he left upstate New York for Philadelphia and the Wharton School of the University of Pennsylvania, Tugwell was ambitious to be one of those "individuals, too, but different." Wharton was then engaged in training a second generation of social critics and expert technicians, with the hope that they would be received as active leaders and managers, rather than as simply academic prophets or mute functionaries.

At Wharton, Tugwell fell under the tutelage of two faculty members who were closely and controversially connected to the advanced reform movements of the Progressive Era, Scott Nearing and Simon Patten. Both Nearing and Patten displayed an evangelical fervor about social problems that linked them closely in tone and sympathy with the Christian socialists and the more religious social workers of the early twentieth century. Both devoted a great deal of effort to inventing quasi-religious appeals to arouse the public's social conscience. They regarded reformers as revivalists who acted out of duty, obligation, and self-sacrifice, and whose job it was to excite similar impulses on the part of the masses. Their own careers, like those of the Progressives, tied this

stance of amateur, advocate, and participant to the disinterested professional role of social scientist. The tie was
loose and strictly personal. Scientific investigation, public arousal, and reforming legislation constituted the
"triune of activities" that Nearing said would insure social
"adjustment" or reform.[7] But there was no reason why the
first and second parts of this trinity, the professional's
responsibility and the amateur's, could not be as separate
from each other as they usually were from the third. Indeed,
given the fragility of academic freedom, the prudent reformer-
academic was careful to maintain the separation of roles.
The professional role was thus the only one officially com-
municated to the students at Wharton, and Tugwell came to
regard the amateur as inappropriate to modern society. When
in 1915 Nearing's non-professional activities became too
prominent for the trustees of the University, he lost his
job. Patten's attempt to defend him on the grounds that
Nearing was simply bringing to the public his professional
knowledge as a social scientist, convinced neither the
trustees, other academics (including the newly formed A.A.U.P.)
nor, finally, Patten himself.[8]

During the years Tugwell was at Pennsylvania, Nearing

was in the middle of a transition from progressive critic of overblown capitalism who saw "science" as a solution to social problems to partisan of the increasingly popular but vague scheme called "industrial democracy," a transition that would lead to his public advocacy of socialism during World War I. His writings were largely a compendium of the insights of others, particularly of Patten and the social workers, grouped around three basic themes: first, the innate capacity of all people at birth for a normal, healthy, and fruitful development, and the corollary environmentalism that traced any lack of fulfillment to economic rather than personal causes; second, the epochal importance of industrialization and the status of technology (the "state of the industrial arts") as an independent variable in economic history and theory; and third, the importance of judging social well-being by measuring two economic factors, standard of living and cost of living, and the relative and class-based nature of both factors.[9]

Except for the last, Nearing carried these themes far enough to see their implications for reform and get himself into trouble as a critic, but not far enough to serve as a firm basis for the work of the technicians who were then emerging from the University's professional business school. Nearing's work was built around themes rather than theses, assertions rather than hypotheses, and it resembled the intellectual equivalent of a social worker's activities more than the work of a professional economist. It was a stabbing out at the world with insights and programs culled from a variety of sources, rarely with any deep or prolonged analysis, and held together only by such vague and often poorly defined terms as "social sanity" and "social adjustment."

Patten was more circumspect in his approach to the establishment and more ambitious and playful in his exploration of ideas in depth, particularly outside his own discipline. Although he was less averse than Nearing to devising a logical theory of the economic order, he was no more successful at it. More important, he was ultimately able to provide a justification for this failure that had a strong impact on the "younger generation" (as Tugwell styled himself and his colleagues in the 1920's).

Patten's thinking revolved around an insight that comported with the Progressives' perception that the modern era was detached from the past, making prior social and economic knowledge irrelevant. According to Patten, society was in the midst of a transition from an era of scarcity, deficit, and pain to an era of abundance, surplus, and pleasure. Industrial technology had finally reached the point, so often predicted in the nineteenth century, at which the productive plant could support all people at a comfortable level of living. Patten's insight created intellectual difficulties for him, centering on the question of whether the values, attitudes, and economic science appropriate to the new age were also appropriate during the transition, and whether, in fact, they would destroy the abundance that the old values had created. He also attributed to the coming "creative economy" the sense of possibility he himself was experiencing in the period of transition, but which in fact could disappear when the transition ended. He saw, but ultimately refused to follow through on, the implications of abundance that several liberal economists, such as Stuart Chase, George Soule, and Rexford Tugwell would take as a major theme in the late 1920's and 30's: that the discovery of abundance was really the discovery of stasis, that, since the mode of production defined eras, abundance meant that a static and non-innovative stage of economic history had been reached, that the future held no surprises as far as the "basis" of modern society was concerned.

There was nowhere to go from industrialism. After much effort, Patten finally stopped trying to identify the values
and economics of the new society because that would bind the
future (the same reason Croly had given), declined to advocate long-range planning on the same grounds, and settled
on the pragmatist's vision of a pluralistic universe and
progress through novelties.[10]

In the face of his conflicting conceptions of society
and social change, it is not surprising that Patten was continually frustrated in his attempts at a _summa_. Yet the
fact that he considered himself a disciple of John Stuart
Mill and did try to make a consistent restatement of economic theory indicated that, at least until 1912, he, like
the Progressives, had not willingly accepted the full implications of what he ultimately saw to be a transition from
rationalism to pragmatism. But in 1912, just when he was
becoming a major influence in Tugwell's life, Patten wrote
a monograph, his last long work, explaining the necessity and
realism of adopting the pragmatistic model.

Patten framed the argument in terms of a conflict between
a "monistic" and "pluralistic" intellectual structure for economics, and he put himself in the camp of the pluralists.

There was no one science of economics, he said, that could cover all areas of economic activity. Static and dynamic analyses, for example, though apparently incompatible, were less antitheses than alternative resources for understanding different problems. Since neither type could be deduced from the other, the monism of neo-classical economic theory was a mistake. Thus, Patten's free-swinging intellectual career, his forays into side issues, his inconsistencies, his acceptance of contradictions, and his inability and final refusal to go back and tie it all together were justified as a manifestation of pragmatism. It was this pluralistic intellectual structure, similar to Nearing's, that Rexford Tugwell remembered and admired--and imitated.[11]

II

Tugwell completed a two-year graduate residency at Penn in 1917, the year Patten was forced into retirement. Resigning his instructorship in economics, Tugwell left Philadelphia to teach marketing for a year at the University of Washington in Seattle. To the extent that Patten and Nearing were his model economists, he could infer that it was not intellectually necessary to develop a consistent, logical, unitary

theoretical structure that would encompass economic life.
Indeed, it was necessary to avoid such structures, since they
did not comport with reality. What Patten and Nearing did
for their students at Wharton was to transform the amateur's
improvisational approach to concrete problems into a model
for a professional intellectual structure, and they labeled
this structure "pragmatism" and "experimentalism." There was
a potential problem for Tugwell, however, in squaring this
model with his ingrained distaste for disorder and irrationality in the external world. That distaste and two years of
practical experience (1918-19) were perhaps the sources of
his interest in scientific management, particularly the work
of Frederick W. Taylor. There was a strong potential for
conflict between the influence of Taylor and that of Patten
and the pragmatists. Patten had been wary of such techniques,
and Jane Addams and Herbert Croly had strongly opposed overt
social manipulation. Tugwell's eventual resolution of the
conflict became one of the dominant strains of New Deal
liberalism.

Taylor had burst into the public consciousness in 1910
when Louis D. Brandeis drew attention to his pioneering work.
In 1911, he published The Principles of Scientific Management,

which Tugwell drew on heavily. Taylor claimed that his principles, if universally adopted, could double productivity.
He thus offered the promise of maintaining an economy of
abundance even if some of the factors Patten had worried
about, such as population growth and the expansion of people's
wants, were not kept under control. Juxtaposing Taylor's
claims to Veblen's argument that while "industry" operated
for productivity, "business" operated for profit and often
(and particularly in the 1920's) kept a stranglehold on production in order to fix prices, one could naturally infer
that only if management were transferred from private to public hands could Taylor's methods and Patten's goals coincide.[12]

Taylor's scientific frame of mind, however, and that of
many of his disciples was closer to the Newtonians' than to
that of post-Darwinians like Patten. Even on the practicing
level, Taylor and his disciples seemed to stand for a new
rationalism. Though scientific management assumed the extreme complexity of even the most simple operations, the conditions in which Taylor operated were relatively fixed and
stable. The environment of a factory performing a given
series of operations, however complex, was not analogous to
the pragmatists' pluralistic universe of novelty, chance,

and unpredictability. For any given set of conditions, Taylor's science assumed that there was one and only one "best" solution and that once the "one best way" (in Gilbreth's phrase) was discovered, the important part of the job was finished. There was no expectation of continual substantive change, and the process of experimentation was not regarded as theoretically endless. The given conditions were fixed, so the solution must be dependable and permanent.

Though there was clearly a potential for conflict between the model of social science implied by scientific management and the one Patten and Tugwell found in pragmatism, the threat need not materialize so long as the conditions the economist or manager dealt with were narrowly circumscribed, local, short-range, and unchanging, so long as society seemed static.

Tugwell's doctoral dissertation, The Economic Basis of the Public Interest (1922) and an article he drew from it were his first extensive works to show the intellectual impact of such a perception of social stasis. His goal was to identify the qualities that vested a business with such a degree of public interest that government regulation of its prices was indicated. His argument was a revealing amalgam of historical, functional, institutional, and neo-classical economics.[13]

By focusing on prices, Tugwell was dealing with the capitalist as a seller of goods and services rather than as a producer of them, and therefore with the arena of neo-classical economics, the market. In the prevailing neo-classical scheme, the classical theory of distribution to the factors of production had been replaced with distribution fixed by supply and demand. In the market place, the antagonists were the seller and the buyer. Tugwell felt he was avoiding neo-classical conservatism by following Patten's dictum that economists should look at their science from the consumer's point of view. He thought that that would allow him to approach "the social problem"--the distribution of wealth--without having to deal with the problems of class conflict implicit in the classical distribution of wealth into wages, interest, and rent.

Setting the producer-as-seller against the consumer, Tugwell found an element of disorder and irrationality in the market, which was supposed to be the classical harmon-izer and rationalizer. Adopting Veblen's idea of a conflict of functions in the capitalist--between productivity and

profit, between "making goods and making money"[14]--Tugwell
argued that when the producer-as-seller was most exploiting
the consumer by limiting the supply of necessities and keeping prices artificially high, he was also hurting himself
in his primary capacity as a producer. There was a natural
harmony between the interests of the consumer and the
producer-as-producer, which the market perverted. If a
regulatory commission had the power to fix prices, it could
set them low enough to call out a sufficient demand to increase output, which would also increase profits.

Tugwell thus seemed to be standing neo-classical price
economics on its head, using it to undermine its own faith
in the market mechanism. But an anti-classicist using a
classical form of argument to subvert classicism would have
persuaded no one, least of all its author, who believed the
free market no longer existed in any case. A thoroughly
classical argument might have been attractive to Tugwell if
in fact it had been congenial to match intellectual structure
to social perception. The institutional school, in which he
had been trained, stressed the connection between theory and
reality. Since Tugwell's "realism" involved a perception of
modern society as fully developed and mature, of the modern

era as static, he could have constructed a theory solely to fit this "real" stasis, which would also have matched the abstract and ideal stasis of classical economics. Tugwell accepted, for example, the notion of a technological frontier, a limit on productive efficiency,[15] which Jane Addams had noticed as early as 1907, a plateau in innovation that meant that society had become the sort of closed system that Frederick Taylor had been able to rationalize in the factory. As long as one regarded the productive system as determinative of the rest of culture, as Tugwell did, then using the consumer's viewpoint implied that the dynamics of economic expansion and substantive economic change were no longer relevant. The disharmony between the producer-as-producer and the producer-as-seller could arise only in a mature economy, where productive capacity was oversufficient.

The solution Tugwell proposed for measuring the public interest--a theory of consumers' disadvantage--revealed a similar perception. Instead of looking for an actual monopoly or a real conspiracy, the government, in enforcing antitrust laws, should apply two functional tests. The first was whether the good or service was a necessity. The second was whether the unregulated market was extracting an "extortionate price," forcing people to do without or allow-ing an "inferior standard of service." Tugwell offered these tests both as his own proposals and as the historic law of regulation. His ability to identify an invented theory, pro-posed as an innovation that realistically fitted distinc-tively modern conditions, with a restatement of the historic law of business regulation arose from his periodization of Anglo-American history. He divided history so that the era of productive revolution, expansion, and development--the era of industrialization--appeared as a brief completed interlude sandwiched between two periods of economic stasis. Tugwell's legal precedents for neo-mercantilism derived from doctrines originated under mercantilist regimes before the Industrial Revolution.[16]

In this context of stasis, the "block universe" of the classical model might have been congenial. There were, in-deed, some strong hints of classical analysis in The Economic Basis, particularly Tugwell's assertion that the standard of price-fixing would in the long run follow the lines of the "natural determination of price" and approach the "natural norm."[17] There was also an apparent indifference to the dynamic impact of the "state of the industrial arts," which

Tugwell's own allies were condemning the classicists for.

Finally, order and rationality, by which Tugwell judged the

economy, were typically classical tests.

But just as classical economics overthrew mercantilism

in favor of an expanding economy, so neo-classical economics

could not be suitable for neo-mercantilism. Thus, Tugwell's

argument for price-control had to be primarily an institu-

tional argument, particularizing the modern era, just as

mercantilism had seemed to rely on particular, constant

oversight by the state. Under mercantilism, it was observed

that monopolies tended to arise where demand was inelastic--

where a necessity was involved--and courts had historically

permitted regulation there. The specifically modern problem

was a general tendency toward combination and monopoly, made

possible by the completion of the productive plant, so that

fixed prices or artificially limited supplies appeared in

sectors of the economy that had not traditionally been con-

sidered necessities. So for modern times, Tugwell proposed

to define "necessity" as "any good or service which contributes

to a psychologically full life." Such a redefinition would

broaden the legal basis for regulation beyond the public

utilities and the staples to almost all of large-scale modern industrialism.[18]

Since the relativity of necessities made the consumer's
choice of goods pivotal, Tugwell was placing a source of
unpredictability at the very center of the economy. Patten
and the reform-institutionalists had made consumption central
because they wanted to judge the economy not by its symmetry
but by the "satisfactions" or "welfare" people derived from
it. In addition, consumer economics was a way virtually to
assume the scientific validity of public control, since it
defined the market, as Tugwell noted, as a "social mechanism
rather than a private one." But even Patten had been wary
of making consumption so important, fearing that its "dynamism" would threaten the maintenance of abundance; and so he
had depended upon education for restraint. He had also re-
frained from offering an analysis of consumption consistent
with his proposed "dynamic" economics. One who did offer
such an analysis--Henry W. Stuart, in a pragmatists' manifesto of 1917--only demonstrated that Patten's fears were well
grounded. Stuart argued that consumption was a motive force
in the progress of society through the consumer's tendency
to accept novelties purely for their novelty and ultimately
to regard as necessities things for which there had been no

previous demand. As the standard of living rose and needs escalated, consumption could make the economy increasingly unpredictable. There were graphic examples of this phenomenon by
the early twenties.[19]

For Tugwell the answer to an unpredictable phenomenon was experimental control, rather than classical laissez-faire. He found
his instrument in a behaviorist economic psychology. The first
step in publicly regulating prices would be to determine the necessary supply. The second would be to set the price at a point that
would allow the marginal producer--the one who rounds out the
supply--to make a profit. The latter would involve a relatively
easy determination of the costs of production. Tugwell offered
two methods for the former. One was the "democratic" method
of using statistics of past consumption as a guide, a method
Tugwell thought unreliable. The second was to have a price-
fixing commission decide, on the advice of experts, which
items constituted the best possible and least costly standard
of living and then fix prices to call out the supply and "to
force consumption habits as gently as possible" into those
channels. Since expertise was neutral, Tugwell had no doubts
that this method was non-authoritarian and non-utopian.
"Men's natures cannot be changed," he had written in 1921,
"but the nature of their stimuli to act can be changed."[20]

Tugwell's shading of price and other economic mechanisms
from economic stimuli into psychological ones derived from
the work of Carleton H. Parker, who had been his chairman
at the University of Washington in 1917-18. The differences
between their two versions of behaviorism, however, graphically illustrate the differences between the Progressives and
the New Dealers. Parker's scholarly output was slender, but
his work was important in the movement, which included Patten,
to find a less simplistic economic psychology than hedonism;
and the standard of a "psychologically full life," which
Tugwell used in defining necessity, was his. After he had
directed the state of California's investigation of the I.W.W.
Wheatland riots in 1913, Parker had turned to psychology for
explanations. He put together a crude behaviorism involving
the interaction of environment and sixteen instincts--a concept just then becoming unfashionable--which he culled from
a variety of sources. Parker was interested in freedom for
the full development of a person's potential rather than in
behavioral control, and that pushed his version of behaviorism closer to Dewey's and Cooley's idea that life was a continuous and indeterminate process of self-realization than
to the idea that it was a simple interaction of stimulus and

response. He was distressed that industrialism twisted personalities on all social levels by persistently thwarting
the expression of instincts--all of which were good, in the
sense of having survival value. He favored an unstructured
environment free of formal discipline and restraint and a
radically new standard of normality--a psychologically full
life--which would break down inhibitions to "experimental
thinking" and to a life led by a method similar to the one
Croly expounded in his biography of Willard Straight.[21]

Parker's behaviorism was useful in undermining the neo-
classical idealization of laissez-faire by destroying its
reliance on hedonism for economic motivation. A theory of
instincts, many of which occurred in conflicting pairs,
rendered meaningless the statement that economic man follows
his self-interest, because it made a general definition of
self-interest nearly impossible. In addition, if people were
at least partly driven by the instinct called "acquisivism,"
rather than by the rational calculation of economic gains,
then the sum total of individual actions could not be automatic social progress, because the sum total of "irrational"
actions was not necessarily rational.

Tugwell used behaviorism for this purpose,[22] but he also

transformed it in a way Parker would not have approved.
While he appropriated the goal of a "psychologically full
life," he made the open-ended process Parker had in mind
into something much less open and much less of a process.
He used Parker's terminology in some of his early published
efforts, a series of articles on Wobblie unrest, employee
turnover, and labor migration, written during the years he
was working on his dissertation. But he tended to see the
problems of the "casuals" from the standpoint of the social
interest in order and stability, rather than from the individual's interest in fulfillment. And he transformed the
primitivism in Parker's instinct-psychology so that the goal
of a "psychologically full life" need not have unpredictable
or, indeed, even progressive effects. Where Parker ascribed
some worth to each of the instincts, Tugwell's articles on
the Wobblies and his later forays into behaviorism indicated
that he valued only some of them. Some were human or social
and had to be cultivated, while others were bestial and were
best repressed. That treatment of instincts, instead of
calling for spontaneity and freedom, as Parker and Jane Addams
and Herbert Croly--and Simon Patten--had desired, contained
an implicit demand for control, order, and restriction. The

individual could not be left free to achieve a psychologically full life on his own. To Tugwell, behaviorism meant that the public's control of the economy was not to be exercised by the public itself, through its choice of goods, but by special individuals like Tugwell himself. "The directive intelligence of our time," he wrote in 1922, was the property of "those specifically trained in the understanding of industrial philosophy and technique." Consumption had theretofore been controlled by the fact of scarcity. The age of abundance demanded other means.[23]

The relativity of necessities was one of two sources of unpredictability that economicst who regarded themselves as pragmatists, such as Patten and Stuart, attributed to the economy. Tugwell showed it could be brought under control. The other source--the state of the industrial arts, the novelty-producing process known as technology--was not a problem for Tugwell. It was rendered impotent by his perception of stasis itself. That perception was grounded--as Tugwell's later work would make even clearer--on the belief that the rise to dominance of technology as a social force was the substantive change from pre-modern to modern times. It was identical with industrialization. Future innovations would only fill in the remaining gaps; they would not produce any substantive or unexpected changes in a context technology itself defined. Technological determinism in the twenties and thirties was a product of the perception of social stasis. Indeed, Tugwell's colleague at both the University of Washington and Columbia, William Fielding Ogburn, believed that a method could be found actually to predict inventions.

The initial institutionalist attacks on classical economics had centered on its indifference to consumption and technology as sources of economic change. In depreciating both of them, while calling them central, Tugwell was leaving an open field for neoclassical economists to continue asserting their own preeminent relevance to modern society. But he was also letting himself use some of the rationalistic language of conventional economists without leaving himself open to charges of rationalism from the younger pragmatists with whom he identified.

In the context of social stasis, Tugwell's transformation of Parker's economic psychology could comfortably end the dualism in the Progressives' early method of reform--the interaction between the "people," whose unconscious actions initiated and revealed substantive changes, and those

who made conscious the tendencies of their actions. There
would be no more such changes; there was nothing more to
learn about the future; and thus the people as an active
force were no longer necessary; in certain areas, such as
consumption, they might even be dangerous. Jane Addams had
made a similar discovery after 1912, but she was never fully
comfortable with it. Tugwell's behaviorism, however,
celebrated it. It precluded independence, spontaneity, and
surprise. It obviated mass movements. It resolved the
Progressives' early "dialectic" of randomness and selectivity,
spontaneity and order; and it bridged the very wide gap between the Progressive's social control and the manager's
social manipulation. When George Herbert Mead began referring to novelties as "repugnant facts," he was using a
metaphor congenial to the younger reformers.

III

If the key to a modern intellect was, as Dewey and
Patten maintained, the reunion of theory and reality, then
the coercive power of any "theory" would be whether the
"reality" it purported to handle coincided with a prevailing
social perception. Tugwell's perception of society, as it

emerged in his writings in the early twenties, described
society as having three characteristics. First, it was distinctively modern; it was a separate era in social history.
Second, it was substantively and irreducibly complex; there
was no going behind the complexity to find simple principles
operating. And third--the feature that distinguished his
perception from the Progressives' before 1910--society was
fully developed or static; its dominant characteristics were
fixed for the foreseeable future; the remaining changes were
limited to filling in gaps and managing the system more efficiently and equitably. Modern society might seem too
fast-changing to be in a static state, Tugwell wrote in
1924, but it was in fact about to repeat, for different
reasons, the stasis of ancient and medieval times. Hence-
forth, he noted, "the changes will perhaps be for a time
more minute, more in the nature of refinements upon already
existing fundamentals, than were those that swung the world
away from medievalism and into what Proudhon so vividly
named 'industrialism.'" The period of transition was over.
Modern times constituted an era, and that era was defined
by a developed industrial system. All contemporary writers,
Tugwell observed, whether they admitted it or not, "recognize

that industry is the force that has shaped the present and
that will create the future." The foreseeable future would
be identical with the present in all its determining characteristics. Tugwell acknowledged that modern society was
substantively complex or "dynamic." The stasis of the modern
age differed from the medieval and ancient in that it was "complicated, intricate, and many dimensioned." Complexity made
specialists necessary. But stasis deprived it of the element
of possible surprise in the Progressives' perception of increasing complexity. Modern society was "vastly complicated,"
but it was "a vastly complicated equilibrium."[24]

What was implicit in Tugwell's dissertation and in his
writings on economic psychology became explicit beginning in
1924: that in the face of this perception he was making a
mode of knowing--"pragmatism" and "experimentalism"--and a
mode of acting--control and management--identical, by attributing to society the very pluralism that he perceived
it no longer to have, that was, indeed, the polar opposite
of the perception of stasis. In 1924, Tugwell first fully
articulated the cognitive mode that he found appropriate to
the social perception--the mode that Patten had labeled
"intellectual pluralism." It had been adumbrated in the

use of apparently incompatible economic styles in his dissertation. In a long essay of 1924, "Experimental Economics," Tugwell asserted the naturalness and realism of such a compendium of styles. The essay was issued as part of a collection called The Trend of Economics, which was intended to be the manifesto of the "younger generation" of professional economists. Tugwell inspired the project and served as its editor. He regarded it as a collective expression of the pluralistic intellectual structure. Each of the contributors, Tugwell noted, was a specialist rather than a generalist, and this comported well with the fact that they were dealing with "the conditions of a more complex life" than their predecessors had faced. An almost random compilation of individual forays into the field with varying methodologies was a more worthy textbook than one that called itself The Principles of Economics and purported to synthesize the nature of the universe.[25]

Tugwell's proposed "experimental economics" epitomized the intellectual pluralism of the collection itself. Instead of defining a coherent discipline or methodology, Tugwell was willing to accept into the fraternity of experimentalism all methods that had any connection with "reality": any data

descriptive of current institutions, any hypothesis not
strictly deduced from first principles, any method, such as
the statistical, that could yield "inductive certainty,"
any theory capable of successful prediction, any procedure
that smacked of trial and error. Thus, "experimental economics" could produce no issue of its own. Tugwell saw his
job as pointing out problems for which other economists
might provide solutions. But he did not see his job as
indicating how the answers could be found. He would offer
no methodology because he could not know what in particular
"experimental economics" was capable of. To do otherwise
would tend to deny the appropriateness of intellectual
pluralism in the modern world. He criticized the classical
school for allowing theory to become detached from reality
by allowing it to persist beyond the context to which it had
been relevant: "the conditions of life in an undeveloped
society." A developed society demanded methodological
pluralism. "Real" stasis could not tolerate a static ideal.
A "vastly complicated equilibrium" was not to be understood
through a theoretical equilibrium.[26]

Tugwell's argument in "Experimental Economics" established his leadership, as an Influential, if not as a research

scholar, in the future of his discipline. Columbia, whose
faculty he had joined in 1920, treated him as a star, though
he was not free of criticism.[27] His reputation also began to
spread beyond academic life, principally through the pages of
the New Republic. His intellectual career was coming to be
testimony to the power of a perception of full development to
promote acceptance of what was conceived to be "pragmatism"
as a mode of approaching modern society.

If stasis made pragmatism congenial, it also allowed it
to become a mode of action that surviving progressives could
not approve. Herbert Croly, for example, struggled in the
1920's against letting the social scientist's interest in
collecting data slip over into the manager's interest in
control. He thought it would make science as restrictive
as the rationalism of the Positivists. He tried to prevent
it by announcing that social scientists had no right to use
their knowledge because none could be authentic and because
pluralism meant that none could be reliable. For Tugwell,
stasis both required and allowed management by people with
stores of reliable knowledge. Modern society was beyond the
ken of ordinary people, he asserted, "partly because they
are ordinary" and partly "because the world has moved away

from and beyond ordinariness." Whatever Croly might claim, stasis meant that knowledge could be accumulated, transferred, and applied beyond the limited spheres from which it had been derived without being subverted by substantive social changes. It meant that Tugwell could take a seemingly rationalistic posture without sacrificing his credibility among younger pragmatists. "There are no Pisan towers as yet in social science," he wrote in 1924; "but they must be acquired so that we may know as Galileo knew, in the face of denial and bitter recrimination, that we are right." That was the only sort of knowledge that comported with his status as a professional. Only when knowledge was transferable and useful would Tugwell regard it as truly scientific.[28]

Thus, the "access of ignorance" that had first accompanied the Progressives' perception of the distinctive modernity of industrial society was not a problem for Tugwell. With no structural changes expected, data about modern life should have been relatively easy to collect. Indeed, since the transition had ended, descriptions of American society, of the type given by Croly and Walter Lippmann in 1914, became increasingly detailed, extensive, and sure. Tugwell himself, with the aid of two colleagues, presented such a

descriptive volume in 1925 as a college economics textbook.
Portrayals of reality could now be issued with as much self-
confidence as restatements of a theoretical order. The sufficiency and dependability of such "qualitative" or "institutional" knowledge was such that Tugwell made no substantial
changes when he issued a similar text nine years later.[29]

But reliable knowledge did not mean rationalism. A
rationalism of the sort that some Taylorites were pushing in
the twenties might have served Tugwell in some respects. It
represented itself as an empirical science rather than one
that was "idealistic" or "theoretical," and it saw no obstacle in the substantive, irreducible complexity of society,
which might have inhibited a revival of the older sort of
rationalism. But while Tugwell later wrote that his Industry's
Coming of Age (1927) was one of his two early works to "derive
directly" from Taylor's influence, the centerpiece of the
volume was actually a neat merger of Taylorism and pragmatism
that rescued scientific management for the purposes of reform,
avoided the Taylorite's neorationalism, and elaborated the
transformation of experimentalism into the mode of action
that Croly had distrusted. It was his first long professional
monograph since his dissertation, and it greatly enlarged his

audience. His impact as a representative of the new liberalism increased when the book sparked an invitation to join the New Republic as a contributing editor later that same year.[30]

Scientific management was important to Tugwell for reasons implicit in the title. Industry's Coming of Age provided a detailed and technical analysis of how American industry had modernized, of how its productive efficiency had accelerated until it had reached its current stage of "maturity," and of what maturity implied for public policy. Businessmen, Tugwell argued, in their pursuit of increased profits, had encouraged piecemeal technological and managerial innovations, until at some critical point the process of development had acquired a momentum of its own, overshadowing the profit motive itself. Industrialization had then turned from an instrument into the domineering fact of modern life, the basis to which all social life had to be accommodated. The persistence of institutions organized on a different basis, such as the business system itself, only created imbalance and messiness. Since the mode of production was the single given of the modern age, the single factor that could not be reversed, Tugwell proposed rationalization of the economy through public control of investment.[31]

Tugwell dated the critical point at which technology had accomplished its reversal of roles and become an imperious and independent force at 1914. That was about the time that the Progressives had noticed the same thing and had capitulated, to the extent that they could, to pragmatism, pluralism, and relativism. Tugwell followed the same path and with less difficulty. On the problem of the relationship between knowledge and action, he submerged Taylorism into pragmatism by emphasizing Taylor's original operations in a circumscribed environment and the local and mutable nature of Taylor's "principles." Maturity might require management; but management was an art, not a science. Its "laws" were in fact only hypotheses--"temporary working rules," "the generalizations of exceptionally well-informed and intelligent technicians." The efficiency movement could not pretend to be, then, anything more than an example of pragmatism in practice. "What is meant [by scientific management] is really only freedom from preconception, not 'scientific' in the strict sense, but depending on active and vigilant intelligence instead of rules-of-thumb." Taylor's idea, according to Tugwell, was "that intelligence could always modify existing practice and improve upon it."[32]

While he squeezed Taylor's method into the pragmatistic
mold, Tugwell's perception of stasis was allowing a recasting
of the intent of pragmatism into a Tayloristic framework.
The problem for both was how to act with incomplete knowledge
of a complicated environment. The "pragmatist's" job was to
increase knowledge by making an experiment to test a hypothesis. The follower of Taylor would make a plan for control on
the basis of whatever knowledge there was. One was a method
of acting in ignorance to increase knowledge; the other a
method of operating with the best available data to accomplish
a defined and concrete goal. The difference between their
practitioners was the difference between hesitancy and self-
assurance. Because of his perception of society, because he
was fairly certain that what dominated the present would
dominate the future, Tugwell was able to combine the pragmatic method with Taylor's concrete type of aim. He was
thus adding what had been the amateur's role (reformer, who
acted) onto the professional's (scientist, who knew), and
calling them both professional. By his willingness to propose concrete actions and institutional overhaul not on the
basis of detailed data, but on the basis of a perception, by
identifying proposals for control with experiments to test

hypotheses, Tugwell was sidestepping all the restrictive implications Croly was drawing from pragmatism in the twenties.
He was also thereby transforming the philosophy of James and
Dewey so that it could become a useful intellectual framework for the New Deal. A version of pragmatism as a mode of
reform was triumphing comfortably for the first time after
the conditions for which it had originally been intended--a
random and unpredictable world with an unknowable future--were
no longer perceived to exist.

With his solid and unassailable conviction that society
had to come to terms with its industrial base, Tugwell could
get along without any hint of the moral absolutes that the
earlier reformers had used both to counterweigh uncertainty
and to define the good society. Instead, he could put social
action at the service of the most factual and arbitrary of
goals: "whatever life seems to men good." "Economic purpose
is to be discovered by asking ourselves first what we want;
we may then inquire the best way to get it," he wrote as
early as 1922. "Finally, and probably not until after a
trial, we inquire whether the satisfaction is worth the
cost. Thus we may adapt institutions to our needs and dis-
card the more costly, the less useful and the outworn."[33]

Despite his recurring equation of economics and ethics and his
call for "moral controls of economic life,"[34] Tugwell's acceptance of arbitrarily chosen goals as legitimate demonstrated a
distinct indifference to "authenticity." The progressives'
ideals had taken on a similar cast of arbitrariness after 1912,
but they had wrestled with the change. Tugwell reveled in it,
and the very structure of his writing reflected it. Where
Bellamy's and George's books had had unitary structures dominated by a single overriding idea, the progressives' had often
"broken" at some point, shifting from a monistic structure,
based on history or a universal, to a pluralistic structure,
focusing on the various aspects of present reality separately.
Tugwell's writings are thoroughly pluralistic. The chapters
are topical, arranged according to no "authentic" organizing
principle; the sequence could easily be changed without altering or obscuring the argument. Often the methodology dif-
fers from chapter to chapter. Tugwell saw neither history
nor the logic of economic theory as sources of understanding,
and so he used neither to structure his works. Most of them
are free of any historical dimension whatever, much less the
extensive inquiries into the past that Croly had made even
when he was rejecting history. The 1925 edition of a text

designed to explain "contemporary civilization" to students

begins with the present; the 1930 edition devotes barely

forty-eight of more than seven hundred pages to "origins."

Nor was the "authenticity" that derived from theory any more

necessary. "In spite of the doubtful points," his 1925 text

noted, "enough facts are known to make intelligent decisions

possible. There are many obvious needs which are obscured

by too much theorizing."[35] Many of Tugwell's articles simi-

larly lack an authentic organizing principle. Digressions

are plentiful. In some ways, his books could be mistaken

for collective works, such as The Trend of Economics, the

number of which seem to abound in the twenties and thirties.

Tugwell's substitute for authenticity was the self-

confidence of specialists--the ultimate expression of "will,"

which had become prominent in the Progressives after 1912.

The social context he perceived was one in which he and

those like him, those "individuals, too, but different,"

could be pivotal, a social context that demanded both ad-

venturousness and expertise. "The conditions of right deci-

sion are clearly, under the circumstances," he wrote, re-

ferring to a complex industrial society, "a forthright

attitude of decision-making and the data requisite for its

completion [i.e., for following through on a decision]."[36]
Just as Tugwell's "Experimental Economics" could produce no
specific issue, his description of "industrial society" could
prescribe no specific reform other than an investment of
power into the hands of those who would control prices and
investment in the public interest. Tugwell was advocating,
not government of laws or principles, but government of men.
While there was little detailed data available to them--and
thus their expertise could be taken as self-assertion--there
was enough "general" or "qualitative" or "institutional"
knowledge to indicate that a "functional" institutional adjustment to industrialism had to be made and that the most
important adjustment was a change of management.

The possibility of such a change first presented itself
in the 1928 presidential campaign between Herbert Hoover and
Al Smith. The publication of Industry's Coming of Age in
1927 had coincided with a renewed public interest in economic management sparked by the Soviet Union's first five-
year plan. Tugwell visited Russia to see the experiment for
himself in the summer of 1927. He had already begun to
reanalyze America's wartime experience with a managed

economy, and the interest in the Russian proposals gave him
an opportunity to score points against laissez-faire. From
Tugwell's viewpoint, the war experience should have ended
doubts about the relevance and practicability of social management and should have illustrated the ease of solving problems of technique once the country stopped sapping its intellectual energies in quarrels about "ends," "ideals," and
"theories." A problem, however, for the advocates of social
management--now coming to call themselves social planners--
lay in the fact that organizing for production in 1917-18
could seem realistic in retrospect from two points of view:
the demands of technology, which was a permanent feature of
modern life, and the demands of war, which was only a temporary emergency. In this context, the Soviet policies seemed
to ratify one of those viewpoints. But the Republican candidate in 1928, who seemed to represent the triumph of technology and a realistic perception of modern society, took
the other point of view. What marked Hoover as a conservative, therefore, was his unwillingness or inability to adjust
his theories and ideals to his social perception. On the
other side, Al Smith's lack of sophistication troubled
Tugwell, and his understanding of modern society was not

apparent. But Tugwell did find Smith's unalloyed "opportunism" attractive. It became an example of the "pragmatic
attitude," though "unconscious of its own experimentalism."
Smith's lack of dogmatic principles made him seem an "instrumentalist" with regard to government; and when he accepted
the Democratic nomination with a speech promising economic
reforms, Tugwell endorsed him and tried to join his campaign
as an expert in agricultural economics.[37]

Since the distinctive modernity of industrial society
had deprived ideals of their authority, Tugwell's reflections
on the early post-war reaction had convinced him that there
were only two remaining forces that could inspire social
reconstruction through management: a profound national
emergency or a charismatic leader. Four years later, he
would have both. In 1928, in the absence of a national
emergency and the unlikelihood of a consensus on an "economic
equivalent of war," Al Smith seemed a likely choice. Hoover's
idealism, like Wilson's, made him unwilling to seek solutions
to problems without reference to a general philosophy.[38]
For Tugwell, a perception of stasis substituted for a general
philosophy, which even the Progressives had never entirely
abandoned. It was indicative of Tugwell's submersion of

Taylorism into pragmatism that he was less willing to take a
chance on Hoover, an accurate perceiver of reality with an
inappropriate intellectual structure, than on Smith, an opportunist with an unknown or outmoded perception of reality.
It was a pattern Tugwell would find himself repeating, and
his later regrets would be salved only by the thought that
a perfect political alternative was not realistically available.

IV

Tugwell's analysis of the milder fluctuations of the
twenties--that the stickiness of prices and wages in a
non-competitive system turned the benefits of large-scale
technology into surplus profits, which were invested in the
expansion of productive capacity beyond conceivable demand--
needed no modification to account for the events that began
with a sudden drop in consumer demand in the spring of 1929.[39]
Underconsumption-overproduction theories of the business
cycle--the emergence of an economy of abundance, the shift
from a seller's to a buyer's market--had become relatively
common fare by the time they were endorsed by the report of
the President's Committee on Recent Economic Changes in 1929.[40]

But the leading members of the Committee--leaders of the economic establishment, including the new President of the United States--refused to seek a "balance" or "continuity" between production and consumption by government control of prices and investment. Their resistance to conscious control of what they themselves called a new "dynamic equilibrium" was supported by a popular economic conservatism deriving from a confusion of the idea of business "cycles" with the neo-classical concept of an ever-disrupted tendency toward a "normal" equilibrium.

That confusion was particularly exasperating to liberal economists, not only because it was an inappropriate way of thinking, but also because it should have been undermined by the very perception of society that had received the imprimatur of the President's committee. Even from the point of view of neo-classical theory itself, not the cycle but prosperity should have been regarded as normal. However regular they appeared, however cyclical business fluctuations may have seemed, the cycles themselves should not have been seen, even by advocates of laissez-faire, as normal or natural. The apparently regular cycles were caused by acknowledged irregularities--discontinuities in production

and consumption. From the laissez-faire standpoint, these
discontinuities were temporary imbalances; from Tugwell's,
they were evidence of the inability of the market to regulate
the economy consistently. More important, the presumption of
an inevitable return to prosperity fitted the experience only
of the nineteenth century, an era of economic expansion and
scarcity (the market kept enlarging beyond the productive
capacity to supply it). Modern society was no longer expansive, and productive capacity was sufficient, indeed excessive,
if uneven. There was no reason to believe, Simon Patten had
shown, that the theories that applied to one age applied to
another. Not only was there no guarantee that the current
depression would end of its own accord, but the excess productive capacity of the mature economy could make depression
more "normal" than prosperity.[41]

The only alternative was "planning." Technology had
passed the point at which production and distribution could
ever be coordinated automatically. Indeed, in a series of
depression inspired papers, culminating in the publication
during the First Hundred Days of The Industrial Discipline
and the Governmental Arts, which was often taken as the
manifesto of the New Dealers, Tugwell extrapolated from his

perception of full development to picture an ultimate society

in which machine production would have usurped all work save

that of management. Technological unemployment was just a

symptom of America's process of "completing" itself industri-

ally, he said; it should be regarded not as a problem, but as

destiny. The detachment of income from work would require

control of all economic functions, including consumption,

from the top. That was the total replacement of spontaneity

by discipline. All freedom was society's.[42]

Tugwell did not conceive of planning as other than a

larger version of experimentalism. While underwritten by the

perception of stasis--"industrialism" would determine its

success or failure--it was geared to the pluralistic universe.

Tugwell looked at history, for example, as a thorough rela-

tivist. Neither the past nor the future had an authentic

order; and so there was, he wrote in a widely discussed paper

on planning in 1932, "the possibility of producing a new

history guided quite consciously toward foreseen ends. . . .

we are at the point where discussion of this possible master-

ing of future history is beginning to assume practical

aspects. . . ." Social science, he said, was not just a mode

of understanding; it was a form of active manipulation of

reality. It was the very act of selecting and arranging
facts so that they took on meaning with respect to some arbitrarily chosen objective. It was what Lester Ward had meant
when he had argued for the modern primacy of the "teleological"
over the "genetic" approach, the conative over the cognitive.
Once the end or purpose was agreed upon--the solution of one
problem, such as the distribution of wealth, rather than
another, such as the maintenance of free enterprise--social
facts acquired meaning in relation to it. Other ends would
give other meanings and would select other facts. This made
economics "the manipulative method." Instrumentalism in
social science meant experimental problem-solving. The
"working hypothesis" or proposed solution was a "plan" of
action. Efficiency, for example, was not a rigid concept
insensitive to human needs; it was just the choice of the
the unique set of facts appropriate to the direct achievement
of any selected goal. Business's failure could thus be seen
as its impossible claim that it could achieve two opposing
objectives--profit and welfare--with a single set of "facts."
According to Tugwell, there was only one alternative "theory
of history" to determinism, and that was "management." A
chosen future would usurp the function of the past or of an

inherently purposeful order in guiding actions. Management
as an "idea" would obviate ideology. A thoroughly modernized
society required only practical technicians, not political or
economic creeds. Tugwell was becoming a living fulfillment
of Veblen's prediction that technology would put an end to
ideology and replace it with "pragmatic," "matter-of-fact"
thinking.[43]

In the five years since Industry's Coming of Age in
1927, Tugwell's identification of the technique of planning
with the free process of experimenting had been increasingly
reinforced by John Dewey's efforts at making the concept of
experiment congenial to planners and by Harlow S. Person's
efforts at redefining Taylorism to make it congenial to experimentalists. Dewey was finding in pragmatism none of the
obstacles to social management that Croly was finding there.
A managed society was one geared to continuous problem-
solving--not a planned society like Bellamy's utopia, but a
continuously planning society. Abandoning pretensions to
authenticity and certainty did not deprive knowledge of its
utility, so long as the limits placed by probabilities, competing knowledge, and recalcitrant facts were understood and
humbly accepted. As Dewey conceived them, planning and

experimenting were a single process. A plan was another label
for a working hypothesis, which could reasonably be accepted
or rejected on the basis of whether or not it worked in the
particular situation.[44]

This was very similar to the redefinition of the Taylorites' "one best way" made by Harlow S. Person, the Managing
Director of the Taylor Society. Tugwell later credited Person
with being the publicist most responsible for making scientific management available for national planning. What Person
really did was validate from the inside Tugwell's treatment
of Taylorism less as a revival of rationalism and more as a
version of experimentalism. In a series of papers from 1929
on, Person played down Taylor's belief that there were "laws"
of industrial action. Like Tugwell, he stressed instead
Taylor's "art." Taylor's own experience, as Person interpreted it, affirmed the individuality and "pluralism" of
each situation. The "relevance" of any facts was decided by
the particular objective in view. Many objectives were possible, and for each there was one best way, just as there
was one best hypothetical solution to a problem. Scientific
management was a problem-solving technique geared not toward
rigidity and formalism but the "individualization" of action.[45]

That was the sort of method that did not require the raising of a movement, a "moral crusade," for each reform; it required only the initial persuasion of the populace to delegate its authority to the experimenters.[46] It would also not produce a utopia. Bellamy's scheme, for example, had been deduced from a universal; it could have been effected at any moment in history and with only one result. For Tugwell, a plan described a factual state; it was inextricably tied to a single era; and it offered a free choice of possible objectives. Once the desirable objectives were agreed upon, the function of management was to experiment with combinations of facts--to see which produced the desired results in the best manner ("best" by whatever standards were chosen; for example, most equitable distribution without violating certain freedoms). The technique was "self-repairing," so that it did not have to claim to be totally free of mistakes before it began operating.[47]

"Self-reparation" indicates that the most crucial support for the method derived from its congeniality to the perception of stasis. A judgment about which experiments led to mistakes could be made only with respect to the premises contained in the initial objective. But the possibility of

trying something else after a failure, depended upon the ability to regard newly discovered facts as reliable, cumulable,
and, most important, reapplicable. It depended even more on
the possibility of believing, first, that society would not
have changed substantially in the interim so that alternative
solutions could still be relevant and, second, that it was
indeed possible to arrive finally at a one-best-way, a most
accurate and direct way, of solving the problem. The scientific manager of the circumscribed environment of a factory
could act that way. With a perception of stasis, the managing
experimentalist in society could also.

In this context, the improvisational style of the early
New Deal was very congenial to Tugwell, just as the possibility of a Smith presidency had been in 1928. But there were
strong reasons within The Industrial Discipline itself why it
could not be sufficient for long. Stasis allowed improvisation to be seen not as self-sufficient, but as a method of
accumulating increasingly reliable data towards more final
and accurate hypotheses or plans. In The Industrial Discipline,
Tugwell went beyond even that and developed in stasis a quality
that completed his perception of society and that would ultimately force the method of experiment to expand from a

succession of increasingly reliable hypotheses to a series
of increasingly wider ones--an expansion of plans from "mere"
experiments to what he would later call "direction" and
"conjunctural control"--what is ordinarily thought of as master
planning. The new quality was the unitary character of modern
society. What Henry George and Edward Bellamy had been able
to find only in theories and fictions, Tugwell was perceiving
in the world around him.

The perception had been, since 1931, his explanation for
the wide reach of the events of 1929-30. Technology had created the ultimate in substantive complexity: thorough "interdependence," "concentration correlated to elaboration"--a
unitary society. The underlying structure of society was
now "continuous," and planning was by definition the method
of maintaining continuity. A "unilateral" would have to replace a "multilateral," or haphazard, course of development.[48]
Harlow Person had repeatedly juxtaposed the history of the
economy and the internal history of scientific management.
The interrelated environment of the factory had required
Taylor and his disciples to expand their control outward
from the workplace to the shop, to the whole factory, and
finally to the entire enterprise from purchasing to marketing.

Controlling one segment proved fruitless if the elements that
affected it were not controlled as well. Tugwell made the
leap from enterprises to industries (the productive sector)
in Industry's Coming of Age, and finally in Industrial
Discipline to the whole economy. And, while he stopped at
national boundaries during the 1930's, in the postwar years
he would include the whole world in a single system. Scientific management, Person had been arguing, was a technique
of progressive--progressively broader--industrial stabilization. Technology, Tugwell agreed, had created an interrelated system, and therefore piecemeal regulation tended
to widen. In a unitary society, any single change could be
disruptive, causing shocks in other parts of the whole. In
the context of transition, such shocks had been regarded as
"openings." From Tugwell's perspective, they could be
dangerous or at best messy; and so planners had to have the
power to adjust, to experiment, and to repair, to keep every
part of the whole within perfect control, even technological
change itself. Tugwell was willing to admit one "law" of
history: In the long run, structure adapted to function.
Technology was the function; "operational wholeness" was
its social expression; and planning was the relevant

structure. Tugwell saw no reason to suffer through to the long run.

The speeches that Tugwell wrote for Franklin Roosevelt after he joined the candidate's Brain Trust in the spring of 1932 and those whose "collectivism" he approved used the perception of stasis as the reason for demanding both "bold, persistent experimentation" and "more imaginative and purposeful planning."[49] It is not surprising that Tugwell's disappointment with the New Deal would take some time to surface. The accumulation of reliable data from lesser experiments would naturally precede the creation of master plans. Almost none of the discussions of national planning in the 1930's, including Tugwell's, did more than describe its "realism" or "necessity" and elaborate its possible institutional framework. Very little was known or said, even on the basis of the Russian experience, about what a plan would look like, how it would be drawn, on what grounds projections would be made, or how alternatives would be chosen.[50]

From the time he burst onto the public scene during the "interregnum" between Roosevelt's election and inauguration, to his retirement from the New Deal following the 1936

election--after serving as Assistant Secretary and Under-
secretary of Agriculture and head of the Resettlement Admin-
istration--Tugwell was to the public the embodiment of the
new liberalism. Though he was not noted in Washington for
circumspection, his public utterances were governed to an
extent by his official positions. He had a strong influence
on the AAA and the NRA; and the RA was his idea. But he was
fully satisfied with none of them.[51] He nevertheless defended them, and on grounds that often varied with his audience. The underlying themes of his academic years, however,
did persist in his public statements and publications during
the New Deal. The arguments for planning and experimentation became, once the planners and experimenters had been
entrusted with the power to solve the problems of the
Depression, a public (and in the long run, impolitic) exaltation of government of men over government of laws. The out-
moding of ideology and authentic values meant that political
decisions had to turn on the character and professional
qualifications of the people who would be given authority.[52]
The New Deal, Tugwell wrote, was simply trying to solve
problems in a way that would satisfy "our undefined sense of
the good life"; and "that life is good which seems good to

the men and women who live it." If that was, as he said, "the
progressive tradition," its lack of "authenticity" would not
have satisfied Addams or Croly. Similarly, theories and histories were irrelevant to Tugwell. "I speak in dispraise of
dusty learning, and in disparagement of the historical technique. . . . It is necessary now to break with the past," he
said. "Are our plans wrong? Who knows? Can we tell from
reading history? Hardly. The only way is to try and see, to
test our opinion in the press of actual events. Was the
opinion wrong? Then alter it. Try another approach. We
have been too long inert." Underlying all this was the perception of stasis. America had "solved the problem of
scarcity." The nation was first "learning to accept the
limitations of maturity." And most graphically, "Our economic course has carried us from the era of economic development to an era which confronts us with the necessity for
economic maintenance. This era of maintenance is the era
of our present and future existence." "For the thesis of
the New Deal is that the United States today confronts a
permanent situation to which we must adjust and that atten-
tive study of the facts will automatically give rise to the
necessary measures."[53]

V

The New Deal did not create to Tugwell's satisfaction, the instruments of control the era of maintenance required. The NRA, as he saw it in retrospect, was dominated by business, when planning was premised on the irrelevancy of the business structure to a mature industrial society. The AAA contained conflicting political and economic impulses. The Resettlement Administration was forced, among other things, to establish new towns complete in themselves, an effort Tugwell thought out of place in modern society. The 1936 election, Tugwell argued, was a mandate for planning, and the New Deal should get on with it. But by that time, he had become too much a target-of-opportunity for conservatives, the "lightning rod" of the administration. Roosevelt could no longer afford to protect him, even though influential liberals measured FDR's liberalism by the extent of Tugwell's influence. He was kept out of the 1936 campaign and eased out of the government after the election. Besides the taint of "radicalism," which was exaggerated by those who were threatened by his sponsorship of a new food and drug law, Tugwell was most hurt by publicity about his "impatience, intolerance, and conceit." In any case, the New Deal seemed to be taking a definitive turn away from planning and toward the antitrust policies that Thurman Arnold was to be put in charge of. At the time of his departure, Tugwell professed to see both policies as reasonable in the current state of society. "I don't care whether we go ahead and bust the trusts or promote monopoly first and then go ahead and regulate it," he told the audience at his farewell dinner; "the only important thing is to make up our minds which course to pursue and then get to the task." But he consistently thereafter derided the antitrust policy as inadequate. The nature of technological reality required planning.[54]

In April 1938, after a year as a business executive with Charles W. Taussig's American Molasses Company, a brain trust refuge, Tugwell got his first crack at planning when Fiorello LaGuardia appointed him chairman of the New York City Planning Commission. The experience was not a thoroughly happy one, as "politics" continually intruded on disinterested expertise, and the political leader failed once again to protect the experimenter. The syndrome was repeated during his tenure as the appointed Governor of Puerto Rico, 1941-46, where his attempts to insulate expertise from politics and to vest power in single-member commissions were often frustrated.

After his return to academic life, to teach government at the
University of Chicago and later to work at the Center for the
Study of Democratic Institutions, he worked on a frame of
government for a world federation and a new constitution for
the United States, which would, among other things, recognize
planning as a separate governmental function entitled to the
protection of the separation of powers in its own branch. He
continued to fill journals and books with arguments for
planning, though often the arguments were couched in bitter
memoirs of his own experience. The Industrial Discipline and
the Governmental Arts of 1933 remained his last book-length
monograph in the field of economics.[55]

In the years after he left the New Deal, Tugwell adopted
from advanced social-science discourse two analytical tools
or analogies that updated the language of the perception and
the argument of The Industrial Discipline and put the New Deal
in a new perspective. The first was the emergent-additive
distinction used by pragmatists in the late thirties; and the
second, in the late forties, was the "organismic" analogy of
"holistic" and "ecological" thinking. Both restated the
static-unitary perception of society that had made pragmatism
attractive and that had justified the expansion outward from

plans as hypotheses to plans as blueprints. Society, he argued, was an "emergent"; it had a "gestalt"; it was a single "organism"; the whole was something other than the sum of its parts. The whole had to be grasped before anything "positive" could be done in the way of reform. To attack social problems piecemeal, Tugwell argued, was to take only an "additive" or "atomistic" approach, to be merely "progressive," to engage only in regulative as opposed to "directive" or "conjunctural" action, to be merely a "negative" reformer rather than a planner. Regulative was to directive as additive was to emergent, as multilateral was to unilateral, as the New Deal, he had come to believe, was to planning. The emergent and ecological models were attractive partly because, in affirming interdependence, they served as countermyths to the competitive model. In addition, by analogizing the social organism to the biological, they relied on a central "directive" center--the brain for the animal; the planning office for society--to keep the organism from destroying itself. Expert intelligence was the means of holding the world together particularly after Hiroshima demonstrated that total destruction was a real possibility. The new models also allowed the argument that planning was not elitist. In an

organism, all parts were vital to the whole; feedback from
the lower centers was necessary for conjuncture; and therefore a planned society had a sort of "physiological democracy."
It was possible, Tugwell argued, to have a government of consent without affirming equality of ability--"all consenting
to others' doing what they could not do for themselves."
"Operational wholeness" outmoded group conflict of all sorts,
including politics. Planning was to be "superpolitical."
The "leadership system," which Tugwell had vainly relied on
for protection, had to be replaced with institutional safe-
guards consonant with the political neutrality of science.
The "displacement of demagogic romancing" would mark the
modernization of social life.[56]

Tugwell confused the issue somewhat by partaking of the
vitriol directed at John Dewey by some leftists and social
scientists in the late thirties. He accepted the confusing
and misdirected condemnation of Deweyism that used "pluralism" as the label for conflict in society (which technology
had outmoded) and "experiment" as a merely negative technique
aimed at eliminating error. Nevertheless, Tugwell clearly
conceived of planning as pragmatism on a grand scale. The
pluralistic universe was the one in which planning operated.

The master plan in city planning and the development plan in social planning were enlarged versions of the smaller hypotheses that selected the facts relevant to their own success. Direction or conjunctural control "is by nature pragmatic," Tugwell wrote in 1939; and, the following year, he argued that the future "can be created." An artificial "monistic conception of the future"--a plan--was possible because the universe was pluralistic, "emergent," ridden with novelties. The triumph of master planning would be the ultimate triumph of the idea that order had to be imposed, not discovered.[57]

Tugwell's perception of society and the metaphysical model that he applied to that society were thus poles apart. His perception of society as static and unitary made planning seem possible and necessary. Planning was not regimentation, Tugwell could argue, because it was merely a recognition of and a submission to the oneness of nature and technology. The facts dictated, not the planner.[58] Necessity ruled, not an ideology. But planning as a mode of thinking and acting was geared to a model of society that, rather than static-unitary, was pluralistic and ever-changing. Only in such a universe was planning--the conscious creation of the future-- possible. Tugwell's perception led him to attribute to

society a "metaphysical" character the polar opposite of his
perception. George and Bellamy had done the same thing; so
had Addams and Croly in a more fluid period. If their experiences were any guide, Tugwell's arguments would be sup-
portable only as long as the social perception persisted.
When that started to disappear, as it did by the mid-1960's,
the arguments would seem less persuasive, even though they
might be needed more than ever.

The pluralistic universe had been useful in breaking
the intellectual rigidity of entrenched conservatism and in
advocating the investment of power in people with Tugwell's
social and professional interests. Tugwell had condemned
monistic thinking because during its ascendancy "chaos in
industrial life was securely enclosed in a shining case of
theoretical justifications." He had thought that pluralistic
economics had triumphed during the the 1930's because in that
mode of thinking "chaos was at last matched with chaos." But
that was not in fact the match that had been made. It had
been the perception of stasis, not chaos, that had underwritten and given resonance to Tugwell's rejection of
ideology, his utilitarianism, his "pragmatic morality," his
ability to function without ideals, his pluralistic

intellectual structure; and when stasis itself finally came
to seem an illusion, then the intellectual and moral "chaos"
of pragmatism was no longer congenial. Tugwell could not
sympathize, for example, with the revival on many fronts
in the late 1960's and 1970's of a sort of moral absolutism
and "ideological" thinking that he had long considered
archaic. He even preferred to the new idealists those who
admitted to a morality of expediency even when their moralism
was revealed as a cover for illegal operations. And the
revival of a movement for planning, while still minor, was
based on an intellectual structure significantly different
from Tugwell's pragmatism. A world gone out of control would
find no comfort in intellectual "chaos" and "utilitarian
tentatives."[59]

CHAPTER IX

PREVENTIVE JUSTICE

Thurman Arnold

In 1923, Roscoe Pound noted that in "a busy age and
crowded urban, industrial society, with complex economic
organization and minute division of labor," traditional legal
practices conflicted with the need for discretionary power,
the need to apply to each new set of facts the results of the
most recent experience. The law's scope would narrow to
nothing, Pound predicted, and extra-legal agencies would take
its place, if lawyers did not start seeing themselves as
social scientists and social engineers.[1] Fitting the law to
the modern social context required shifting jurisprudence
from a rationalistic science to a pragmatistic one. What
lawyers did, rather than what judges did, had to become the
intellectual model: the active arranging of facts and principles to suit each case. But since practicing lawyers were
partisans with limited concern for larger social issues, the
pivotal figure had to be the legal scholar, whose professional

disinterest allowed the combination of consciousness and
activism that the progressives had recently discovered was
necessary in the modern age.

Thurman Arnold, with a touch of contrariness, called the
combination "opportunism" and expounded it in two books that
came to be seen as the major statements of New Deal political
theory. It was, as he saw it, as far from the pattern of
nineteenth-century reform as an intellectual model could be.
"Philosophy was for them more important than opportunism,"
he said of Edward Bellamy among others, "and so they
achieved in the end philosophy rather than opportunity."[2]
The new model helped prepare liberal lawyers who could take
over from liberal economists in a Second New Deal after 1935;
and it justified a liberal opportunity for more than thirty
years thereafter, until opportunity without philosophy seemed
suddenly to lose its appeal.

I

Thurman Arnold's autobiography, like Rexford Tugwell's
used the pattern of a single life to illustrate the difficulties America faced in adjusting to reality as an industrial
society because of the persistence of values fitted for a

different era. The years of America's coming of age, they
saw in retrospect, were the very years of their own approach
to maturity--the two decades ending in 1912. Born in the
same year as Tugwell, 1891, Arnold also grew up in a small
town the child of a prosperous, independent, and respected
family. But where Tugwell's Sinclairville was a farming community of settled relationships, Arnold's home was Laramie,
Wyoming, a town caught between the desire to "settle down"
and the centrifugal pulls of the isolated cattle ranches,
for which it was only a service center. In his father's
career, Arnold saw that an unsettled society could force the
repression of civilized qualities. In his own early career
in Laramie, however, he found that modernization not only
settled social patterns; it also shifted control of those
patterns away from local elites, so that civilization itself
became stifling.[3]

Like Tugwell's father, Arnold's loomed blindingly large
in his youth. Where Tugwell's mother appeared in her son's
autobiography as an interesting but sometimes troubled
creature to be gently controlled and manipulated by her men,
Arnold's mother did not figure at all in her son's memoirs.
Toward his father, however, he displayed, as a friend

recalled, "an authentic and well-deserved case of hero-worship." Constantine Peter Arnold, a leader of the Wyoming bar, appears to have been a man of extravagant personality, with a special flare for the theater of the courtroom and for the dramatic exaggeration that was one of the mythic modes of discourse in the western landscape. Thurman Arnold apparently admired these qualities in his father, but also felt that "CPA" was limited by his undeveloped environment. The elder Arnold does seem to have exhibited poles in personality which might indicate repressed potential. Pulling against the forced public excesses of the rancher-lawyer was a genuine romanticism that expressed itself in three small volumes of verse, and he was apparently later subject to depression. In Arnold's youth, however, he appeared a supremely self-confident man, successful by any standards, sure of his code of conduct, demanding and judgmental in his treatment of people, and strongly independent--the sort of father a son can flourish under best by imitating from far away.[4]

Thurman Arnold's celebrated irony was perhaps a refined version of his father's exaggeration. It could also have been a way of maintaining distance. Arnold's autobiography itself used irony and humor to avoid revealing much about its author;

and the few surviving letters from his student days--at Princeton, class of 1911, and then at Harvard Law School-- avoided personal matters, presenting instead highly detailed and sarcastic descriptions of social relations. While irony and sarcasm are fitting modes of discourse for one who finds it more congenial to attack certainties than to expound them, they may also be useful in camouflaging intellectual experi- mentation. The inability to tell whether or not the writer is serious allows him to try out ideas without taking full responsibility for them, a weapon that Arnold would later wield to the delight and confusion of many of his readers.

After graduating from Harvard Law, Arnold practiced in Chicago, served reluctantly with the Illinois National Guard at the Mexican border in 1916, and then joined the American war effort in France as an artillery officer. After the war, he joined his father's law office in Laramie, had a brief political career there--one term each as Democratic mayor and state representative--and then in 1927 became Dean of West Virginia University Law School. In 1930, he moved to Yale, from which he took on occasional jobs in the New Deal and wrote his two most famous books. In 1938, he was appointed Assistant Attorney General in charge of the Antitrust

Division, becoming a symbol of the Brandeisianism of the
Second New Deal, and five years later became a Justice of the
Federal Appeals Court for the District of Columbia. He re-
signed from the bench after three years to begin a highly
successful Washington law practice closely aligned with
Democratic interests, which lasted until his death in 1969.

While Arnold did not record his service in World War I
as having had any effect on him, he was apparently strongly
influenced by postwar revisionism. In 1936, in response to
a favorable mention of The Symbols of Government, Arnold wrote
Harry Elmer Barnes, the most prolific and wide-ranging of the
revisionists, that he recalled "very distinctly, when I was
practicing law in Wyoming how your writings on the World War
were the first breath of fresh air which I had had. It completely changed my own point of view because I had been
caught, as most other people had, in the war psychology."
Arnold noted that Barnes's early works had pioneered in using
the "same point of view" that Arnold was then using in his
own books--the scientific, objective viewpoint of an observer
detaching himself from public prejudices. While Barnes's
Genesis of the World War (1926) fueled the general deflation
of "idealism" in the wake of Versailles, "disillusionment"

was too negative a word for both Barnes and Arnold. It implied a resigned passivity that they did not feel would result from the removal of wartime illusions. Since Barnes's
work, like Arnold's, treated all "biological, social, economic, or political" reality as grounded in psychology, the
revelation that high-mindedness did not motivate people, the
contrast between ideals and reality, should, they felt, promote neither passive irrationalism nor active anti-
intellectualism, but rather a liberation that was the first
step toward social control.[5]

Thus, Barnes's praise of the new field of intellectual
history could be seen as defining the task that Arnold and
other analysts of public opinion set for themselves in the
twenties and thirties, as well as defining the audience they
tried to reach. It was, Barnes said, "the most interesting
and promising" of the new histories because it rested upon
"the belief that general opinions and attitudes of mind on
the part of the educated classes are the chief unifying and
causative factors in historical development." The "vital
classification of society," he wrote, should be into that of
"the able, intelligent, informed and experienced, on the one
hand, and the mediocre, stupid, ignorant, and incompetent on

the other," because the unprecedented complexity of modern
society required the preeminence of expertise as much in
economic and political matters, where the people were resisting it, as in medicine, science, and technology, where they
were not. The vitality of elitism could be asserted by contrasting "scientifically"--through the new anthropology--the
persistent primitivism of the former fields with the modernism of the latter. Thus the adoption of the "scientific attitude," the anthropological-psychological point of view in
political and economic theory would constitute, for both
Barnes and Arnold, the modernization of intellectual life.[6]

The unmasking of idealism affected Arnold at the same
time that modernization reached Laramie. He was ready to
leave the town in 1926 when the call from West Virginia came
because, he recalled, of his growing realization that the
town's pioneer phase had ended in an unexpected and ugly way.
He saw in his law practice that Wyoming had been drawn into,
and become the victim of, invisible, impersonal, and complex
webs of dependence whose control was in distant centers. In
addition, he felt that the new system was marked by stagnation and standardization, by the absence of variety and
pluralism, and by a sense of being closed in, even in the

wide open spaces of the West. The opportunities in this static and interdependent society would come to those closest to the centers of power and to those whose expertise would allow them to claim a corner on at least one method of understanding its complex organization.[7]

II

Between 1912 and 1933 academics moved from the periphery to the center of social reform efforts in America, and in launching a career as an academic lawyer, Arnold was also launching a career as a reformer. Soon after his return to Laramie after the war, he had become a prime mover in an effort to establish a law school at the University of Wyoming. The school was begun in 1920 with fourteen students and half a dozen part-time faculty and administrators, including Arnold himself. In the 1920's, at Wyoming and West Virginia, he endorsed and even proposed to exceed the recommendations of the American Bar Association and the Association of American Law Schools for raising entrance requirements to both law school and the bar.[8]

The twentieth-century movement for further professionalization of the old liberal callings was complex in motivation and effect. The desires to limit access to certain classes and to detach one's livelihood from public control no doubt were as strong in many cases as the desire to raise the standards of practice and the calibre of practitioners. But Arnold had no substantial stake in the former category of motives, and in any case, the arguments for professionalization through formal schooling tied to universities, were phrased in some words and not in others; and the spread of the movement, as well as the persuasiveness of its arguments, depended upon things other than the internal dynamics of the profession itself. They depended, at least in part, on their relevance to prevailing social perceptions. The attack on the apprenticeship system of legal education, still regarded as a bulwark of democracy, especially in a state like Wyoming, which had had no law school until 1920, could be laid only to the fact that "the times have changed." The world, Arnold noted, was different from his father's. "The great complexity of modern legal regulations," he wrote in 1923, "requires for the proper performance of legal services lawyers of broad general education and thorough legal training. The legal education which was fairly adequate under simpler economic conditions is inadequate today."[9]

As Arnold conceived it, professionalization was a reform of society at large partly because, in tying legal training to universities and having a faculty devoted to research,
he was elevating the law above the status of both trade and
profession and treating it instead as a social science.
More important, he was treating it as a science that comported
with the distinctive character of modern society. Historic
jurisprudence, the "science of the law," had always claimed
to be a social science, a body of rules governing the legal
order in general and not simply the outcome of litigation.
The legal science that Arnold was taking for granted in urging
professionalization (and that made professionalization seem
natural) had fewer pretensions. The complexity of modern
society wrote a vast new program for legal research, demanding specialization and expertise: a concentration of effort
and a limiting of scope, an abandonment of claims to the
truth of any attempt to synthesize society as a whole with a
single methodology. It also denied in turn the reliability
of simple common sense, which seemed just a label for limited
experience, limited observation, and limited research.[10]

Arnold's assumptions derived largely from the work of
Roscoe Pound, who had arrived at Harvard Law School as a

teacher in 1910, the year before Arnold arrived there as a
student. While Arnold was enrolled, Pound taught two required courses in Equity, which Arnold took with him, and a
third-year elective in Jurisprudence and Law Reform in
America. In the same years, he published his promise of a
summa, "The Scope and Purpose of Sociological Jurisprudence,"
which discovered and promoted a revolution in modes of
thinking about law analogous to the revolution promoted by
the institutional economists who trained Rexford Tugwell.
Pound's essay rejected the notion that the law was a complete
and consistent set of logical precepts that governed society
the way the set of natural laws was thought to govern the
material universe. Instead, he urged the less pretentious
study of the law as a branch of sociology, as one among many
methods of social control.[11]

Sociological jurisprudence was the explicit expression
of pragmatism in law, and it was the attribution to society
of the pluralistic universe that made this program of research
seem identical with a program of reform. There was a telling
confusion in the jurist's use of the term "teleological"
that nicely illustrated the identification. On the one hand,
it was applied to research as a synonym for functional

analysis--a technically inaccurate use, but common in modern sociology and biology--what Lester Ward and Albion Small had originally meant by "genetic." On the other hand, "teleological" was used in the Dynamic Sociologists' more precise sense: the ability to fulfill chosen purposes. To impose chosen purposes on a moving stream of events was the obverse of the sociological researchers' use of hypotheses in understanding current legal institutions and in finding a fruitful sociological legal history. It was the expression of Ward's elevation of "conation" over "cognition," the rise of the pragmatic will over the limitations of rationalism.

Pound's analysis of the historic schools of jurisprudence, their origins and roles, and their rooting in the context of their times, clearly tied to his own school to a particular perception of social transition. As Pound saw it, the distinctive modernity of industrial society had undermined the persuasiveness of the older system of mechanical deduction from rules authenticated by centuries of historic use. And the increasing complexity of modern industrial organization and the variety and continual novelty of its conflicting interests demanded the flexibility offered by methodological pluralism. For Pound, the sense of a society in the making, rather than fully made, with a future partly known and partly unknown, made the law an instrument for the social "control" of a moving stream rather than for either the simple discovery and application of preexisting principles or the manipulation of a static existential condition.[12]

In addition, like the early institutionalists--indeed like his progressive contemporaries--Pound's thinking contained dualisms that were relevant to a period of transition but that a period of "maturity" would regard as unnecessary. His sense of the illegitimacy of certainty and absolutes was balanced by his simultaneous refusal to reject the desire for authentic values as governing forces in legal decisions or in the hypotheses that effected teleological reform itself. It was balanced as well by his search for ways to give authority to the popular conception of substantive justice. He later resolved the dualism by dividing the law itself into two fields, one requiring certainty, the other requiring flexibility. He opposed the idea that legal rules could be deduced from certain existing social "facts" or perceptions, such as, in the twenties, "interdependence," because, he said, he favored empiricism over deduction even in details; and yet his empiricism was not the historical relativism of the

New Deal generation. He went to history and comparative
studies not for the purpose of finding facts that fitted
consciously chosen preconceptions, but to give some degree of
authenticity to hypotheses about values. As well, his sense
of historic continuity, even of evolutionary progress, was
very strong.[13]

Arnold, Tugwell, and their allies differed from their
mentors in what they were willing to live without--the theoretical certainty and authenticity that Patten and Pound
could not completely abandon, the limitation on the total
freedom that the mentors' pragmatism otherwise seemed to
promise and which was undeniably present in the attribution
to society of the pluralism of the universe. From the perspective of the younger generation, it was the flexibility
to meet modern problems that seemed the contribution of the
pre-World War I thinkers, and it was the remnants of the
monistic modes of thought, the residual desires for authenticity and certainty, that seemed to outdate them. It was
the mentors who had noted the conflict between the pluralistic universe and the rigidity of economic and legal scholar-
ship, and the protegés who wanted the conflict fought to a
conclusion. That conflict determined the character of the

legal reform movements of the late 1910's and 1920's, which can be seen as the bridge between the two reform generations. Professionalization as Arnold conceived it was one such movement. Arnold became active in others, and the continuity among them might be expressed by classifying them together under the label "preventive justice."

The label was Pound's[14] and though he used it in a restricted sense he did apply it to proposals for law reform whose major element was part of a larger reform tendency. That was the attempt to provide the methodological pluralism that could satisfy the distinctive and complicated demands of modern society. Indeed, his initial concern had been to give such flexibility to jurisprudence and thereby revive the role in social engineering that changing times had begun to transfer from the law to other institutions. Pound repeatedly referred to a dualism in law resulting from conflicting tendencies toward what he called in 1913 "the technical" and the "discretionary," and, in the 1920's, "generaliation" and "individualization." The problem was to what extent cases should be referred to general categories and then decided according to fixed rules whatever the affront to common standards of justice and to what extent each case should be treated as unique and decided with reference to its special

facts. Pound noted that in his own time there was a tendency toward greater discretion or individualization and that
such a tendency had always been the result of the pressures
of transition to a new age. The nineteenth-century attempt
to reduce both substantive law and procedure to rules that
could be applied mechanically to every situation, he wrote,
had made the court system extremely rigid, unable to individualize or to reflect a distinctively modern social
ethic similar to Jane Addams's: "the ideal of social
justice of the twentieth century." It also denied the
courts the ability to handle the distinctively modern questions to which the old rules did not apply and to handle
them with the speed demanded by their impact in complex
conditions.[15]

Thus, at least partly because of "the increasing
complexity of life" and the law's failure to deal with
it, the people were turning to what Pound called "justice
without law," "executive justice" and, later, "administration" (as opposed to "adjudication"), "preventive
justice" (as opposed to "remedial" justice), and government
of men. Equity, which had been the judicial system's own
remedy for excessive "generalization" in an earlier period,

had itself been reduced to a fixed set of rules, making it
as rigid as the law itself, and so a new set of institutions
had arisen outside the courts. That was always true of
periods of transition, Pound noted, and it accounted for the
rise of commissions and administrative tribunals with summary powers in the period just before World War I. Pound
did not approve such a thorough passage of power away from
the courts, however, and he did not regard it as an inevitably increasing trend. Using the progressive dual standard,
he favored "judicial justice" because it combined "the possibilities of certainty and of flexibility better than any
other form of administering justice." He thought that sociological jurisprudence could break the rigidity of the
courts and give them back the flexibility to do many of
the things the commissions had taken on by default, until a
better balance among the two sets of institutions could be
achieved.[16]

As a reform movement, preventive justice clearly aimed
at flexibility in "procedure" at least as much as in "substantive law." Indeed, sociological jurisprudence saw "the
limitations upon effective legal action" as much in the law's
machinery as in its rules or "substance." In terms of

intellectual structure, sociological jurisprudence made no greater separation between procedure and substance than mechanical jurisprudence did. The latter had rigidified procedure the way it had rigidified substance into a set of rules whose smallest violation could determine the outcome of a case as forcefully as could the substantive question. The former treated both as processes, as instruments, whose use had to be geared to the social and individual facts of the case and so had to remain discretionary. Pound noted that the real reason modern society turned to administrative commissions was less the rigidity of "the law" than the time-consuming complications of court procedure.[17]

Rexford Tugwell and Thurman Arnold had identical feelings about the law's use and potential. In his only major achievement as a Wyoming legislator, Arnold took a lesson from Pound in authoring an abatement bill under which certain laws could be enforced through equity proceedings initiated by offended private parties rather than by officers of the law. The bill sought to rescue "judicial justice" from the charge of uncertainty and weakness--since juries and prosecutors might refuse to enforce or convict if the law (prohibition, for instance) was unpopular. At the same time, it

would give the law the flexibility Arnold repeatedly admired
in the British tradition of private prosecution.[18]   But where
Pound would retain his faith in judicial justice because of
inherent values he found in the law as a system, both Tugwell
and Arnold would willingly seek flexibility elsewhere when
the courts seemed to persist in their obsession with certainty. They did not share Pound's desire for a balance
between certainty and flexibility in the courts; they were
willing to live without the former in order to secure the
latter.

There was nothing inherently conservative in the procedural reform aspect of the movement for preventive justice.
It was just an attempt to enable the court system to deal
with a complicated form of social life. Nor was it solely
an intra-professional reform. The increasing number of
cases, the long delays in coming to trial, the turning of
decisions on complicated technicalities, and the statement
of principles adversely affecting unrepresented parties,
made court machinery in the first third of the century an
obstacle to fluidity in society; and so reform of the
"tyranny of procedure" could be as liberal as any other.[19]

The contention that procedural reform is inherently

conservative depends upon attributing to procedural reformers
a maxim to the effect that there is no substantive social
problem that cannot be solved by a change in legal (or political) procedure (or the more venal assumption that reforms of
legal procedure divert attention from substantive social
problems). But neither the progressives nor the preventive
justice reformers subscribed to such a maxim. It had some
credence in mechanical jurisprudence, which identified itself with political theory and regarded "substantive law"
as a set of quasi-natural laws. In that conception, the
"science of law" was the, not a, science of society, and it
was separate from the practical "art" of litigation, which
dealt with the rules and procedures of legal institutions
alone. But sociological jurisprudence reduced the pretensions of substantive law to a set of rules relevant only to
the conduct and decision of controversies reaching the courts.
It was not the same as the "substance" of society and therefore had no greater fundamentality than procedure. The sociological jurist had two goals: to increase the range of
things the courts included when considering the merits of a
case, which focused on appellate courts and substantive law;
and to get the courts to decide cases on their merits, which

focused on trial courts and the rules of procedure. In both
cases, the goal was the flexibility, the methodological
pluralism, that modern society needed and that the people
were demanding and getting in administrative tribunals. The
courts were not to stand in the way of either justice, as the
people newly defined it, or progress. But they could not--
not yet at least--be left out in the cold.

III

Like his father, Thurman Arnold was primarily concerned
with the trial process. He had been a trial lawyer in
Wyoming, and he taught trial methods at West Virginia and
Yale. In 1936, he produced an innovative casebook on the
subject.[20] He was naturally most concerned with court procedure, and his role in the movement for preventive justice
in West Virginia was notable in two areas: simplification of
code and common-law pleadings, and the establishment of a
state judicial council. Both reflected the concern for flexibility, for bringing law into closer coordination with a
pluralistic "reality." Arnold limited his early focus to
legal reform--no more limited in scope than an economist's
concentration on economic reform, considering the nature of

American institutions--until he came to believe that there
might be something inherent in the courts as an institution
that precluded the methodological pluralism needed for social
management, at which time he carried the effort and the analysis over to a larger field.

In both of his preventive justice efforts, Arnold at
West Virginia was following the lead of Roscoe Pound, but
especially of Charles E. Clark of Yale Law School (later
Chief Justice of the Second Circuit Court of Appeals) and
Edson R. Sunderland of the University of Michigan. Clark
was a prime mover in the major procedural reform of the
century, the Federal Rules of Civil Procedure of 1937. For
both Clark and Sunderland, as for Pound and Arnold, the impact of legal procedure on the life of society was as great
as when Jeremy Bentham had first distinguished between
"adjective" and "substantive law." While "mere procedure"
was said to be only a "means" and not an "end," in everyday
life the distinction was not so clear. Since the courts
dealt with controversies, the rules governing the presentation of a case could have a determining impact on its outcome.
"Pleadings" was the "science" of the rules for identifying
contested facts and issues. Its purpose was to save the

court's time by forcing the parties to limit their focus,
present juries with simple alternatives, and allow judges to
find and apply the appropriate substantive rule easily and
efficiently. By the early twentieth century, the forms had
become so rigid that they were defeating the ends of justice.
Cases were being decided on technicalities of pleadings instead of on the merits; trials were being delayed by the
ritual exchange of endless pieces of paper; the determination
of the issue or disputed facts was in many instances a fiction contradicting the interests of both parties; and the
limitations on joinder prevented disposition of cases that
should have been tried together. When people complained of
legal technicalities, they were often complaining of pleadings. Clark's proposal for modernization, considered the
most important procedural reform of the 1920's, was the summary judgment, in which a decision was entered without trial
if after the filing of affidavits it was clear that there
was no real defense to the plaintiff's claim. The reform
aimed at efficiency and flexibility by increasing the discretionary power of judges.[21]

Arnold's proposals for West Virginia included such a
motion-for-judgment procedure, simple "notice pleading" (as

opposed to drawn-out attempts to reach specifics) and liber-
alization of rules for joinder that similarly increased the
discretionary or administrative abilities of the courts.
The only way to keep pleadings simple, he argued, was to
make it "comparatively unimportant," and to give the courts
the power to control it. Similarly, he would solve the problems of joinder by ignoring archaisms derived from trial by
combat (in which only one issue could be tried at a time because a man could not be both a loser and a winner) and giving the judge the discretionary power to decide joinder
solely on the basis of trial convenience. Discretion,
Arnold analogized, "is fundamentally the reason why football
games, in spite of a volume of complicated rules, can nevertheless be played without several days of preliminary adjudication. The contesting teams must trust the umpire instead
of the rules. The emphasis is on getting the game played."[22]

Arnold's argument for judicial discretion, like Clark's
and Sunderland's, was grounded on the attribution of pluralism to the social order. The possibility of continual novelties required flexible procedures. Logic, which Edward
Bellamy had relied on as the source of all advance, Arnold
saw as inconsistent with reality and as an obstacle to

progress. In a constantly changing world, he wrote,the belief that logic reflected reality resulted in confusion, for
a logical system could account for novelties only with epi-
cycles of thought; and so the law should abandon "the attempt to provide in advance for all contingencies." The
ability to get along without rules of procedure was the attraction of administrative tribunals and regulatory commissions. The concern, Clark and Sunderland had repeatedly
argued, should be with the "product," not the process; the
consequence, not the premise. Judges should likewise be regarded as experts and allowed to function more freely in
satisfying society's standards of justice and law. Arnold
was asking for "government of men" in the sphere where
"government of laws" was enshrined.[23]

The need for procedural pragmatism to cope with a
pluralistic universe also underlay Arnold's other major proposal, the judicial council. The council movement originated
in nineteenth-century English reforms, and the modern movement was sparked by Roscoe Pound and Benjamin Cardozo.
Arnold came to it by way of Sunderland. The goal was to find
a method of keeping procedure continually abreast of unexpected social changes and of the lessons learned from the

changing experience under any set of rules.[24] No one questioned "the need for modernizing our methods," Sunderland
wrote, to make them suit "the growing complexities" of modern
society. But lawyers and judges had a professional stake in
keeping archaic procedures complicated and mysterious, and
so the source of change had to be disinterested outsiders.
To prevent flagrant discrepancies between theory and reality,
Sunderland proposed a ministry of justice on the continental
model, a political office with public accountability for
legal administration to make rules for court procedure.
Sunderland would take the rule-making power away from the
courts because they had a tendency either to ignore the problem or to devise rigid solutions. Similarly, he opposed
legislative control of procedure not because it would be too
liberal, but precisely because it could not be pragmatistic.
Legislative control was sporadic, ill informed, tended
toward detail and rigidity, and was detached from practice.
"[E]fficient methods are the joint product of technical training and practical experience," he wrote. Legislative rules
would "not grow spontaneously out of the exact requirements
of actual practice. . . . Procedure requires constant attention, and no method of regulation will suffice which cannot

function steadily."[25]

No ministries of justice were established in the United States, but eleven states had Judicial Councils by 1929. Clark was a member of Connecticut's, and Sunderland regarded them as viable compromises between court-made rules and political ministries of justice. The typical council contained judges, practicing lawyers, and academics to recommend rules of procedure to the judges, who kept the final rule-making power. Arnold's plan for West Virginia, which he cleared with Sunderland, included two significant innovations. First, the law school of West Virginia University was to serve as a permanent research staff for the council, which would move the academic into the center of legal reform under the guise of scientist. And second, the council itself was to have the power to make the rules, not just to recommend changes to the courts. It would have been the judicial version of the regulatory commission. Those who, as disinterested experts, kept surveillance over reality, also had to be given control over it. Consciousness and activity had to be united.[26]

In setting up trial convenience as the determining factor of court procedure, Arnold was identifying efficiency

with "individualization." The two were not in opposition.
"Efficiency" was not necessarily a new formalism. Indeed,
efficiency of procedure was not the rigid imposition of rules
and regulations, however "practical," but the opposite:
functionalism or experimentalism, what Arnold later liked to
call "opportunism." The dichotomy was, as Sunderland expressed it, between "efficiency" and "regularity." Regularity meant obedience to rules and forms; efficiency, the disregard of rules and forms so that the courts could focus on
the goal of justice in particular cases. Procedure would
be made efficient not through formalism, but through flexibility for pragmatic adaptation to individual sets of facts.[27]

In fact, efficiency in procedure was, far from a new
rationalism, the counterpart of the methodological or intellectual pluralism introduced by sociological jurisprudence.
In its most general terms, the law, as Arnold conceived and
practiced it, was a perfect field for someone for whom a
pluralistic intellectual structure was congenial. On the
level of trial practice, at which Arnold excelled, the
preparation and presentation of a variety of cases afforded
the psychic satisfactions of particularization and "occasional" thinking. For Arnold, the law was litigation. On

the academic level, the proliferation and upgrading of law
reviews--which Arnold promoted at both Wyoming and West
Virginia--provided a medium for striking out in various directions with brief jabs and experimental forays occasioned
by recent events, by legislation, or by judicial decisions.
They made "opportunistic" intellectual effort possible and
respectable in the law for those who found elaborately
logical treatises uncongenial. Efficiency in action was
opportunistic or experimental control by experts. Efficiency in intellectual life was, similarly, not streamlined
and rigid thinking, but the abandonment of unitary truths
and monistic intellectual structures.

The same considerations--efficiency as individualization,
pluralism, and "opportunism"--affected Arnold's more technical thinking about issues of substantive law. An analysis
of the law of criminal attempts, for example, his first such
effort, was a case study of the confusion created by generalization and abstraction in an area of the law requiring individualization and concreteness. "Criminal attempts" as a
field dealt with society's desire to punish attempts at certain crimes even though they did not succeed. Under the influence of mechanical jurisprudence, this desire had led to

an obsession with the definition of an "attempt" in general
apart from the particular crime attempted, producing a series
of decisions whose absurdity Arnold's irony effectively dis-
closed.[28]

Arnold was attacking the very animus of mechanical
jurisprudence, which inhibited judicial opportunism by seeking a monistic intellectual structure to cover all areas of
human behavior. Because the generalizations of mechanical
jurisprudence resulted from a process of abstraction from
particular cases, the result had to be totally arbitrary, he
argued; they ignored the probability of novelties; and so
their application to new cases had to result in hopeless
confusion. Once begun, the processes of logic and generalization escalated into "a cumbersome metaphysical machine,"
and could be ended only by ignoring the abstractions and
giving judges the discretion to decide whether the policy
of a statute or of a common law prohibition should cover the
facts of a particular attempt at a crime. General concepts
had to be regarded solely as rhetorical instruments for presenting particular sets of facts, Arnold asserted. The
weight of authority need not burden judges "if they prefer
a more realistic treatment."[29]

At bottom, Arnold believed, the refusal to regard legal labels instrumentally, rather than as names for some pre-existing reality, derived from the refusal to admit that people could live without certainty and that generalization was a habit of mind that the world could safely abandon. It was a refusal, he noted, that characterized not only criminal law, which was squarely in the common-law tradition, but equity as well, one of whose original functions had been to provide flexibility to handle novel situations. Arnold criticized Austin Scott's draft Restatement of the Law of Trusts, for example, on the grounds that it fell into all the traps laid by the desire for logical certainty and for a monistic structure--"a seamless web"--for the law. Scott's "definitional" or "conceptual" approach, Arnold argued, wrongly assumed that a legal concept--in this case the trust-- really governed society and therefore that its disparate uses had to be logically reconciled. Arnold proposed in its place a "descriptive" or functional approach, which regarded the concept as a verbal device useful only for certain purposes in particular types of litigation. Only such a approach could restore to equity the flexibility it was intended to have. "Of course, a descriptive restatement of the law will not

have the appearance of a set of rules, because the inevitable
uncertainties in the law will appear without concealment."
But the sacrifice of certainty would give the courts the
freedom to treat novel cases. There was no sense, Arnold
said, in putting "modern ideas and current problems in the
garb of ancient language."[30]

                              IV

    Arnold reclassified trusts into two functional categor-
ies[31] in a grudging attempt to show the logical classifiers
how the problems of generalization could be eased with a
"teleological" (in this case, really genetic or functional)
viewpoint. The attempt was grudging because, at bottom,
Arnold was questioning the whole tendency toward generalization. He wanted to extend modernization--the ability to
live without fixed rules and authenticated certainties--from
procedure to substantive law; and that involved an entirely
different view of the real world from the one that inspired
the search for rules. Indeed, Scott's response to Arnold,
indicated that the opponents were talking across each other
and using incompatible intellectual structures. As Thomas
Reed Powell, a Harvard ally of Arnold's, wrote him, he and

Scott had different universes of discourse.[32]   Powell was
among the twenty jurists whom Karl Llewellyn had examined
in order to define the ideas of a "rising generation" of
jurists given the label "legal realists." Llewellyn counted
Arnold's articles on Criminal Attempts and the Restatement
of Trusts among those that had to be examined for the "common points of departure" of the movement.[33]

Some of the language, concepts, and historical under-
pinnings ultimately used by the realists in defining and demanding the radical modernization of legal and political
thought during the 1930's derived from a series of lectures
delivered by the historian Carl Becker at the Yale Law
School in April 1931. Later published as <u>The Heavenly City</u>
<u>of the Eighteenth-Century Philosophers</u>, Becker's lectures
were based on the idea that the persuasiveness of arguments
depended upon the universe of discourse or intellectual struc-
ture--Becker used the phrase "climate of opinion"--in which
they were conducted. He contrasted two such universes, the
medieval and the modern; and he set the advent of the latter
at so recent a point in time that even those who were ordinarily taken as its progenitors--the philosophers of the
Enlightenment--were revealed as sharing the medieval mode.

The contrast between reason and faith usually employed to distinguish the thirteenth century from the eighteenth, Becker argued, was invalid. Both periods were thoroughly rationalistic and both supplemented reason with a passionate faith that gave authenticity and authority to the "old absolutes" on which their world-systems were based. In contrast to the premise that there was an essential order to the universe discoverable by reason, the "modern mind" saw that the world was in fact "a continuous flux, a ceaseless and infinitely complicated process of waste and repair." Consequently, the "modern climate of opinion" was "factual rather than rational"; it had little use for theology or philosophy or logic or theory. It did not need first prin-ciples, so it did not need passionate faith to authenticate them. "The atmosphere which sustains our thought," Becker observed, "is so saturated with the actual that we can easily do with a minimum of the theoretical." Becker's anti-rationalism did not, of course, include a hostility to science. Indeed, the choice was between "reason" and "science." The modern substitute for theology was the "historical approach"--by which Becker meant the genetic or functional method. The substitute for philosophy was the "scientific approach"--detached and disinterested observation of facts rather than their rationalization or generalization. Science was for a pluralistic universe, the real universe; reason was for a mythical monistic universe. Becker saw science in a pragmatistic mold, the substitution of "will" and control for mere cogitation, for the latter embodied universalism and therefore, as he saw it, determinism.[34]

Becker's attack on determinism indicated that he saw modern thought not only in a historical context, but in a political one as well. The complete modernization of social thought would be more than a prescription for reform; it would also be an antidote to revolution. Both the French and the Russian Revolutions, he claimed, derived from rationalistic pretensions, from an attempt to do too much with reason, and from the claim that a universal philosophy could be put into practice. Because rationalism was always accompanied by some passion--as opposed to "science," which could be objective, detached, and disinterested--Marxism, like medievalism and Enlightenment, could not escape religiosity, dogmatism, theological argument, millenialism, saints, ceremony, and ritual--things whose power over the masses Becker found repulsive. The discovery that the most modern

of revolutions was actually medieval in its foundations implied either that modernism was inherently impotent or that
it was incomplete. The message for modernists like Arnold
was clear. Find a method of propagating modernism in the
interests of reform, or face a revolution.

The first and the most graphic exposition of the modernist's intellectual structure for the sake of legal reform had
been Jerome Frank's widely circulated Law and the Modern Mind,
published in late 1930. Frank's underlying concern, like
Thurman Arnold's, was the problem of individualization versus
generalization. Frank brought to the surface the incompatibility of the two, the metaphysical impossibility, for example,
of Pound's attempt to retain both, to allot to each its own
sphere in an attempt to express that combination of continuity
and change, relativity and absolutism, flexibility and certainty, that had been fitting for an age of transition. To
Frank it was evident that the two were geared to different
and exclusive universes. The universe of generalization was
the orderly universe of Newton and mechanical jurisprudence,
of preexisting and essential absolutes, of certainty and
universals. The universe of individualization was the
pragmatist's universe of chance, novelty, and unpredictability,

of, at best, "modest probabilities." "Modern civilization,"
Frank said, required the acceptance of the pragmatist's universe as the real one.[35]

In jurisprudence, Frank argued, pragmatism meant that
the law was what happened in trial courts, that law was by
definition judicial conduct in litigation, that rules were
at best hypotheses and fictions (and more often mere ration-
alizations of hunches), and that judging, whatever its pretensions, involved discretion and individualization. It
meant that the distinction between procedure and substance
was not useful. All cases--all combinations of facts--had
to be seen as novel; rules were abstractions from facts and
therefore imperfect and constantly upset by novelties.
"Experience reveals," he noted, "the fact that concrete situations are always individual, so that truth with respect
to them is always relative." Monistic intellectual structures based on a monistic universe had to be replaced with
a pluralistic intellectual structure based on a pluralistic
universe. As Frank analyzed recent legal thinking, the
limitations of Pound, Cardozo, and other apparent modernizers
(Holmes alone was a model realist) derived from their failure
to make the changeover complete.[36]

Like Arnold's, Frank's view belied the idea that efficiency was a new formalism, that it somehow was a flaw in
modern liberalism. Efficiency was individualization, flexibility, a focus on particulars, on novelties and tentative-
ness. Its opposite was the attempt at regularity, uniformity,
and certainty in the law. Efficiency, geared to a pragmatistic universe, and theoretical certainty, geared to a
rationalistic universe, could not be achieved together. And
modern man had to learn to live without certainty. He had to
be free to act. The persistent myth that the law could be or
was in fact certain and predictable Frank laid to the sublim-
ation of childish attitudes toward the all-knowing father.
To immature minds, the law was a father-substitute. But
modern life, he argued, looking to William James, required an
emotionally mature adult, one who was flexible, adaptable,
realistic, and experimental, one who delighted in contingency
and uncertainty. The mature adult in modern society had to
be, in effect, an opportunist, a person whose consciousness
of self liberated him from the bonds of authority, whose
self-confidence and self-authority, indeed adventurous
arrogance, substituted for the false certainty of a monistic
universe.

Arnold praised Frank's book for its dismissal of the childish need for certainty. He wrote Frank that he particularly liked his praise of Leon Green, who had advised Arnold on legal reform, as "one of the most clearheaded yet subtle exponents of the new realistic school."[37] Green had bluntly asserted in 1929, when made Dean of Northwestern's law school, that the pragmatistic attribution of pluralism to the modern world made intellectual opportunism the only sound and congenial stance for lawyers. Life, he had observed, was "neither controlled nor protected by rules." The modern substitution of science and expertise for political methods of control deprived legal rules of their authenticity, exposed the uselessness of most of them in modern society, and treated them at best as instruments for selecting facts and justifying decisions often made on other grounds. Law had to be conceived, he had argued, as simply the power of certain institutions to pass judgments on human conduct that were acceptable for the time and place in which they were made. The law was only a set of procedures, and the good jurist was the one who knew how to manipulate them. The great judges and the great lawyers in modern times would be the great opportunists. "Thus, the emphasis changes from the rule

as an instrumentality to the individual as an instrumentality,"
Green had said, "and instead of having 'a government of laws'
as the corollary political slogan suggests, we have a 'government of men.'"[38]

Arnold's acceptance of Frank's dismissal of certainties
as childish and of Green's deflation of substantive law into
an aspect of procedure only heightened a major problem that
had grown out of the initial thrust of sociological jurisprudence. That was not simply the problem of how judges should
make decisions if rules were demystified--the focus of much
contemporary criticism of the realists. It was also, to the
extent that legal realists identified themselves as social
reformers, as most did, the problem of the locus of their own
concern with the legal process in the program of social analysis as a whole. Sociological jurisprudence had deflated substantive law effectively. Though there were strong differences over the necessity for and the ability to attain predictability and certainty in the law, there was agreement
among the "rising generation" that the pretensions of "substantive law" to being the governor of society outside the
courts--the natural laws of society--were nonsense. Given
that agreement, indeed given the escalating attack on the

notion of substantive law, the continued exclusive focus on
the internal processes of the courts vitiated the realists'
social concerns. Legal realists like Llewellyn, Green, and
Frank displayed a concern with the legal process as if it were
the whole of society, which belied their dismissal of the fundamentalists' conception of the legal order. The realization of
this "mistake," of the narrowness of this concern with the
"law" as what the courts did, of the fact that the realists
and sociological jurists, for all their realism, were imitating the arrogance of mechanical jurists, came slowly, emerging
in clear form only once the New Deal had gotten under way. It
never emerged fully: that was part of the impact of professionalization in such socially pivotal disciplines as law and
economics. But tendencies toward it had appeared earlier, in
a reduction of the importance of the courts, if not of the law
itself.

In West Virginia, for example, while working to restore
flexibility to the judicial process, Arnold, unlike Pound in
1913, had a strong sense that the control of many of the
cases that had passed out of the courts should not be given
back to them. The social pressures for preventive justice
had enlarged extra-judicial agencies, and that could not be

reversed. There were, he was discovering, limits to legal reform inherent in the courts as institutions, and there consequently should be limits to the kinds of issues that courts should decide for society. No matter how flexible and practical pleadings were made, for example, and no matter how much discretion was given the judge, the court's function was to settle only those issues that were presented by the litigants. This function had two consequences for Arnold's liberalism and professionalism. The first and most important was that a decision was ordinarily based on the rights and obligations of the litigants alone, even though the people most affected by it might be the vast majority who were not parties to the case. The concern for the representation of the unrepresented, which Llewellyn said was characteristic of the realists, connected Arnold's professional focus on judicial processes to the problem of social reform--the inequitable distribution of wealth and power-- and it remained an overriding concern, through his later antitrust activities for Roosevelt. Second, and correctively, the court was an adjudicating and not an investigating institution, a fact that determined its procedures in individual cases and limited its role in society. The court was a

passive institution--though passive aggression was not
uncommon--it could not conduct its own research and it had a
commitment to consistency that prevented methodological
pluralism. It was hard for courts to change their minds.[39]

The consequences of these two insights, taken together,
was a growing sense of the limited role of the "law," as
what the courts do, in society and an increasing approval
of that limitation. The law, if broadly conceived as government, could remain pivotal--more particularly, politically
active and socially conscious legal scholars could become
pivotal--but the function of judicial bodies was to be limited
to the adjudication of disputes, and Arnold protested any attempted enlargement beyond that function to include investigation, administration, or regulation. Those tasks--by far
the larger share of legal and political affairs--belonged to
the activist.[40]

Even before the New Deal began, however, and he became
active in its defense, Arnold found that this stratification
of roles was working to the benefit of the institution he had
hoped to restrict. And it became increasingly clear after
1933 that the courts had been able to use their rather per-
ipheral function--the settlement of the exceptional disputes

that happened to come to trial--to acquire a strategic position in keeping the functions they could not perform from
being performed at all. It was particularly irritating that
the judiciary had become the arena of appeal from the decisions of regulatory agencies; and that court procedure--
passivity until a case arose, decision of only one issue at
a time, settlement of the rights of only the immediate parties,
determination of the relevant facts and issues by the parties
themselves, the difficulty of reversal--meant that administrative actions were always under a cloud, often even after
a case had been decided. Moreoever, in those instances in
which the court was finally settling such issues, it was usually declaring that opportunism--freedom of action--was inconsistent with accepted legal-political theories and social
ideals.[41]

In a series of ironic and increasingly angry articles
that he drew together into The Symbols of Government in 1935,
Arnold traced this persistent imperialism of generalization
over individualization to the court's use of the ideals of
"substantive law" and "law enforcement" to make its decisions
acceptable to litigants, in the process convincing society at
large (potential litigants) that it was a governing

institution. To deflate the court's importance, Arnold argued that "substantive law" had no fundamentality, that it was merely the language in which lawyers presented their cases, and that it did not govern human conduct outside of courts. He argued that even if "law enforcement" was a governing ideal, it was not the courts that governed, but the prosecutors, because they had the ability to individualize, to decide which behavior would be brought to trial. He argued that the two ideals involved a desire for certainty and predictability that were dangerous and irrelevant to modern society, and that the court was using the ideals in a "romantic" attempt to obstruct "pragmatic" or benevolent action by the government. He argued that "theory" and "idealism" in general, with their demands for logical consistency and their pretensions to universalism, could never be reliable guides to actions because the real world was a pluralistic world of chance and novelty. Only where theory and idealism were ignored could there be efficiency--individualization, opportunism, the experimental matching of means to ends.[42]

Thus nearly every paradox, conflict, and distinction in The Symbols of Government expressed the dichotomy of preventive justice, between individualization, flexibility, administration, government of men, practical necessity, convenience, and pluralistic reality, on the one hand, and on the other, generalization, rigidity, adjudication, government of laws, theoretical certainty, moral universals, and idealistic monism. Unlike Jane Addams and Herbert Croly and Roscoe Pound (and Arnold himself in his early abatement law), who had had a use for interweaving the two positions, Arnold came down squarely on the side of the former, and the trajectory of his arguments pointed toward the total destruction of "monism" as the final modernization of intellectual life.

But Arnold's arguments, like Barnes's in the 1920's, were in fact directed at a very limited audience, the independent, especially academic, lawyer, whom he wanted to make the agent of modernity and the repository of professional reform, just as Tugwell had elevated the academic economist. The larger public, Arnold believed, was not as mature as the legal realists in outgrowing the need for certainty. In the absence of a referendum on the New Deal, which would not occur until 1936, he could not tell how "modern" the masses were. And if the public had not, the courts certainly would not willingly accept the deflation of the ideals that give them power. Arnold concluded, perhaps from his contacts with

Harry Stack Sullivan and Edward S. Robinson, that the roles
performed by actors in a social ritual limited their candor.
If judges self-consciously rid themselves of the ideals they
embodied, as Green and Frank had proposed, they would be
paralyzed. The pivot of the judicial and ultimately the
governmental process therefore had to shift to an outsider,
someone who could see both the objective appeal of ideals
and their objective falsity, and whose interest lay in individualizing rather than in generalizing, in conforming the
process to the pluralism of the world rather than conversely.
A modernist outsider would see that legal rules and political
theories were arbitrary "teleologies," like Tugwell's experimental hypotheses or plans: statements that selected the
facts that verified them. The rule for deciding a particular
case was never implicit within it; it was always arbitrarily
imposed from without; and it ought to be imposed by someone
with a larger perspective than a judge could have. For
ordinary litigation, Arnold urged that the disinterested
academic scholar be the arbiter of rules, telling judges
when it was socially desirable to treat cases with the
inflexible "attitude of substantive law" and when with the
"attitude of 'procedure.'" In larger social controversies,

the legal modernist was to function as a broad-range social
activist, a litigating lawyer with society as his client.[43]

Because a completely candid opportunism--to run society
the way physicians ran an insane asylum--would not, Arnold
concluded, persuade either the public or the courts, he urged
the activist to develop a "technique of public acceptance,"
an ability to use popular symbols as camouflage, the way a
lawyer manipulated legal ideals in court. He criticized the
NRA, for example, as too much of a hodgepodge of conflicting
symbols to retain popular approval for long; he attributed
the AAA's failure to its excessive candor, which made it efficient but left it open to attack from idealists; and he
praised the SEC and the social security bill for their expedient use of old symbols as protective cover for innovations.[44]

For the ultimate camouflage, Arnold devised a counter-
theory and counter-ideal of his own. To satisfy the public's apparent residual need for theories and ideals while
subverting its loyalty to them, Arnold proposed a "theory of
emergency" based on the war experience. It was in fact a
negation of theory, but phrased to function as a countermyth.
At first he presented it as a temporary expedient, but he

quickly saw the usefulness of a theory of permanent emergency, which in fact became his version of continual
"emergence," thereby bringing "theory" into line with pluralistic reality.[45]

His counter-ideal expressed the same pragmatism: the
efficient and individualizing "humanitarian," "benevolent,"
or "practical" impulse--the necessity to distribute purchasing power--embodied by the technicians of social-welfare
institutions. It was not a concept that George and Bellamy
or Croly and Addams before 1912 would have called an ideal.
Arnold presented it explicitly as an arbitrary choice of his
own, a hypothesis or plan similar to what the Progressives'
ideals had become after 1912, to be socially accepted as a
result of the leadership, the will, of the people standing
for them. It was a negation of idealism, as the theory of
permanent emergency was a negation of theory. But if the
courts and the public would let "emergency" and "benevolence"
satisfy their "spiritual" need for theory and ideals, then
both theory and reality would be the exclusive province of
the individualizers, and the New Deal would set the permanent pattern for legitimate governmental action. Tugwell
had said society should make necessity a virtue. Arnold

proposed calling it an ideal.[46]

Arnold's version of the activist role thus differed
from the one Croly and Addams had conceived for the independent critic thirty years before--that of serving as the consciousness for the real dynamic forces making the future.
It was rather an extension of the role the progressives had
envisaged after 1912--critics as the choosers and imposers
of the future, directing the other actors according to freely
chosen plots or plans.

The structure of Arnold's writing itself was silent support for his argument. His taste for the theater analogy
refelected his disbelief in a universe that had authentic
order. And, like the articles that went into it, The Symbols
of Government had a casual lack of an authentic organizing
principle. Neither logic nor chronology dictated the order
in which issues were discussed. There were numerous repeti-
tions and digressions, possibly deliberate imprecisions and
lacunae. That such an anarchically structured book--Leon
Green's and Jerome Frank's were much the same--could seem to
be a book was testimony to the conflicting intellectual
structures that Thomas Reed Powell had identified as the
source of the juristic conflict and to the congeniality of a

pluralistic intellectual structure to those on Arnold's side.

That the activism of the early New Deal was the "reification" of that structure was clear to Arnold and his allies. They saw that a revolution in the universe of discourse was also a revolution in the forms of action. Edward S. Robinson, for example, whose Law and the Lawyers (1935) was the "companion volume" to Arnold's, saw no distinction between radical empiricism as a form of knowing and as a mode of action. Their common refusal to distinguish between hypotheses for understanding and plans for control made the roles of objective scientist and reformer identical. As Morris R. Cohen pointed out, neither Arnold nor Robinson understood--or perhaps more accurately admitted--the distinction between pure and applied science. The New Deal, Robinson said, was seeking "to popularize the idea that the experimental, fact-dominated, forward-looking view of natural science is relevant to the process of social adjustment."[47] Arnold in turn praised Roosevelt from the beginning of his term for his random experimentalism. And while he called his own economic proposals "planning," Arnold, like other New Dealers, used planning only as a label for individualization, experiment, random functionalism, "mobility," "frankly trying one thing

and then trying another, without being unduly disturbed."
New Deal "opportunism," as Arnold came to call it, was attractive because it was pure--experiments without generalizations. And the "objective scientist" posture of <u>The Symbols</u>
<u>of Government</u> was attractive because it was its equivalent in
intellectual structure--the mind of the "tolerant adult"--a
series of "guesses," "assertions," "illustrations," "analogies,"
"observations," and "parables," which needed no backing except
the author's self-confidence and which were valued apart from
their accuracy. As in Bellamy's and George's monism and
Croly's and Addams's dualism, so in Arnold's and Tugwell's
pluralism, the pattern of action and the intellectual structure were identical.[48]

They were, however, polar with their perception of society. Intellectual pluralism accompanied social stasis.
The theoretical or "spiritual" obstacles to an opportunistic
government had been relatively harmless, Arnold observed,
during the previous era of prosperity, when the practical or
"temporal" needs of society had been met well enough to keep
people from seeking practical guidance in the monistic
theories they worshipped. The problems of the Depression, he
hoped, would force people to discover that monism was no help

in a pluralistic universe. But Arnold quickly concluded that
the Depression was significant not because it was a depression, but because it had occurred during an era of stasis,
after the productive machine had been built and productive
capacity had passed the saturation point. Arnold admired and
corresponded with Tugwell, Stuart Chase, and George Soule,
the major exponents of the liberal version of the economy of
abundance: the end of all the social, economic, and geographical frontiers that had marked an expanding society, one
in which demand always exceeded supply. Arnold's own economic proposals--a series of credit reforms he devised with
Wesley Sturges--were set in that context of economic maturity.
The emphasis, he wrote, had to shift from expansion to stabilization and finally to a wider distribution of purchasing
power. The minor welfare efforts of political machines and
business organizations could not make a dent in that problem
in a mature interdependent economy. Stasis was a permanent
emergency.[49]

Roscoe Pound caught the opportunism of the "rising generation." Sociological jurists, he noted, aimed at a jurisprudence that, while socially oriented, would have the traditional focus on the "general security" of the economic order.

Legal realists, however, denied themselves even that center
of stability by emphasizing instead its "exigencies." Individualization and generalization, instead of compromising on
a division of territory, as Pound had wanted, were engaged in
their own trial by combat for exclusive control of the adjustment to modern industrialism.[50]

The polarity between Arnold's perception and his intellectual structure may have been the safeguard that kept what
some critics saw as a dangerous moral relativism from bearing
poisonous fruit. Arnold and Tugwell may have had the ability
to get along without the principles, moral absolutes, and
ordered systems that had provided certainty in chaos to the
readers of Henry George and Edward Bellamy, because their perception provided an underlying certainty about social reality
that George and Bellamy had lacked. The New Dealers' self-
assurance--a government of men, of us, rather than of laws--
reflected that certainty and obviated moral absolutes. It
appeared in their assumption that expertise, which they had,
was all that was necessary for modern society and that,
given modern social complexity and the roles it forced on
people, true expertise could center only in a disinterested
class of academics. That, in turn, was grounded in the

perception of social stasis. "Science" might not be able
to tell what was a good or bad reform, what was "socially
useful," but the prevailing perception could, because the
standard was, as Green had put it, what was acceptable and
fitting "for the time and place." The perception also kept
the bonds on because it determined the characteristics of
an acceptable expert; because, by providing a ground of
unchanging reality, it made experimentation appropriate and
its results reliable; and because, by defining the modern era
as the end of productive growth, it declared that the goal of
reform could only be the democratization of the economy.

V

Arnold ended The Symbols of Government with the hope
that a detached, objective viewpoint, when adopted by opinion
leaders, would eliminate "fanatical alignments between opposing political principles." His "science about law"--his and
Robinson's alternative to the "science of law"--was to be a
third way, an alternative to the perfectionism of the left
and the right, an ultimate replacement for trial by combat,
indeed for politics itself.[51]

In the two years between the publication of The Symbols

of Government (1935), which was well received, and the great
popularity of The Folklore of Capitalism (1937), two events
conspired to shift Arnold's focus slightly and to provide the
climate for an increased receptivity to his form of argument.
The first was the hysterical rhetoric used by conservatives
against Roosevelt in the 1936 campaign, and yet the President's overwhelming popular victory. The second was the
controversy over FDR's court-packing plan, in which Arnold
found many fellow liberals sympathizing with conservative
myths about the sanctity of the Supreme Court and the
supremacy of law. Arnold liked the candor of Roosevelt's
opportunism; he even advised against the President's having a
program. But he saw that some liberals were concerned about
Roosevelt's inconsistencies. Arnold defended the court plan
as a way to appoint Justices who understood the Court's
symbolic role and who would be statesmanlike enough to avoid
imposing a single economic theory on America. But he found
some liberals, who opposed such a theory, siding with its
major exponents to defend the court against the attempt to
make it a practical institution for a highly organized society.
These remnants of utopian perfectionism on the left and right
and the means of eliminating them became the foci of Arnold's

most popular book.[52]

Roosevelt's massive victory in 1936 seemed to Arnold a partial solution to the problem he had attacked in The Symbols of Government. As the referendum he had earlier lacked, it seemed to show a shift in popular attitudes from a romantic concern with universals to a pragmatic focus on distinctively modern problems. He concluded that the early New Deal had taught the masses that political theory was a sham, that government could be a practical institution rather than just a spiritual center, that democracy was just effective leadership--government of men--responding to people's needs. But the rhetoric of 1936-37 convinced him that his own audience, as identified by Harry Elmer Barnes in the twenties--the scholars and intellectuals, the opinion leaders and "respectable people"--had not yet been converted to the "objective point of view," and therefore politics had continued. More particularly, he saw that his own exclusive focus on the law was insufficient. There were two, rather than one, focal disciplines; politics could not be adjourned by disposing of political-legal theory alone. Traditional economic theory had continued to limit the opportunism of government, to protect narrow interest groups, and to obstruct the complete

modernization of social thought. The Folklore of Capitalism--
Arnold first proposed calling it The Symbols of Finance--would
therefore do for economics what The Symbols of Government had
done for law.[53]

Economic theory, like legal and political theory, could
be demystified, Arnold and Robinson had been arguing, simply
by treating it as subject to scientific dissection. But dissection had to have some particular point of view to be effectively revelatory, and Arnold had two. In both, the perception of stasis was central. The first emphasized the
anachronistic character of the major defenses of capitalism.
The courts and other defenders of business were using concepts fitted for a nation of individual producers, Arnold
argued, long after that era had disappeared. All the old
notions--private property, the protection of the individual,
antitrust, fresh-start bankruptcy--instead of describing an
expanding free economy, simply served as convenient masks
for exploitation when applied to the static setting of large
corporate businesses. The economy was no longer a free-
wheeling theater of individualism. America was instead in
an "age of organization," a "world of specialized organization," the "most highly organized and specialized society

the world has ever known," a "regimented industrial structure,"
an "industrial feudalism," and an "industrial army." The lesson of Berle and Means was well taken. The rise of finance
capitalism, he observed, had shifted the focus away from
production, characteristic of a developing economy, and toward marketing and fiscal manipulation, characteristic of a
developed economy. This new condition of stasis had caused
the excessive elaboration of "logical" economic theory--and
would topple it. "[W]hen the great industrial organization
ceased to expand and became faced with new problems," Arnold
wrote, economic theory had become so out of touch with
reality that it had begun imitating the epicyclic inflation
that mechanical jurisprudence had undergone in its own futile
battle against pragmatism.[54]

The second mode of dissection was to interchange the
symbols of politics and law with those of economics and business. The revelation that political machinations among competing groups were a stronger factor in corporate reorganiza-
tions than the economic viability of the company; the demon-
stration that industrial pricing and investment policies were
really forms of taxation; the argument that, despite claims
of applying economic principles to government, conservative

theorists denied government the ability to imitate business by denying it the right to include capital improvements in its balance sheets--these were the most prominent and successful examples of Arnold's analytic technique. Indeed, Arnold said, there was no difference in terms of role behavior between politics and economics. The only real differences lay between "business" and "politics" on the one hand and "government" on the other. The people in charge of the former did not ordinarily feel public responsibility, while those in charge of the latter were held to public account.[55]

Arnold's social perception was crucial to this analytic technique. The interchange of categories was an expression of his attack on the compartmentalization of social roles, which he claimed was characteristic of a premodern, rationalistic age. In a society that worshipped universals, practical needs and the emotional demand for ideals had to be handled by separate institutions, since practical needs had to be met in a pluralistic world, where universals were irrelevant. In such a society, the government (primarily through the courts) was limited to the symbolic role of embodying ideals, while the practical needs--production for an

expanding society and welfare for underclasses--were met
irresponsibly or poorly by businesses, political machines,
and private charity. The whole thrust of Arnold's "principles
of political dynamics," his "science about," was to force the
reader to conclude that the unification of these three roles--
the economic, the humanitarian, and the symbolic--in a single
responsible institution--the government--was the only road to
a truly modern society. In a thoroughly opportunistic society, the emotional and the practical needs could be met
together and therefore the separate categories of reasoning
that had been applied to them could be abandoned. Where the
ideal and the practical need did not conflict, Arnold said,
there the universe of discourse was modernized and there the
most efficient organization arose.[56]

The argument could be convincing because the economic
"realities" of the interwar decades had led Arnold to conclude
that since the problem of production had been solved, unregulated business was out-dated. The modern problem was the
distribution of purchasing power: the humanitarian problem
of reform. Since efficient distribution and humanitarianism--
the practical need in modern times and the appropriate modern
"ideal"--were identical, they belonged in the same institution.

In a thoroughly modern society, he said, disinterested technicians would wield economic as well as political power.
They would avoid "theory" and "learning"; they would experiment and individualize freely, respond to day-to-day needs,
avoid long-range plans, be publicly responsible, and show the
utility of "opportunistic action or judgment."[57]

By the mid-thirties, Arnold noted, the old organizations
had clearly failed to satisfy practical needs; but they still
had the advantage of familiar slogans, while the new organizations had none. With all his inconsistencies, Franklin
Roosevelt, Arnold suggested, had been serving as an interim
symbol for the inchoate new philosophy of government, and
thus the 1936-37 struggle over the Supreme Court was a symptom
of a possible "catharsis," which was all the more violent because it was fought between symbols. "A social need which
runs counter to an abstract ideal will always be incompe-
tently met," Arnold asserted as Principle Number 20, "until
it gets a philosophy of its own. The process of building
up new abstractions to justify filling new needs is always
troublesome in any society, and may be violent." But in a
caveat to Principle 20, Arnold indicated the pivotal role of
the reformer-scientist during the modernizing process: "This

principle does not apply in situations toward which men can take a fairly objective attitude." Thus the easy deflation of old slogans was one advantage of an objective attitude. Another was the ability to manipulate old slogans for the sake of social reforms. The sanctity of the corporation, for example, could be exploited through the fiction of a federal corporation. Arnold's own later use of antitrust sentiment was another example. So, too, was his advocacy of the social budgeting of Leon Keyserling. "Objectivity" obviated revolution as a means of modernization.[58]

In the 1920's, Herbert Croly had feared that such "manipulation" of science was implicit in the combination of the perception of stasis and the pragmatism that had accompanied it after the war. He had vainly tried to prevent it by asserting that knowledge could only be a catalyst, because the pluralistic universe made it untransferable. Arnold, however, took that universe as permission to identify "objective science" with a pluralistic intellectual structure, a series of "half truths" and "guesses," illustrations and analogies, imprecisions and demands for the reader's consent to the failure to be precise. The underlying structure of modern society was fixed. Random functionalism and radical

empiricism were appropriate to that structure, not because
they offered real control, but because hypotheses selected
their own appropriate facts and therefore permitted candid
attention to problems in any order that happened to be convenient.[59]

They also would eliminate politics. Government of men
with the "objective viewpoint," Arnold argued, would end the
social blindness, sub rosa corruptions, and intellectual
rigidities of government of laws. Such rigidities Arnold
found on both the left and the right, among legal realists
as well as legal fundamentalists. He told Americans that if
they needed parables, they should look to Sweden, a functioning opportunistic society that showed how to avoid the
ideological struggles that occurred when the choices seemed
to be only Nazism or Bolshevism. Since there was nowhere to
go from industrialism, a thoroughly modernized and opportunistic society, patterned after preventive justice, would put
a permanent end to ideology.[60]

VI

The reception of The Folklore of Capitalism among New
Dealers and their intellectual supporters was strongly

favorable. Conservatives, to Arnold's delight, reacted pre-
dictably in the very fashion he had been analyzing. The most
thoughtful critiques came from analysts who were more guarded
in their support of or opposition to the New Deal and who
were troubled by Arnold's pure opportunism, his lack of belief in theories, universals, or even hypotheses, his lack of
a theory of history, or his lack of an authentic organizing
principle. Arnold had no sympathy for such points of view.
He was offering an intellectual structure, a mode of analysis; and it was this that the public apparently found infec-
tious, as Max Lerner noted that it became commonplace to
imitate it. Lerner also neatly captured the appeal of its
pluralistic intellectual structure. "It is characteristic
of the book that one's first impulse is not to tell what it
says but to give examples," Lerner reported. "The book is
molecular. . . . The beautiful thing about it is that the
author has violated every rule on how to write a treatise--
which may account for his brilliant achievement." The book
made the New York Times list of best sellers, and Arnold was
even mentioned for the Supreme Court.[61]

The possible irony in that appointment was surpassed by
his nomination the following March (1938) to become Assistant

Attorney General in charge of the Antitrust Division. The
irony derived from his treatment of the Sherman Antitrust
Act in both Symbols and Folklore as an example of the compartmentalization of roles that occurs in a rationalistic
society, whose monistic ideals conflict with pluralistic
reality. The antitrust law and its very sporadic enforcement satisfied the folklore of a competitive expanding
economy of individuals, while it inhibited realistic measures
geared to a developed economy of increasingly interdependent
organizations. The law's treatment of corporations as persons, its concern with intentions, and its imposition of
criminal penalties, he had argued, made antitrust a form of
moral preaching, which satisfied the public's emotional needs,
while the large-scale organizations necessary for modern society were allowed to grow up without interference. The
modern situation, he had concluded, required responsible
governmental organizations to replace the private ones.

Since Arnold's analysis of antitrust bordered on ridicule
--his intention in all cases of compartmentalization--it
naturally aroused fear in those who took the antitrust law
seriously. Senator William E. Borah in particular came to
Arnold's confirmation hearing armed with quotations from

Folklore. Arnold drew on the protective robes of the scientist and explained that he had only described how the
Sherman Act had functioned, that the failure of enforcement,
not its impossibility, had been the problem; and he assured
Borah that he "sincerely believe[d] in the philosophy of the
antitrust laws."[62] Certainly, Arnold's claim of concern for
the competitive economy had legitimate roots in his personal
history.[63] And the recurrent use of the phrase "industrial
feudalism" in Folklore had echoed a favorite slogan of
Southern and Western antimonopolists. His fascination with
the Swedish system had also centered on the use of governmental power to make the productive system competitive. But
the lesson of Folklore for an "objective observer" interested
in immediate practical reform was to use available ideals for
one's own purposes. The ideals of a people should not be attacked as illegitimate, Arnold had advised. One might weaken
them by objective analysis, but only practical necessity
could cause their demise. In the meantime, realizing the
"absolute necessity" of making the system work with the tools
at hand, Arnold took the Sherman Act as an "available weapon"
that he could turn to the service of reform--the distribution
of economic power. It was "an elastic procedure backed by

tradition."[64]

Arnold's modes of action as antitrust prosecutor followed the discretionary pattern first seen in preventive justice. He switched the focus of investigation from the "moral" to the "practical," from a determination of the "intent" of the parties to the "results" of their actions, and thereby switched the goal of enforcement from punishing evil men to achieving an economic objective. He made the test of prosecution not size, but consumers' disadvantage. Instead of using the Act to protect small business, he used it to maximize distribution. Mass production increased efficiency, he said, but only "up to a certain point." Where size went beyond efficiency, where an industry was monopolistic but inefficient, and where the benefits of efficiency were not passed on to the consumer, an investigation was in order. That meant looking at the particular facts of particular situations case-by-case.[65]

Thus, the dichotomy between individualization and generalization was crucial to Arnold's policy. Litigation as the mode of enforcement naturally involved some individualization, just as it did in ordinary criminal prosecutions. But Arnold went further and refused to announce prosecution

policy in advance. The ineffectiveness of previous antitrust enforcement, he claimed, was traceable to its tendency
toward generalization--its capitulation to business demands
for certainty, and its attempt to treat all business organizations alike. Since litigation was his ultimate weapon, it
had the protective symbolism of the courts. But Arnold had
absorbed his own earlier analysis of law enforcement. It
was the prosecutor, not the court--the individualizing agency,
not the generalizing--who had discretion and who therefore
had power. It was he who made economic policy.[66]

Similarly in the preventive mode, Arnold favored a role
for the Division analogous to the declaratory judgment and to
the minor role in the reform process he had once proposed
for the Supreme Court.[67] He argued that a version of the
controversial "consent decree"--the advance submission of a
plan by business, conditional permission to proceed, plus
continual oversight by the Justice Department--would allow
freedom to experiment. Since he was judging violations by
their effects, conditional permission was necessary; if the
plan proved to be a restraint, it would be stopped without
criminal penalty. The antitrust law, he wrote, was a
"flexible instrument" by whose use "general regulation

becomes less necessary." Since the American people were not
yet ready to delegate economic power to the only organization
that was inherently responsible (the government), antitrust
procedure would try to make private enterprise conform to the
public interest. Arnold identified both planning and
laissez-faire as generalizations suited only to a rationalistic universe; his "case-by-case method" was pure opportunism,
under the protection of an ancient slogan.[68]

Free trade never meant to Arnold an unregulated economy.
Arnold was no classical economist, and he was not capitulating to the conservatives whose laissez-faire rigidities he
had effectively demolished. Free enterprise was not to be
confused with laissez-faire. Free trade meant simply free
trade--the absence of private and artificial restraints on
distribution. It was necessary for the operation of any
economic scheme, he assumed, including the sort of "non-
utopian" planning he approved of, that of the National
Resources Planning Board and Leon Keyserling--"limited planning for specific industrial problems . . . against a broad
background of free enterprise."[69]

The rise of totalitarianism sealed Arnold's position.
There were, he argued in 1940, only two methods of

distribution: the army system and free trade. He carried out this durable lesson of nineteenth-century social science by associating each method with a form of government. "Industrial democracy," as he called it, was the foundation of political democracy. He associated the distribution of economic power with the distribution of political power, and thus World War II became a war of production between the different distribution systems. Carrying these dichotomies into the post-war period, Arnold applied them to the Cold War. Since a free trade economy was an opportunistic society, the ideological conflict that its adoption would obviate in domestic politics could be legitimate in foreign affairs until the whole world was a free trade area.[70]

The key to Arnold's mounting concern for "free trade" and the ease with which he could transfer it to a world scale lay in the perception of stasis. The concern for distributing economic and political power, besides being the concern of social reform, was occasioned by the ability of the economy permanently to over-produce. "Development" was completed. The new context made administered prices seem necessary to businessmen; it made monopolization possible; it had caused the depression; and it required continuous policing of the market by a disinterested organization. It was required, he wrote, by "the realization that our economic frontier has disappeared and that our population curve is flattening out."[71]

During World War II, when effective demand was vastly expanded by government spending, Arnold briefly argued that fears of postwar overproduction and depression were groundless, since "surpluses distribute themselves in the absence of restricted control." In the bureaucratic struggle over economic policy, the fears of postwar overproduction defeated Arnold's version of a free market, so he resigned his post in early 1943 and accepted a seat on the Federal bench. But he continued to expound his views even during his judicial tenure (which lasted until 1946) and beyond. His version of Say's law, however, could have been convincing only in the special circumstances of the war; and after that brief exposition of the argument, he never expounded it so boldly. For the next twenty-five years, he based his arguments for a free market on the perception of stasis implied by the reality of overproduction and interdependence. It served as the basis for his internationalism, his support of the Cold War, and his arguments for what some called economic

imperialism. "The techniques of the twentieth century," he
wrote in 1950, "have made our present free trade area too
small." In 1953, "our great domestic market, which in the
last century seemed to be limitless, seems suddenly too
small to absorb the vastly accelerated productive capacity
of the twentieth-century industrial revolution without the
stimulus of huge government spending. We are haunted by the
specter of overproduction and underconsumption whenever this
government spending ends." The remedy was the export of
American capital and the creation of a vast free trade area
encompassing the whole western world, which would force the
decentralization of industry and serve as a market for
American goods. In the spring of 1967, in a widely publi-
cized Law Day address at Valparaiso University, Arnold argued
that the tremendous expansion of productive capacity in the
twentieth century would allow the United States to satisfy
domestic demand, end poverty at home, and fight a major war
in Vietnam.[72]

Arnold's lack of sympathy with those who criticized the
Vietnam War on practical grounds matched his inability to
understand those who opposed it on moral grounds as well.
In the years after World War II, he began noting that when

men forget their ideals, they erode the cement that binds civilized societies together. He remembered the usefulness of the instrumental conception of law in the 1930's, but noted that the non-ideal ideal he and Jerome Frank had proposed during that decade was ill-suited to maintaining the prestige of an independent judiciary. That, of course, had been precisely the reason Arnold had advocated it during the New Deal. His turnabout during the 1950's derived from the political realities of the post-war decades. Arnold's Washington law firm--a partnership with Abe Fortas and Paul Porter--was active in defending the civil liberties of the victims of McCarthyism, and the most useful defense was the ideal of a fair trial. Later it became apparent that the Supreme Court under Earl Warren was the only agency of government with the flexibility to bring America up-to-date in such areas as civil rights and reapportionment. Thus the ideals of an independent judiciary and of a rule of law above men were weapons in defending a liberal, pragmatic Court against attack from the right. They were no more "authentic" than antitrust had been. Similarly, in 1967, Arnold used the precedent of the Nuremberg tribunals to justify the Vietnam conflict as a war to repel aggression,

while two years earlier he had seemed to hold the tribunals
up to disdain for their impotence.[73]

Despite Arnold's statement that he had come to believe
that deeply felt ideals were necessary, his attitude toward
them always remained distant, ready to use them when the
need was there, to abandon them when it was not. Absolutes
of any sort were unnatural to him. His arguments for them
lacked the firmness and specificity of deep belief. And he
would never give any indication, either in the thirties or
the sixties, what they were. Ideals never had authenticity
for Arnold; they had relevance. They were weapons for use
in specific contexts. His style of analysis was congenial
for an age that could live without ideals because it did not
need them. Its certainty derived not from moral absolutes,
but from the social perception of static modern industrialism, a system fixed for the foreseeable future and with
imperatives of its own. Arnold did not distinguish among
World War I, World War II, Korea, and Vietnam, because in
his eyes all had occurred during the same era. During the
Vietnam War, though not necessarily because of it, there
seemed to be a growing perception that the era of stasis had
ended in a new era of chaos. The consequent groping for a

new approach to this new perception and for a new intellectual structure appropriate to it was all the more uncongenial to Arnold and Tugwell because it seemed to portend a revival of intellectual structures like those of the 1870's and 1880's, which they thought Americans had outgrown and which they and their mentors had discarded as idealistic and simple-minded.

CONCLUSION

The Postmodernization of American Reform

The modernized liberalism of the New Deal was not immune to criticism in the 1930's, even from those who would
have been its allies on the left; and as the fascist threat
became more apparent in Europe, the criticisms increased
in harshness and intensity. Abstracted out of their intellectual setting, the emphasis on expediency and technique,
the melding of freedom and control, the demystification of
theory and ideals, and the exaltation of government-of-men
over government-of-laws were attacked for blurring the distinctions between liberalism and authoritarianism, leaving
the former defenseless against the new barbarism. The
modern liberals were accused of indifference not only to absolutes and universals, but to moral and cultural values of
any sort and thus of having no intellectual or moral arsenal
to direct against the authoritarian menace.

Yet it was the New Dealers, not least Franklin Roosevelt
himself, who were the earliest segment of the political

mainstream to appreciate the external dangers. Modern reform
was not ideological or political, Tugwell and Arnold had been
arguing; it was experimental and scientific; and science
meant operating in a context of freedom. Their domestic political context was the controversy between one kind of freedom and another. Their intellectual context was the controversy between a free universe and a domineering one, between
a pluralistic universe that allowed itself to be freely transformed by human action and a block universe that forbade such
action, between a universe in which knowledge had no meaning
apart from its use and a universe that offered at best passive understanding. It is not surprising, therefore, that
they would be sensitive to the challenge of an illiberal
system that seemed based on a similar perception of social
stasis but that was also actively anti-intellectual, emotionally charged, and tyrannical, a system that was not polar
with stasis, as American reform was, but, in an extreme form,
congruent with it. They therefore did not have to hunt for
new absolutes to resist the challenge. "Democracy" was less
a form of compensation for the values they had ignored, than
the banner under which they could defend their universe of
discourse.

When an expansive Soviet Communism took the place of the defeated Axis, a literature analyzing both the fascist and Bolshevik regimes as examples of the single phenomenon of totalitarianism found their common characteristic in the subordination of intellectual pluralism to the rigidities of ideology. A corollary, and sometimes competing, literature used a form of technological determinism to foresee a "convergence" of opposing systems toward the single appropriate method of governing "modern industrial society," a pattern that seemed confirmed by the emergence of "mixed economies" in western nations after the war. Since the perception indicated that modern industrial society was unitary and indivisible, the permanent coexistence of competing systems was precluded, and the issue of freedom vs. determinism emerged as the salient point of contention. The "end of ideology in the West," elaborated most notably by Daniel Bell, thus seems to have resulted less from any misconception that all problems had been solved, would solve themselves, or would be solved by affluence, than from the idea that solutions in this last era of social history were a matter of science, knowledge, and technique, not a matter of politics.

The "cold war consensus," however unattractive it

became in some respects, thus allowed New Deal reformers
not only to continue to play a substantial role in shaping
the themes of American foreign policy, but also to maintain
the legitimacy of both the agenda and the style of New Deal
reform through the period of postwar reaction. The apparent quiescence of debate about social issues among liberals
of the period may have derived less from a loss of interest,
imagination, or courage, than from a general agreement
on the appropriate structure of reform in an industrial
society. The literature of social analysis was in fact
rich and creative in the thirty years after the New Deal;
it was fundamentally continuous with it in both structure
and perception; and a good deal of the richness and creativity came from former members of the New Deal, from its
active supporters, and from those who considered themselves
its heirs.

New Left critics of this consensus in the early sixties
rejected both the perception of stasis as a "dead end" and
the pluralistic intellectual structure that accompanied it.
The SDS Port Huron Statement of 1962, for example, declared
of modern liberalism: "Theoretic chaos has replaced the
idealistic thinking of old--and, unable to reconstitute

theoretic order, men have condemned idealism itself. . . .
The decline of utopia and hope is in fact one of the defining
features of social life today." By reinjecting ideals and
values, though not yet an ideology or a utopia, into social
policy, the universe of discourse and therefore the modes of
action could be transformed, and social history might begin
again. The method of reform could revert from scientific objectivity to personal involvement; the goal, from centraliza-
tion to participation; the control, from disinterested expertise to the victims themselves.[1]

Specific failures of liberal policy that were visible by
the early 1960's do not seem sufficient to account for either
the timing or the extent of liberalism's later vulnerability
to this sort of attack. Prior criticisms in the same vein
and prior failures of policy had resulted only in revised
experiments. Its sudden loss of resonance may be more directly attributable to the factor that had energized the declines of the monistic and dualistic structures: a relatively
rapid change in social perception. In 1968, for example, more
than half a century after his first public success as a social
critic, Walter Lippmann observed that "the country has entered
a period of revolutionary change of which no one can foresee

the course or the end or the consequences." The "modern
revolution," he said, "is far deeper and more overwhelming,
more rapid and more unpredictable than any other general experience of the human race."[2] Even if Lippmann had been
given to hyperbole, his description of a new era of chaos,
of rapid and unpredictable changes, of social disorder following social disorder, was repeated countless times in the
half-dozen years after 1967 in the organs of liberal opinion,
in the general public media, and even in forums apparently
remote from social issues.

It was a far-reaching change of mood from that of only
two or three years earlier. The self-assurance with which
reformers had faced the deeper material crisis of the early
1930's, for example, was profoundly lacking, and the intellectual framework that had more recently been able to assimi-
late episodes of social and racial unrest, issues of nuclear
warfare, a presidential assassination, the beginnings of
American involvement in Vietnam, and even the rediscovery
of widespread poverty, broke down under a series of challenges
that arose in rapid succession beginning in 1965 and that
seemed to reach a breaking point in 1967 or 1968. The outbreak of massive and violent urban racial protests in the

North, which challenged not only the efficacy, but the good
will, of social experimentalism and planning; the widespread
student resort to civil disobedience, whose moral absolutism
could not be resisted with "utilitarian tentatives"; the
sudden visibility of domestic and international undergroups
whose "untidy assumptions" were abstracted into ideologies
for new world systems; the revelation of CIA funding of anti-
communist intellectual activities, which seemed to reveal a
political and ideological side to apolitical and anti-
ideological knowledge; and the escalation of the war, which
fragmented the leadership of liberal opinion--created a con-
centrated sense of social and moral anarchy within a period
of not much more than two years. In the reflected light of
the more glaring social disorders, the cumulative impact of
social changes traceable to the early postwar period also
acquired sudden visibility: the decay of the cities, the
breakdown of the family, the change in the distribution of
industrial occupations, the growth of dependent populations,
the continual outdating of conventional knowledge by revolutions in information technology, the development of a fragile
and uncontrollable global economy. Other, apparently more
sudden reversals and surprises also challenged the fundamental

characteristics of the perception of stasis: the discovery
that technological advances could produce disaster, that the
problem of production had not in fact been solved, that contemporary society, unlike "modern" society, was based on
scarcity and shortages rather than on abundance and surpluses,
that rates of population growth had gotten out of hand in the
most unexpected ways, that nature could take revenge when it
was exploited. "[Y]ou wake up on the morning of a new
decade," Benjamin Demott wrote in 1970, "resolved to explain
to yourself as clearly as you can exactly what happened during the ten-year night before and you can't say a word."[3]

The sense of a radical and very recent discontinuity
between past and present had created a similar speechless-
ness in the late 1870's and 1880's. The resonant cures in
that era had been monistic intellectual structures that denied the discontinuity by permanently embedding traditional
values in theoretically perfect social orders. A hundred
years of intervening history have radically altered both the
intellectual and the social contexts, but if the polarity
between structure and perception in American reform persists
beyond the period of modernization, then structures resem-
bling monism that also take account of the altered context

might be expected to have some degree of appeal in the new era of chaos. The literature of "post-modern," "post-civilized," and "post-industrial" society, for example, reinforces the discontinuity by identifying the new era according to what has ended, at the same time that it seeks to relieve uncertainty by identifying the determining features of the emerging order, which are not in fact substantially different from the descriptions of the modern era in Rexford Tugwell's writings: the necessity and ability to control nature and society according to plans, the shift in emphasis away from production, the supremacy of technical expertise, the adequacy, indeed amplitude, of physical resources (muted in later expositions), and the necessity to overcome political and ideological conflicts, which hamper efficient organization.[4] The pressures toward something like the monistic pattern among segments of a potential reform constituency may also be part of the revival of religious appeals, the founding of single-concept "intentional communities," the renewed interest in Marxism, the reversion to "fundamentalist Constitutionalism" during the Watergate affair, and, more profoundly and in the long run perhaps more consequentially, the modern contract theory of John Rawls and the various forms of

structuralism in the social and humanistic disciplines.
Structuralism particularly may be attractive because of its
initial appearance as an "ultra-relativism"[5] and its later
appeal as a new universalism. In the American setting, the
transformational linguistics and radical politics of Noam
Chomsky symbolize a connection between post-modern reformism
and the impulse toward a new universalism. The theory first
attracted attention outside its discipline through its rejection of behaviorism, which had come to be feared as the
ultimate development of the modern combination of a pluralistic universe and the need for imposed order. Chomsky
offered to reverse the emphasis, from control to individual
creativity, and (to invert an early formula of pragmatism)
from "consequences" (unpredictable in a chaotic era) to
"premises" or internal structure, and from empiricism to
theory. As the genius of Henry George and Edward Bellamy
was to transform a chaotic era's desire for limits into a
reform impulse, so structuralism and transformational linguistics offer models that are both restrictive and creative; and
their use by other social scientists indicates that at least
one of their attractions is the promised ability to identify
a finite set of rules behind even the most complex social

activities, even behind discontinuities. The model has been explicitly connected to a reform agenda demanding decentralization, personal participation, and the devolution of power.[6] But its emergence as a coercive truth is still unclear. That will depend, at least in part, upon configurations perceived in current and future events; and history has ways of playing tricks on the living.

NOTES

Introduction

[1]The Trouble Makers: Dissent over Foreign Policy, 1792-1939 (Bloomington, Ind., 1958), 23.

[2]David A. Wells, Recent Economic Changes (New York, 1890), v, 465.

[3]President's Conference on Unemployment, Committee on Recent Economic Changes, Recent Economic Changes in the United States (New York, 1929), I, ix.

Chapter I (Modern Industrial Society)

[1]Tarbell, "New Dealers of the 'Seventies: Henry George and Edward Bellamy," Forum, XCII (Sept. 1934), 133-139; Albert E. Schalkenback, Letter to the Editor, Forum, XCII (Oct. 1934), xi-xiii.

[2]Parrington, Main Currents in American Thought (New York, 1930), III, 302, 136; Tugwell, "Henry George," Encyclopedia of the Social Sciences (New York, 1931), VI, 631.

[3]Beard, Syllabus of a Course of Six Lectures on Industrialism and Democracy, Columbia University Extension Syllabi, Series B, No. 16 (New York, 1905); Beard, Contemporary American History, 1877-1913 (New York, 1914), esp. chs. iv, v; Lippmann, Preface to Politics (New York, 1913), 27; John G. Sproat, "The Best Men": Liberal Reformers in the Gilded Age (New York, 1968), 280.

[4]Rollo Ogden, ed., <u>Life and Letters of Edwin Lawrence</u>
<u>Godkin</u> (New York, 1902), I, 11.

[5]Marxists, for example, object to the label because it
puts American capitalism and Soviet communism in the same
category. See the discussion in Raymond Aron, <u>The Industrial</u>
<u>Society: Three Essays on Ideology and Development</u> (New York,
1967).

[6]Frank E. Manuel, <u>The New World of Henri Saint-Simon</u>
(Cambridge, Mass., 1956), 219-242. Saint-Simon has also
been credited with inventing the words "industrial" and
"industrielisme," though claims have been advanced on behalf
of Benjamin Constant, J-B. Say, and de Montlosier; <u>ibid.</u>,
189, 403n. Rexford Tugwell attributed "industrialism" to
Proudhon; <u>The Trend of Economics</u> (New York, 1924), 375.

[7]Raymond Aron, <u>War and Industrial Society</u> (London,
1958), 7-12; Auguste Comte, <u>The Positive Philosophy of</u>
<u>Auguste Comte</u>, freely translated and condensed by Harriet
Martineau, 2d ed. (London, 1875), II, 302.

[8]<u>The Principles of Sociology</u>, authorized ed. (New York,
1896), I, Part I, ch. xxvii, and Part II. This edition
comprises the third edition of volume I (1st ed., 1876; no
significant changes except as noted in note 13, below), the
second edition of volume II (1st ed., 1882), and the first
edition of volume III.

[9]A third system--the distributing system--develops
later, but does not become one of the societal types.
<u>Ibid.</u>, I, Part II, chs. vi, viii.

[10]<u>Ibid.</u>, 1, Part II, and II, Part V.

[11]<u>Ibid.</u>, I, 599.

[12]<u>Ibid.</u>, III, 327 ff.

[13]Ibid., I, 599-600; emphasis his. It is that
italicized clause which was added in the third edition;
cf. The Principles of Sociology (New York, 1881), I, 618b.
Other than a few grammatical changes, changes in some examples, and the substitution of "militant" for "predatory"
in many places, there seem to be no other significant differences between the first and third editions. One indication of the changing uses of "industrial society" is Jane
Addams's adoption of Spencer's last schema, but with reverse causation. In Newer Ideals of Peace (New York, 1907),
she did not argue that when peace replaced war industrialism
would replace militarism; rather, she argued that since
industrialism had replaced militarism, peace ought to replace
war.

[14]"The Influence of Commercial Crises on Opinions about
Economic Doctrines (1879)," in The Forgotten Man, and Other
Essays, A. G. Keller, ed. (New Haven, 1918), 217. This
essay had not been previously published.

[15]Outline of Lectures upon Political Economy (Baltimore,
1881), 13, 29.

[16]Outline of Lectures upon Political Economy, 2d ed.
(Ann Arbor, 1886), 67-68. Cf. "Economics and Jurisprudence"
and "Another View of Economic Laws and Methods," in Science
Economic Discussion (New York, 1886), 81, 99.

[17]Comparative Wages, Prices, and Cost of Living (Boston,
1889), Part I; the quotations are from pages 4, 36, 3. This
volume was reprinted from the Massachusetts Labor Census,
issues in 1885.

[18]"Introduction" to Jane Addams, et al., Philanthropy
and Social Progress (New York, 1893), vi, vii.

[19]Studies in the Evolution of Industrial Society (New
York, 1903); the quotations are from pp. 12, 13. There is
a summary list of stages on p. 26. There is a table

summarizing the various ways in which economic history has been periodized, by Ely and others, on p. 71.

[20]Arnold Toynbee, Lectures on the Industrial Revolution in England (London, 1884). Evidence of other and earlier uses of the term can be found in Anna Beyanson, "Early Use of the Term Industrial Revolution," Quarterly Journal of Economics, XXXVI (1922), 343; George N. Clark, The Idea of the Industrial Revolution (Glasgow, 1953).

[21]Henry F. May, The Protestant Churches and Industrial America (New York, 1948), 91.

Chapter II (Henry George)

[1]Richard T. Ely, Ground under Our Feet: An Autobiography (New York, 1938), 65-66

[2]Lester F. Ward, "Politico-Social Functions," Penn Monthly, XII (May 1881), 373-397, reprinted in Glimpses of the Cosmos (New York, 1913-18), II, 335-337.

[3]Dynamic Sociology (New York, 1883), I, 16. The date of its completion is in Glimpses of the Cosmos, II, 269. On cataclysmic thinking in the late 19th and early 20th centuries, see Frederic C. Jaher, Doubters and Dissenters (Glencoe, Ill., 1964).

[4]Tugwell, "Wesley Mitchell, An Evaluation," New Republic, XCII (October 6, 1937), 240.

[5]Sumner, "The Influence of Commercial Crises on Opinions about Economic Doctrines" (1879), The Forgotten Man, and Other Essays, A. G. Keller, ed. (New Haven, 1918), 235. Even his later moral relativism seems to have been at bottom an evolutionary determinism.

[6] Sumner, What Social Classes Owe to Each Other (New York, 1883), 126, 132, 133.

[7] The definitive biography of George is Charles A. Barker, Henry George (New York, 1955), the source of many of the biographical details below. See also, Henry George, Jr., The Life of Henry George, in The Complete Works of Henry George (Garden City, N.Y., 1911), IX and X. References to George's writings in this edition will hereafter be cited as Works, with the volume number.

[8] The Sunday school anecdote is recalled in George, Jr., Life, 6; see also Henry George, "The Crime of Poverty" (1885), Works, VIII, 185-218.

[9] Diary, December 25, 1864, and February 17, 1865, in Henry George Papers, New York Public Library (hereafter cited as George Papers); "On the Profitable Employment of Time," March 25, 1865, George Papers, is the source of the quotation.

[10] "What the Railroad Will Bring Us," Overland Monthly, I (October 1868), 297-306. On the importance of George's reaction to the California experience, see Kevin Starr, Americans and the California Dream, 1850-1915 (New York, 1973), 134-141.

[11] Henry George to Thomas Dawson, February 1, 1883 (date uncertain), George Papers; Works, VI: The Science of Political Economy, I, 163, 201 (unfinished at George's death, 1897); Henry George, Jr., Life, 191-193, 210.

[12] Works, VIII: Our Land and Land Policy, 119; first published in San Francisco, 1871.

[13] Ibid., 75, for the quoted definition. George R. Geiger, The Philosophy of Henry George (New York, 1933), ch. iv, distinguishes the different labor-value theories, though his use of the distinction is different from the one here.

[14] *Our Land and Land Policy*, 75, 98-99.

[15] George did distinguish between a "necessary or real value of land," which is derived from the specific lot's advantages, and an "unnecessary or fictitious value," which results from the artificial scarcity that monopoly creates. The former is, however, negligible; the difference between the two is "most enormous" and constitutes the unnecessary tax upon labor. *Ibid*., 84-85.

[16] *Ibid*., 9-10, 31.

[17] *Ibid*., 121, 122.

[18] *Ibid*., 85-87.

[19] "The Study of Political Economy," *Works*, VIII, 135-153; quotations from pp. 137, 152.

[20] See Ely, "Introduction," *Science Economic Discussion* (New York, 1886), vii; Ely, *The Past and the Present of Political Economy* (Baltimore, 1884), 17-20; Ely, "Ethics and Economics," *Science Economic Discussion*, 46; H. C. Adams, "Economics and Jurisprudence," *ibid*.; Adams, *Outline of Lectures upon Political Economy* (Baltimore, 1881; 2d ed., Ann Arbor, 1886); E. R. A. Seligman, "Continuity of Economic Thought," *Science Economic Discussion*, 22-23.

[21] Ely, *The Past and the Present*, 17; Richmond Mayo-Smith, "Methods of Investigation in Political Economy," *Science Economic Discussion*, 113; Adams, *Outline of Lectures* (1st ed.), 14, (2d ed.) 4. Since among the lego-historical facts, the economic policies of governments had to be included, there were few, if any, "natural" limits (the anti-laissez-faire argument ran) to what a government could do. Thus, what had, since Mill, been called the "art" of political economy had to be included within the "science." Classical economists had used the distinction both to preserve the purity of their science and to use science as a limit on art or policy. George

would try to use the distinction for a different purpose in his last book, The Science of Political Economy.

[22] Ely, The Past and the Present 46, 64; Mayo-Smith, "Methods of Investigation," 116; Ely, The Past and the Present, 40; Adams, "Economics and Jurisprudence," 85, citing Ward specifically, Sumner, "The Influence of Commercial Crises" is a good example of the classicists' arguments about complexity's precluding induction.

[23] See Robert V. Bruce, 1877, Year of Violence (Indianapolis, 1959); John G. Sproat, "The Best Men": Liberal Reformers in the Gilded Age (New York, 1968), 225ff.

[24] "Why Is Economics Not an Evolutionary Science?" Quarterly Journal of Economics, XII (July 1898), 373-397.

[25] George, "The Study of Political Economy," 141, 135, 149; Ely, The Past and the Present, 50.

[26] Works, I: Progress and Poverty, 539-540, emphasis his; "Preface to the 4th Edition . . . November 1880," ibid., xiv. Works reprints the "4th Edition" (i.e., fourth printing) of November 1880, the edition with the widest circulation. Only a few minor verbal corrections had been made. The first printing was issued in January 1880. George had printed an author's edition of 500 copies in 1879.

[27] On the rise in real wages: Phyllis Deane and W. A. Cole, British Economic Growth, 1688-1959: Trends and Structure (Cambridge, End., 1962, 18-28); C. D. Long, Wages and Earnings in the United States, 1860-1890 (Princeton, 1960). S. Lebergott, "Wage Trends, 1800-1900," in National Bureau of Economic Research, Trends in the American Economy in the Nineteenth Century (Princeton, 1960), 466-471, claims that real wages changed by only small amounts or fell between 1800 and 1880. For authorities contemporary to George, see, for example, David A. Wells, "Influence of the Production

and Distribution of Wealth on Social Development,"
Journal of Social Science, VIII (May 1876), 1-22. The
British economist J. E. Cairnes was the authority most fre-
quently cited in the 1880's (as was Henry George himself):
for example, Washington Gladden, Working People and Their
Employees (Boston, 1876), 204-206, and Applied Christianity
(Boston, 1886), 13-14; Josiah Strong, Our Country (New York,
1885), 103-104; H. C. Adams, "The 'Labor Problem,'"
Scientific American Supplement, XXII (August 21, 1886),
8861. "Scientific" confirmation came with J. E. Thorold
Rogers, Six Centuries of Work and Wages (London, 1884),
Preface, ch. xviii, ch. xix (for England), and Carroll D.
Wright, Comparative Wages, Prices, and Cost of Living
(Boston, 1889), 33 (for the United States).

   [28]In his last book, The Science of Political Economy,
Book II, ch. xix, George gave a definition of poverty which
was compatible with even a comfortable standard of living.
He defined "service" as "all things which indirectly satisfy
human desire." The "normal line" of service is "equality
between giving and receiving." A rich man is then one who
can command more than he need give; a poor man is one who
gives more than he receives. Changing conceptions of
poverty are discussed in Robert Bremner, From the Depths
(New York, 1956).

   [29]Progress and Poverty, 9.

   [30]Ibid., 10, 403-404, emphasis his.

   [31]Ibid., 12, 26.

   [32]Ibid., 204; see also 11, 217, and passim.

   [33]Ibid., Book I, for the refutation of the wage-fund;
Book II, for Malthus.

   [34]Ibid., Books III-VII; the quotation is from p. 326.

[35]For example, _ibid._, Book III, chs. vii, viii.

[36][Sumner], "Henry George's 'Progress and Poverty' and 'The Land Question,'" _Scribner's Monthly_, XXII (June 1881), 312-313.

[37]"A Concurrent Circulation of Gold and Silver" (1878), _The Forgotten Man, and Other Essays_, 187; "The Influence of Commercial Crises on Opinions about Economic Doctrines" (1879), _ibid._, 215-216. Herbert Spencer's reception in America seems to have derived from his reputation as a unifier of knowledge. See _Herbert Spencer on the Americans and the Americans on Herbert Spencer_ (New York, 1883), 71 and _passim_; Chauncey Wright, "German Darwinism," _Nation_, XXI (Sept. 9, 1875), 168; Josiah Royce, _The Spirit of Modern Philosophy_ (Boston, 1892), 296-297.

[38]_Forgotten Man_, 222, 224-225.

[39]Charles A. Barker, _Henry George_, ch. x, sees _Progress and Poverty_ as in constant tension because of two conflicting assumptions: the assumption of selfishness underlying the economic argument and the assumption of unselfishness underlying the moral argument. For the reasons stated below, it seems that _Progress and Poverty_ resolves the tension in the same way that the small enterpriser morality of St. Paul's Episcopal Church did.

[40]John Dewey, "An Appreciation of Henry George," in H. G. Brown, ed., _Significant Paragraphs from Progress and Poverty_ (New York, 1928); and Dewey, Foreword, to Geiger, _The Philosophy of Henry George_, xi-xiii. On George and the Social Gospel, see James Dombrowski, _The Early Days of Christian Socialism in America_ (New York, 1936); Charles H. Hopkins, _The Rise of the Social Gospel in American Protestantism, 1865-1915_ (New Haven, 1940); Fred Nicklason, "Henry George: Social Gospeller," _American Quarterly_, XXII (Fall 1970), 649-664.

[41]Progress and Poverty, 128.

[42]Ibid., "Conclusion: The Problem of Individual Life."

[43]For example, ibid., 461, 549. For a discussion of George's fraternity in a larger context (and differing in several respects), see Wilson Carey McWilliams, The Idea of Fraternity in America (Berkeley, 1973), 385-386.

[44]Youmans, "The Forces of Human Progress," Popular Science Monthly, XXVIII (February 1881), 553-556; Henry George to Edward R. Taylor, January 21, 1881, George Papers; George, Works, III: The Land Question, 103 (first published in 1881, for the Irish Land League agitation).

[45]Works, II: Social Problems, 4 (recourse). Social Problems was first published in 1883 as a series in Leslie's magazine in response to Sumner's articles in Harper's Weekly, which were published as What Social Classes Owe to Each Other.

[46]Social Problems, ch. ix, esp. p. 84.

[47]"Progressive societies outgrow institutions as children outgrow clothes. Social progress always requires greater intelligence in the management of public affairs; but this is the more as progress is rapid and change quicker. . . . To adjust our institutions to growing needs and changing conditions is the task which devolves upon us." Ibid., 7.

[48]Ibid., 241 (keener sense), 9, 85-86.

[49]Ibid., 85-86; see also Works, IV: Protection or Free Trade? (1886), 305.

[50]In at least two speeches, for instance, in 1884 and 1885, George rephrased the two halves of the Sunday-school

commandments to identify duty with justice: thou shalt not steal, and thou shalt not suffer thyself <u>or others</u> to be stolen from. (Private property in land <u>is</u> theft.) "The Crime of Poverty" (1885), <u>Works</u>, VIII, 185-218; "The Eighth Commandment" (1884), George Papers.

[51]<u>Protection or Free Trade</u>, 302-306.

[52]For example, <u>Works</u>, III: <u>The Condition of Labor</u>, 61-63 (first published in 1891 in response to the Papal encyclical <u>Rerum Novarum</u>).

[53]On the redefinition of cooperation, <u>ibid</u>.; also, <u>The Science of Political Economy</u>, Book III, chs. ix-x.

[54]<u>Protection or Free Trade</u>, Introductory, ch. iii, and p. 31. Cf. George to E. R. Taylor, September 14, 1884, George Papers: "I do not think that induction employed in such a question as the tariff is of any use. What the people want is theory and until they get a correct theory into their heads all citing of facts is useless. . . . All the facts, in California especially, are for free trade, but people continue to believe in protection because they have a wrong theory in their heads."

[55]George to T. F. Walker, August 23 and 28, 1890, George Papers (copy): "The name 'single tax' is new; but the thing as I am now advocating it is what I first proposed. If I am wrong now the wrong is in my original thinking not in my subsequent deviation." George felt that he had never swerved "one hair's breadth in this matter from what so far as God gave me power to see--I saw to be true."

[56]For example, <u>The Conditions of Labor</u>, 62. For a more extensive discussion, see <u>The Science of Political Economy</u>, Book III, chs. ix-x.

[57]For example, <u>Social Problems</u>, 9, and chs. viii-ix; "England To-day," <u>The Times-Star</u> (n.p. [England], n.d. [c. 1882-84]), in the Henry George Scrapbooks, V, 13, in the

Economics Division, New York Public Library; "'Thou Shalt Not Steal'" (1887) and "Thy Kingdom Come" (1889), in Works, VIII, 241-262, 279-293, respectively; The Single Tax Faith (n.p., 1889).

[58]For example, Works, V: A Perplexed Philosopher, 273 and passim (first published in 1892).

[59]Geiger, for example, a disciple of Dewey's, in The Philosophy of Henry George sees George as an example of the instrumentalist outlook: scientific means for moral ends. Significantly, when Geiger attempts to show what George "really" thought, he uses George's last book, The Science of Political Economy, to a much greater extent than Progress and Poverty.

[60]For example, The Science of Political Economy, Book III, ch. v.

[61]The work was first published, posthumously, in 1898, since George had died in 1897 during his second campaign for Mayor of New York. See George's Preface and Henry George, Jr.'s Prefatory Note on the purpose of the treatise, in Works, VI. The labels "science" and "art" are used in Book I, ch. xiv; but the substance is discussed throughout Book I, "The Meaning of Political Economy." It seems likely that George took the distinction from John Stuart Mill, whom he had read extensively, rather than from, for instance, his contemporary, Lester Ward. The quotations are from pp. 102, 73.

[62]On production, ibid., Book III; see also Book I, ch. xii. On distribution, Book IV, esp. ch. iv. The quotation is from p. 452.

[63]For example, from his analysis: his discussion of the difference between "value from production" and "value from obligation" in ibid., Book II, ch. xiv. His rejection of other sciences: Book II, chs. iii-x. His rejection of other arts: Book II, chs. v-viii, esp. ch. vii.

[64] *A Perplexed Philosopher*, Part II, ch. iii; *The Science of Political Economy*, 74-76.

Chapter III (Edward Bellamy)

[1] *Equality* (New York, 1897), 324.

[2] Ibid., 331 and ch. xxxv. Other printings substitute "clamor" for "creeds."

[3] Gronlund, *The Cooperative Commonwealth*, Stow Persons, ed. (Cambridge, Mass., 1965), 8, 238, 63, 247. The volume was first published in 1884; this edition reprints the original edition and appends the "Introduction to the Revised Edition, 1890," which contains Gronlund's claims to origination.

[4] Strong, *Our Country: Its Possible Future and Its Present Crisis* (New York, 1885), iii, v, 111, 91, 112, 143, 144. The revised edition of 1891 was republished with an introduction and notes by Jurgen Herbst (Cambridge, Mass., 1963).

[5] Gladden, *Recollections* (Boston, 1909), 291; Gladden, *Working People and Their Employers* (Boston, 1876), 34; Gladden, *Applied Christianity* (Boston, 1886), 213, 161.

[6] Henry David, *The History of the Haymarket Affair* (New York, 1958); Frederic C. Jaher, *Doubters and Dissenters: Cataclysmic Thought in America, 1885-1918* (Glencoe, Ill., 1964), 37-40; John G. Sproat, *"The Best Men": Liberal Reformers in the Gilded Age* (New York, 1968), 232-235.

[7] Carnegie, "Results of the Labor Struggle," *Forum*, I (Aug. 1886), 538-551; Howells to Hamlin Garland, Jan. 15, 1888, in Mildred Howells, ed., *Life in Letters of William*

Dean Howells (Garden City, N.Y., 1928), I, 407-408
(indefinitely widened); Howells to Edward Everett Hall, Aug.
30, 1888, ibid., 416 (warfare); Howells to Henry James,
Oct. 10, 1888, ibid., 417 (illogical). Of his first novel
after these events, A Hazard of New Fortunes (1889), Howells
wrote twenty years later: "It became, to my thinking, the
most vital of my fictions, through my quickened interest in
the life about me, at a moment of great psychological import.
We had passed through a period of strong emotioning in the
direction of the humaner economics, if I may phrase it so;
the rich seemed not so much to despise the poor, the poor
did not so hopelessly repine. The solution of the riddle
of the painful earth through the dreams of Henry George,
through the dreams of Edward Bellamy, through the dreams
of all the generous visionaries of the past, seemed not
impossibly far off. The shedding of blood which is for the
remission of sins had been symbolized by the bombs and
scaffolds of Chicago, and the hearts of those who felt the
wrongs bound up with our rights, the slavery implicated in
our liberty, were thrilling with griefs and hopes hitherto
strange to the average American breast." "Bibliographical"
(dated July 1909), A Hazard of New Fortunes (New York, 1911),
vi.

[8] Adams, "The 'Labor Problem,'" Scientific American
Supplement, XXII (Aug. 21, 1886), 8862; Walker, "Mr. Bellamy
and the New Nationalist Party," Atlantic Monthly, LXV
(Feb. 1890), 255.

[9] Nationalist Club of Boston, Declaration of Principles
[and] Constitution (Boston, 1889), 1.

[10] Biographical details from Arthur E. Morgan, Edward
Bellamy (New York, 1944); Mason A. Green, "Edward Bellamy:
A Biography of the Author of Looking Backward" (unpublished
typescript, n.d. [1925?], in Edward Bellamy Papers, Houghton
Library, Harvard University [hereafter cited as Bellamy
Papers; quoted by permission of Houghton Library, Harvard
University]); Sylvia Bowman, The Year 2000: A Critical
Biography of Edward Bellamy (New York, 1958). For a stimu-
lating recent interpretation of Bellamy's career, see

John L. Thomas, "Introduction," to Edward Bellamy, <u>Looking Backward</u> (Cambridge, Mass., 1967).

[11] Green, "Edward Bellamy," 12.

[12] "Autobiographical Sketch," Bellamy Papers. All page references to the Bellamy Papers will be to the typewritten copies, where they exist.

[13] Notebook I, Sept. 1871, p. 5 (pelf), Bellamy Papers; <u>ibid</u>., May 1873, pp. 24-26 (mediocre); <u>ibid</u>., Feb. 1874, pp. 30-31 (vague); <u>ibid</u>., Feb. 1872, pp. 7-8 (disappointment); <u>ibid</u>., Nov. 1871, pp. 5-6 (literary life).

[14] For example, <u>ibid</u>., 1872, pp. 15-17; Notebook IV, before 1877, pp. 17, 23-24; Notebook C, date uncertain, p. 32; all in Bellamy Papers.

[15] On passivity and self-assertion: "Autobiographical Sketch"; Notebook IV, before 1877, pp. 13, 17, 23-24. On his cognitive style: Notebook I, Aug. 1871, p. 3 (least inclination); <u>ibid</u>., Jan. 1874, pp. 29-30 (intensely practical); Notebook II, between 1870 and 1875, pp. 1-5, 8-10 (law of the mind; logical people); all in Bellamy Papers.

[16] Notebook I, c. Jan. 1873, pp. 22-23 (loyalty); Notebook II, between Sept. 1874 and Nov. 1875, p. 27 (revenge); both in Bellamy Papers.

[17] <u>Six to One: A Nantucket Idyl</u> (New York, 1878).

[18] <u>The Religion of Solidarity</u>, Arthur E. Morgan, ed. (Yellow Springs, Ohio, 1940), 43.

[19] On privacy: Notebook I, Aug. 1871, pp. 4-5; Notebook II, between Sept. 1874 and Nove. 1875, pp. 28-29; in Bellamy Papers. On death: Notebooks, passim, Bellamy

Papers; <u>Religion of Solidarity</u>, 25.   On retreat from material
world: <u>ibid.</u>, 16.   On time: <u>ibid.</u>, 12-13; "Almost a Suicide";
in Bellamy Papers.   On change: Notebook II, p. 29, Bellamy
Papers.

[20]Bellamy denied the reality of the abstraction Humanity
in Notebook C, date uncertain, p. 10, Bellamy Papers.   On
esthetics as the closest approximation: <u>Religion of
Solidarity</u>, esp. 11, 12, 17, 22, 26-27.   On love and the
remedies: Notebook I, Oct. 1872, p. 17; Notebook VI, 188-?,
Bellamy Papers; similar comments abound in all the notebooks
kept before <u>Looking Backward</u>.   Contrasting interpretations
of this point can be found in Morgan and Thomas.

[21]"Story of Eliot Carson" (#1), pp. 4-5, Binder 2 (poor
mechanic); "Story of Eliot Carson" (#2), p. 30, Binder 2
(cultivation); both in Bellamy Papers.   There are variant
spellings of Eliot's name.

[22]"Story of Eliot Carson" (#3), pp. 19-21, 38-39, 45-46,
101, Binder 1, Bellamy Papers.

[23]<u>Ibid.</u>, 134 (she felt).   On the security of inaction,
cf. the situation in "Almost a Suicide," Bellamy Papers.
The religion also cultivated emotional passivity: "Story
of Eliot Carson" (#3), 71.

[24]<u>Religion of Solidarity</u>, 36.

[25]"Story of Eliot Carson" (#3), 109-111.

[26]For a contrasting interpretation, see George
Fredrickson, <u>The Inner Civil War</u> (New York, 1965), 226

[27]"How Many Men Make a Man," 10, Bellamy Papers; see
also Notebook IV, before 1877, pp. 6-8, Bellamy Papers.
The theory was used in two of his short stories: "Lost"
(1877) and "The Old Folks' Party" (1876); reprinted in
<u>The Blindman's World, and Other Stories</u> (Boston, 1898).

[28] _Dr. Heidenhoff's Process_ (New York, 1880), 86, 105, 121.

[29] Bellamy to Ripley Hitchcock, May 19, 1897, Ripley Hitchcock Papers, Columbia University Library.

[30] _Miss Luddington's Sister_ (Boston, 1884), 183.

[31] "The Blindman's World," _The Blindman's World, and Other Stories_, 16, 29.

[32] _Looking Backward, 2000-1887_, J. L. Thomas, ed. (Cambridge, Mass., 1967), 100, 102, 102, 123, 102, for the direct quotations. This edition is a variorum edition, comprising the first two editions of the book, both published in 1888.

[33] Joseph Schiffman, ed. (Cambridge, Mass., 1962). The novel was first published in book form in 1900, expurgated by Francis Bellamy.

[34] _Looking Backward_, 98, 99.

[35] _Ibid._, 285.

[36] _Ibid._, 215, 212, 180. There are no loose ends in the story either. Julian has only two personal ties to the nineteenth century: his servant Sawyer and his fiancee Edith Bartlett. Sawyer died in the fire that destroyed Julian's home the night he was hypnotized. Dr. Leete's daughter, with whom Julian falls in love, turns out to be Edith Bartlett's great-granddaughter.

[37] "How I Came to Write 'Looking Backward.'" _Nationalist_, I (May 1889), 1, 3, 1.

[38] "How I Wrote 'Looking Backward,'" _Ladies Home Journal_, XI (Apr. 1894), 2.

[39]On emulation and other incentives, <u>Looking Backward</u>, 171-178; on duty, 151-153; on punishment, 175; on the family, 179, 261. The long quotation is from 131-132.

[40]"How I Came to Write 'Looking Backward.'"

[41]"The Blindman's World," 25.

[42]<u>Looking Backward</u>, 122, 126.

[43]<u>Ibid</u>., 126.

[44]<u>Ibid</u>., 308.

[45]<u>Ibid</u>., 260.

[46]For example, "The Programme of the Nationalists," <u>Forum</u>, XVII (Mar. 1894), 86; "Introduction," to <u>Socialism: The Fabian Essays</u>, G. B. Shaw, ed. (Boston, 1894); Edward Bellamy to W. D. Howells, June 17, 1888, Howells Papers, Houghton Library, Harvard University.

[47]"Nationalism--Principles and Purposes," <u>Nationalist</u>, II (Apr. 1890), 179; "Progress of Nationalism in the United States," <u>North American Review</u>, CLIV (June 1892), 746. See also "First Steps Toward Nationalism," <u>Forum</u>, X (Oct. 1890), 183.

[48]"The Programme of the Nationalists," 90.

[49]On becoming a religion: the pamphlet <u>Plutocracy or Nationalism--Which?</u> (Boston, 1889); "Progress of Nationalism in the United States," 747-748; "Christmas in the Year 2000," <u>Ladies Home Journal</u>, XII (Jan. 1895), 6. For the criticism and Bellamy's decision for universality: Francis A. Walker, "Mr. Bellamy and the New Nationalist Party," <u>Atlantic Monthly</u>, LXV (Feb. 1890), 258-259; Bellamy, "'Looking Backward' Again,"

North American Review, CL (Mar. 1890), 357-358; Bellamy,
"Looking Forward," Nationalist, II (Dec. 1889), 2.

[50]Edward Bellamy to Ripley Hitchcock, Jan. 8, 1898,
Ripley Hitchcock Papers, Columbia University Library.

[51]Equality, 309, 327; the story of the revolution is
is chs. ii, xxxiv, xxxv, xxxvii.

[52]Ibid., 375

[53]Ibid., 350-352.

Chapter IV (Understanding Transition)

[1]Drift and Mastery (New York, 1914), 184, 329, 179,
179, 318.

[2]For example, the announcement written (probably by
Albion Small) to introduce the first issue of the American
Journal of Sociology: "The Era of Sociology," American
Journal of Sociology, 1 (July 1895), 1-15.

[3]For example, Lyman Abbott, Christianity and Social
Problems (Boston, 1896), 357-360; Josiah Royce, The
Philosophy of Loyalty (New York, 1908), 212.

[4]For example, Charles H. Cooley, Human Nature and the
Social Order (New York, 1902), ch. xii; Frederick Jackson
Turner, "Pioneer Ideals and the State University" (1910),
The Frontier in American History (New York, 1920), 287.
Turner's essay had not been previously published.

[5]Glimpses of the Cosmos (New York, 1913-18), V, 1.

[6]The Psychic Factors of Civilization (Boston, 1893);
Dynamic Sociology, 2 v. (New York, 1883). Cf. Walter E. Weyl,

The New Democracy (New York, 1912), 354-355: "The mortal
defect of Utopias is that they are too static. The kingdom
of heaven on earth is always a permanent, unchanging, perfect, and unutterably stupid place, than which our present
society, with all its imperfections, is vastly superior.
Utopias break down because they represent attainment, fulfillment. But society does not strive towards fulfillment,
but only towards striving. It seeks not a goal, but a
higher starting point from which to seek a goal. [New
Paragraph] Opposed to such Utopias our present ideal of a
socialized democratic civilization is dynamic. It is not
an idyllic state in which all men are good and wise and
insufferably contented. It is not a state at all, but a
mere direction."

[7] John Dewey, Review of L. F. Ward, The Psychic Factors
of Civilization; B. Kidd, Social Evolution; G. B. Adams,
Civilization during the Middle Ages; R. Flint, History of
the Philosophy of History, Psychological Review, 1 (July
1894), 400-411.

[8] The Principles of Psychology (New York, 1890), I, 8,
142, 141, 144, 78.

[9] "What the Will Effects," Scribner's Magazine, III
(February 1888), 249-250. Cf. "The Will to Believe," New
World, V (1896), 327-347; reprinted in The Will to Believe,
and Other Essays in Popular Philosophy (New York, 1897,
1-31.

[10] "Social Consciousness," American Journal of Sociology,
SII (March 1907), 686.

[11] The Complete Works of Henry George (Garden City,
New York, 1911), VI: The Science of Political Economy,
148-149.

[12] Review of Jane Addams, The Spirit of Youth and the
City Streets, American Journal of Sociology, XV (January
1910), 553.

[13] Twenty Years at Hull-House (New York, 1910), ch. ix.

[14] The New Era (New York, 1893), esp. chs. i, vii-ix; quotations are from pp. v, 1, 2.

[15] William James in 1880 and Charles Cooley in 1897 used the Darwinian model to argue, in opposition to Spencer, that social changes derived from the intersection of individual innovations and a complex, changing social environment. William James, "Great Men, Great Thoughts, and the Environment," Atlantic Monthly, XLVI (October 1880), 441-459; Charles H. Cooley, "The Process of Social Change," Political Science Quarterly, XII (March 1897), 63-81

[16] The Spirit of Modern Philosophy (Boston, 1892), ch. viii. Jane Addams cites it in Newer Ideals of Peace (New York, 1907), 32.

[17] The World and the Individual (New York, 1899-1901), I, Introduction. A. W. Moore, "Some Logical Aspects of Purpose," in John Dewey, et al., Studies in Logical Theory (Chicago, 1903), 349, identifies Royce's concept with "working hypotheses," the "scientific conception" of ideas.

[18] The Philosophy of Loyalty (New York, 1908), ch. i. The quotation is from p. 22.

[19] The phrase is Graham Taylor's: Pioneering on Social Frontiers (Chicago, 1930), 116.

[20] Twenty Years at Hull-House, 190, 197.

Chapter V (Jane Addams)

[1] Social Facts and Forces (New York, 1897), 17, 37, 72, 198.

[2]The Theory of Social Forces (Philadelphia, 1896), 5-6, 109-115, 119-126, 141-143.

[3]"The Significance of the Frontier in American History," American Historical Association, Annual Report for the Year 1893, 227; "Social Forces in American History," American Historical Review, XVI (Jan. 1911), 220, 225. See also "The West and American Ideals" (1914) and "Pioneer Ideals and the State University" (1910), in The Frontier in American History (New York, 1920).

[4]The best biography is Allen Davis, American Heroine (New York, 1973). Biographical information can also be found in James W. Linn, Jane Addams (New York, 1935), and Jane Addams, Twenty Years at Hull-House (New York, 1910). The quotation is the title of ch. i of Twenty Years. The analysis that follows is based on these sources as well as on scattered reminiscences elsewhere; for example, Addams, "The Progressive Party and the Negro," The Crisis, V (Nov. 1912), 30-31.

[5]Jane Addams to Ellen Starr, August 11, 1879, and January 29, 1880, Ellen Starr Papers, Sophia Smith Collection (Women's History Archive), Smith College; emphasis hers.

[6]Jane Addams to Ellen Starr, November 3, 1883, August 12, 1883, and July 11, 1883, Starr Papers; emphasis hers. Compare this excerpt from Addams's commonplace book, quoted in Linn, Jane Addams, 10: "The difficulty is not in bearing our ills, but in knowing what ills are necessary, not in doing what is right but in knowing what is right to do. I suppose to say that I do not know just what I believe is a form of cowardice, just going on trying to think things out instead of making up my mind, but then why am I happier when I am learning than when I am trying to decide? For I do not think there could be any happiness in being a coward." Davis, 24-27, 51, corrects Jane Addams's own recollections of the dates of her breakdown and baptism.

[7]Twenty Years at Hull-House, 78-79.

[8] Jane Addams to Mary Addams Linn, April 1, 1889, Swarthmore College Peace Collection (microfilm of Jane Addams, Letters, Schlesinger Library, Radcliffe College).

[9] Ellen Starr to Mary Blaisdell, February 23, 1889, Starr Papers.

[10] "How Would You Uplift the Masses?" Sunset Club, Chicago, Yearbook (1891-92), 118; Jane Addams's address was given Feb. 4, 1892.

[11] "The Subjective Necessity for Social Settlements," in Jane Addams, et al., Philanthropy and Social Progress (New York, 1893), 26 (moving and living; she omitted this passage when she reprinted the paper in Twenty Years, ch. vi), 23 (solidarity), 1 (endeavors); "A Function of the Social Settlement," Annals of the American Academy of Political and Social Science, XIII (May 1899), 345 (geographical salvation); "How Would You Uplift the Masses?" 119 (theory).

[12] "The Subjective Necessity," 21; "How Would You Uplift the Masses?" 120. Cf. "The Objective Value of a Social Settlement," in Philanthropy and Social Progress, 33, and Twenty Years, 94, in reference to Hull-House itself.

[13] Twenty Years, 64.

[14] For example, Robert A. Woods, "The University Settlement Idea," in Philanthropy and Social Progress, passim, esp. 68-71.

[15] "The Objective Value," 48.

[16] For example, Twenty Years, ch. vii.

[17] "The University Settlement Idea," 60. Addams discusses the conference in Twenty Years, 113-115.

[18]Twenty Years, 259.

[19]Twenty Years, 186. See especially, ibid., 56-57
and ch. ix; and "The Settlement as a Factor in the Labor
Movement," in Jane Addams, et al., Hull-House Maps and
Papers (New York, 1895), 191-192.

[20]For a contemporary view of the limitations of the
word "social," see Albion W. Small, "'Social' vs.
'Societary,'" Annals of the American Academy of Political
and Social Science, V (May 1895), 948-953.

[21]For example, "A Modern Lear," Survey, XXIX (Nov. 2,
1912), 134-135; "The Settlement as a Factor in the Labor
Movement," passim. "A Modern Lear" was written in 1894;
no one would publish it at the time; in a note to the
article, she indicated that she was publishing it
unchanged.

[22]"The Subjective Necessity," 26.

[23]"A Modern Lear."

[24]Pioneering on Social Frontiers (Chicago, 1930), 111,
116.

[25]The Story of My Life (New York, 1932), 52-55 and chs.
vii, viii.

[26]Forty Years of It (New York, 1914), 89-90. There
is a significant exception to this pattern that must be
noted. Frederic C. Howe studied at Johns Hopkins under
Richard T. Ely in the early 1890's. Howe said that Ely's
theories taught him that modern society was unique and
complex and did not fit any of the modes of thinking about
society that he had absorbed in his small-town boyhood.
Howe thus rejected George's teachings in Progress and
Poverty as too simple. Through his later connection with

Tom Johnson, however, and the latter's fight against en-
trenched interests in city real estate and utility franchises,
Howe was converted to the Single Tax and remained an ardent
Single Taxer to the end of his life. Howe, Confessions of a
Reformer (New York, 1925).

[27]"Social Education of the Industrial Democracy:
Labor Museum at Hull House," Commons, V (June 30, 1900), 2;
and Twenty Years, 235-246. Cf. John Dewey, The School and
Society (Chicago, 1899), 33-34.

[28]An assortment of roles and postures can be seen in
"Social Settlements," National Conference of Charities and
Corrections, Proceedings (1897), 339-346; "Ethical Survivals
in Municipal Corruption," International Journal of Ethics,
VIII (April 1898), 273-291; "A Function of the Social
Settlement"; "The College Woman and Christianity," Inde-
pendent, LIII (Aug. 8, 1901), 1852-55.

[29]"The Child and the Curriculum," University of Chicago
Contributions to Education, Number V (Chicago, 1902), 17-20.
Dewey's pedagogy seems a particularly fitting analogy to
Jane Addams's social theory--as well as a possible example
of the distant reverberations an idea can have--in light of
his list of the "fundamental divergences" between the child
(the starting point of educational development) and the curriculum (its goal): "first, the narrow but personal world
of the child against the impersonal but infinitely extended
world of space and time; second, the unity, the single whole-
heartedness of the child's life, and the specializations and
divisions of the curriculum; third, an abstract principle of
logical classification and arrangement, and the practical
and emotional bonds of child life." Ibid., 11.

[30]Addams, "A Function of the Social Settlement," 335;
Dewey, The School and Society, 39 (for Dewey's characterization of the changes--similar to Jane Addams's--see pp. 17-22);
Small, The Significance of Sociology for Ethics (Chicago,
1902), 113, 118; Dewey, "Intelligence and Morals" (1908),
The Influence of Darwin on Philosophy (New York, 1910), 60;
cf. Dewey, "The Significance of the Problem of Knowledge,"

University of Chicago Contributions to Philosophy, Number III
(Chicago, 1897), 16-20.

[31] Social Control (New York, 1901), 84, 426-427, 64.
Cf. Ross, Sin and Society (Boston, 1907), ch. 11-19, and
ch. iii, 40-42.

[32] Democracy and Social Ethics, A. F. Scott, ed.
(Cambridge, Mass., 1964), 93 (complicated). This edition is
a photographic reproduction of a 1907 printing, identical
with the first edition of 1902. The phrase "moral dynamic"
is used in the brochure that she wrote for the course of
lectures on which the book was based; Democracy and Social
Ethics (Chicago, n.d.), 5.

[33] Mead, "The Working Hypothesis in Social Reform,"
American Journal of Sociology, V (Nov. 1899), 367-371.

[34] Small, The Methodology of the Social Problem (Chicago,
1898), 131; Small, The Significance of Sociology for Ethics,
144. See also, B. J. Stern, ed., "Letters of Albion W. Small
to Lester F. Ward: II," Social Forces, XIII (March 1935),
332-333. When Ward had proposed the working hypothesis as
the reform instrument six years before Mead, he had seen it
as the scientific alternative to the closed systems of dogmatic reformers, who were not scientific precisely because
they offered "pure theory and a priori deductions." But Ward,
like Small, saw it as a method of research and as a stop-gap
until the "scientific period" was reached, not as an indication of permanent ignorance. Ward, The Psychic Factors of
Civilization (Boston, 1893), 330-331.

[35] Democracy and Social Ethics, 1, 276-277.

[36] Ibid., 12, 274, 272, 152.

[37] "The College Woman and Christianity," 1852-55.

[38] The phrase (indirection) is Dewey's: "The Child and
the Curriculum," 39.

[39] *Democracy and Social Ethics*, 211.

[40] *Human Nature and the Social Order* (New York, 1902), 325.

[41] *The New Nationalism* (New York, 1910), 37.

[42] *Newer Ideals of Peace* (New York, 1907), 20, 60, 163, 217, 122, 121.

[43] "The Present Crisis in Trades-Union Morals," *North American Review*, CLXXIX (Aug. 1904), 191 (America). Technological frontier: "How Shall We Approach Industrial Education?" *Educational Bi-Monthly*, I (Feb. 1907), 190; cf., *The Spirit of Youth and the City Streets* (New York, 1909), 131.

[44] *Newer Ideals of Peace*, 3 and passim (dynamic pacifism); 28-30, 60, 86 (human nature); 27-28, 60, 63, 119, 214 (nurture, evolutionary; the quotations are from pp. 65, 213).

[45] *The Spirit of Youth and the City Streets* (New York, 1909).

[46] *Democracy and Social Ethics*, 211 (offset); *Spirit of Youth*, 124.

[47] *Spirit of Youth*, 152 and ch. vi. Cf. "The Reaction of Modern Life upon Religious Education," *Religious Education*, IV (April 1909), 23-29, and "The Reaction of Moral Instruction upon Social Reform," *Survey*, XXII (Apr. 3, 1909), 17-19.

[48] "Charity and Social Justice," *Survey*, XXIV (June 11, 1910), 441-449; "The Call of the Social Field," National Conference of Charities and Corrections, *Proceedings* (1911), 370-372; "Religious Education and Contemporary Social Conditions," *Religious Education*, VI (June 1911), 145-162.

[49] Newer Ideals of Peace, 122 (compulsion); Twenty Years at Hull-House (New York, 1910).

[50] "The Reaction of Modern Life upon Religious Education"; "The Reaction of Moral Instruction upon Social Reform"; "Charity and Social Justice"; "The Call of the Social Field'; "Religious Education and Contemporary Social Education."

[51] "The Progressive Party and the Negro," The Crisis, V (Nov. 1912), 31 (remarkable); "Social Justice through National Action," Nationalism . . . Speeches at the Second Annual Lincoln Day Dinner of the Progressive Party (New York, 1914), 9 (perhaps); "Speech Seconding the Nomination of Theodore Roosevelt at the Progressive Convention, 1912," Congressional Record, 62 Cong., 2 Sess., Vol. XII, Appendix, 564-565 (Aug. 12, 1912) (endowed); "The Progressive's Dilemma: The New Party," American Magazine, LXXV (Nov. 1912), 14 (longing) and cf. her description of Lincoln in "Social Justice through National Action," 9; "The Woman in Politics," Progress, I (Nov. 1912), 40 (new order); "The Progressive Party and the Negro," 30; "My Experiences as a Progressive Delegate," McClure's, XL (Nov. 1912), 14 (emergence).

[52] "Lessons of the Election," City Club Bulletin, V (Nov. 27, 1912), 363-364; "Introduction," to Graham Taylor, Religion in Social Action (New York, 1913), xx-xxi.

[53] "The Revolt against War" and "Factors in Continuing the War," in Jane Addams et al., Women at the Hague (New York, 1915); "Women and War, Address Given at the Hague, May 1, 1915," in L. A. Mead, ed., The Overthrow of the War System (Boston, 1915).

[54] "Patriotism and Pacifists in War Time," City Club Bulletin, X (June 16, 1917), 184-190; "The Revolt against War," 57; "Factors in Continuing the War"; "World's Food and World's Politics," National Conference of Charities and Corrections, Proceedings (1918), 650-656.

[55] *Peace and Bread in Time of War* (New York, 1922), 145-146, 150-151.

[56] *Peace and Bread*, 151; an example of her reexamination of the progressive movement is *The Second Twenty Years at Hull-House* (New York, 1930), ch. ii.

[57] *The Excellent Becomes the Permanent* (New York, 1932), 5.

[58] "Why I Shall Vote for LaFollette," *New Republic*, XL (Sept. 10, 1924), 36-37; *Democracy and Social Ethics*, 270; "The Settlement as a Way of Life," *Neighborhood*, II (July 1929), 139-146.

[59] "The Spirit of Social Service," National Conference of Social Work, *Proceedings* (1920), 41-43; "How Much Social Work Can a Community Afford?" *Survey*, LVII (Nov. 15, 1926), 199-201; "Pioneers in Sociology," *Neighborhood*, I (July 1928), 6-11; *The Second Twenty Years at Hull-House*, ch. vi; "Social Workers and the Other Professions," National Conference of Social Work, *Proceedings* (1930), 50-54.

[60] "The Settlement as a Way of Life," 141; cf. *The Excellent Becomes the Permanent*, 134-135.

[61] "Opening Address," Women's International League for Peace and Freedom, *Report of the Fourth Congress*, IV (1924), 1-3; "New Methods of Procedure," WILPF, *Report of the Fifth Congress*, V (1925), 63-65; "President's Address," WILPF, *Report of the Sixth Congress*, VI (1929), 13-15.

[62] "Tolstoy and Gandhi," *Christian Century*, XLVIII (Nov. 25, 1931), 1485-88.

[63] Address (no title), Oct. 30, 1933, Jane Addams Collection, Sophia Smith Collection, Smith College.

Chapter VI (Herbert Croly)

[1] *The New Freedom* (New York, 1913), 3-4, 20, 37.

[2] "The Social Settlement: Its Basis and Function,"
The University Record of the University of Chicago, XII
(January 1908), 108-110.

[3] *The Theory of Business Enterprise* (New York, 1904),
322, 318, 319, 341, 321n, 346, and ch. ix, *passim*.

[4] Doubting and Working," *The Californian*, III (March
1881), 235; cf. *The World and the Individual* (New York,
1899-1901), I, xi.

[5] At the time Croly and Jane Addams were writing,
"authentic" and "inauthentic" were characteristics of standards,
and the problem of "authenticity" was thus the problem of
moral and intellectual authority. In recent years, accompanying the popularity of existentialism and existential psychi-
atry, the word "authenticity" has become associated with
"personal authenticity," the idea that a "real self" would
emerge if modern society did not repress or alienate it.
See, Marshall Berman, *The Politics of Authenticity* (New York,
1970), Introduction; Amitai Etzioni, *The Active Society*
(New York, 1968), Epilogue and Glossary.

[6] *Christianity and the Social Crisis* (New York, 1907),
chs. v, vi (the quotation is from p. 356); Chapman, *Practical
Agitation* (New York, 1900), 142, 140.

[7] Christopher Lasch, in *The New Radicalism in America,
1889-1963* (New York, 1965), ch. v, has said that the
"manipulative mind" is characteristic of Progressivism.

[8] Biographical details from Muriel Shaver, "David Goodman
Croly," *Dictionary of American Biography* (New York, 1930),
IV, 560; Muriel Shaver, "Jane Cunningham Croly," *ibid.*, IV,
560-561; Oswald Garrison Villard, "Herbert David Croly,"

Dictionary of American Biography, Supplement One (New York, 1944), 209-210; [Caroline M. Morse, ed.], Memories of Jane Cunningham Croly, "Jennie June" (New York, 1904); "Herbert Croly, 1869-1930" (Special Supplement), New Republic, LXIII (July 16, 1930), 243-271. The only full length study of Croly and his parents is David W. Levy, "The Life and Thought of Herbert Croly, 1869-1914," unpub. Ph.D. diss., University of Wisconsin, 1967.

[9]Quoting herself in Jane C. Croly to E. C. Stedman, Oct. 27, no year (after 1885), Stedman Papers, Columbia University Libraries.

[10]Essays and letters by Jane Croly in Morse, ed., Memories, 89-141. The quotations are from pp. 122, 123, 110. Jane Croly was also attracted by Edward Bellamy's Nationalism: Jennie June, "The New Point of View," Nationalist, I (Oct. 1889), 195-197.

[11]John Cunningham, "A Brother's Memories," in Morse, ed., Memories, 7. The following material on David Croly's Positivism is from David G. Croly (D. Goodman, pseud.), The Modern Thinker, I-II (1870, 1873); and David G. Croly (C. G. David, Pseud.), A Positivist Primer (New York, 1871).

[12]See, especially, A Positivist Primer, 39-43; "What of the Future," The Modern Thinker, I (1870), 73-92. The quotation is from A Positivist Primer, 56.

[13]A Positivist Primer, 86-87, 24.

[14]"What of the Future," The Modern Thinker, I (1870), 74.

[15]Herbert Croly, "From a Testimonial [to David Croly] by Herbert D. Croly," in Morse, ed., Memories, 61-64; David G. Croly, Extracts from letters . . . to his son Herbert Croly, 1886-87 and 1888, Houghton Library, Harvard University.

[16]Herbert Croly, "From a Testimonial," 62-63.

[17] Lovett, "Herbert Croly's Contribution to American Life," New Republic, LXIII (July 16, 1930), 245.

[18] Herbert Croly, A.B. 1890 (1910), Transcript, Biographical File, Harvard University Archives.

[19] "Originality and Consciousness," Harvard Monthly, XXIV (June 1897), 133.

[20] For example, "The New World and the New Art," Architectural Record, XII (June 1902), 135-153; and "A New Use of Old Forms," Arch. Rec., XVII (Apr. 1905), 271-293.

[21] For example, "American Artists and Their Public, Arch. Rec., X (Jan. 1901), 256-262.

[22] "American Architecture of Today," Arch. Rec., XIV (Dec. 1903), 431-432.

[23] Ibid., 432. See also the story of the changes in architectural standards in Croly and H. W. Desmond, Stately Homes in America, from Colonial Times to the Present Day (New York, 1903); and Croly (William Herbert, pseud.), Houses for Town or Country (New York, 1907).

[24] Stately Homes in America, 211, 532; Croly, "Henry James and His Countrymen," Lamp, XXVIII (Feb. 1904), 47-53.

[25] Croly discussed the social changes most fully in Stately Homes and "New York as the American Metropolis," Arch. Rec., XII (March 1903), 193-206.

[26] See, for example, "American Artists and Their Public" and "Rich Men and Their Houses," Arch. Rec., XII (May 1902), 27-32. Croly later said he was also influenced in 1900 by Robert Grant's novel Unleavened Bread, in which the conflict between commercialism and art bulked large: "The Architect in Recent Fiction," Arch. Rec., XVII (February 1905), 137-139,

and "Why I Wrote My Latest Book," <u>World's Work</u>, XX (June 1910), 13086.

[27] See especially, "The New World and the New Art," and "American Architecture of Today. The quotation is from (Wm. Herbert, pseud.), "Some Business Buildings in St. Louis," <u>Arch. Rec.</u>, XXIII (May 1908), 391

[28] See, for example, "Henry James and His Countrymen"; "Criticism That Counts," <u>Arch. Rec.</u>, X (April 1901), 398-405; and "A New Use of Old Forms."

[29] The sense of transition can be seen, in addition to the items cited in note 25, in his objections to long-range planning that would bind the future, see "What Is Civic Art?" <u>Arch. Rec.</u>, XVI (July 1904), 47-52, especially 50, and "The Promised City of San Francisco," Arch. Rec., XIX (June 1906), 425-436.

[30] "Criticism That Counts," <u>Arch. Rec.</u>, (Apr. 1901), 398-405.

[31] "New York as the American Metropolis," 202-203; <u>Stately Homes</u>, 107; "New World and New Art," 153. The theme of a national culture is also present in all the items cited above.

[32] "Some Really Historical Novels," <u>Lamp</u>, XXVI (July 1903), 509-510.

[33] <u>The Promise of American Life</u>, A. M. Schlesinger, Jr., ed. (Cambridge, Mass., 1965). This is a photographic reproduction of a 1911 printing, identical with the first edition, published by Macmillan in 1909.

[34] "[We] may somewhat indefinitely mark off the last three decades of the nineteenth century as a transition period in America. By 1869 the Union Pacific Railroad had narrowed the continent to a week's journey; by 1901 the

main outlines of our new trust system had become apparent."
Walter Weyl, <u>The New Democracy</u> (New York, 1912), 64. Weyl
subsequently became Croly's colleague on <u>The New Republic</u>.

[35]<u>The Promise of American Life</u>, 101.

[36]<u>Ibid</u>., 53, 88.

[37]<u>Ibid</u>., 27, 104.

[38]<u>Ibid</u>., 27.

[39]Some Business Buildings in St. Louis," 391.

[40]<u>Promise</u>, 4-5.

[41]"Natural Law, Ethics, and Evolution," <u>International
Journal of Ethics</u>, V (July 1895), 489-500. Royce had pre-
sented a similar argument in <u>The Spirit of Modern Philosophy</u>
(Boston, 1892), Part II.

[42]"The New University of California," <u>Arch Rec</u>., XXIII
(April 1908), 272.

[43]<u>Promise</u>, 17.

[44]The issue of continuity is illuminated by contrasting
Royce's article in Note 41 with the reply by J. Mark Baldwin,
"The Cosmic and the Moral," <u>International Journal of Ethics</u>,
VI (Oct. 1895), 93-97. Both Royce's and Baldwin's articles
were part of a widely discussed series of articles on ethics
and evolution. See also, Baldwin, "The Origin of a 'Thing'
and Its Nature," <u>Psychological Review</u>, II (Nov. 1895), 551-
573.

[45]<u>Promise</u>, 139.

[46]On the talented person, ibid., ch. xiii, parts ii and iv, and pp. 190-191, 196. On the critic, ibid., 452, 420-421, 451, 139, 435.

[47]Cf. Charles H. Cooley, Human Nature and the Social Order (New York, 1902), ch. xii. Like Croly, Cooley felt that complexity was not sufficient, that something had to hold society together if complexity were to be useful for individual development. Cooley's answer was "communication"; Croly's was common loyalty to an authentic ideal.

[48]Promise, 439, 449.

[49]"Democratic Factions and Insurgent Republicans," North American Review, CXCI (May 1910), 626-635; "A Great School of Political Science," World's Work, XX (May 1910), 12887-888; "A Test of Faith in Democracy," American Magazine, LXXV (Nov. 1912), 21-23; Croly to Theodore Roosevelt, June 25, 1912, Theodore Roosevelt Papers, Series 1, Box 216, Library of Congress, Manuscript Division.

[50]Croly turned down an official position in the party so that his work would not be seen as mere propaganda. Croly to Theodore Roosevelt, January 3, 1913 (misdated by Croly as 1912), Theodore Roosevelt Papers, Series 1, Box 186; Theodore Roosevelt to Croly, January 7, 1913, Theodore Roosevelt Papers, Series 2, Volume 94.

[51]Progressive Democracy (New York, 1914), 1.

[52]Croly himself minimized the shift: "I hope you will like my book," Croly wrote T. R. in November 1914. "It carries the argument somewhat further that it was carried in The Promise of American Life, but it remains in my mind as only a supplement thereto. I wish the two books had been combined into one." Croly to Theodore Roosevelt, November 5, 1914, Theodore Roosevelt Papers, Series 1, Box 276.

[53]Progressive Democracy, 175, 177-178, 28.

[54]Briefly summarized, Croly's history is as follows:
At the time the state and national constitutions were made,
the democratic forces asserted supremacy only in the fact
that the constitutions were made in conventions and submitted to a popular vote. The democrats shared the conservative idea that social reason could be embodied in law,
and they lacked a conception of a positively socialized
will. Thus, both sides came to see the free and active
assertion of the public will as inimical to the embodiments
of reason. This played into the hands of the anti-
democrats, who wanted to subordinate the exercise of the
popular will to an actual written law and to turn respect
for order into "reverence for an established order." Thus,
Constitution-worship was born. The "people" did not
redirect this tendency when they gained power under the
Jeffersonians, because they were more interested in the
pursuit of individual economic gain. They were concerned
about government's strength, not its democratic or undemo-
cratic character. The vast undeveloped natural resources
thus prompted a temporary alliance between the partisans of
localism and individual economic freedom and the partisans
of rigid legal protection of property interests. The active
use of the government under the National Republicans produced the resurgence of the democracy under Jackson. The
pioneer farmers wanted a firmly established national law
for the sake of cohesion, but they also wanted feeble execution so that local interests would have freedom of action.
Retention of the Constitution meant that government would
have to be democratized and humanized by an extra-
governmental organ: the Democratic Party. The early
Republicans combined the party organization invented by
the Democrats to hobble government with an active goal of
national welfare and humane ideals, rather than with Law
and Constitutionalism. Republican economic nationalism effectively promoted abundant production, which terminated
the conditions of equal opportunity which it had arisen to
develop. The party could not adjust to the new conditions.
The Democratic idea of party organization was fitted for a
balance between strong law and weak government, but
Republican policies kept strengthening the government. At
the same time, the organ which was to control the govern-
ment--the party--fell into the control of an alliance of

businessmen and professional politicians. The evidence of
the need for a "new economic nationalism"is that the old is
producing rigid class divisions rather than unifying society.
The new economic nationalism must be based on the recognition
that privileges cannot be abolished--because private property
cannot be abolished for the foreseeable future--but that they
can be made socially useful and responsible. A revised distribution of privileges in the interest of the disenfran-
chised classes and "a system of special discipline" to make
all holders of privileges socially responsible will dampen
class conflict. These necessarily entail the acceptance of
the "enhancement of human life" as the common purpose of all
actions in a democracy, and an active government, liberated
from the obstructive supremacy of a final law and from party
control, constantly to appraise the equity of the distribution of privileges. The problem then becomes to find a
method for the restoration of strong government to popular
control.

[55] *Progressive Democracy*, 184 (compensation); 184-193
(allegory); 168 (power of faith); 278 (fund); 370 (more
complex); 404 (relatively). See also 405 and chs. viii and
ix.

[56] *Ibid*., 384, 385; also, 15-19, 97, 111, 116-118, 411,
416.

[57] *A Preface to Politics* (New York, 1913), 209, 273,
213.

[58] *Drift and Mastery* (New York, 1914), 62, 64, 152,
170-171, 262.

[59] *Ibid*., 276, 278.

[60] Groff Conklin, ed., *The New Republic Anthology*
(New York, 1936), xxxii-xxxv.

[61] "The End of American Isolation," *New Republic*, I
(Nov. 7, 1914), 9-10; "The Meaning of It," *New Republic*, IV

(Aug. 7, 1915), 10-11; "Our Relations with Great Britain," New Republic, V (Jan. 22, 1916), 290-292; "The Effect on American Institutions of a Powerful Military and Naval Establishment," Annals of the American Academy of Political and Social Science, LXVI (July 1916), 157-172. His rejection of the Democrats is in "Unregenerate Democracy," New Republic, VI (Feb. 5, 1916), 17-19. He announced his support of Wilson in "The Two Parties in 1916," New Republic, VIII (Oct. 21, 1916), 286-291. On a league: "The Structure of Peace," New Republic, IX (Jan. 13, 1917), 287-291; the quotation is from pp. 290-291. For discussions of The New Republic as a whole during the war, see Charles Forcey, The Crossroads of Liberalism (New York, 1961); David Noble, The Paradox of Progressive Thought (Minneapolis, 1958), ch. ii; Eric F. Goldman, Rendezvous with Destiny (New York, 1952), ch. xi; Christopher Lasch, The New Radicalism in America (New York, 1965), ch. vi; Robert E. Osgood, Ideals and Self-Interest in America's Foreign Relations (Chicago, 1953), 121-125, 275-276. Unsigned articles and editorials by Croly are identified as his by The New Republic Book (New York, 1916) and by Forcey.

[62]Progressive Democracy, 404-405, 426; Jane Addams, Peace and Bread in Time of War (New York, 1922), 122.

[63]"The Future of the State," New Republic, XII (September 15, 1917), 179-183; the quotation is from p. 182. Croly proposed the same method as a way to prevent war in "Counsel of Humility," New Republic, XIII (December 15, 1917), 173-176.

[64]Croly, "A School of Social Research," New Republic, XVI (June 8, 1918), 167-171. Dewey's views are in "A New Social Science," New Republic, XIV (April 6, 1918), 292-294, and "Political Science as a Recluse," New Republic, XIV (April 27, 1918), 383-384.

[65]"The Obstacles to Peace," New Republic, XVIII (Apr. 26, 1919), 403-407; "Disordered Christianity," New Republic, XXI (Dec. 31, 1919), 136-139; "Liberalism vs. War," New Republic, XXV (Dec. 8, 1920), 35-39.

[66] In 1919, Croly wrote, but never published, The Breach in Civilization, an attempt to combine the relativism in his conception of science with the moral authority of Christianity. The incomplete galleys are in Houghton Library, Harvard University.

[67] "The Eclipse of Progressivism," New Republic, XXIV (October 27, 1920), 210.

[68] "Hope, History, and H. G. Wells," New Republic, XXIX (November 30, 1921), 12; "The New Republic Idea," New Republic, XXXIII (December 6, 1922; Part II), 5, 13; "Why I Shall Vote for LaFollette," New Republic, XL (October 29, 1924), 223; "Surely Good Americanism," New Republic, XXXII (November 15, 1922), 294-296; "Social Discovery," New Republic, XXXIX (May 28, 1924), 18-20.

[69] "The Eclipse of Progressivism," 210-216; "The Better Prospect," New Republic, XXVII (August 24, 1921), 344-349; "The New Republic Idea," 1-16; "Why I Shall Vote for LaFollette"; "The Outlook for Progressivism in Politics," New Republic, XLI (December 10, 1924), 60-64.

[70] "The Progressive Voter: He Wants to Know!" New Republic, LV (July 25, 1928), 242-247.

[71] "Disordered Christianity," New Republic, XXI (December 31, 1919), 136-139; "Behaviorism in Religion," New Republic, XXIX (February 22, 1922), 367-370; "Reply to C. S. Macfarland," New Republic, XXX (March 29, 1922), 141-143; "The Reconstruction of Religion," New Republic, XXXI (June 21, 1922), 101-103; "Naturalism and Christianity," New Republic, XXXIV (February 28, 1923), 9-11.

[72] "Behaviorism in Religion"; "Reply to C. S. Macfarland"; "Naturalism and Christianity."

[73] "The New Republic Idea," 10.

[74]"Christianity as a Way of Life," New Republic, XXXIX (July 23, 1924), 230-237.

[75]"Christians, Beware!" New Republic, XLV (November 25, 1925), 12-14. The quotation is from p. 14.

[76]"Consciousness and the Religious Life," New Republic, XLV (January 27, 1926), 264.

[77]"Liberalism vs. War," New Republic, XXV (December 25, 1920), 38; "Social Discovery," New Republic, XXXIX (May 28, 1924), 18.

[78]Marcus Alonzo Hanna: His Life and Work (New York, 1912), 39, 111. See also "Introduction" and "Conclusion."

[79]"What Ails American Youth," New Republic, XLI (February 11, 1925), 303.

[80]Willard Straight (New York, 1924), especially ch. xvi, "An Interpretation," 547-560. The quotation is from p. 42, quoting Straight's sister.

[81]"Consciousness and the Religious Life," 265. Cf. "What Ails American Youth," 301-303.

[82]"Social Discovery." The quotation is from p. 19. This article was the Introduction to Eduard C. Lindeman, Social Discovery (New York, 1924). The term "superpragmatism" is Lindeman's: E. C. Lindeman, "Emerging American Philosophy," New Republic, XL (November 19, 1924), 291.

[83]"The Human Potential in the Politics of the Pacific," New Republic, LII (October 5, 1927), 171.

[84]Bayard Rankin, "The History of Probability and the Changing Concept of the Individual," The Journal of the History of Ideas, XXVII (October 1966), 483-504.

Chapter VII (The Mature Society)

[1]Stuart Chase, A New Deal (New York, 1932), 68. Chase noted the effect of cities on population decline in ibid., 70. The major summary statement is Louis Wirth, "Urbanism as a Way of Life," American Journal of Sociology, XLIV (1938), 1-24. See also, President's Research Committee on Social Trends, Recent Social Trends in the United States (New York, 1933), I, xx, ch. i.

[2]President's Conference on Unemployment, Recent Economic Changes in the United States (New York, 1929), I, 81-82; II, 910.

[3]Social Change (New York, 1922), 200-201; Ogburn, "A Reply," Journal of Political Economy, XLI (April 1933), 218; President's Research Committee on Social Trends, Recent Social Trends in the United States (New York, 1933), esp. I, xiii-xiv.

[4]Recent Economic Changes, I, ch. i and pp. 81-82, 842-910 (Mitchell).

[5]Chamberlain, Farewell to Reform (New York, 1933), 323; Ann Rochester, Rulers of America (New York, 1936); Lewis Corey, The Decline of American Capitalism (New York, 1934); Lawrence Dennis, The Coming American Fascism (New York, 1936), 12; George Soule, A Planned Society (New York, 1933) and The Coming American Revolution (New York, 1934); Stuart Chase, A New Deal, 74.

[6]S. Kesselman, "The Frontier Thesis and the Great Depression," Journal of the History of Ideas, XXIX (April 1968), 253-268.

[7]Turner, "Problems in American History" (1906), The Significance of Sections in American History (New York, 1932), 6. See also James C. Malin, "Space and History: Reflections of the Closed-Space Doctrines of Turner and Mackinder and

the Challenge of Those Ideas by the Air Age," <u>Agricultural History</u>, XVIII (April 1944), 65-74 and (July 1944), 107-126.

[8]Dewey, <u>The Quest for Certainty</u> (New York, 1929); Kemler, <u>The Deflation of American Ideals</u> (Washington, 1941).

[9]<u>New York Times</u>, February 3, 1935, Section II, p. 1.

[10]Mead, <u>The Philosophy of the Act</u> (Chicago, 1938), 95; Mead, <u>Philosophy of the Present</u> (Chicago, 1932), 174.

[11]Soule, "The Prospects for General Economic Planning," in F. Mackenzie, ed., <u>Planned Society, Yesterday, Today, Tomorrow</u> (New York, 1937), 915.

Chapter VIII (Rexford Tugwell)

[1]Hoover, <u>The Challenge to Liberty</u> (New York, 1934), 147-148; Hoover, <u>Addresses upon the American Road</u> (New York, 1938), 15.

[2]Stuart Chase, <u>A New Deal</u> (New York, 1932), 137; Rexford Tugwell, "Social Objectives in Education," in <u>Redirecting Education</u>, R. G. Tugwell and L. H. Keyserling, eds. (New York, 1934), I, 5; Tugwell, "After the New Deal," <u>New Republic</u>, XCII (July 26, 1939), 323-325; Tugwell, <u>The Battle for Democracy</u> (New York, 1935), 318-319; Tugwell, "Henry George," <u>Encyclopedia of the Social Sciences</u> (New York, 1931), VI, 631.

[3]Biographical information from Rexford Tugwell, <u>The Light of Other Days</u> (Garden City, New York, 1962); Bernard Sternsher, <u>Rexford Tugwell and the New Deal</u> (New Brunswick, New Jersey, 1964); Russell Lord, <u>The Wallaces of Iowa</u> (Boston, 1947); Russell Lord, "Rural New Yorker," <u>New Yorker</u>, XI (March 23, 1935), 20-24 and (March 30, 1935), 22-24. The quotation is from <u>Light of Other Days</u>, 59.

[4]They were Democrats in a heavily Republican area; ibid., 57.

[5]Ibid., 275 (rattles); 77-80 (on his mother); 307 (different).

[6]Ibid., 62.

[7]Scott Nearing, Social Adjustment (New York, 1911), 374 and chs. xv-xvii.

[8]See the account in Daniel Fox, The Discovery of Abundance: Simon N. Patten and the Transformation of Social Theory (Ithaca, New York, 1967), 125-126, 215.

[9]Scott Nearing, Social Adjustment (New York, 1911), Social Sanity (New York, 1913), Reducing the Cost of Living (Philadelphia, 1914), Poverty and Riches (Philadelphia, 1916). For Nearing's view of Patten, see Nearing, Educational Frontiers (New York, 1925).

[10]Daniel Fox, The Discovery of Abundance; David Noble, The Paradox of Progressive Thought (Minneapolis, 1958), ch. viii; Tugwell, "Some Formative Influences on the Life of Simon Nelson Patten," American Economic Review, XIII (March 1923), Supplement, 273-285; Tugwell, "Notes on the Life and Work of Simon Nelson Patten," Journal of Political Economy, XXXI (April 1923), 153-208; Patten, The New Basis of Civilization (New York, 1907), reprinted, with an introduction by Daniel Fox (Cambridge, 1968); Patten, Essays in Economic Theory, R. G. Tugwell, ed. (New York, 1924); Stuart Chase, The Economy of Abundance (New York, 1934).

[11]Patten, "The Reconstruction of Economic Theory," Essays in Economic Theory, 273-276; Tugwell, "Notes on the Life and Work of Simon Nelson Patten," 206.

[12]Taylor, The Principles of Scientific Management (New York, 1911), 142; Veblen, The Theory of Business

Enterprise (New York, 1904); Veblen, Engineers and the Price System (New York, 1921).

[13] The Economic Basis of Public Interest (Menasha, Wisconsin, 1922); "The Economic Basis for Business Regulation," American Economic Review, XI (December 1921), 643-658.

[14] The famous phrase used by Tugwell's Columbia colleague, Wesley C. Mitchell, in 1922; Mitchell, The Backward Art of Spending Money, and Other Essays (New York, 1937), 137.

[15] For example, Economic Basis of Public Interest, 30; "Economic Basis for Business Regulation," 654.

[16] Economic Basis of Public Interest, 104; 2, chs. iv and vi; ch. ix and passim.

[17] Economic Basis of Public Interest, 35; "Economic Basis for Business Regulation," 656. Tugwell explained this as the relative favor in which various products were held by nature, but gave no method of determining it as an alternative to the market.

[18] Economic Basis of Public Interest, 103. The case of Tyson and Bro. v. Boulton, 273 U.S. 418 (1927), finally convinced him of the futility of relying on an expansion of common-law regulation by the courts, which based decisions on nineteenth-century principles. Tugwell, "That Living Constitution," New Republic, LV (June 20, 1928), 120-122.

[19] Ibid., 22. Henry Waldgrave Stuart, "The Phases of Economic Interest," in John Dewey, et al., Creative Intelligence: Essays in the Pragmatic Attitude (New York, 1917), 282-253. Tugwell was familiar with the essay; he discussed it in "Human Nature in Economic Theory," Journal of Political Economy, XXX (June 1922), 327, and he assigned it to his students: Course Syllabus, 1921, Rexford Tugwell Papers, Franklin D. Roosevelt Library.

[20]"Economic Basis for Business Regulation," 656;
"The Gipsy Strain," Pacific Review, II (September 1921),
196. See also, "The Distortion of Economic Incentive,"
International Journal of Ethics, XXXIV (April 1924), 272-
282.

[21]Parker presented his theories in three essays.
The first, "Toward an Understanding of Labor Unrest," was
presented as an address to members of the Wharton School
in January 1917, while Tugwell was still on the faculty there.
The other two--a piece sympathetic to the Wobblies and a general theoretical statement--were produced and published during the year Tugwell was Parker's colleague in Seattle. They
were collected posthumously in Carleton H. Parker, The Casual
Laborer, and Other Essays (New York, 1920).

[22]Tugwell, "Human Nature in Economic Theory," 339-342.

[23]Tugwell, "The Casual of the Woods," Survey, XLIV
(July 3, 1920), 472-474; "The Outlaw," Survey, XLIV (August
16, 1920), 641-642; "The Philosophy of Despair," New York Call
Magazine (October 17, 1920), 4, 9; "The Gipsy Strain";
"Country Life for America," Pacific Review, II (March 1922),
566-586; "The Distortion of Economic Incentive"; "Human
Nature and Social Economy," Journal of Philosophy, XXVII
(August 14 and 28, 1930), 449-457, 477-492. The quotation
is from "Human Nature in Economic Theory," 343.

[24]The quotations are from Tugwell, "Experimental
Economics," in The Trend of Economics, R. G. Tugwell, ed.
(New York, 1924), 375, 382, 375, 376.

[25]Rexford G. Tugwell, ed., The Trend of Economics
(New York, 1924). Tugwell wrote the "Introduction"; his
"Experimental Economics" appears on pages 371-422; the quo-
tation is from p. ix. Wesley C. Mitchell and Albert B.
Wolfe were included among the "younger generation" because
of their "mental flexibility"; ibid., x. See also, Tugwell,
"Economic Theory and Practice--Discussion," American Economic
Review, XIII (March 1923), Supplement, 107-109.

[26]For example, "Experimental Economics," 407-409 and ch. iv. The quotations are from pp. 401, 382, 389.

[27]Sternsher, Rexford Tugwell and the New Deal, 7; Russell Lord, "Rural New Yorker," New Yorker, XI (March 23, 1935), 23; Tugwell to Horace Taylor, March 12, 1929, Tugwell Papers.

[28]"Experimental Economics," 376, 387, emphasis his.

[29]Tugwell, Munro, and Stryker, American Economic Life; Tugwell and Howard C. Hill, Our Economic Society and Its Problems (New York, 1934).

[30]Industry's Coming of Age (New York, 1927); The Light of Other Days, 329n. The other work cited as influenced by Taylor was The Industrial Discipline and the Governmental Arts (New York, 1933).

[31]Industry's Coming of Age, 265. The requisite control over the economy could not be exercised through consumption, which Tugwell had been at such pains to render static earlier, because consumption was "selective, not initiative or creative" and was primarily an instrument with which the individual adjusted to, rather than controlled, the world; ibid., 107.

[32]Ibid., 30, 124.

[33]"Experimental Economics," 422; "Guild Socialism and the Industrial Future," International Journal of Ethics, XXXII (April 1922), 286.

[34]Industry's Coming of Age, 262. See also, "Economics and Ethics," Journal of Philosophy, XXI (December 4, 1924), 682-690.

[35]Tugwell, Munro, and Stryker, American Economic Life, 2d and 3d eds. (1925, 1930); quotation is from 2d ed., 4.

[36] *Industry's Coming of Age*, 246.

[37] For the war and Russian experiences, see, "The Paradox of Peace," *New Republic*, LVI (April 18, 1928), 262-267; "America's War-Time Socialism," *Nation*, CXXIV (April 6, 1927), 364-367; "Economics as the Science of Experience," *Journal of Philosophy*, XXV (January 19, 1928), 29-40; "Discussion of 'Must Prosperity Be Planned?'" *Bulletin of the Taylor Society*, XIII (February 1928), 19-21; "Communism: Reality and Theory," *New Republic*, LIV (February 22, 1928), 22-23; "Russian Agriculture," in Stuart Chase, *et al.*, *Soviet Russia in the Second Decade* (New York, 1928), 55-102; "Experimental Control in Russian Industry," *Political Science Quarterly*, XLIII (June 1928), 161-187.
    For the political campaign, see, "The Liberal Choice," *New Republic*, LVI (September 5, 1928), 74-75; "Platforms and Candidates," *ibid.*, LV (May 30, 1928), 44-45; "Hunger, Cold, and Candidates," *ibid.*, LIV (May 2, 1928), 323-325; "Governor Smith's Dilemma," *ibid.*, LV (August 1, 1928), 276-277.

[38] "Governor or President?" *New Republic*, LIV (May 16, 1928), 381-382; "The Paradox of Peace," 267; "Platforms and Candidates."

[39] For example, "Flaws in the Hoover Economic Plan," *Current History*, XXXV (January 1932), 525-531; "Discourse in Depression," 1932, mimeographed, New York Public Library; *Mr. Hoover's Economic Policy* (New York, 1932 [John Day Pamphlet]).

[40] President's Conference on Unemployment, Committee on Recent Economic Changes, *Recent Economic Changes in the United States*, 2 v. (New York, 1929).

[41] "The Theory of Occupational Obsolescence," *Political Science Quarterly*, XLVI (June 1931), 226; "Discourse in Depression," 11-16.

[42]Industrial Discipline and the Governmental Arts (New York, 1933), 67-68, 223; "Theory of Occupational Obsolescence," 171-227. On the book's reception as a New Deal manifesto: Walton H. Hamilton, "The Credo of Recovery," New Republic, LXXV (June 1933), 185.

[43]"The Principle of Planning and the Institution of Laissez-Faire," American Economic Review, XXII (March 1932), Supplement, 91-92. By "foreseen," Tugwell meant not predicted or predestined, but consciously chosen. See also Industrial Discipline, 22-23. Manipulative method: "Economics," in Roads to Knowledge, W. A. Neilson, ed. (New York, 1932), 108. Management vs. determinism: "Social Objectives in Education," in Redirecting Education, R. G. Tugwell and L. H. Keyserling, eds. (New York, 1934), I, 90; this essay was written in 1932.

[44]For example, Dewey, Philosophy and Civilization (New York, 1931), last ch., cited by Tugwell in "Social Objectives in Education," 29; Dewey, Review of The Art of Thought by Graham Wallas, New Republic, XLVII (June 16, 1926), 118-119, cited by Tugwell in "Economics as the Science of Experience," Journal of Philosophy, XXV (January 19, 1928), 33. See also, Dewey, "Justice Holmes and the Liberal Mind," New Republic, LIII (January 11, 1928), 210-212; "Social Science and Social Control," New Republic, LXVII (July 29, 1931), 276-279; The Public and Its Problems (New York, 1927), 163, 197-203.

[45]Tugwell, The Place of Planning in Society (San Juan, Puerto Rico, 1954), 81, on Person's role. For Person's ideas: Harlow S. Person, ed., Scientific Management in American Industry (New York, 1929), chs. i and ii are by Person; "Scientific Management as a Philosophy and Technique of Progressive Industrial Stabilization," World Social Economic Congress (Hague, 1931), 153-204; "Principles of Planning and Control Derived from American Experience," Bureau of Personnel Administration, Economic and Social Planning, Conference 4, November 5, 1931, pp. 28-36. For the professional context of the reformism of efficiency

experts, see Edwin Layton, The Revolt of the Engineers
(Cleveland, 1971).

[46]Tugwell, "Social Objectives in Education," 70.

[47]Ibid., 66-69.

[48]Industrial Discipline, 218; "Social Objectives in
Education," 12.

[49]Oglethorpe University Address, March 22, 1932, Public
Papers and addresses of Franklin D. Roosevelt, S. Rosenman,
ed. (New York, 1938), I, 646; Jefferson Day Address, April
18, 1932, ibid., I, 631. See also, Commonwealth Club
Address, September 23, 1932, ibid., I, 742-756. Tugwell
identified himself as a writer of the second and third;
Tugwell, The Democratic Roosevelt (Garden City, New York,
1957), 217-219. He later disputed the idea that he agreed
with the stasis implied in the maturity thesis; ibid., 246.
But his desire for "expansion" or "growth" did not contra-
dict stasis, which, as used here, implies not stagnation,
but the emergence of society as a completed "type" in
people's minds. It could easily include "growth," because
growth did not imply substantive change, but increased productive efficiency of "industrial society."

[50]See, for example, Lewis Lorwin, "Comment," American
Economic Review, XXII (March 1932), Supplement, 94; and
the volume, Planned Society, Yesterday, Today, Tomorrow,
F. P. Mackenzie, ed. (New York, 1937). For modern discus-
sions of planning in the New Deal, see Ellis Hawley, The
New Deal and the Problem of Monopoly (Princeton, 1966), and
Otis L. Graham, Jr., "The Planning Ideal and American Reality:
The 1930's" in The Hofstadter Aegis: A Memorial, S. Elkins
and E. McKitrick, eds. (New York, 1974), 257-299.

[51]For his career as an administrator and his private
opinions of the measures, see Sternsher, Rexford Tugwell and the
New Deal; Paul K. Conkin, Tomorrow a New World: The New Deal

Community Program (Ithaca, New York, 1959); Charles T.
Goodsell, Administration of a Revolution: Executive Reform
under Governor Tugwell, 1941-1946 (Cambridge, 1965); and
Tugwell's own quasi-memoirs, beginning with The Stricken
Land (Garden City, New York, 1947).

[52]For example, Tugwell and Hill, Our Economic Society
and Its Problems, 541ff.; Tugwell, "Address to Editors,"
New York Times, April 22, 1934, p. 30; "Are the Increasing
Powers of the President Improving the American Government,"
Congressional Digest, XII (November 1933), 270; "The Ideas
Behind the New Deal," New York Times Magazine, July 16, 1933,
p. 17; "The Economics of the Recovery Program" (November 16,
1933), in Tugwell, The Battle for Democracy (New York, 1935),
94.

[53]"The Progressive Tradition," Atlantic, CLV (April
1935), 414, 418 (good life); "The Prospect for the Future"
(October 29, 1933), in Battle for Democracy, 70-71 (dispraise). Quotations on stasis are from, in sequence:
"Bread or Cake" (May 12, 1934), ibid., 290; "Ideas Behind
the New Deal," 1; "Are the Increasing Powers of the President," 268; "Le Role de l'etat dans la vie economique des
Etats-Unis," L'Esprit Internationale, VIII (April 1934),
206. See also, "Government in a Changing World," Review
of Reviews, LXXXVIII (August 1933), 33; "Design for Government," in Battle of Democracy, 7-8.

[54]"The Future of National Planning," New Republic,
LXXXIX (December 9, 1936), 162-164, on mandate for planning.
For the reaction to him: Editorial, New York Times,
January 17, 1937, IV, 9; "Tugwell to the Wolves?" New
Republic, LXXXV (December 25, 1935), 186-187; "Editorial
Note," ibid., LXXXIX (December 2, 1936), 128; Arthur Crock,
Column, New York Times, January 17, 1937, IV, 3; Delbert
Clark, "Brain Trusters Make Way for Executives," New York
Times Magazine, March 7, 1937, p. 16. His parting remarks
were reported in New York Times, January 14, 1937, p. 3.

[55]Tugwell's proposed new constitution for the United
States is in The Center Magazine, III (September/October

1970). The idea was adumbrated in his reflections as a
planner in New York City: "The Fourth Power," Planning and
Civic Comment, V (April-June 1939), Part III, 1-39; "The
Superpolitical," Journal of Social Philosophy, V (January
1940), 97-114; "Implementing the General Interest," Public
Administration Review, I (Autumn (1940), 32-49; "The
Directive," Journal of Social Philosophy and Jurisprudence,
VII (October 1941), 5-36. For Tugwell as a planner, see
also his Changing the Colonial Climate (San Juan, Puerto
Rico, 1942); The Stricken Land (New York, 1947); The Art of
Politics (Garden City, New York, 1958). The memoirs include
the series of articles in the Western Political Quarterly
and other journals in the late forties and fifties, which
then were incorporated into The Democratic Roosevelt.

[56]"The Directive," Journal of Social Philosophy and
Jurisprudence, VII (October 1941), 5-36; "The Utility of the
Future in the Present," Public Administration Review, VIII
(Winter 1948), 49-59; "Notes on Some Implications of Oneness
in the World," Common Cause, I (November 1947), 165-172; The
Place of Planning in Society (San Juan, Puerto Rico, 1954);
and the items in note 55.

[57]"On the Troublesome 'X,'" Philosophy of Science, IV
(October 1937), 412-426; "The Fourth Power," 22; "The
Superpolitical," 113-114; "The Utility of the Future in the
Present"; "The Directive."

[58]For example, "The Fourth Power," 30. Cf. George
Soule, "Toward a Planned Society," New Republic, CI
(November 8, 1939), 29-33.

[59]"Wesley Mitchell: An Evaluation," New Republic,
XCII (October 6, 1937), 240 (chaos; tentatives); "The
Fourth Power," 4 (pragmatic morality); Letter to the
Editor, New York Times, June 28, 1973, p. 46.

Chapter IX (Thurman Arnold)

[1]Roscoe Pound, "Preventive Justice and Social Work,"
National Conference of Social Work, Proceedings (1923),
156.

[2]Thurman Arnold, The Folklore of Capitalism (New Haven,
1937), 220-221.

[3]Thurman Arnold, Fair Fights and Foul: A Dissenting
Lawyer's Life (New York, 1965). Biographical information
can also be found in Edward N. Kearny, Thurman Arnold,
Social Critic: The Satiric Challenge to Orthodoxy
(Albuquerque, 1970); Douglas Ayer, "In Quest of Efficiency:
The Ideological Journey of Thurman Arnold in the Interwar
Period," Stanford Law Review, XXIII (June 1971), 1049-1086;
Gene Gressley, Introduction, to Voltaire and the Cowboy:
Letters of Thurman Arnold (Boulder, 1977).

[4]Philo Calhoun, "Foreword," to C. P. Arnold, Crannies
and Horizons: A Memorial Edition of the Poems of Constantine Peter Arnold, 1860-1943, Selected by Thurman
Arnold (n.p., 1962), 5. See also, F. L. Arnold, "Biographical Note," in ibid.; and T. W. Arnold, Fair Fights and Foul,
ch. i.

[5]Arnold, Symbols of Government (New Haven, 1935);
Arnold, New Haven, to Harry Elmer Barnes, January 27, 1936,
Harry Elmer Barnes Papers, Coe Library, University of
Wyoming,also reprinted in Gressley, 218-219; Barnes, The
Genesis of the World War (New York, 1926), 14, 697-698.

[6]Barnes, The New History and the Social Studies
(New York, 1925), 56, 687-589, 596.

[7]Arnold, Fair Fights and Foul, ch. iv.

[8]Arnold, "The Law School of the University of Wyoming,"
Wyoming State Bar Association, Proceedings of the Eighth

Annual Meeting (1921), 49-52; "Report of the Committee on
Legal Education and Admission to the Bar," Wyoming State
Bar Association, Proceedings of the Tenth Annual Meeting
(1923), 75-79; "College of Law Registration--Raising Requirements for Entrance," West Virginia Law Quarterly, XXXV
(December 1928), 53-54; "Review of the Work of the College
of Law," West Virginia Law Quarterly, XXXVI (June 1930),
319-329.

[9]"The Law School of the University of Wyoming," 49;
"Report of the Committee on Legal Education and Admission
to the Bar," 76. For a stimulating discussion of professionalization and related issues, see Jerold S. Auerbach,
"Enmity and Amity: Law Teachers and Practitioners, 1900-
1922," Perspectives in American History, V (1971), 551-601.

[10]On the relation of professionalism to reform, see his
"Review of the Work of the College of Law"; Arnold, Morgan-
town, to H. F. Goodrich, Oct. 18 and 24, 1928, Arnold
Papers; Johns Hopkins University, Institute of Law, Current
Research in Law for the Academic Year 1928-1929 (Baltimore,
1929), 7, 25, 43, 114, 155; and same, . . . for the
Academic Year 1929-1930 (Baltimore, 1930), 14, 33. For the
context of Arnold's efforts, see Auerbach, "Enmity and
Amity"; and Robert Stevens, "Two Cheers for 1870: The
American Law School," Perspectives in American History, V
(1971), 405-548.

[11]Information from Registrar's Office, Harvard Law
School; Harvard University Catalogue, 1912-1913, 691ff,
and 1913-1914, 681ff. Roscoe Pound, "The Scope and Purpose
of Sociological Jurisprudence," Harvard Law Review, XXIV
(June 1911), 591-619; XXV (December 1911), 140-168; XXV
(April 1912), 489-516. Arnold was not always aware of intellectual debts, and the only Pound mentioned in his autobiography in Ezra. But his repeated use of Roscoe Pound's
classifications and aphorisms (without citation) bespeaks
a considerable indebtedness.

[12]In addition to Pound's, "Scope and Purpose," see
also his "Justice According to Law," Columbia Law Review,

XIII (December 1913), 696-713; XIV (January 1914), 1-26;
XIV (February 1914), 103-121, especially pp. 706, 713, 120.

[13]For example, "A Theory of Social Interests," American
Sociological Society, Papers and Proceedings of the 15th
Annual Meeting, December 1920, XV (May 1922), 16-45, espe-
cially pp. 17-19.

[14]"Preventive Justice and Social Work," National
Conference of Social Work, Proceedings (1923), 151-163.

[15]In addition to the previously cited works, the ensuing discussion is based on the following by Pound:
Interpretations of Legal History (New York, 1923); "Jurisprudence," in H. E. Barnes, ed., The History and Prospects
of the Social Sciences (New York, 1925), 444-479; "The
Decadence of Equity," Columbia Law Review, V (January 1905),
20-35; "Justice according to Law" (Dec. 1913), 696, and
(January 1914), 20-21; "Jurisprudence," in Barnes, ed., The
History and Prospects of the Social Sciences, 472.

[16]"Justice according to Law" (Jan. 1914), 18 and (Feb.
1914), 108; and "The Decadence of Equity." Pound acknowledged the perception of complexity, but his own interests
in judicial reform led him to prefer the explanation that
justice without law increases whenever the legal system
fails to fulfill its purpose and was therefore not incurable.

[17]Pound, "Preventive Justice and Social Work," 154;
"Justice According to Law" (January 1914), 20.

[18]For a different view of this episode see Ayer, "In
Quest of Efficiency," Stanford Law Review, XXIII (June 1971),
1053-1054. See also Pound, "Justice According to Law,"
Columbia Law Review, XIV (February 1914), 109-110.

[19]For example, Robert F. Wagner, "The Law's Delays,"
in H. Oliphant and P. T. Moon, ed., Law and Justice,
Proceedings of the Academy of Political Science, X (July
1923), 184-188.

[20]Arnold and Fleming James, Jr., Cases and Materials on Trials, Judgments, and Appeals (St. Paul, Minn., 1936).

[21]The discussion is based on the following by Charles E. Clark: "The Code Cause of Action," Yale Law Journal, XXXIII (June 1924), 817-837; "History, Systems and Functions of Pleading," Virginia Law Review, XI (May 1925), 517-552; "The Complaint in Code Pleading," Yale Law Journal, XXXV (January 1926), 259-291; "The New Summary Judgment Rule in Connecticut," A.B.A. Journal, XV (February 1929), 82-85; "Summary Judgment," Encyclopedia of the Social Sciences (New York, 1934), XIV, 461-462; "Methods of Legal Reform," West Virginia Law Quarterly, XXXV (December 1929), 106-118; Handbook of the Law of Code Pleading (St. Paul, Minn., 1928), ch. i.

[22]Arnold, J. W. Simonton, and H. C. Havighurst, "Report to the Committee on Judicial Administration and Legal Reform," West Virginia Law Quarterly, XXXVI (December 1929), 27, 34.

[23]Ibid., 37.

[24]The ensuing discussion is based on the following by Edson R. Sunderland: "The Machinery of Procedural Reform," Michigan Law Review: XXII (February 1924), 293-311; "The English Struggle for Procedural Reform," Harvard Law Review, XXXIX (April 1926), 725-748; "The Regulation of Legal Procedure," West Virginia Law Quarterly, XXXV (April 1929), 301-322; "Comments on Proposed Changes in Procedure in West Virginia," West Virginia Law Quarterly, XXXVI (December 1929), 119-132.

[25]Sunderland, "The English Struggle for Procedural Reform," 745, 746 (modernizing; insight); "The Regulation of Legal Procedure," 314 (efficient); "The Machinery of Procedural Reform," 298, 299 (grow; procedure).

[26]Arnold, "The Collection of Judicial Statistics in West Virginia," West Virginia Law Quarterly, XXXVI (February 1930), 184-194; "Judicial Councils," West Virginia Law Quarterly, XXXV (April 1929), 193-238. The

West Virginia legislature passed the bill after Arnold had
left the state, but it was vetoed by the Governor, primarily,
Arnold thought, because of the connection to the law school,
whose studies had angered powerful interests; Arnold,
New Haven, to Edward C. Dickinson, March 10, 1931, Arnold
Papers.

[27]Sunderland, "The Regulation of Legal Procedure," 314.

[28]"Criminal Attempts--The Rise and Fall of an Abstraction," Yale Law Journal, XL (November 1930), 53-80.

[29]Ibid., 70, 79.

[30]"The Restatement of the Law of Trusts," Columbia
Law Review, XXXI (May 1931), 821, 802.

[31]For a pragmatic, descriptive restatement of trusts,
Arnold looked at the actual operation of the rules in different circumstances, then classified cases according to
the purposes for which the trust was used. He thereby
found two functional classes of trusts: one in which the
parties intended to set one up (the owner of property
having given one person the benefit of it and another
control of it), and a second in which courts used the device
as a fiction to avoid undesirable results from another rule
or statute. The attempt of the definitional restaters to
reconcile the two classes in disregard of their functional
differences, produced unnecessary confusion. Judges should
not have to consider decisions in the second class as precedents for cases belonging in the first, since they had
neither the same purpose nor the same effect; they only had
the same name. Such a method would permit the elimination
of useless formulas. Ibid., passim.

[32]On generalization: Arnold, New Haven, to Thomas Reed
Powell, n.d., Powell Papers, Harvard Law School. Scott's
reply to Arnold is in: Austin W. Scott, "The Restatement
of the Law of Trusts," Columbia Law Review, XXXI (December
1931), 1266-1285. Powell's comments are in: T. R. Powell,

Cambridge, Mass., to Arnold, May 27, 1931, Arnold Papers.
Arnold's criticism and Scott's reply had been first presented during the spring of 1931.

[33]Llewellyn, "Some Realism about Realism--Responding
to Dean Pound," Harvard Law Review, XLIV (June 1931),
1222-1264; the quotation is from pp. 1235-1236, n. 36.
Pound's criticisms were in "The Call for a Realist Jurisprudence," Harvard Law Review, XLIV (March 1931), 697-711,
which had, in turn, apparently been prompted by Llewellyn's,
"A Realistic Jurisprudence--The Next Step," Columbia Law
Review, XXX (April 1930), 431-465. Arnold later liked to
distinguish himself from the Realists on the grounds that
most Realists were cynical and disillusioned and took the
law as seriously as the Fundamentalists. For helpful and
accessible discussions of Legal Realism, see Wilfred E.
Rumble, American Legal Realism (Ithaca, N.Y., 1968);
G. Edward White, "From Sociological Jurisprudence to
Realism," Virginia Law Review, LVIII (September 1972),
999-1028; Edward A. Purcell, Jr., "American Jurisprudence
between the Wars," American Historical Review, LXXV
(December 1969), 424-446.

[34]The Heavenly City of the Eighteenth-Century Philosophers (New Haven, 1932); the longer phrases and the sentence
quoted are from ibid., 12, 27.

[35]Law and the Modern Mind (New York, 1930). Modest
probabilities is Dewey's phrase, quoted in ibid., 263.

[36]The quotation is from ibid., 73.

[37]Arnold, Review of Law and the Modern Mind by Jerome
Frank, Saturday Review of Literature, VII (March, 1931),
644; Arnold, New Haven, to Jerome Frank, January 13, 1931,
Arnold Papers. The quotation is from Frank, Law and the
Modern Mind, 283. Arnold admired Green greatly, though he
became defensive about his praise of Green's work when

Felix Frankfurter said it was shallow; Frankfurter,
Cambridge, to Arnold, December 22, 1931, Arnold Papers;
Arnold, New Haven, to Frankfurter, Cambridge, to Arnold,
December 22, 1931, Arnold Papers; Arnold, New Haven, to
Frankfurter, January 9, 1932, Arnold Papers.

[38]Leon Green, Scientific Methods in Law, Northwestern
University School of Law, Bulletin, No. 1 (1929), 12, 20.
Arnold commended this piece in Arnold, New Haven, to Leon
Green, February 4, 1930, Arnold Papers. Arnold's review
of Green, Judge and Jury (Kansas City, Mo., 1930) is in
Yale Law Journal, XL (March 1931), 833-835. Most of Judge
and Jury had appeared earlier as articles, so that Frank
could comment on Green's work even though Law and the Modern
Mind was published a few months before Judge and Jury.

[39]The issue of representation was a major impulse be-
hind Arnold's "An Inequitable Preference in Favor of Surety
Companies," West Virginia Law Quarterly, XXXVI (April 1930),
278-288. Llewellyn commented on it in "Some Realism about
Realism," 1255. The court as passive is an issue in
Arnold, "The Changing Law of Competition in Public Service--
A Dissent," West Virginia Law Quarterly, XXXIV (February
1928), 183-188.

[40]For example, ibid.; also, "Contempt--Evasion of
Criminal Process as Contempt of Court," West Virginia Law
Quarterly, XXXIV (February 1928), 188-192; "The Lake Cargo
Rate Case of February 1928," ibid., XXXIV (April 1928),
272-282; "The Lake Cargo Rate Controversy," ibid., XXXIV
(June 1928), 365-366. The last two involved the ICC, which
Arnold felt was stepping outside its intended adjudicating
function and attempting to regulate the national economy
according to its own limited ideal. The case involved the
welfare of West Virginia, so Arnold was also a partisan in
the articles. See also Arnold's "Comparative Procedure,"
Connecticut Bar Journal, V (July 1931), 247.

[41]Arnold, "Trial by Combat and the New Deal," Harvard
Law Review, XLVII (April 1934), 913-947. In late 1933,

Arnold represented the government in cases involving the
constitutionality of the AAA and also wrote an amicus
curiae brief for the Nebbia case (which the AAA did not use);
Arnold, New Haven, to F. L. Lowmaster, October 9, 1933;
Arnold, New Haven, to T. B. Jackson, October 30, 1933;
Arnold to A. B. Curtiss, December 7, 1933 (all Arnold
Papers). See also, Arnold, "The New Deal Is Constitutional,"
New Republic, LXXVII (November 15, 1933), 8-10, an attempt
to show that the AAA could satisfy all the canons of traditional legal logic and that it did not require a revolution
from the courts to keep it going.

[42]"The Role of Substantive Law and Procedure in the
Legal Process," Harvard Law Review, XLV (Feb. 1932), 617-
647; "Law Enforcement--An Attempt at Social Dissection,"
Yale Law Journal, XLII (Nov. 1932), 1-24.

[43]"The Role of Substantive Law," 647; "Law Enforce-
ment," 24; Harry Stack Sullivan, New York, to Arnold,
October 10, 1932, Arnold Papers; Arnold, New Haven, to
Harry Stack Sullivan, October 18, 1932, Arnold Papers;
Arnold, "Law Enforcement," 1, n. 1; Arnold, "The Juris-
prudence of Edward S. Robinson," Yale Law Journal, XLVI
(June 1937), 1282-1289.

[44]"Law Enforcement," 4, 23, 24; see also Arnold,
Review of Studies in Law and Politics by Harold J. Laski,
Columbia Law Review, XXXIII (February 1933), 377-378. His
analysis of New Deal measures is in Symbols of Government,
107-123. The analogy to an insane asylum is in ibid., 232-
236.

[45]Arnold and W. A. Sturges, "The Progress of the New
Administration," Yale Review, n.s., XXII (June 1933), 673-
674; Arnold, "Theories about Economic Theories," Annals of
the American Academy of Political and Social Science, CLXXII
(March 1934), 32-36.

[46]Symbols of Government, 258-271, on the humanitarian
ideal; 263-266, on ideals as arbitrary choice.

[47]Edward S. Robinson, Law and the Lawyers (New York, 1935), 6 (popularize); Arnold, "Institute Priests and Yale Observers," University of Pennsylvania Law Review, LXXXIV (May 1936), 812. See also, Arnold, "The Jurisprudence of Edward S. Robinson," Yale Law Journal, XLVI (June 1937), 1282-1289. Morris R. Cohen, Review of The Symbols of Government, Illinois Law Review, XXXI (November 1936), and Review of Law and the Lawyers, Cornell Law Quarterly, XXII (1936); both are reprinted in Cohen, Reason and Law (Glencoe, Ill., 1950), 137-148, 173-181.

[48]Arnold's praise of FDR: "Progress of the New Administration," 656, 676-677; "Theories about Economic Theory," 34; Symbols of Government, 247; "How They are Voting" (letter), New Republic, LXXXVIII (September 30, 1936), 233; "What I Expect of Roosevelt," Nation, CXLIII (November 28, 1936), 62. On planning as experiment: "Progress of the New Administration," 674, 677; "Theories about Economic Theory," 35. On the intellectual structure and lack of a need for accuracy: "Institute Priests and Yale Observers," 822; "The Parable of the Bright Swede," Yale Review, n.s., XXV (March 1936), 613-614; Symbols of Government, passim.

[49]On economic maturity: Symbols of Government, 100, 260-263. The earliest hint of this idea in Arnold is in "Review of A Treatise on the Law of Oil and Gas by W. L. Summers," West Virginia Law Quarterly, XXXIV (June 1928), 413-415. His connection to the theorists of the economy of abundance: "A Criticism of the Critics of Stuart Chase," Yale Review, n.s., XXIII (June 1934), 835-838; James B. Angell, New Haven, to Arnold, March 28, 1934, Arnold Papers, referring to an invitation from Arnold to Tugwell to visit Yale; Arnold, "Theories about Economic Theory," Annals of the American Academy of Political and Social Science, CLXXII (March 1934), 26-36; The Symbols of Government, 4. His economic proposals: Arnold and W. A. Sturges, "The Progress of the New Administration," Yale Review, n.s., XXII (June 1933), 656-677, esp. 672, 676, 677. See also "RCS" (Research Assistant to Arnold and Sturges), New Haven, to C. A. Wilson, March 20, 1933; Arnold, New Haven, to Senator E. B. Smith,

March 21, 1933; Arnold, New Haven, to A. G. Crane, March 9, 1933; Carl Arnold, Laramie, to Arnold, March 13, 1933; Frank Evans, Washington, to Arnold, March 13, 1933; Arnold to George Longan, April 4, 1933 (all in Arnold Papers).

[50] Pound, "Jurisprudence," Encyclopedia of the Social Sciences (New York, 1933), VIII, 485; cf. Pound, "The Call for a Realist Jurisprudence," 708, where Pound saw that emphasis as "business"-oriented.

[51] Symbols of Government, 270-271.

[52] "How They are Voting"; "What I Expect of Roosevelt"; "A Reply," A.B.A. Journal, XXIII (May 1937), 364-368, 393-394. Arnold wrote this article at the urging of the Attorney General; Arnold, Washington, to Charles E. Clark, April 30, 1937, Arnold Papers. See also Arnold to James M. Landis, March 23, 1937, and Arnold to W. D. Lewis, March 23, 1937, Arnold Papers.

[53] Eugene Davidson, New Haven, to Arnold, May 24, 1937, Arnold Papers.

[54] The Folklore of Capitalism (New Haven, 1937), 47 (dissection); 121, 270, 333, 108, 185, 118 (age of organization, etc.); 364 (ceased to expand).

[55] The interchange was noted by Felix Cohen, Review of The Folklore of Capitalism by T. W. Arnold, National Lawyers Guild Quarterly, I (March 1938), 161-164.

[56] Folklore of Capitalism, ch. xiv, 376.

[57] Ibid., 58; see also 38-39.

[58] Ibid., 378 (Principle 20), 328 (catharsis); also 390-392, 326-328, 151, 345.

[59]For example, ibid., 349, 59, 137, 179, 162.

[60]Ibid., 9, 12, 333. See also, "The Parable of the Bright Swede," Yale Review, n.s., XXV (March 1936), 612-615.

[61]Arnold, Fair Fights and Foul, 135; Arnold, Letter to the Editor, New York Times Book Review, March 6, 1938, p. 23; Max Lerner, "The Shadow World of Thurman Arnold," Yale Law Journal, XLVII (March 1938), 687-703; Harold Laski, Review of Folklore of Capitalism, Brooklyn Law Review, VII (May 1938), 535-537; Sidney Hook, "The Politician's Handbook," University of Chicago Law Review, V (April 1938), 341-349, together with Arnold's reply, pp. 349-353, and Hook's rejoinder, 354-357; Arnold to J. R. Sullivan, January 26, 1938, Arnold Papers. The quotation is from Lerner, "Capitalism as Magic," Nation, CXLVI (Jan. 8, 1938), 46.

[62]"Nomination of Thurman W. Arnold," Hearings before a Subcommittee of the Senate Committee of the Judiciary, 75 Cong., 3 sess., March 11, 1938, p. 3, a question of Borah's, to which Arnold replied, "Certainly."

[63]For example, "The Changing Law of Competition in Public Service--A Dissent," West Virginia Law Quarterly, XXXIV (February 1928), 183-188; "The Lake Cargo Rate Case of February 1928," ibid., XXXIV (April 1928), 272-282.

[64]The Bottlenecks of Business (New York, 1940), 10, 91, 97. Arnold wrote many articles and made many speeches during his tenure in the Justice Department; there is a substantial collection in the Arnold Papers. The most accessible collections of his views are The Bottlenecks of Business and Democracy and Free Enterprise (Norman, Okla., 1942). Ellis Hawley discusses antitrust under Arnold in The New Deal and the Problem of Monopoly (Princeton, 1966). See also Gene Gressley, "Thurman Arnold, Antitrust, and the New Deal," Business History Review, XXXVIII (Summer 1964), 214-231.

[65]"Fair and Effective Use of Present Antitrust Procedure," Yale Law Journal, XLVII (June 1938), 1297.

[66]Bottlenecks of Business, 99-111.

[67]In "Trial by Combat and the New Deal," 926-931, Arnold had briefly capitulated to the legitimating power of the Court and proposed a method analogous to, though weaker than declaratory judgments, as a way of giving the courts a more orderly but weaker role in the regulatory process. He called for methods of advance tentative approval of regulatory schemes during an experimental period, as well as methods of considering the needs of all interested groups, and quick appeals. Roscoe Pound had pointed to declaratory judgments as examples of preventive justice, and Edson Sunderland saw them as a way to make the court useful in "modern civilization." Pound, "Jurisprudence," in Barnes, ed., The History and Prospects of the Social Sciences, 467; Sunderland, "A Modern Evolution in Remedial Rights--The Declaratory Judgment," Michigan Law Review, XVI (December 1917), 68-69.

[68]"Antitrust Activities of the Department of Justice," Oregon Law Review, XIX (December 1939), 27; "Fair and Effective Use," 1294; Bottlenecks of Business, 274.

[69]For example, Radio Broadcast for Freedom House, December 19, 1944, Arnold Papers; Folklore of Capitalism, 173, 277, 312; Bottlenecks of Business, 14-19; Democracy and Free Enterprise, 59-62; "The Folklore of Capitalism Revisited," Yale Review, n.s., LII (December 1962), 188-204. The quotation is from Bottlenecks of Business, 19.

[70]Bottlenecks of Business, 10.

[71]Ibid., 278.

[72]Democracy and Free Enterprise, 62; "The Sherman Act on Trial," Atlantic, CXCII (July 1953), 39. See also, "The

Economic Purpose of the Antitrust Laws," Mississippi Law
Journal, XXVI (May 1955), 207-214; "The Folklore of Capi-
talism Revisited"; "The Preservation of Competition," in
T. W. Arnold, et al., The Future of Democratic Capitalism
(Philadelphia, 1950), 10; Speech on the Cold War at Emory
University, May 5, 1950, Arnold Papers; "The Growth of
Awareness," International Lawyer, I (July 1967), 546-547
(the address was delivered April 28, 1967).

[73]"How Not to Get Investigated," Harper's, CXCVII
(November 1948), 61-63; "Mob Justice and Television,"
Atlantic, CLXXXVII (June 1951), 68-70; "The American Ideal
of a Fair Trial," Arkansas Law Review, IX (Summer 1955),
311-317 (Summer 1957), 633-642; "Professor Hart's Theology,"
Harvard Law Review, LXXIII (May 1960), 1298-1317; "The
Growth of Awareness," 538-540; Fair Fights and Foul, 84-86,
230-231.

Conclusion

[1]C. Wright Mills, "On the New Left," Studies on the
Left, II (1961), 63-72; cf. Mario Savio, "An End to History"
(Dec. 1964), in M. Cohen and D. Hale, eds., The New Student
Left (Boston, 1967); Port Huron Statement, in Cohen and
Hale, 11.

[2]Lippmann, "The Dismal Choice," Newsweek (Sept. 23,
1968), 23; Column, New York Post, May 18, 1968, p. 8.

[3]Demott, Surviving the Seventies (New York, 1971), 13.

[4]Daniel Bell, The Coming of Post-Industrial Society
(New York, 1973); Kenneth Boulding, The Meaning of the
Twentieth Century (New York, 1964); Harrison Brown, et al.,
The Next Hundred Years (New York, 1957); Harrison Brown,
et al., The Next Ninety Years (Pasadena, 1967); Zbigniew
Brzezinski, Between Two Ages: America's Role in the Tech-
netronic Era (New York, 1970); Peter Drucker, The Age of
Discontinuity (New York, 1969); Amitai Etzioni, The Active

Society (New York, 1968).

[5]H. Stuart Hughes, The Obstructed Path (New York, 1968), 274.

[6]For example, Robert Sklar, "Chomsky's Revolution in Linguistics," Nation (Sept. 9, 1968); Chomsky, "Language and Freedom," in his For Reasons of State (New York, 1973), 387-408.

A NOTE ON BIBLIOGRAPHY

The nature of this study required principal reliance
on the printed works of the six reformers and on unpublished
works of a public nature, such as speeches and lectures.
Manuscript materials proved useful largely for the private
years of their lives, and here a major gap exists only in
Herbert Croly's life before 1901.

The New York Public library has the major collection
of Henry George materials, including notebooks and diaries,
early articles and unpublished writings, a vast number of
letters, scrapbooks of newspaper clippings, and transcripts
of unpublished speeches. Most of the available Bellamy
materials are in Houghton Library, Harvard University. A
substantial portion of his later papers were destroyed by
an accidental fire after having been gathered by his colleague Mason Green. Jane Addams's papers are scattered, but
many of the larger collections are available on microfilm,
and the whole is being prepared for publication at the
University of Illinois. The known remnants of Herbert
Croly's papers are scattered as well. The University of
Wyoming has Thurman Arnold's complete collection, which is
thin on the 1920's and earlier; and the Franklin D. Roosevelt
Library has Rexford Tugwell's. Both collections include
large numbers of letters, as well as drafts of articles,
speeches, and books; and both are now completely open.

The biographical record is uneven. George left no
autobiography, but his son's study provides useful personal
reminiscences. Charles Barker's biography of George is
thorough and definitive, worthy of its subject. Geiger's
admiring study is discriminating on the intellectual context
of George's ideas, but relies too heavily on what he regards
as George's most "mature" statements. For Bellamny, Arthur
Morgan's biography is especially useful on the very early
years and on the influence of transcendentalism and theosophy.

Sylvia Bowman's The Year 2000 is indispensable for the
history of Bellamy's ideas before 1888. Of the shorter
studies, John L. Thomas's introduction to the John Harvard
Library edition of Looking Backward is the best piece on
Bellamy, and Daniel Aaron's essays on both George and
Bellamy in Men of Good Hope are still required reading.

Jane Addams left two volumes of useful and interesting
autobiography, but until very recently there was only one
significant biography, written in the 1930's by her nephew,
James Weber Linn. Though Linn's book has held up, Allen
Davis's American Heroine, while controversial in some respects, is solid and persuasive and deals extensively with
Addams's public persona. John Farrell's Beloved Lady is a
thorough intellectual biography, arranged topically. Of
the shorter works, Christopher Lasch's New Radicalism in
America has a perceptive chapter on Addams's early years;
Anne F. Scott's introduction to Democracy and Social Ethics
is a good overview of Addams's ideas; and Jill Conway's
essay is tough-minded and interesting. Other than the
Articles in the D.A.B., the only source for Croly's early
life is an unpublished dissertation by David Levy, which
also deals very nicely with Croly's parents. Charles
Forcey's Crossroads of Liberalism is the major study of the
intellectual changes in the years 1900-1925. A briefer
introduction is the essay by Arthur M. Schlesinger, Jr., in
the John Harvard Library edition of Promise of American
Life.

Both Tugwell and Arnold have published autobiographies,
though Arnold's is a cursory effort. Many of Tugwell's post-
New Deal writings have important autobiographical elements,
and he is still writing. Bernard Sternsher's book is a
thorough study of Tugwell's career, and there is an informa-
tive essay on his thought in Gruchy's volume. Kearny's study
is the one long monograph on Arnold, though Ayer's and
Gressley's shorter pieces are important.

For the intellectual and social context, the most useful works are the writings of their contemporaries, a number
of which are listed below. On Darwinism and pragmatism,
Hofstadter's Social Darwinism and Wiener's Evolution and the
Founders of Pragmatism are still standard references; and

Lovejoy's essay of 1913 remains the best brief introduction. Morton White's Social Thought in America has long dominated our understanding of the intellectual revolution. It ought to be read in conjunction with two very different recent approaches to the intellectual changes: Lasch's New Radicalism and Edward Purcell's Crisis of Democratic Theory. Hofstadter's Age of Reform and Goldman's Rendezvous with Destiny still set the terms of debate about the intellectual side of social reform, though they have been supplemented and challenged by an enormous literature on both Progressivism and the New Deal. David Thelen's The New Citizenship and Richard Pells' Radical Visions and American Dreams are the most appealing of these newer works. Wiebe's Search for Order is the most stimulating synthesis of the earlier part of the period. Effective counterpoints to the reformers can be found in Robert McCloskey's studies of conservatism, Sproat's study of the "old" liberals, Jaher's examination of cataclysmic literature, Wilson's study of the issue of community, Graham's work on the old progressives during the New Deal, Lawson's study of independent liberalism, and Gilbert's study of selected reactions to collectivism. In terms of a larger historiographical context, no one could have escaped the direct or indirect impact of the work of Thomas Kuhn, Raymond Williams, and Michel Foucault. I found Stephen Toulmin's studies of science particularly useful, especially Foresight and Understanding. The phrase "ideal of natural order," used in defining intellectual structure, is his.

I would like to thank Agnes George DeMille and the New York Public Library for permission to quote from the Henry George Papers; Joan Bellamy May, Houghton Library of Harvard University, and Columbia University Libraries, Manuscripts Division, for permission to quote from Bellamy manuscripts; Elizabeth Linn Murray and the Sophia Smith Collection (Women's History Archive), Smith College, for permission to quote from Jane Addams's letters; Josephine Starr and the Sophia Smith Collection for permission to quote from the Ellen Starr Papers; and Gerald Gunther for permission to consult the Learned Hand Papers at Harvard Law School. The curators of manuscripts and their staffs at the Harvard Law School Library, the University of Wyoming, and the Franklin D. Roosevelt Library were also very helpful.

This manuscript was, in its first incarnation, a doctoral dissertation at Harvard University, 1971. I am grateful to Donald Fleming, as principal adviser, and Frank Freidel for their advice and criticism. A year at the Charles Warren Center for Studies in American History, Harvard University, not only provided the time for further work, but also gave me the benefit of the criticisms and suggestions of eight interesting scholars. I also profited from the comments of Jon Saari, David Thelen, Geoffrey Blodgett, and Phyllis Vine, who read parts of the manuscript at various stages. Richard Ellis provided aid and advice of many sorts over a long period, for which I am very grateful. Anne Pippin typed the index. Bertha S. Mintz of Newton, Mass., typed the manuscript, in both its incarnations, with skill and good humor under pressure. My greatest debt is to my wife Anne, without whose patience, care, and encouragement it would never have been finished.

BIBLIOGRAPHY

I. PRIMARY SOURCES

A. Henry George

1. Manuscripts

Garrison, William Lloyd II, Papers, Sophia Smith Collection, Smith College Library.

Gay Family, Papers, Columbia University Library.

George, Henry, Papers, New York Public Library, Manuscript Division.

George, Henry, Henry George Scrapbooks, 27 v., New York Public Library, Economics Division.

George, Henry, Pamphlet Volumes, New York Public Library, Economics Division.

George, Henry, Henry George Letters, C. W. Barrett Library, University of Virginia.

George, Henry, Correspondence from Henry George to Hamlin Garland, 1888-1895, American Literature Collection, University of Southern California Library [microfilm].

Jay Family, Papers, Columbia University Library.

Lazarus, Emma, Papers, Columbia University Library.

Seligman, E. R. A., Papers, Columbia University Library.

2. Published Writings

>   (in order of publication. The numbers in brackets refer
>   to the appropriate volume of The Complete Works of Henry
>   George, 10 v. [Garden City, New York, 1911]. Articles
>   and speeches reprinted in Works, VIII, are not listed.)

"What the Railroad Will Bring Us," Overland Monthly, I
    (October, 1868), 297-306.

Our Land and Land Policy. San Francisco, 1871. [VIII]

Progress and Poverty: An Inquiry into the Cause of Industrial
    Depression, and of Increase of Want with Increase of
    Wealth--The Remedy. San Francisco, 1879 [author's
    edition]; New York, 1880. [I]

The Land Question: What It Involves and How Alone It Can Be
    Settled. New York, 1881. [III]

Social Problems. New York, 1883. [II]

Protection or Free Trade? An Examination of the Tariff Ques-
    tion with Especial Regard to the Interests of Labor.
    New York, 1886. [IV]

The Condition of Labor: An Open Letter to Pope Leo XIII.
    New York, 1891. [III]

A Perplexed Philosopher: Being an Examination of Mr. Herbert
    Spencer's Various Utterances on the Land Question, with
    Some Incidental Reference to His Synthetic Philosophy.
    New York, 1892. [V]

The Science of Political Economy. Henry George, Jr., ed.
    New York, 1898. [VI, VII]

3. Newspapers edited by Henry George

The Daily Evening Post (San Francisco), 1871-1873.

The Standard (New York), 1887-1890.

B. <u>Edward Bellamy</u>

1. <u>Manuscripts</u>

Aldrich, Thomas Bailey, Papers, Houghton Library, Harvard
University.

Bellamy, Edward, Papers, Houghton Library, Harvard University.

Bellamy, Edward, Papers, C. W. Barrett Library, University of
Virginia.

Bok-Alexander Correspondence, C. W. Barrett Library,
University of Virginia.

Clark, John B., Papers, Columbia University Library.

Higginson, Thomas Wentworth, Papers, Houghton Library,
Harvard University.

Hitchcock, Ripley, Papers, Columbia University Library.

Howells, William Dean, Papers, Houghton Library, Harvard
University.

2. <u>Books</u>

(in order of first publication)

<u>Six to One: A Nantucket Idyl</u>. New York, 1880.

<u>Miss Luddington's Sister: A Romance of Immortality</u>. Boston,
1884.

<u>Looking Backward, 2000-1887</u>. Boston, 1888.

<u>Equality</u>. New York, 1897.

<u>The Blindman's World, and Other Stories</u>. Boston, 1898.

The Duke of Stockbridge: A Romance of Shays' Rebellion.
   Joseph Schiffman, ed. Cambridge, Mass., 1962.
   [An incomplete edition was published in 1900.]

3. Articles and other short works

   (in order of publication and excluding articles published
   in the New Nation)

Plutocracy or Nationalism--Which? Boston, 1889.

"How I Came to Write 'Looking Backward,'" Nationalist, I
   (May, 1889), 1-4.

"Our Prospective Sovereigns," Nationalist, I (July, 1889),
   68-69.

"Looking Forward," Nationalist, II (December, 1889), 1-4.

"'Looking Backward' Again," North American Review, CL (March,
   1890), 351-363.

"Nationalism--Principles and Purposes," Nationalist, II
   April, 1890), 174-180.

"What 'Nationalism' Means," Contemporary Review, LVIII (July,
   1890), 1-18.

"First Steps toward Nationalism," Forum, X (October, 1890),
   174-184.

"Woman in the Year 2000," Ladies Home Journal, VIII
   (February, 1891), 3.

"Progress of Nationalism in the United States," North American
   Review, CLIV (June, 1892), 742-752.

"Introduction" to Socialism: The Fabian Essays. G. B. Shaw,
   ed. Boston, 1894.

"The Programme of the Nationalists," Forum, XVII (March,
   1894), 81-91.

"How I Wrote 'Looking Backward,'" <u>Ladies Home Journal</u>, XI
    (April, 1894), 2.

"Christmas in the Year 2000," <u>Ladies Home Journal</u>, XII
    (January, 1895), 6.

"How We Shall Get There," <u>Twentieth Century</u>, II (May, 1889),
    166-167.

<u>The Religion of Solidarity</u>. Arthur E. Morgan, ed. Yellow
    Springs, Ohio, 1940.

4. <u>Periodicals</u>

<u>Nationalist</u>, I-III (1889-1891).

<u>New Nation</u>, I-IV (1891-1894). Edited by Edward Bellamy.

C. Jane Addams

1. <u>Manuscripts</u>

Addams, Jane, Correspondence in the Jane Addams Papers,
    Swarthmore College Peace Collection (microfilm).

Addams, Jane, Jane Addams Collection, Sophia Smith Collection,
    Smith College Library.

Addams, Jane, Copies of letters from Jane Addams to her sister,
    S. Alice Haldeman, and others, 1883-1885, 1887-1888,
    University of Kansas Library (microfilm).

Addams, Jane, Jane Addams Correspondence in the Ada James
    Papers, et al., in the State Historical Society of
    Wisconsin (microfilm).

Addams, Jane, Twenty Letters in the Davidson, House, Warburg,
    and Kent Papers, Sterling Memorial Library, Yale
    University (microfilm).

Bourne, Randolph, Papers, Columbia University Library.

Kelley, Florence, Papers, Columbia University Library.

Meloney, Marie, Papers, Columbia University Library.

Nevins, Allan, Papers, Columbia University Library.

Ordway, Edward, Papers, New York Public Library, Manuscript Division.

Roosevelt, Theodore, Papers, Library of Congress, Manuscript Division.

Seligman, E. R. A., Papers, Columbia University Library.

Smith, D. E., Papers, Columbia University Library.

Starr Ellen Gates, Correspondence of Jane Addams and Ellen Gates Starr, 1879-1931, Starr Papers, Sophia Smith Collection, Smith College Library.

Steffens, Lincoln, Papers, Columbia University Library.

Wald, Lillian, Papers, New York Public Library, Manuscript Division.

2. <u>Books</u>

(in order of first publication)

<u>Democracy and Social Ethics</u>. New York, 1902.

<u>Newer Ideals of Peace</u>. New York, 1907.

<u>The Spirit of Youth and the City Streets</u>. New York, 1909.

<u>Twenty Years at Hull-House, with Autobiographical Notes</u>. New York, 1910.

<u>A New Conscience and an Ancient Evil</u>. New York, 1917.

The Long Road of Woman's Memory. New York, 1917.

Peace and Bread in Time of War. New York, 1922.

The Second Twenty Years at Hull-House. New York, 1930.

The Excellent Becomes the Permanent. New York, 1932.

My Friend, Julia Lathrop. New York, 1935.

3. Articles, speeches, and other short works

   (in order of publication)

"How Would You Uplift the Masses?" Sunset Club, Chicago,
    Yearbook (1891-1892), 118-121. An address given
    February 4, 1892.

"The Subjective Necessity for Social Settlements," in Jane
    Addams, et al., Philanthropy and Social Progress.
    New York, 1893.

"The Objective Value of a Social Settlement," in Jane Addams,
    et al., Philanthropy and Social Progress. New York,
    1893.

"What Shall We Do for Our Unemployed?" Sunset Club, Chicago,
    Yearbook (1893-1894), 81-82. An address given December
    21, 1893.

"The Settlement as a Factor in the Labor Movement," in
    Residents of Hull-House, Hull-House Maps and Papers.
    New York, 1895.

"The Art Work Done by Hull-House, Chicago," Forum, XIX
    (July, 1895), 614-617.

"Social Settlements," National Conference of Charities and
    Correction, Proceedings (1897), 338-346, 472-476.

"Discussion on After-Care of the Convalescent Insane,"
    National Conference of Charities and Correction,
    Proceedings (1897), 464-466.

"Ethical Survivals in Municipal Corruption," International Journal of Ethics, VIII (April, 1898), 273-291.

"The College Woman and the Family Claim," Commons, III (September, 1898), 3-7.

"Trade Unions and Public Duty," American Journal of Sociology, IV (January, 1899), 448-462.

"The Subtle Problems of Charity," Atlantic Monthly, LXXXII (February, 1899), 163-178.

"A Function of the Social Settlement," Annals of the American Academy of Political and Social Science, XIII (May, 1899), 323-345.

"What Peace Means," Unity, XLIII (May 4, 1899), 178. An address given April 30, 1899.

"Social Education of the Industrial Democracy: Labor Museum at Hull-House," Commons, V (June 30, 1900), 1-4.

"Respect for Law," Independent, LIII (January 3, 1901), 18-20.

"One Menace to the Century's Progress," Unity, XLVII (April 4, 1901), 71-72. An address given February 14, 1901.

"The College Woman and Christianity," Independent, LIII (August 8, 1901), 1852-1855.

Democracy and Social Ethics: A Syllabus of a Course of Twelve Lectures. Chicago, no date [1901?].

"Neighborhood Improvement," National Conference of Charities and Correction, Proceedings (1904), 456-458, 560-562.

"Larger Social Groupings," Charities, XII (June 25, 1904), 675.

"The Present Crisis in Trades-Union Morals," North American Review, CLXXIX (August, 1904), 178-193.

"Problems of Municipal Administration," American Journal of
    Sociology, X (1905), 425-444. An address given
    September, 1904.

"Class Conflict in America--Remarks," American Sociological
    Society, Publications, II (1907), 152-155.

"How Shall We Approach Industrial Education?" Educational
    Bi-Monthly, I (February, 1907), 183-190. An address
    given November, 1906.

"Woman's Conscience and Social Amelioration," in Charles
    Stelzle, et al., The Social Application of Religion.
    Cincinnati, 1908.

"The Relation of 'Settlements' and Religion; or, The Place
    of Religion As It May Be Experienced in the Settlement,"
    Unity, LX (January 9, 1908), 295, and LX (January 16,
    1908), 311, 312. Remarks made November 8, 1907.

"The Chicago Settlements and Social Unrest," Charities and
    the Commons, XX (May 2, 1908), 155-166.

"The Reaction of Modern Life upon Religious Education,"
    Religious Education, IV (April, 1909, 23-29.

"The Reaction of Moral Instruction upon Social Reform,"
    Survey, XXII (April 3, 1909), 17-19.

"Charity and Social Justice," Survey, XXIV (June 11, 1910),
    441-449.

"Standards of Education for Industrial Life," National Con-
    ference of Charities and Correction, Proceedings
    (1911), 162-164.

"The Call of the Social Field," National Conference of Char-
    ities and Correction, Proceedings (1911), 370-372.

"Social Control," The Crisis, I (January, 1911), 22-23.

"Religious Education and Contemporary Social Conditions,"
    Religious Education, VI (June, 1911), 145-152.

"The Humanitarian Value of Civil Service," Survey, XXVIII
    (April 6, 1912), 14-16.

"A Challenge to the Contemporary Church," Survey, XXVIII
    (May 4, 1912), 195-198.

"Votes for Women and Other Votes," Survey, XXVIII (June 1,
    1912), 367-368.

"Speech Seconding the Nomination of Theodore Roosevelt at
    the Progressive Convention, 1912," U.S., Congressional
    Record, 62 Cong., 2 Sess., Vol. XII, Appendix, 564-565
    (August 12, 1912).

"Pragmatism in Politics," Survey, XXIX (October 5, 1912),
    11-12.

"The Progressive's Dilemma; The New Party," American Magazine,
    LXXV (November, 1912), 12-14.

"The Progressive Party and the Negro," The Crisis, V
    (November, 1912), 30-31.

"My Experience as a Progressive Delegate," McClure's, XL
    (November, 1912), 12-14.

"The Woman in Politics," Progress, I (November, 1912), 37-40.

"A Modern Lear," Survey, XXIX (November 2, 1912), 131-137.
    Originally written as an address in 1894.

"Lessons of the Election," City Club Bulletin, V (November
    27, 1912), 361-364.

"Has the Emancipation Act Been Nullified by National Indif-
    ference?" Survey, XXIX (February 1, 1913), 565-566.

"Miss Addams," Ladies Home Journal, XXX (January-August, 1913).
    A monthly column.

"Introduction," to Graham Taylor, Religion in Social Action.
    New York, 1913. The introduction is dated September,
    1913.

"Humanitarian Aspects of the Merit System," National Civil Service Reform League, Proceedings (1914), 108-113.

"Democracy and Social Ethics," Cyclopedia of American Government, A. C. McLaughlin and A. B. Hart, eds. (New York, 1914), I, 563-564.

"Social Justice through National Action," in Nationalism, Its Need in Our Social, Industrial, and Political Growth; Speeches at the Second Annual Lincoln Dan Dinner of the Progressive Party, February 12, 1914 (New York, 1914), 6-9.

"Women and War; Address Given at the Hague, May, 1915," in Lucia A. Mead, ed., The Overthrow of the War System. Boston, 1915.

"The Revolt against War," "Factors in Continuing the War," and "Women and Internationalism," in Jane Addams, et al., Women at the Hague. New York, 1915.

"Patriotism and Pacifists in War Time," City Club Bulletin, X (June 16, 1917), 184-190.

"Tolstoy and the Russian Soldiers," New Republic, XII (September 29, 1917), 240-242.

"World's Food and World's Politics," National Conference of Charities and Correction, Proceedings (1918), 650-656.

"Americanization," American Sociological Society, Publications, XIV (1919), 206-214.

"The Spirit of Social Service," National Conference of Social Social Work, Proceedings (1920), 41-43.

"The Immigrants and Social Unrest," National Conference of Social Work, Proceedings (1920), 59-62.

"Feed the World and Save the League," New Republic, XXIV (November 24, 1920), 325-327.

"Disarmament and Life," National Peace Council, Disarmament Pamphlet No. 2. An address given September 18, 1921.

"The Aftermath of the War," Christian Century, XXIX (January 5, 1922), 10-12.

"Preface" and "Opening Address," Women's International League for Peace and Freedom, Report of the Fourth Congress, IV (1924), vii-xi, 1-3.

"Why I Shall Vote for LaFollette," New Republic, XL (September 10, 1924), 36-37.

"Impressions of Mexico," Women's International League for Peace and Freedom, United States Section, Bulletin, XIV (April-May, 1925), n.p.

"New Methods of Procedure," Women's International League for Peace and Freedom, Report of the Fifth Congress, V (1926), 63-65.

"How Much Social Work Can a Community Afford?" Survey, LVII (November 15, 1926), 199-201.

"A Book That Changed My Life," Christian Century, XLIV (October 13, 1927), 1196-1198.

"Introduction," to Abraham Epstein, The Challenge of the Aged. New York, 1928.

"Pioneers in Sociology," Neighborhood, I (July, 1928), 6-11.

"President's Address," Women's International League for Peace and Freedom, Report of the Sixth Congress, VI (1929), 13-15.

"After Sixty-Five," Survey, LXII (June 1, 1929), 303.

"The Settlement as a Way of Life," Neighborhood, II (July, 1929), 139-146.

"A Toast to John Dewey," Survey, LXIII (November 15, 1929), 203-204.

"Social Workers and the Other Professions," National Conference of Social Work, Proceedings (1930), 50-54.

"Jane Addams Delivers the Ware Lecture [A Needed Implement to Social Reform]," Christian Register (June 4, 1931), 464-465.

"Tolstoy and Gandhi," Christian Century, XLVIII (November 25, 1931), 1485-1488.

"Social Consequences of the Depression," Survey, LXVII (January 1, 1932), 370-371. Originally written in 1931.

"The Process of Social Transformation," in Charles A. Beard, ed., A Century of Progress. New York, 1933.

"The Social Deterrent of Our National Self-Righteousness, with Correctives Suggested by the Courageous Life of William Penn," Survey Graphic, XXII (February, 1933), 98-101.

"Pioneering in Social Work," Federation News, I (November, 1933), 1-2. An address given June, 1933.

"Old Age Security," Booklist, XXXI (March, 1935), 215.

D.   Herbert Croly

1.   Manuscripts

Bourne, Randolph, Papers, Columbia University Library.

Conway, Moncure D., Papers, Columbia University Library.

Crane, Stephen, Papers, Columbia University Library.

Croly, David G., Extracts from letters to Herbert Croly, 1886-87 and 1888, Houghton Library, Harvard University.

Croly, Herbert, Extracts from letters and two manuscripts by Herbert Croly, Houghton Library, Harvard University.

General Manuscript Collection, Columbia University Library.

Hand, Learned, Papers,Harvard Law School Library.

Lowell, Amy, Papers, Houghton Library, Harvard University.

Roosevelt, Theodore, Papers, Library of Congress, Manuscript
  Division.

Seligman, E. R. A., Papers, Columbia University Library.

Stedman, E. C., Papers, Columbia University Library.

Steffens, Lincoln, Papers, Columbia University Library.

3. Books by Herbert Croly

    (in order of first publication)

(with Desmond, Harry W.), Stately Homes in America, from
  Colonial Times to the Present Day. New York, 1903.

(William Herbert, pseud.), Houses for Town or Country.
  New York, 1907.

The Promise of American Life. New York, 1909.

Marcus Alonzo Hanna: His Life and Work. New York, 1912.

Progressive Democracy. New York, 1914.

The Breach in Civilization. New York, 1920. Not published;
  galley proofs of pp. 1-152 in Houghton Library,
  Harvard University.

Willard Straight. New York, 1924.

3. Articles by Herbert Croly

    (in order of publication; NRA, below, refers to The New
    Republic Anthology, 1915-1935 [New York, 1936]; NRB,
    below, refers to The New Republic Books: Selections
    from the First Hundred Issues [New York, 1916])

"Art and Life," Architectural Record, I (October-December, 1891), 219-227.

"American Artists and Their Public," Architectural Record, X (January, 1901), 256-262.

"Criticisms That Counts," Architectural Record, X (April, 1901), 398-405.

"Rich Men and Their Houses," Architectural Record, XII (May, 1902), 27-32.

"The New World and the New Art," Architectural Record, XII (June, 1902), 135-153.

"New York as the American Metropolis," Architectural Record, XIII (March, 1903), 193-206.

"Some Really Historical Novels," Lamp, XXVI (July, 1903), 509-513.

"American Architecture of Today," Architectural Record, XIV (December, 1903), 413-435.

"Henry James and His Countrymen," Lamp, XXVIII (February, 1904), 47-53.

"An American Farmer," Lamp, XXVIII (July, 1904), 477-478.

"What Is Civic Art?" Architectural Record, XVI (July, 1904), 47-52.

"The Architect in Recent Fiction," Architectural Record, XVII (February, 1905), 137-139.

"A New Use of Old Forms," Architectural Record, XVII (April, 1905), 271-293.

"The Promised City of San Francisco," Architectural Record, XIX (June, 1906), 425-436.

"'Civic Improvements'" The Case of New York," Architectural Record, XXI (May, 1907), 347-352.

"What Is Indigenous Architecture?" Architectural Record, XXI
(June, 1907), 434-442.

(William Herbert, pseud.) , "An American Architecture,"
Architectural Record, XXIII (February, 1908), 111-122.

"The New University of California," Architectural Record,
XXIII (April, 1908), 269-273.

(William Herbert, pseud.), "Some Business Buildings in
St. Louis," Architectural Record, XXIII (May, 1908),
391-396.

"How to Get a Well-Designed House," Architectural Record,
XXV (April, 1909), 221-234.

"Democratic Factions and Insurgent Republicans," North
American Review, CXCI (May, 1910), 626-635.

"A Great School of Political Science," World's Work, XX
(May, 1910), 12887-888.

"Why I Wrote My Latest Book: My Aim in 'The Promise of
American Life,'" World's Work, XX (June, 1910), 13086.

"Portland, Oregon: The Transformation of the City from an
Architectural and Social Viewpoint," Architectural
Record, XXXI (June, 1912), 591-607.

"The Building of Seattle," Architectural Record, XXXII
(July, 1912), 1-21.

"A Test of Faith in Democracy," American Magazine, LXXV
(November, 1912), 21-23.

"The End of American Isolation," New Republic, I (November
7, 1914), 9-10. Identified by NRB.

"Lincoln," New Republic, II (February 6, 1915), 1.
Identified by NRB.

"Examples of the Work of Otis and Clark," Architectural
Record, XXXVII (May, 1915), 385-409.

(H. C.), "The Meaning of It," New Republic, IV (August 7, 1915), 10-11.

"The Obligation to Vote," New Republic, IV (October 9, 1915), Part II, 5-10.

"Reconciling Irreconcilables," New Republic, V (November 20, 1915), Part II, 2-3.

"Our Relations with Great Britain," New Republic, V (January 22, 1916), 290-292. Identified by NRB.

"Unregenerate Democracy," New Republic, VI (February 5, 1916), 17-19.

"Submarines as Commerce Destroyers," New Republic, VI (March 4, 1916), 116-117. Identified by NRB.

"The Ultimate Controversy," New Republic, VII (May 27, 1916), 76-78. Identified by NRB.

"Sovereign Mexico," New Republic, VII (June 10, 1916), 132-134.

"The Effect on American Institutions of a Powerful Military and Naval Establishment," Annals of the American Academy of Political and Social Science, LXVI (July, 1916), 157-172.

(H. C.), "The Commonwealth of Greater Britain," New Republic, VII (July 22, 1916), 309-312.

"Voting for President," New Republic, VIII (August 5, 1916), 5-7. Identified by NRB.

"Unionism vs. Anti-Unionism," New Republic, VIII (September 23, 1916), 178-180. Identified by NRB.

"The Two Parties in 1916," New Republic, VIII (October 21, 1916), 286-291.

"The Structure of Peace," New Republic, IX (January 13, 1917), 287-291.

"The Future of the State," New Republic, XII (September 15, 1917), 179-183.

"Counsel of Humility," New Republic, XIII (December 15, 1917), 173-176.

"A School of Social Research," New Republic, XV (June 8, 1918), 167-171.

(H. C.), "Victory without Peace," New Republic, XVII (January 11, 1919), 301-303.

"The Obstacles to Peace," New Republic, XVIII (April 26, 1919), 403-407.

"Disordered Christianity," New Republic, XXI (December 31, 1919), 136-139.

"The Paradox of Lincoln," New Republic, XXI (February 18, 1920), 350-353.

"The Residence of the Late F. W. Woolworth," Architectural Record, XLVII (March, 1920), 195-213.

"Pidgeon Hill," Architectural Record, XLVIII (September, 1920), 178-191.

"Regeneration," New Republic, XXIII (June 9, 1920), 40-47.

"The Eclipse of Porgressivism," New Republic, XXIV (October 27, 1920), 210-216.

"Liberalism vs. War," New Republic, XXV (December 8, 1920), 35-39.

"The Better Prospect," New Republic, XXVII (August 24, 1921), 344-349.

"The Meaning of the Conference," New Republic, XXVIII (November 16, 1921), Part II, 1-14.

"Hope, History and H. G. Wells," New Republic, XXIX (November 30, 1921), 10-12.

"In Memoriam--Willard Straight," New Republic, XXIX
(December 21, 1921), 94-96.

"Behaviorism in Religion," New Republic, XXIX (February 22,
1922), 367-370.

"Reply to C. S. Macfarland on American Protestant Churches
during the War," New Republic, XXX (March 29, 1922),
141-143.

"The Reconstruction of Religion," New Republic, XXXI (June
21, 1922), 101-103.

"Surely Good Americanism," New Republic, XXXII (November 15,
1922), 294-296.

"The New Republic Idea," New Republic, XXXIII (December 6,
1922), Part II, 1-16.

"Naturalism and Christianity," New Republic, XXXIV (February
28, 1923), 9-11.

"American Withdrawal from Europe," New Republic, XXXVI
(September 12, 1923), 65-68.

"The Reclamation of a Business Slum," Architectural Record,
LIV (December, 1923), 587-588.

"Education for Grown-Ups," New Republic, XXXVII (December 12,
1923), 56-61.

"The Skyscraper in the Service of Religion," Architectural
Record, LV (February, 1924), 203-204.

"The Paradox of Woodrow Wilson," New Republic, XXXVII
(February 13, 1924), 299-300. Identified by NRA.

"Economics and Statesmanship," New Republic, XXXVIII
(February 27, 1924), 17-19.

"The Architect's Interest in Low-Rent Dwellings," Architectural Record, LV (March, 1924), 307-308.

"Social Discovery," <u>New Republic</u>, XXXIX (May 28, 1924), 18-20.

"Christianity as a Way of Life," <u>New Republic</u>, XXXIX (July 23, 1924), 230-237.

"Controlling Economic Factor in Current Building," <u>Architectural Record</u>, LVI (August, 1924), 185-186.

"Why I Shall Vote for LaFollette," <u>New Republic</u>, XL (October 29, 1924), 221-224.

"The Outlook for Progressivism in Politics," <u>New Republic</u>, XLI (December 10, 1924), 60-64.

"What Ails American Youth," <u>New Republic</u>, XLI (February 11, 1925), 301-303.

"Architectural Response to Social Change," <u>Architectural Record</u>, LVIII (August, 1925), 186-187.

"Christians, Beware!" <u>New Republic</u>, XLV (November 25, 1925), 12-14.

"Consciousness and the Religious Life," <u>New Republic</u>, XLV (January 27, 1926), 262-265.

"Architects and State Aid to Housing," <u>Architectural Record</u>, LIX (March, 1926), 293-294.

"Architectural Counterpoint," <u>Architectural Record</u>, LIX (May, 1926), 489-490.

"Religion as a Method," <u>New Republic</u>, XLVII (June 30, 1926), 174-177.

"Mexico and the United States," <u>New Republic</u>, L (March 30, 1927), 159-164.

"The Human Potential in the Politics of the Pacific," <u>New Republic</u>, LII (October 5, 1927), 164-172.

"Smith of New York," <u>New Republic</u>, LIV (February 22, 1928), 9-14.

"How Is Hoover?" New Republic, LV (June 27, 1928), 138-140.

"The Progressive Voter: He Wants to Know!" New Republic,
     LV (July 25, 1928), 242-247.

E. Rexford Tugwell

1. Manuscripts

Frank, Jerome, Papers, Sterling Memorial Library, Yale
     University.

Bingham, Alfred, Papers, Sterling Memorial Library, Yale
     University.

Tugwell, Rexford G., Papers, Franklin D. Roosevelt Library,
     Hyde Park, N.Y.

Tugwell, Rexford G., Reminiscences, Oral History Research
     Office, Columbia University, 1972.

2. Books

     (in order of first publication)

The Economic Basis of Public Interest. Menasha, Wisconsin,
     1922.

(editor and major contributor), The Trend of Economics.
     New York, 1924.

(with Munro, Thomas, and Roy Stryker), American Economic
     Life and the Means of Its Improvement. 2nd ed.
     New York, 1925. First edition privately circulated
     only.

Industry's Coming of Age. New York, 1927.

The Industrial Discipline and the Governmental Arts.
     New York, 1933.

(with Keyserling, L. H.), Redirecting Education. Vol. I.
    New York, 1934.

(with Hill, H. C.), Our Economic Society and Its Problems.
    New York, 1934.

The Battle for Democracy. New York, 1935.

Puerto Rican Public Papers. San Juan, P.R., 1945.

The Stricken Land: The Story of Puerto Rico. Garden City,
    N.Y., 1947.

The Place of Planning in Society. San Juan, P.R., 1954.

A Chronicle of Jeopardy: 1945-55. Chicago, 1955.

The Democratic Roosevelt. Garden City, N.Y., 1957.

(with Dorfman, Joseph), Early American Policy: Six Columbia
    Contributors. New York, 1960.

The Light of Other Days. Garden City, New York, 1962.

Off Course: From Truman to Nixon. New York, 1971.

3. Articles and other short works

   (in order of publication)

"The Casual of the Woods," Survey, XLIV (July 3, 1920), 472-
    474.

"The Outlaw [Letter to the Editor]; Survey, XLIV (August 16,
    1920), 641-642.

"The Philosophy of Despair: Outlawing the I.W.W.," New York
    Call: The Call Magazine (October 17, 1920), 4, 9.

"The Gipsy Strain," Pacific Review, II (September, 1921),
    177-196.

"The Economic Basis for Business Regulation," American
    Economic Review, XI (December, 1921), 643-658.

"Country Life for America," Pacific Review, II (March, 1922), 566-586.

"Guild Socialism and the Industrial Future," International Journal of Ethics, XXXII (April, 1922), 282-288.

"Human Nature and Economic Theory," Journal of Political Economy, XXX (June, 1922), 317-345.

"Economic Theory and Practice-Discussion," American Economic Review, XIII (March, 1923), Supplement, 107-109.

"Some Formative Influences in the Life of Simon Nelson Patten," American Economic Review, XIII (March, 1923), Supplement, 273-285.

"Notes on the Life and Work of Simon Nelson Patten," Journal of Political Economy, XXXI (April, 1923), 153-208.

"The Distortion of Economic Incentive," International Journal of Ethics, XXXIV (April, 1924), 272-282.

"The Problem of Agriculture," Political Science Quarterly, XXXIX (December, 1924), 549-591.

"Economics and Ethics," Journal of Philosophy, XXI (December 4, 1924), 682-690.

"The Woman in the Sunbonnet," Nation, CXX (January 21, 1925), 73-74.

"The Hired Man," Nation, CXXI (August 5, 1925), 164-166.

"An Economist Reads Dark Laughter," New Republic, XLV (December 9, 1925), 87-88.

"Henry Ford in This World," Saturday Review of Literature, III (August 7, 1926), 17-19.

"Chameleon Words," New Republic, XLVIII (August 25, 1926), 16-17.

"The End of Laissez-Faire [letter]," New Republic, XLVIII (October 13, 1926), 222.

"America's War-Time Socialism," Nation, CXXIV (April 6, 1927), 364-367.

"What Will Become of the Former?" Nation, CXXIV (June 15, 1927), 664-666.

"Russian Agriculture," in S. Chase, R. Dunn, and R. G. Tugwell (eds.), Soviet Russia in the Second Decade. New York, 1928.

"Economics on the Science of Experience," Journal of Philosophy, XXV (January 19, 1928), 29-40.

"Discussion of 'Must Prosperity Be Planned?' by H. B. Brougham, and 'High Wages and Prosperity' by Henry H. Williams," Bulletin of the Taylor Society, XIII (February, 1928), 19-21.

"Communism: Reality and Theory," New Republic, LIV (February 22, 1928), 22-23.

"The Paradox of Peace," New Republic, LIV (April 18, 1928), 262-267.

"Hunger, Cold and Candidates," New Republic, LIV (May 2, 1928), 323-325.

"Governor or President?" New Republic, LIV (May 16, 1928), 381-382.

"Contemporary Economics," New Republic, LIV (May 16, 1928), 397-398.

"Platforms and Candidates," New Republic, LV (May 30, 1928), 44-45.

"Experimental Control in Russian Industry," Political Science Quarterly, XLIII (June, 1928), 161-187.

"What Is a Scientific Tariff?" New Republic, LV (June 13, 1928), 92-93.

"That Living Constitution," New Republic, LV (June 20, 1928),
    120-122.

"A Plant on Agriculture," New Republic, LV (July 4, 1928),
    161-163.

"Wage-Pressure and Efficiency," New Republic, LV (July 11,
    1928), 196-198.

"Governor Smith's Dilemma," New Republic, LV (August 1, 1928),
    276-277.

"The Liberal Choice," New Republic, LVI (September 5, 1928),
    74-75.

"Bankers' Banks," New Republic, LVII (December 12, 1928),
    95-96.

"This Ugly Civilization, by Ralph Borsodi [review]," in
    Henry Seidel Canby, et al. (eds.), Designed for Reading.
    New York, 1934. Written in 1930.

"The Agricultural Policy of France" (3 parts), Political
    Science Quarterly, XLV (June, September, and December,
    1930), 214-230, 405-428, 527-547.

"Human Nature and Social Economy," Journal of Philosophy,
    XXVII (August 14 and 28, 1930), 449-457, 477-492.

"Elements of a World Culture; II. Economics," World Unity
    (November, 1930; December, 1930), 95-105; 202-207.

"Henry George," Encyclopedia of the Social Sciences. Vol. VI.
    New York, 1931.

"The Theory of Occupational Obsolescence," Political Science
    Quarterly, XLVI (June, 1931), 171-227.

"Economics," in Neilson, William Allan, Roads to Knowledge.
    New York, 1932.

"Discourse in Depression" (Mimeograph). New York, 1932.

Mr. Hoover's Economic Policy (Pamphlet). New York, 1932.

"Flaws in the Hoover Economic Plan," Current History, XXXV
    (January, 1932), 525-531.

"The Principle of Planning and the Institution of Laissez-
    Faire," American Economic Review, XXII (March, 1932),
    Supplement, 75-92.

"The New Deal Interpreted: Its Basic Policies Viewed by
    Aides of Roosevelt," New York Times, May 28, 1933;
    Section VIII, p. 6. Includes brief statements by
    Tugwell, Raymond Moley, Harold L. Ickes, Henry Wallace,
    Henry Morgenthau Jr., Daniel C. Roper, and John Dickinson.

"The Ideas behind the New Deal," New York Times Magazine,
    July 16, 1933, pp. 1, 2, 17.

"Government in a Changing World," Review of Reviews, LXXXVIII
    (August, 1933), 33-34, 56.

"Are the Increasing Powers of the President Improving the
    American Government?" Congressional Digest, XII
    (November, 1933), 268, 270, 272.

"Resettling America: A Vast Land Program," New York Times,
    January 14, 1934; Section VIII, p. 1.

"'The Great American Fraud,'" American Scholar, III (Winter,
    1934), 85-95.

"La Rôle, de l'état dans la vie économique des États-Unis,"
    L'Esprit International, VIII (April, 1934), 202-207.

"Professor Tugwell's Address to Newspaper Editors at the
    Capital," New York Times, April 22, 1934; p. 30.

"The Progressive Tradition," Atlantic Monthly, CLV (April,
    1935), 409-418.

"Should the Administration's Housing Policy Be Continued?"
    Congressional Digest, XV (April, 1936), 114-116.

"Down to Earth," Current History, XLIV (July, 1936), 33-38.

"Changing Acres," Current History, XLIV (September, 1936), 57-63.

"The Future of National Planning," New Republic, LXXXIX (December 9, 1936), 162-164.

"Behind the Farm Problem: Rural Poverty," New York Times Magazine, January 10, 1937, pp. 4-5, 22.

"Cooperation and Resettlement," Current History, XLV (February, 1937), 71-76.

"The Meaning of the Greenbelt Towns," New Republic, XC (February 17, 1937), 42-43.

"On the Troublesome 'X'," Philosophy of Science, IV (October, 1937), 412-426.

"Wesley Mitchell: An Evaluation," New Republic, XCII (October 6, 1937), 238-240.

"Land of Plenty," Current History, XLVIII (February, 1938), 18-21.

Annual Report of the City Planning Commission. New York, 1938.

"Veblen and 'Business Enterprise.'" in Cowley, Malcolm, and Smith, Bernard (eds.), Books That Changed Our Minds. New York, 1939.

"Notes on the Uses of Exactitude in Politics," Political Science Quarterly, LIV (March, 1939), 15-28.

"The Fourth Power," Planning and Civic Comment, V (April-June, 1939), Part II, 1-31.

"Frightened Liberals," New Republic, XCVIII (April 26, 1939), 328-329.

"After the New Deal," New Republic, XCIX (July 26, 1939), 323-325.

Annual Report of the City Planning Commission. New York, 1939.

"The Superpolitical," Journal of Social Philosophy, V (January, 1940), 97-114.

"Planning in New York City," The [American Institute of] Planners' Journal, VI (April-June, 1940), 33-34.

"Parts of a New Civilization," Saturday Review of Literature, XXI (April 13, 1940), 3-4.

"Must We Draft Roosevelt?" New Republic, CII (May 13, 1940), 630-633.

"Planning for Living," Child Study, 17 (Summer, 1940), 102-103.

"Implementing the General Interest," Public Administration Review, I (Autumn, 1940), 32-49.

Annual Report of the City Planning Commission. New York, 1940.

"The Directive," Journal of Social Philosophy and Jurisprudence, VII (October, 1941), 5-36.

"Notes on Some Implications of Oneness in the World," Common Cause, 1 (November, 1947), 165-172.

"The Utility of the Future in the Present," Public Administration Review, VIII (Winter, 1948), 49-59.

"Open Reply to Mr. Borgese," Common Cause, II (October, 1948), 81-84.

"Beyond Malthus: Numbers and Resources," Common Cause, II (May, 1949), 375-377.

"Variation on a Theme by Cooley," Ethics, LIX (July, 1949), 233-243.

"The New Deal: The Progressive Tradition," Western Political Quarterly, III (September, 1950), 390-427.

"The New Deal: The Rise of Business," Western Political Quarterly, V (June, 1952), 274-289; 5 (September, 1952), 483-503.

"The Two Great Roosevelts," Western Political Quarterly, V (March, 1952), 84-94.

"The Compromising Roosevelt," Western Political Quarterly, VI (June, 1953), 320-431.

"The Sources of New Deal Reformism," Ethics, LXIV (July, 1954), 249-276.

"The President and His Helpers: A Review Article," Political Science Quarterly, LXXXII (June, 1967), 253-267.

F. Thurman Arnold

1. Manuscripts

Arnold, Thurman W., Papers, Coe Library, University of Wyoming.

Bingham, Alfred, Papers, Sterling Memorial Library, Yale University.

Frank, Jerome, Papers, Sterling Memorial Library, Yale University.

Hand, Learned, Papers, Harvard Law School Library.

Powell, Thomas Reed, Papers, Harvard Law School Library.

2. Books

   (in order of publication)

[American Law Institute and The National Commission on Law
  Observance and Enforcement], <u>A Study of the Business of
  the Federal Courts</u>. Part I: <u>Criminal Cases</u>.
  Philadelphia, 1934.

<u>The Symbols of Government</u>. New Haven, 1935.

(with James, Fleming, Jr.), <u>Cases and Materials on Trials,
  Judgments and Appeals</u>. St. Paul, Minn., 1936.

<u>The Folklore of Capitalism</u>. New Haven, 1937.

<u>The Bottlenecks of Business</u>. New York, 1940.

<u>Democracy and Free Enterprise</u>. Norman, Okla., 1942.

<u>Selections from the Letters and Legal Papers of Thurman Arnold</u>.
  Victor H. Kramer, ed. Washington, D.C., 1961.

<u>Jingles, Jeers, and Jeremiads</u>. Privately Printed, 1962.

<u>Fair Fights and Foul</u>. New York, 1965.

<u>Voltaire and the Cowboy: The Letters of Thurman Arnold</u>.
  Edited with an Introduction by Gene M. Gressley.
  Boulder, 1977.

3. <u>Articles and other short works</u>.

   (in order of publication)

"The Law School of the University of Wyoming," Wyoming State
  Bar Association, <u>Proceedings</u> of the Eighth Annual
  Meeting, January 13-14, 1921. Cheyenne, Wyo., 1921.

"Report of Committee on Legal Education and Admission to the
  Bar," Wyoming State Bar Association, <u>Proceedings</u> of the
  Tenth Annual Meeting, January 11-12, 1923. Cheyenne,
  Wyo., 1923.

Review of <u>The Living Constitution</u> by Howard Lee McBain, <u>West
  Virginia Law Quarterly</u>, XXXIV (December, 1927), 119-121.

"The Changing Law of Competition in Public Service--A Dissent,"
West Virginia Law Quarterly, XXXIV (February, 1928),
183-188.

"Contempt-Evasion of Criminal Process as Contempt of Court,"
West Virginia Law Quarterly, XXXIV (February, 1928),
188-192.

"The Lake Cargo Rate Case of February, 1928," West Virginia
Law Quarterly, XXXIV (April, 1928), 272-282.

"The Lake Cargo Rate Controversy," West Virginia Law Quarterly,
XXXIV (June, 1928), 365-366.

Review of The Business of the Supreme Court by Felix Frankfurter
and Jonas M. Landis, West Virginia Law Quarterly, XXXIV
(June, 1928), 408-410.

Review of The Elements of Crime by Boris Brasal, West Virginia
Law Quarterly, XXXIV (June, 1928), 410-413.

Review of A Treatise on the Law of Oil and Gas by Walter L.
Summers, West Virginia Law Quarterly, XXXIV (June, 1928),
413-415.

"College of Law Registration--Raising Requirements for
Entrance," West Virginia Law Quarterly, XXXV (December,
1928), 53-54.

"A New Dormitory to Commemorate the Fiftieth Anniversary of
the College of Law," West Virginia Law Quarterly, XXXV
(December, 1928), 54-56.

Review of Jural Relations by Albert Kocourek, West Virginia
Law Quarterly, XXXV (December, 1928), 98-99.

"Judicial Councils," West Virginia Law Quarterly, XXXV
(April, 1929), 193-238.

"Should the Jury System Be Abolished?" West Virginia Law
Quarterly, XXXV (April, 1929), 277-279.

"Success of Bar Association Amendments to the Constitution,"
West Virginia Law Quarterly, XXXV (April, 1929), 280-282.

Arnold, Thurman W. Review of Law of Engineers and Architects
by Laurence P. Simpson and Essel R. Dillavon, West
Virginia Law Quarterly, XXXV (April, 1929), 298-299.

(with Simonton, James W.; Havighurst, Harold C.), "Report to
the Committee on Judicial Administration and Legal
Reform," West Virginia Law Quarterly, XXXVI (December,
1929), 1-102.

"The Collection of Judicial Statistics in West Virginia,"
West Virginia Law Quarterly, XXXVI (February, 1930),
184-194.

"An Inequitable Preference in Favor of Surety Companies,"
West Virginia Law Quarterly, XXXVI (April, 1930), 278-288.

Review of How to Conduct a Criminal Case by William Harmon
Black, Yale Law Journal, XXXIX (May, 1930), 1083-1084.

"Review of the Work of the College of Law," West Virginia
Law Quarterly, XXXVI (June, 1930), 319-329.

"Criminal Attempts--The Rise and Fall of an Abstraction,"
Yale Law Journal, XL (November, 1930), 53-80.

"Court Martial," Encyclopedia of the Social Sciences, Vol. IV.
New York, 1931.

Review of Judge and Jury by Leon Green, Yale Law Journal, XL
(March, 1931), 833-835.

Review of Law and the Modern Mind by Jerome Frank, Saturday
Review of Literature, VII (March 7, 1931), 644.

"The Restatement of the Law of Trusts," Columbia Law Review,
XXXI (May, 1931), 800-823.

"Comparative Procedure [Title supplied]." Connecticut Bar
Journal, V (July, 1931), 244-255.

"Progress Report on Study of the Federal Courts - No. 7," American Bar Association Journal, XVII (December, 1931), 799-802.

Review of Essays in Jurisprudence and the Common Law by Arthur L. Goodhart, Yale Law Journal, XLI (December, 1931), 318-320.

Review of The Law of Martial Rule by Charles Fairman, Harvard Law Review, XLV (December, 1931), 400-402.

"The Rôle of Substantive Law and Procedure in the Legal Process," Harvard Law Review, XLV (February, 1932), 617-647.

Review of Conflicting Penal Theories in Statutory Criminal Law by Mabel A. Elliott, Illinois Law Review, XXVI (February, 1932), 719-722.

Review of The Story of My Life by Clarence Darrow, Yale Law Journal, XLI (April, 1932), 932-933.

Review of Soviet Administration of Criminal Law by Judah Zelitch, Columbia Law Review, XXXII (May, 1932), 923-925.

"Law Enforcement--An Attempt at Social Dissection," Yale Law Journal, XLII (November, 1932), 1-24.

"Law Enforcement," Encyclopedia of the Social Sciences. Vol. IX. New York, 1933.

"Martial Law," Encyclopedia of the Social Sciences. Vol. X. New York, 1933.

(with Brand, C. E.), "Military Law," Encyclopedia of the Social Sciences. Vol. X. New York, 1933.

Review of The Trial of Joanne D'Arc by W. P. Barrett, Yale Law Journal, XLII (January, 1933), 459-462.

Review of Studies in Law and Politics by Harold J. Laski, Columbia Law Review, XXXIII (February, 1933), 377-378.

"The Code 'Cause of Action' Clarified by United States
Supreme Court," American Bar Association Journal, XIX
(April, 1933), 215-218.

(with Sturges, Wesley A.), "The Progress of the New Administration," Yale Review, n.s., XXII (June, 1933), 656-677.

"The New Deal Is Constitutional," New Republic, LXXVII
(November 15, 1933), 8-10.

"Theories about Economic Theory," Annals of the American
Academy of Political and Social Science, CLXXII (March,
1934), 26-36.

"Trial by Combat and the New Deal," Harvard Law Review, XLVII
(April, 1934), 913-947.

"A Criticism of the Critics of Stuart Chase," Yale Review,
n.s., XXIII (June, 1934), 835-838.

Review of Precedent in English and Continental Law by
L. Goodhart, Columbia Law Review, XXXV (February, 1935),
311-313.

"Apologia for Jurisprudence," Yale Law Journal, XLIV (March,
1935), 729-753.

"Reform from the Left Bank," Yale Review, n.s., XXV
(December, 1935), 411-414.

"The Parable of the Bright Swede," Yale Review, n.s., XXV
(March, 1936), 612-615.

Review of Ford on Evidence, Yale Law Journal, XLV (March,
1936), 959.

Review of The Law of Trusts and Trustees by George Gleason
Bogert, Columbia Law Review, XXXVI (April, 1936), 687-
690.

"Institute Priests and Yale Observers--A Reply to Dean
Goodrich," University of Pennsylvania Law Review and
American Law Register, LXXXIV (May, 1936), 811-824.

"How They Are Voting [Letter]," New Republic, LXXXVIII (September 30, 1936), 223.

"What I Expect of Roosevelt," Nation, CXLIII (November 28, 1936), 628.

"Back to the Constitution," New Republic, LXXXIX (December 16, 1936), 222.

"A Reply [to Journal's Position against Roosevelt's Court Plan]," American Bar Association Journal, XXIII (May, 1937), 364-368, 393-394.

"The Jurisprudence of Edward S. Robinson," Yale Law Journal, XLVI (June, 1937), 1282-1289.

"Labor Technique," Yale Review, n.s., XXVII (December, 1937), 418-420.

United States, 75th Congress, 3rd Session, Senate, Committee on the Judiciary, Hearings on the Nomination of Thurman W. Arnold to be Assistant Attorney General. March 11, 1938.

"The Folklore of Mr. Hook--A Reply," University of Chicago Law Review (April, 1938), 349-353.

"Fair and Effective Use of Present Antitrust Procedure," Yale Law Journal, XLVII (June, 1938), 1294-1303.

"Antitrust Activities of the Department of Justice," Oregon Law Review, XIX (December, 1939), 22-31.

"Free-Wheeling among Ideas and Ideals," Saturday Review of Literature, XXVIII (June 23, 1945), 10.

"Leon Green: An Appreciation," Illinois Law Review, XLIII (March-April, 1948), 1-4.

"How Not to Get Investigated," Harper's Magazine, CXCVII (November, 1948), 61-63.

"Mr. Justice Murphy," Harvard Law Review, LXIII (December, 1949), 289-293.

"The Preservation of Competition," in Arnold, Thurman, et al., The Future of Democratic Capitalism. Philadelphia, 1950.

"Mob Justice and Television," Atlantic, CLXXXVII (June, 1951), 68-70.

"Bullying the Civil Service," Atlantic, CLXXXVIII (September, 1951), 45-46.

"The Sherman Act on Trial," Atlantic, CLCII (July, 1953), 38-42.

"The Economic Purpose of Antitrust Laws," Mississippi Law Journal, XXVI (May, 1955), 207-214.

"The American Ideal of a Fair Trial," Arkansas Law Review, IX (Summer, 1955), 311-317.

"Judge Jerome Frank," University of Chicago Law Review, XXIV (Summer, 1957), 633-642.

"Walton Hale Hamilton," Yale Law Journal, LXVIII (January, 1959), 399-400.

"Professor Hart's Theology," Harvard Law Review, LXXIII (May, 1960), 1298-1317.

"The Playboy Panel: Sex and Censorship in Literature and the Arts," Playboy, XIII (July, 1961), 27-28, et al.

"The Folklore of Capitalism Revisited," Yale Law Review, n.s., LII (Winter, 1963), 188-204.

"Wesley A. Sturges," Yale Law Journal, LXXII (March, 1963), 640-642.

"In Contempt of Justice," New Republic, CL (March 17, 1964), 32-33.

"Roosevelt's Contribution to Our Competitive Ideal,"
    Centennial Review, IX (1965), 192-208.

"The Growth of Awareness," _International Lawyer_, I (July,
    1967), 534-547.

II.   SECONDARY MATERIAL

A.   Selected Published Works by Contemporaries

Adams, Henry C., "An Interpretation of the Social Movements
    of Our Time," _Publications of the Church Social Union_,
    Cambridge, Mass., Series B, N. 2, May 15, 1895.   A
    lecture originally delivered August 12, 1891.

Adams, Henry C.   "The 'Labor Problem,'" _Scientific American
    Supplement_, XXII (August 21, 1886), 8861-8863.

Adams, Henry C.   _Outline of Lectures upon Political Economy_.
    Baltimore 1881; 2d ed., Ann Arbor, 1886.

Baldwin, James Mark, "The Cosmic and the Moral," _Interna-
    tional Journal of Ethics_, VI (Octtober, 1895), 93-97.

Baldwin, James Mark, "The Origin of a 'Thing' and Its
    Nature," _Psychological Review_, II (November, 1895),
    551-573.

Barnes, Harry Elmer, _The New History and the Social Studies_.
    New York, 1925.

Barnes, Harry Elmer, _The Genesis of the World War_.   New York,
    1926.

Beard, Charles, _The Industrial Revolution_.   London, 1901.

Beard, Charles A., _Contemporary American History, 1877-1913_.
    New York, 1914.

Carnegie, Andrew, "Results of the Labor Struggle," Forum, I (August, 1886), 538-551.

Chapman, John Jay, Practical Agitation. New York, 1900.

Chase, Stuart, A New Deal. New York, 1932.

Chase, Stuart, The Economy of Abundance. New York, 1934.

Clark, Charles E., "The Code Cause of Action," Yale Law Journal, XXXIII (June, 1924), 817-837.

Clark, Charles E., "History, Systems and Functions of Pleading," Virginia Law Review, XI (May, 1925), 517-552.

Clark, Charles E. "The Complaint in Code Pleading," Yale Law Journal, XXXV (January, 1926), 259-291.

Clark, Charles E., "An Experiment in Studying the Business of the Courts of a State," American Bar Association Journal, XIV (June, 1928), 318-319.

Clark, Charles E., "The New Summary Judgment Rule in Connecticut," American Bar Association Journal, XV (February, 1929), 82-85.

Clark, Charles E., "Methods of Legal Reform," West Virginia Law Quarterly, XXXVI (December, 1929), 106-118.

Clark, Charles E., "Summary Judgment," Encyclopedia of the Social Sciences. New York, 1934. XIV, 461-462.

Clark, Charles E., Procedure--The Handmaid of Justice: Essays of Judge Charles E. Clark. Eds., Charles Alan Wright and Harry M. Reasoner. St. Paul, Minn., 1965.

Clark, J. M., et al., "Long-Range Planning for the Regulariaztion of Industry," New Republic, LXIX (January 13, 1932), Part Two.

Cohen, Felix S., Review of The Folklore of Capitalism by T. W. Arnold, National Lawyers Guild Quarterly, I (March 1938), 161-164.

Cohen, Morris R., "Change and Fixity in the Law," Nation, CXXXIII (September 9, 1931), 259-260.

Cohen, Morris R., Law and the Social Order: Essays in Legal Philosophy. New York, 1933.

Cohen, Morris R. The Faith of a Liberal: Selected Essays. New York, 1946.

Cooley, Charles Horton, Human Nature and the Social Order. New York, 1902.

Cooley, Charles H., "The Process of Social Change," Political Science Quarterly, XII (March, 1897), 63-81.

Cooley, Charles H., "Social Consciousness," American Journal of Sociology, XII (March, 1907), 675-687.

Corey, Lewis, The Decline of American Capitalism. New York, 1934.

Cowley, Malcolm, and Smith, Bernard (eds.), Books That Changed Our Minds. New York, 1938.

Dennis, Lawrence, The Coming American Fascism. New York, 1936.

Dewey, John, Review of L. F. Ward, The Psychic Factors of Civilization, et al., Psychological Review, I (July, 1894), 400-411.

Dewey, John, "Evolution and Ethics," The Monist, VIII (April, 1898), 321-341.

Dewey, John, The School and Society. Chicago, 1899.

Dewey, John, "The Child and the Curriculum," University of Chicago Contributions to Education, Number V. Chicago, 1902.

Dewey, John, The Influence of Darwin and Philosophy, and Other Essays in Contemporary Thought. New York, 1910.

Dewey, John, "The Pragmatic Acquiescence," New Republic, XLIX (January 5, 1927), 186-189.

Dewey, John, "Justice Homes and the Liberal Mind," New Republic, LII (January 11, 1928), 210-212.

Dewey, John, et al., Creative Intelligence: Essays in the Pragmatic Attitude. New York, 1917.

Ely, Richard T., The Past and the Present of Political Economy. Baltimore, 1884.

Frank, Jerome, Law and the Modern Mind. New York, 1930.

Giddings, Franklin H., "The Theory of Sociology," Annals of the American Academy of Political and Social Science, Supplement, V (July, 1894), 7-80.

Gladden, Washington, Applied Christianity. Boston, 1886.

Gladden, Washington, Social Facts and Forces. New York, 1897.

Gladden, Washington, Working People and Their Employers. Boston, 1876.

Green, Leon, "Scientific Methods in Law," Northwestern University School of Law, Bulletin No. 1, 1929.

Green, Leon, Judge and Jury. Kansas City, Mo., 1930.

Gronlund, Laurence, The Cooperative Commonwealth in Its Outlines. New York, 1884.

Gronlund, Lawrence, Insufficiency of Henry George's Theory. New York, 1887.

Gronlund, Laurence, Socialism vs. Tax Reform: An Answer to Henry George. New York, 1887.

Harris, Abram L., "Types of Institutionalism," Journal of Political Economy, XL (December, 1932), 721-749.

Herbert Spencer on the Americans, and the Americans on Herbert Spencer. New York, 1883.

Hook, Sidney, *Reason, Social Myths, and Democracy*. New York, 1940.

Hoover, Herbert, *The Challenge to Liberty*. New York, 1934.

Howells, Mildred, ed., *Life in Letters of William Dean Howells*. 2 v. Garden City, N.Y., 1928.

James, William, "What the Will Effects," *Scribner's Magazine*, III (February, 1888), 240-250.

James, William, *The Principles of Psychology*. 2 v. New York, 1890.

Kemler, Edgar, *The Deflation of American Ideals*. Washington, D.C., 1941.

Laveleye, Emile de, "Two New Utopias," *Contemporary Review*, LVII (January, 1890), 1-19.

Lerner, Max, *Ideas for the Ice Age*. New York, 1941.

Lerner, Max, "The Shadow World of Thurman Arnold," *Yale Law Journal*, XLVII (March, 1938), 687-703.

Lippmann, Walter, *A Preface to Politics*. New York, 1913.

Lippmann, Walter, *Drift and Mastery*. New York, 1914.

Lorwin, Lewis L., "The Problem of Economic Planning," in World Social Economic Congress, 1931, *World Social Economic Planning*. The Hague, 1931.

Mackenzie, Findlay, ed., *Planned Society, Yesterday, Today, Tomorrow*. New York, 1937.

Malin, James C., "Space and History," *Agricultural History*, XVIII (April, 1944), 65-74 and (July, 1944), 107-26.

Mead, George Herbert, "The Working Hypothesis in Social Reform," American Journal of Sociology, V (November, 1899), 367-371.

Mead, George Herbert, Review of Jane Addams, The Newer Ideals of Peace, American Journal of Sociology, XIII (July, 1907), 121-128.

Mead, George Herbert, "The Social Settlement: Its Basis and Function," The University Record of the University of Chicago, XII (January, 1908), 108-110.

Mead, George H., Philosophy of the Present. New York, 1932.

Mead, George H., The Philosophy of the Act. Chicago, 1938.

Mitchell, Wesley C., The Backward Art of Spending Money, and Other Essays. New York, 1937.

Morgenthau, Hans J., "The Limitations of Science and the Problem of Social Planning," Ethics, LIV (April, 1944), 174-185.

Nearing, Scott, Social Adjustment. New York, 1911.

Nearing, Scott, Poverty and Riches. Philadelphia, 1916.

Ogburn, William F., Social Change with Respect to Culture and Original Nature. New York, 1922.

Ogburn, William F., "The Psychological Basis for the Economic Interpretation of History," American Economic Review, IX (March, 1919), Supplement, 291-305.

Parker, Carleton H., The Casual Laborer and Other Essays. New York, 1920.

Patten, Simon N., The Theory of Social Forces. Philadelphia, 1896.

Patten, Simon N., The New Basis of Civilization. Daniel M. Fox, ed. Cambridge, Mass. 1968. Orig. pub. 1907.

Patten, Simon N., Essays in Economic Theory. Essays in Economic Theory. R. G. Tugwell, ed. New York, 1924.

Person, Harlow S., ed., Scientific Management in American Industry. New York, 1929.

Person, Harlow S., "Scientific Management as a Philosophy and Technique of Progressive Industrial Stabilization," World Social Economic Congress, 1931, World Social Economic Planning. The Hague, 1931.

Person, Harlow S., "Nature and Technique of Planning," Plan Age, 1 (December, 1934), 4-7.

Post, Louis F., Henry George's 1886 Campaign. New York, 1961 [reprint of edition of December, 1886].

Pound, Roscoe, "The Scope and Purpose of Sociological Jurisprudence," Harvard Law Review, XXIV (June, 1911), 591-619; XXV (December, 1911), 140-168; XXV (April, 1912), 489-516.

Pound, Roscoe, "Justice According to Law," Columbia Law Review, XIII (December, 1913), 696-713; XIV (January, 1914), 1-26; XIV (February, 1914), 103-121.

Pound, Roscoe, An Introduction to the Philosophy of Law. New Haven, 1922.

Pound, Roscoe, "A Theory of Social Interests," American Sociological Society, Papers and Proceedings, XV (May, 1922), 16-45.

Pound, Roscoe, "Preventive Justice and Social Work," National Conference of Social Work, Proceeding (1923), 151-163.

Pound, Roscoe, "Jurisprudence," in Harry Elmer Barnes, ed., The History and Prospects of the Social Sciences. New York, 1925.

Pound, Roscoe, "The Call for a Realist Jurisprudence," Harvard Law Review, XLIV (March, 1931), 697-711.

Powell, Thomas Reed, "An Imaginary Judicial Opinion," _Harvard Law Review_, XLIV (April, 1931), 889-905.

President's Conference on Unemployment, Committee on Recent Economic Changes, _Recent Economic Changes in the United States_. 2 v. New York, 1929.

President's Research Committee on Social Trends, _Recent Social Trends_. 2 v. New York, 1933.

Rauschenbusch, Walter, _Christianity and the Social Crisis_. New York, 1907.

Robinson, Edward S., "Psychology and the Law," _Journal of Social Philosophy_, 1 (April, 1936), 197-217.

Robinson, Edward S., _Law and the Lawyers_. New York, 1935.

Roosevelt, Theodore, _The New Nationalism_. New York, 1910.

Roosevelt, Theodore, "Two Noteworthy Books on Democracy," _Outlook_, CVIII (November 18, 1914), 648-651.

Ross, Edward A. _Social Control_. New York, 1901.

Royce, Josiah, _The Spirit of Modern Philosophy_. Boston, 1892.

Royce, Josiah, "Natural Law, Ethics, and Evolution," _International Ethics_, V (July, 1895), 489-500.

Royce, Josiah, "Originality and Consciousness," _Harvard Monthly_, XXIV (June, 1897), 133-142.

Royce, Josiah, _The Philosophy of Loyalty_. New York, 1908.

Royce, Josiah, "The Mechanical, the Historical and the Statistical," _Science_, n.s., XXXIX (April 17, 1914), 551-566.

Science Economic Discussion. New York, 1886.

Small, Albion, _The Methodology of the Social Problem_. Chicago, 1898.

Small, Albion W., The Significance of Sociology for Ethics. Chicago, 1902.

Sorokin, Pitirim, "Recent Social Trends: A Criticism," Journal of Political Economy, XLIV (April, 1933), 194-210, 210-221 (Ogburn), 400-404.

Soule, George, A Planned Society. New York, 1933.

Soule, George, "Toward a Planned Society," New Republic CI (November 8, 1939), 29-33.

Spencer, Herbert, The Study of Sociology - London 1873; New York, 1883.

Spencer, Herbert, The Principles of Sociology. 3 v. New York, 1896.

Stern, B. J., ed., "The Letters of Albion W. Small to Lester F. Ward," Social Forces, XII (December, 1933), 163-173; XIII (March, 1935), 323-340; XV (December, 1936), 174-186.

Strong, Josiah, The New Era. New York, 1893.

Strong, Josiah, Our Country. New York, 1885.

Sumner, William G., "Sociology," Princeton Review, LVII (November, 1881), 303-323.

Sumner, William G., What Social Classes Owe to Each Other. New York, 1883.

Sumner, William G., The Forgotten Man, and Other Essays. A. G. Keller, ed. New Haven, 1918.

Sunderland, Edson R., "A Modern Evolution in Remedial Rights,-- The Declaratory Judgment," Michigan Law Review, XVI (December, 1917), 69-89.

Sunderland, Edson R., "The Machinery of Procedural Reform," Michigan Law Review, XXII (February, 1924), 293-311.

Sunderland, Edson R., "The English Struggle for Procedural Reform," Harvard Law Review, XXXIX (April, 1926), 725-748.

Sunderland, Edson R., "The Regulation of Legal Procedure," West Virginia Law Quarterly, XXXV (April, 1929), 301-322.

Sunderland, Edson R., "Comments on Proposed Changes in Procedure in West Virginia," West Virginia Law Quarterly, XXXVI (December, 1929), 119-132.

Taylor, Frederick W., Scientific Management. New York, 1947. Includes Shop Management, 1903; The Principles of Scientific Management, 1911; Testimony before the Special House Committee, 1912.

Veblen, Thorstein, The Theory of Business Enterprise. New York, 1904.

Veblen, Thorstein, "Why Is Economics Not an Evolutionary Science?" Quarterly Journal of Economics, XII (July, 1898), 373-397.

Walker, Francis A., "Mr. Bellamy and the New Nationalist Party," Atlantic Monthly, LXV (February, 1890), 248-262.

Ward, Lester F., Dynamic Sociology. 2 v. New York, 1883.

Ward, Lester F., The Psychic Factors of Civilization. Boston, 1893.

Weyl, Walter E., The New Democracy. New York, 1912.

Wilson, Edmund, "Hull-House in 1932," New Republic, LXXIII (January 18, 1933), 260-262; (January 25, 1933), 287-290; (February 1, 1933), 317-321.

Wilson, Woodrow, The New Freedom. Garden City, 1913.

Woods, Robert A., "The University Settlement Idea," in Jane Addams, et al., Philanthropy and Social Progress. New York, 1893.

B. Selected Historical Works: Autobiography,
Biography, and Background

Aaron, Daniel, Men of Good Hope. New York, 1951.

Aaron, Daniel, "Bellamy--Utopian Conservative," Edward
Bellamy, Novelist and Reformer; Union Worthies, Number
23. Schenectady, N.Y., 1968.

Ackerman, Bruce A., "Law and the Modern Mind by Jerome Frank,"
Daedalus, CIII (Winter, 1974), 119-130.

Auerbach, Jerold S., "Enmity and Amity: Law Teachers and
Practitioners, 1900-1922," Perspectives in American
History, V (1971), 551-601.

Ayer, Douglas, "In Quest of Efficiency: The Ideological Journey
of Thurman Arnold in the Interwar Period," Stanford Law
Review, XXIII (June, 1971), 1049-1086.

Barker, Charles Albro, Henry George. New York, 1955.

Becker, George J., "Edward Bellamy: Utopia, American Plan,"
Antioch Review, XIV (Summer, 1954), 181-194.

Bell, Daniel, "The Background and Development of Marxian
Socialism in the United States," in D. Egbert and S. Persons,
Socialism and American Life. Princeton, N.J., 1952.
I, 213-405.

Bowman, Sylvia, The Year 2000: A Critical Biography of Edward
Bellamy. New York, 1958.

Bruce, Robert V., 1877: Year of Violence. Indianapolis, 1959.

Commons, John R., Myself. New York, 1934.

Conkin, Paul K., Tomorrow a New World: The New Deal Community
Program. Ithaca, N.Y., 1959.

Conway, Jill, "Jane Addams: An American Heroine," Daedalus,
XCIII (Spring, 1964), 761-780.

Curti, Merle, "Jane Addams on Human Nature," Journal of the History of Ideas, XXII (April-June, 1961), 240-253.

Darrow, Clarence, The Story of My Life. New York, 1932.

David, Henry, The History of the Haymarket Affair. New York, 1936.

Davis, Allen F., Spearheads for Reform: The Social Settlements and the Progressive Movement, 1890-1914. New York, 1967.

Davis, Allen F. American Heroine: The Life and Legend of Jane Addams. New York, 1973.

de Mille, Anna George, Henry George: Citizen of the World. Chapel Hill, 1950.

Dombrowski, James, The Early Days of Christian Socialism in America. New York, 1936.

Dorfman, Joseph, The Economic Mind in American Civilization. New York, 1949, 1959. Vols. III-V.

Dorfman, Joseph, et al., Institutional Economics: Veblen, Commons, and Mitchell Reconsidered. Berkeley, 1963.

Ely, Richard T., Ground under Our Feet: An Autobiography. New York, 1938.

Farrell, John C. Beloved Lady: A History of Jane Addams' Ideas on Reform and Peace. Baltimore, 1967.

Filler, Louis, "Edward Bellamy and the Spiritual Unrest," American Journal of Economics and Sociology, VIII (April, 1949), 239-249.

Forbes, Allyn B., "The Literary Quest for Utopia, 1880-1900," Social Forces, VI (December, 1927), 179-189.

Forcey, Charles, The Crossroads of Liberalism: Croly, Weyl, Lippmann, and the Progressive Era 1900-1925. New York, 1961.

Fortas, Abe, "Thurman Arnold and the Theatre of the Law," Yale Law Journal, LXXIX (May, 1970), 988-1004.

Fox, Daniel M., The Discovery of Abundance: Simon N. Patten and the Transformation of Social Theory. Ithaca, 1967.

Franklin, John Hope, "Edward Bellamy and the Nationalist Movement," New England Quarterly, XI (December, 1938), 739-772.

Freidel, Frank, Franklin D. Roosevelt: Launching the New Deal. Boston, 1973.

Geiger, George Raymond, The Philosophy of Henry George. New York, 1933.

George, Henry Jr., The Life of Henry George. New York, 1900.

Gilbert, James, Designing the Industrial State: The Intellectual Pursuit of Collectivism in America, 1880-1940. Chicago, 1972.

Gladden, Washington, Recollections. Boston, 1909.

Graham, Otis L., Jr., An Encore for Reform: The Old Progressives and the New Deal. New York, 1967.

Graham, Otis L., Jr., "The Planning Ideal and American Reality: The 1930's," in Stanley Elkins and Eric McKitrick, eds., The Hofstadter Aegis: A Memorial. New York, 1974.

Green, Mason A., "Edward Bellamy: A Biography of the Author of Looking Backward." Unpublished typescript. Houghton Library, Harvard University. c.1925.

Goldman, Eric F., Rendezvous with Destiny: A History of Modern American Reform. New York, 1952.

Goodsell, Charles T., Administration of a Revolution: Executive Reform in Puerto Rico under Governor Tugwell, 1941-1946. Cambridge, Mass., 1965.

Gressley, Gene. "Thurman Arnold, Antitrust and the New Deal," Business History Review, XXXVIII (Summer, 1964), 214-231.

Gressley, Gene, "Introduction," to Voltaire and the Cowboy: Letters of Thurman Arnold. Boulder, 1977.

Gruchy, Allan G., "The Concept of National Planning in Institutional Economics," Southern Economic Journal, VI (October, 1939), 121-144.

Gruchy, Allan G., Modern Economic Thought: The American Contribution. New York, 1947.

Hawkins, Richmond L., Positivism in the United States, 1853-1861. Cambridge, Mass., 1938.

Hawley, Ellis, The New Deal and the Problem of Monopoly. Princeton, N.J., 1966.

"Herbert Croly, 1869-1930," New Republic, LXIII (July 16, 1930), 243-271 (Special Supplement).

Hill, Warren P., "The Psychological Realism of Thurman Arnold," University of Chicago Law Review, XXII (Winter, 1955), 377-396.

Hofstadter, Richard, The Age of Reform: From Bryan to F.D.R. New York, 1955.

Hofstadter, Richard, Social Darwinism in American Thought. Revised Edition. Boston, 1955.

Hopkins, Charles Howard, The Rise of the Social Gospel in American Protestantism, 1865-1915. New Haven, 1940.

Howe, Frederic C., The Confessions of a Reformer. New York, 1925.

"Introduction to the Issue" [Dedication to Thurman W. Arnold], Yale Law Journal, LXXIX (May, 1970), 979-981.

Jaher, Frederic C., Doubters and Dissenters: Cataclysmic Thought in America, 1885-1918. Glencoe, Ill., 1964.

Jaher, Frederic C., ed., The Age of Industrialism in America: Essays in Social Structure and Cultural Values. New York, 1968.

Kearny, Edward N., Thurman Arnold, Social Critic: The Satirical Challenge to Orthopoxy. Albuquerque, 1970.

Lasch, Christopher, The New Radicalism in America, 1889-1963. New York, 1965.

Lasch, Christopher, The Agony of the American Left. New York, 1969.

Lasch, Christopher, ed., The Social Thought of Jane Addams. Indianapolis, 1965.

Lawson, Alan, The Failure of Independent Liberalism, 1930-1941. New York, 1971.

Layton, Edwin T., Jr., The Revolt of the Engineers. Cleveland, 1971.

Leuchtenburg, William E., Franklin D. Roosevelt and the New Deal. New York, 1963.

Levi, Edward H., "Thurman Arnold," Yale Law Journal, LXXIX (May, 1970), 983-984.

Levin, Harry, "Some Paradoxes of Utopia," Edward Bellamy, Novelist and Reformer, Union Worthies, Number 23. Schenectady, N.Y., 1968.

Levine, Daniel, Varieties of Reform Thought. Madison, 1964.

Levy, David W., "The Life and Thought of Herbert Croly, 1869-1914." Ph.D. diss., Univ. of Wisconsin, 1967.

Lindsey, Almont, The Pullman Strike, Chicago, 1942.

Linn, James Weber, Jane Adams: A Biography. New York, 1935.

Lord, Russell, "Rural New Yorker," New Yorker, XI (March 23 and 30, 1935).

Lord, Russell, The Wallaces of Iowa. Boston, 1947.

Lovejoy, Arthur O., "The Thirteen Pragmatisms," Journal of Philosophy, Psychology and Scientific Method, V (1908), 5-12, 29-39.

Lovett, Robert M. All Our Years. New York, 1948.

Lubove, Roy, The Progressives and the Slums. Pittsburgh, 1962.

Lubove, Roy, The Professional Altruist, Cambridge, Mass., 1965.

Lugo-Silva, Enrique, The Tugwell Administration in Puerto Rico, 1941-1946. Rio Piedras, P. R., 1955.

Lynd, Stoughton, "Jane Addams and the Radical Impulse," Commentary, XXXII (July, 1961), 54-59.

MacNair, Everett W., Edward Bellamy and the Nationalist Movement, 1889 to 1894. Milwaukee, 1957.

McCloskey, Robert G., American Conservatism in the Age of Enterprise, 1865-1910. New York, 1951.

Moley, Raymond, After Seven Years. New York, 1939.

Morgan, Arthur E., Edward Bellamy. New York, 1944.

Morgan, Arthur E., The Philosophy of Edward Bellamy. New York, 1945.

Nicklason, Fred, "Henry George: Social Gospeller," American Quarterly, XXII (Fall, 1970), 649-664.

Noble, David W., The Paradox of Progressive Thought. Minneapolis, 1958.

Pells, Richard H. Radical Visions and American Dreams: Culture and Social Thought in the Depression Years. New York, 1973.

Purcell, Edward A., "American Jurisprudence between the Wars," American Historical Review, LXXV (December, 1969), 424-446.

Purcell, Edward A., The Crisis of Democratic Theory. Lexington, Ky., 1973.

Rostow, Eugene V., "American Legal Realism and the Sense of the Profession," The Sovereign Prerogative: The Supreme Court and the Quest for Law. New Haven, 1962.

Rostow, Eugene V., "Thurman Arnold," Yale Law Journal, LXXIX (May, 1970), 985-987.

Rumble, Wilfred E., American Legal Realism. Ithaca, 1968.

Schiffman, Joseph, "Edward Bellamy's Religious Thought," PMLA, LXVIII (September, 1953), 716-732.

Schiffman, Joseph, "Edward Bellamy's Altruistic Man," American Quarterly, VI (Fall, 1954), 195-209.

Schiffman, Joseph, "Edward Bellamy: Realist and Utopian," in Bellamy, Edward, The Duke of Stockbridge: A Romance of Shays' Rebellion. Cambridge, Mass., 1962.

Schlesinger, Arthur M., Jr., The Age of Roosevelt. 3 v. Boston, 1957-1960.

Schneider, Robert E., Positivism in the United States. Rosario, Argentina, 1946.

Scott, Anne Firor, "Introduction," to Jane Addams, Democracy and Social Ethics. Cambridge, Mass., 1964.

Shapiro, Edward S., "Decentralist Intellectuals and the New Deal," Journal of American History, LVIII (March, 1971), 938-957.

Shaver, Muriel, "Jane Cunningham Croly," Dictionary of American Biography, IV, 560-561. New York, 1930.

Shaver, Muriel, "David Goodman Croly," Dictionary of American Biography, IV, 560. New York, 1930.

Sproat, John G., "The Best Men": Liberal Reformers in the Gilded Age. New York, 1968.

Sternsher, Bernard, Rexford Tugwell and the New Deal. New Brunswick, N.J., 1964.

Stevens, Robert, "Two Cheers for 1870: The American Law School," Perspectives in American History, V (1971), 405-548.

Sutherland, Arthur E., The Law at Harvard. Cambridge, Mass., 1967.

Taylor, Graham, Pioneering on Social Frontiers. Chicago, 1930.

Taylor, Walter F., The Economic Novel in America. Chapel Hill, 1942.

Thelen, David P., The New Citizenship: Origins of Progressivism in Wisconsin, 1885-1900. Columbia, Mo., 1972.

Thomas, John L., "Introduction," to Bellamy, Edward, Looking Backward, 2000-1887. Cambridge, Mass., 1967.

"Utopia," Daedalus, XCIV (Spring, 1965).

Villard, Oswald Garrison, "Herbert David Croly," Dictionary of American Biography, Supplement One, pp. 209-210. New York, 1944.

Wald, Lillian D., The House on Henry Street. New York, 1915.

Ward, Lester F. Glimpses of the Cosmos. v. 2,5. New York, 1913, 1917.

Warren, Frank A., Liberals and Communism: The "Red Decade" Revisited. Bloomington, Ind., 1962.

Warren, Frank A., An Alternative Vision: The Socialist Party in the 1930's. Bloomington, Ind., 1974.

White, G. Edward, "From Sociological Jurisprudence to Realism: Jurisprudence and Social Change in Early Twentieth-Century America," Virginia Law Review, LVIII (September, 1972), 999-1028.

White, Morton, Social Thought in America: The Revolt Against Formalism. 2d. ed. Boston, 1957.

Wiebe, Robert H., The Search for Order, 1877-1920. New York, 1967.

Wiener, Philip P., Evolution and the Founders of Pragmatism. Cambridge, Mass., 1949.

Wigdor, David, Roscoe Pound, Philosopher of Law. Westport, Conn., 1974.

Wilson, R. Jackson, In Quest of Community: Social Philosophy in the United States, 1860-1920. New York, 1968.

Woodard, Calvin. "Reality and Social Reform: The Transition from Laissez-Faire to the Welfare State," Yale Law Journal, LXXII (December, 1962), 286-328.

Young, Arthur N., The Single Tax Movement in the United States, Princeton, 1916.